TIMES L

YOUR COMPLETE FORECAST 2012 HOROSCOPE

Bejan Daruwalla

Shri Ganeshaya Namah!

The 2012 Horoscope Book

First Edition 2010
ISBN : 978-93-80483-44-3

Publishers

Ranvir Books

B-50/200, Siddha CHS,
Road No. 4, Siddharth Nagar part 2,
Goregaon-(W), Mumbai- 400 104
Tel : 022 28777111 / 0124 4308888
Mob.: +91 9716974444
www.ranvirbooks.com

Printed at : Narain Printers, Noida

Assisted by : Namita Rajhans & Nidhi Vyas

Marketed and distributed exclusively by

Times Group Books
(A division of Bennett, Coleman and Company Limited)
Times Annexe, Express Building,
9-10, Bahadur Shah Zafar Marg, New Delhi - 110002.

A Disclaimer from Bejan

My regular (and new, I hope) readers will be somewhat familiar with my style. I wrote the horoscopes from 2010 with a new publisher. However, I need to point out that the zodiac itself does not change. The qualities and the predictions for each sun sign are unchanged.

Since the author/astrologer is also the same, the style and language are therefore bound to be similar to what was seen in earlier books.

Any perceived similarities are merely co-incidental and not deliberate plagiarising. In any case, an author/writer can't possibly be said to have plagiarised himself. Moreover, forecasts for previous years no longer have any relevance, and copying from them would be an exercise in futility. Any such claim about these books deserves to be thrown out forthwith.

Foreword

(For the 2010 and subsequent horoscopes)

Ancient Indian thought traditionally and historically quantifies longer spells of time according to *yugas,* each of which is approximately twelve years. For example, the present era or *yuga* we are living in is considered to be the *yuga* of *kali (Kalyug)* in which all kinds of iniquities, sins, malpractices flourish.

There is a reason for this little preamble that I have written. I wrote my books for my previous publishers for more than one '*yuga*' – sixteen years or so. It was time for a change. Remember, greater philosophers than I can ever pretend to be have said that change is the only constant in life. However, my changeover has resulted in some degree of acrimony and heart-burning. Perhaps it was necessary to accomplish it. Whatever it may be, I hope that all these factors will not affect the loyalty of my regular readers or the interest of my new ones. Ultimately, you are the ones who matter. Now, having crossed 80, only the future of the world excites me. Before my eyes are closed and I go to meet my boss Ganesha, I hope to predict world peace and compassion. That's all.

I dedicate the new, changed version of my books not only to my Lord Ganesha, as always, but also to all my readers, both old and new, and hope you will enjoy them. The contents – astrology - is as old as time itself.

BEJAN DARUWALLA UP CLOSE - NEW MILESTONES

ACHIEVEMENTS

Excelsior! It is the motto of the New York State. It means ever upwards and that is what our astrologer does in his predictions. It is like Batsman Gayle hitting 37 runs in one over on 8th May 2011. But our Bejan only says, "fais ce que dois". It means, "Do your duty". Ganesha wants me to throw light on future events. Sometimes, it feels I am in Elysium or in heaven. Sometimes, I am shattered by it.

As early as 19th February, Bejan predicted in the Bombay Times that India will win the World Cup. He repeated it twice on **Times Now, NDTV Profit, CNN IBN, CNBC Awaaz and India TV.** It was a fantastic performance.

Bejan predicted in his 2010 annual book on page 9, "The poor, the downtrodden, the weak will find prosperity and peace. Justice will be done to them and that, to me, is of vital importance". In his 2010 annual book, on page 10, Bejan explained, "The main result of this will be the end of tyranny and brute force all over the world".

We have seen the rebellion and the awakening in Syria, Egypt, Yemen and all over the Middle East. Bejan finds sweet satisfaction in his predictions. And please remember that the 2010 book came out in September 2009.

On page 519 of his 2010 annual book, Bejan said, "Yes, if anybody can save the world and succeed in bringing nations closer, it will be him. He should succeed in this by 2011-2012."

He further clarified on page 524 of his 2011 book, "Before that, Jupiter will be in Aries from 23rd January 2011 to 4th June 2011. Another, and earlier, lucky period for Obama! Obama will deliver the goods; that is the bottom line!" Osama Bin Laden was killed on 2nd May 2011 i.e. between 23rd January and 4th June 2011. It is a remarkably accurate prediction. And the prediction was underlined in the book! Bejan says, Ganesha be praised.

On Tuesday, 3rd May 2011, Bejan went on a mini pilgrimage to the mighty God Hanuman at Sahalangpur, near Botad in Saurashtra. He had a great darshan of Hanumanji and Kothari Swami, the Head Priest, blessed Bejan and gave him a picture of the mighty Lord Hanumanji. Bejan described it all as, "Sweetness and light". Bejan has been a Hanuman devotee for about 60 years or so.

On 14th April 2011, the Metro Rotary Club of Ahmedabad made Bejan an Honorary member. President Mehul Shah, secretary Jamin and past district Governor Dr Shashank Rathod presented him with a beautiful memento. Rotarians are well known for their social and welfare activities. Bejan had a mile-long smile.

Bejan was on Bigg Boss twice, namely at the beginning and at the very end. He had great fun with the debonair Salman Khan, who sat at his feet. Bejan predicted that Salman would once again be on Bigg Boss. Bejan also predicted that Libran lady Shweta Tiwari would bag the big prize.

Saurav Ganguly was NOT selected for the IPL championship. But our Bejan told ace sportswriter Ayaz that Ganguly would definitely play. Ayaz immediately tweeted about it. We all know that Ganguly did play for Pune Warriors. Ayaz again tweeted Bejan's correct prediction on Twitter. A remarkable prediction against all odds!

He is acknowledged as one of the 100 great astrologers in the last 1,000 YEARS in the great Millennium Book of Prophecy, published by Harper Collins, USA.

1) Awarded the highest degree of Vedic astrology, "Jyotish MAHAHOPADHAYA" by the Federation of Indian Astrologers.
2) He was the astrologer in residence at Manila Hotel, Philippines.
3) Bejan featured on Hard Talk India on the BBC channel in August 1999. He was born on the 11th of July, 1931. He has a family of five, including his wife and 3 children.
4) On 10th December 2010, Bejan featured in **The Job: Corporate Astrologer** in The Financial Times, London. The interviewer was Rhymer Rigby.

Bejan Daruwalla is one of 100 eminent Zoroastrians of the world in a book being brought out by Meher Besania, the chairperson of the World Zoroastrian Congress.

Important Announcement

Our Ganesha devotee Bejan Daruwalla has moved from Mumbai to Ahmedabad. His Ahmedabad address is:

Bejan Daruwalla

Astrologer & Columnist
C/o Nastur Daruwalla,
A-5, Spectrum Towers,
Opposite Police Stadium,
Shahibaug, Ahmedabad - 380004, India.
Tel: 079 32954387
Nastur's tel: 09825470377
Meetu's tel: 09974031159
Call: Between 2-5 pm and 8-11 pm
Email: info@bejandaruwalla.com
bejandaruwalla@rediffmail.com

CONTENTS

The Planets and their Indications 10

Aries 13

Taurus 61

Gemini 103

Cancer 145

Leo 191

Virgo 231

Libra 271

Scorpio 313

Sagittarius 353

Capricorn 393

Aquarius 435

Pisces 481

Nastur - Bejan's Hanuman 521

Mamata - Queen of Bengal 522

World Predictions 523

Astro - Analysis of Suicide Bombers 527

THE PLANETS AND THEIR INDICATIONS

Mars – Body, ego, brother, force, technical education, arrogance, anger, *tamas* (ignorance), blood, blood relatives. Energy produces power, and power is the rate of energy, and power is Mars.

Mercury – *Buddhi*, intelligence. The whole universe is covered by intelligence. Intelligence is essential for education, discretion, business dealings, and business acumen. Also younger siblings and friendship.

Jupiter – Is the *Jeevatma, Jeevakaraka*, preacher, *Guru*, children, money and nobility.

Sukra – Wife, *Jeevakaraka* for females, luxury, vehicles, *bhoga* or materialistic pleasures and learning.

Saturn – *Karma*, profession, lethargy, lazy, slow moving.

Rahu – *Apasavya Karma*, poison, pain, foreign, unethical things and materialism.

Ketu – Binding, wiry, imprisonment, trying for *mukti*, rejection of materialistic pleasures.

Rahu and Ketu are called destiny breakers while the moon is considered a destiny modifier.

The order of existence in the universe is rooted in acting for the sake of other. The world of true peace, love and the ideal is both the ideal of god's creation and the desire of humankind. Therefore the origin of happiness and peace lies in the living for the sake of others

– (Sun Myung Moon).

Aries

March 21 - April 19

ARIES

(March 21 – April 19)

ELEMENT AND RULING PLANET: Fire and Mars.

STRENGTHS: Aries is active, energetic, excitable and impulsive, optimistic; open to change and new experiences.

WEAKNESS: Haste, impetuousness, rashness, over aggression. Prone to accidents involving fire and high speed.

SYMBOL: The Ram – Assertive, sexual and able to climb to great heights.

MATCHING SIGN: Libra.

MAGICAL BIRTHSTONE: Coral and Diamond – attracts love, financial success, and brings luck in new ventures.

 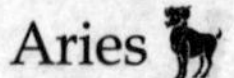

ARIES

YEARLY FORECAST

Warrior, leader, pioneer, commander. To top it all, a great artist. That's the real Arian.......

Main Trend

A time to assess past achievements and set fresh goals and objectives. Ganesha assures you that you will make the right decisions and choices. The reason is simple and you don't have trouble finding it. Your own greatly enhanced spirituality and faith guide you. Moral values, you're already strong on.

The combination will be deadly, unbeatable, and you annihilate any wrong tendencies before they have chance to grow, thanks to the blessings of Ganesha, who is truly benevolent and kind to a fault! We can all take a lesson from Him so that we can truly have the life we want.

Kindness, caring, sharing seems to be what you desire to achieve the most. It will have a greatly pleasing and beneficial effect on your personal life and on your professional interactions. Let's just carry on looking at your sphere of personal relationships for a while more. Your ideas could be confused, perhaps mixed up with powerful sexual attractions. Alarming, and certainly strong, passions are experienced, either within marriage or outside it. Don't take offence or turn puritanical on me. I'm just telling you the astro-indications!

Ultimately, of course, you see through things and gain superb

strength, power and creative union so that true love is felt deeply and solid ideas are shared in a setting that increases affection and caring. Moving on to other matters, gains, and acquisitions will figure largely, but finances will present a somewhat confused picture. Loans, funds, capital, joint-finances are favoured, but so are the possibilities of huge expenses and outlays or perhaps even a debt-trap. It will pay to be careful, cautious, conservative - new C's to describe an attitude that will yield better - and more lasting - material gains.

Jupiter:

Ganesha says Jupiter, the planet of great good, fortune and mighty achievements will be moving in your 3rd angle. It promises tremendous potential, which can, and must, be converted into actual performance. You Arians have a chance to show the world just how good and great and capable you are. It is time to come into your own. Connectivity, collective, consciousness make up the three C's. The fourth C will be contracts. If you learn to be good at it, the years ahead will hum and glow with promise and achievement. Ganesha says, you Arians are achievers and love perfection; this should serve as a great motivating factor for you.

How come I have singled out communication for you? Jupiter, I said, will zoom in your 3rd angle from January 19, 2010 to January 22, 2011. Jupiter stands for good luck, success and expansion.
The additional goodies of Jupiter will be courage and valour, physical fitness, hobbies, talent, education, good qualities, siblings, longevity of parents, tolerance, capability, quality and nature of food, selfishness, sports, fights, refuge, trading, dreams, sorrows, and stability of mind, the neighbourhood, near relations, friends, army, inheritance, ornaments, cleverness, and short journeys. What a list!

The additional highlights are:

a) This is the right time to take a crash course in matters which interest you, develop self-expression, and cultivate opinions;

b) Play chess or bridge, enter quiz shows, Sudoku contests, in short, all mental games;

c) Learn to get along with relatives and neighbours;

d) Try not to have mental strain, because this is where you are weak and therefore vulnerable; be ready to listen to others, though I know you are both able and discriminating;

e) Enrich your mind and enhance your knowledge.

I have mentioned this in earlier writings. Major climatic changes are happening, with dire consequences, on planet Earth. Jupiter in the 3rd angle shows research, intelligence and the trust to help people realise that we are all a family. Ganesha says, Jupiter in your 3rd angle could help in shrinking the size of the microelectronics packed into silicon chips. It could help enhance memory and the processing of talk. More accurate weather/climate/ and geological predictions could perhaps be made, too. Perhaps artificial intelligence could be the final gift of Jupiter in the 3rd angle. All these could be the brainchild or handiwork of your sign.

Let me summarise what the 3rd angle is all about. Mainly it is about outlets/media of expression and ideas. Trips and ties form an integral part of it. News, views, messages through faxes, mobiles and the latest technology are the modern ways of achieving this. The writing of books, pamphlets, flyers, mental gymnastics in games such as chess and bridge are good illustrations of it. Every salesman knows that CREATIVE LISTENING is a pivotal part of selling, marketing, and advertising. The 3rd angle has much to do with it.

Improving the vistas of your knowledge and information through books, research, even trade and travel, and interactions with people also come under the sway and domain of Jupiter (in terms of wisdom and spirituality) in your 3rd angle. Jupiter also has reference, very specially, to brothers and sisters, relatives and neighbours.

As a former professor of English, I have a theory about how the word "neighbour" came about. It came from the neigh or cry of a horse. The cry of a horse can be heard for some distance. Therefore, the cry or neigh could be heard in the neighbourhood. I wonder how far I'm right! A neighbour is the person living next door or near us. I could be wrong about my interpretation of the word "neighbour", or I could be right. It's up to you to take it or leave it.

Lets us now assess the minor planets Mercury, Venus and Mars.

Mercury:

Mercury is in charge of publicity, alliance, marriage and travel. From 3rd March to 23rd March and 17th April to 9th May, Mercury performs marvels, resulting in the achievement of goals and victories. You will balance work and pleasure in almost ideal proportions. There is also a chance of wedlock, an engagement, a business deal, or major contract or a hugely successful publicity campaign coming through. You will gatecrash headlong into the corridors of fame. Travel and collaborations are likely. Yes, you can start a project. This is a time when you will have renewed vigour and verve, and feel at your optimistic, ebullient best. Attitude spells attainment, and you will personify this now.

Venus:

Venus moves in your sign from 9th February to 5th March. You will have a chance to marry, love well, if not entirely wisely (there can never be both), an opportunity for warm emotional bonds and relationships to develop. We achieve true comfort and solace in love. Relationships of all kinds will be in strong focus. Collaborations and ties, journeys and publicity, rivalry and competitions, legal cases and confrontations, ventures and adventures, are the other salient features. You sporty Arians usually like to take chances in life.

Mars:

Mars does NOT TRANSIT or enter your sign this year. But Mars will help you till 3rd July. This planet helps you in different ways. If married, your spouse could have a minor or major wish coming true, your children and you might be involved in a major shift. Professionally, there could be important changes in your work area and you will have to work that much harder and possibly longer.

Uranus:

The planet of rebellion, erratic behaviour, contrariness, moodiness and sudden as well as drastic upheavals and emotional as well as intellectual tsunamis will be in your own sun sign. BEWARE, this warning is given with good intensions. Also, I admit that I could be wrong.

Uranus is in a bad formation with both Saturn and Pluto. This means sudden and complete changes of fortune.

Neptune:

Neptune will be in your hidden angle from 4th February. It will lead to secrecy and strange meetings with strange people. Sex, spirituality, journeys and inspirations will be in a very unusual mix-n-match for you. A weird, roller-coaster ride! Luckily from 12th June 2012, that is, this year, Jupiter will be in fine formation with Uranus. I know we are talking about Neptune. But this fine formation of Uranus and Jupiter after 12th June will mitigate, or lessen the bare influence of Uranus and Neptune. In other words, Jupiter is your saviour.

Pluto:

Pluto moves in your 10th angle of profession, prestige, parents, power and in-laws. This will most certainly give you an overdrive of ambition. How you use it will decide your destiny. My suggestion is: Go slow, be sweet to people, do not be egoistic and selfish. You have so much to give to the world. Learn to have control and sweetness in relationships. This applies to personal and professional ties, contacts and links. Believe me. You will be happier for it.

Saturn:

Let me give you an extract from my 2010-2011 books.
Your astrologer is only pointing out very humbly and very gently what may happen. That's all.

Saturn is the planet of limitation and sorrow. Libra is the sign of expansion and joy i.e. the 7th house or sign. This is planetary placing by western astrology only. A few of your desires and goals will be realised, but a few will flop and fail. Once you know this, you will be prepared for any eventuality. The result will be less hurt, less disappointments, less frustration. This is what astrology is all about. It is about making you happier at times, and guiding you to be less unhappy at other times. In other words, it is about guiding you on the path of life. I reiterate: No discipline is perfect; astrology is not perfect either.

Here is special advice for you, Arians. You must learn to do well in group activities, be part of the team in large organisations, fit into the social circle in short, and not be a loner. Let me put it differently. THE SECRET OF YOUR SUCCESS WILL BE IN YOUR ABILITY TO ADJUST AND ACCOMMODATE. If you do so, your gains and your joy, your profit and your pleasure, will be doubled. Otherwise, expenses and losses are likely. Finally, the choice is yours. The stars only impel, they do not compel.

But this is not the complete story; your tormentor Saturn leaves you alone and moves in your 8th angle. From 6th October 2012, Saturn will remain in your 8th angle for about two and a half years. Saturn moves slowly but surely. At the end of roughly two and a half years, that is, about December end 2014, there will be deep transformations or changes in your life. Saturn in your 8th angle refers to money, property, loans, funds, family and food. Insurance and pension, credit cards, mortgage and shares, stocks, securities. Saturn also signifies life-death-regeneration. Yes, it is quite a list. We will talk in detail about all this in our 2013 forecast. Till then, keep smiling. The Arians' smile is pure sunshine.

ARIES

MONTH-BY-MONTH

JANUARY

The ram is usually ambitious and energetic and will brook no opposition to achieve whatever he or she wants. It is a flying start to the year. You are pushing ahead on all cylinders and Ganesha is with you. You get off to a good start in 2012. You have a lot of ground to cover and things are moving fast. You will be a busy bee in this productive period. You exhibit great skills at work and also have deep bonding with loved ones. If interested in any sort of partnership or business/ collaborations/ connections, this is the right time to go ahead and take it all head-on. Journeys, meetings and conferences will produce pleasing results.

There could be many changes in the domestic scene; what these are likely to be, I am not in a position to say in a general forecast. But there will be growth in parental ties and duties, and a new attitude of pooling, caring and sharing. There will be deep bonding, wonderful family interactions and a happier home environment. You move to more stable ground.

You have gained in the belief in yourself and faith in those you care for. You learn to take setbacks calmly, especially when plans don't quite work out the way you had anticipated and friends don't live up to your hopes and dreams. You have the ability to change the situation with your own efforts and not allow delays, problems and snags hold you back. You have the vision and perseverance to achieve magical results at work. There is applause and you spruce up your persona. You want to present the world a better image of yourself and so take up a gym membership, yoga or meditation and find the time to concentrate on improving your health with a lifestyle and fitness regimen. You also attempt to resolve personal problems and are on a rapid growth trajectory. Take Ganesha's blessings and sally forth.

FEBRUARY

There will be many new affiliations and associations, says Ganesha. You will be crowded out, or should I say, crowded in by people. You will be meeting many new and interesting people and also making old associations work for you. Friendships, ties, travel and correspondence are what February and March 2012 will be about. Introspection and insight will run this year round, if not longer, for you. February is for relationships at every level. It emphasizes an expanding social and family circle also. Even the community and neighbourhood will assume greater importance in your life. You will be made very aware of your role and its requirements. You try hard to fulfil these, not just adequately, but really well. Ganesha is with you right through. Life now is large and fabulous. You think big and plan big. You also execute big. You recently embarked on a programme of self-improvement and now you are ready to claim your treasure chest. There is a great desire to work harder, earn more and build assets. You are satisfied with life and there are massive gains in business. You experience great camaraderie, shared dreams, true love and support, and a grand vision of life. Ganesha blesses you as there is visible all-round progress.

You revamp your finances as the month advances and it leads to greater prosperity. You focus strongly on property, gains, friendship and fraternity. Loans and funds also come your way easily. There could also be an addition to the family, even an adoption. There are several soft and emotional moments and deep intimate bonding with your special partner. If newly married, this will be a blissful period.

Finances, funding, capital-raising, investments come to the fore towards the end of February. You will also focus on building strong family ties, bonds of love and caring. Buying and selling are all-important, whether of assets, shares or real estate. Elders, parents, in-laws, siblings and extended family will also be in the picture. Your determination and enterprise will ensure that you pull through difficult situations.

MARCH

You will be looking at life with new eyes. You will move beyond the mundane and look at spirituality and other aspects of life with a new vision. The action-oriented side of your nature comes to the fore this month. In a few cases, a complete overhaul of goals and values will be part of the fare that March serves up to you. This month, the new and special trend of insights and introspection, spirituality and evolution of the spirit will be in full manifestation. There are some other concerns to think about, as well. Hospitalization and Medicare are best taken care of in the first 20 days of March, reminds Ganesha. You need to cultivate both patience and forbearance which will be your best armour against the smite of Saturn. Also, trips and ties and expenses will fill your cup to overflowing, as the Bible says, though in a different context, evidently! This is a period of ideas and growth. There is harmony at home and accolades, rewards and awards at work. This is a magical period and Ganesha hopes that you make the most of it. Mercury, the mighty planet, is all-powerful. Mercury is turbo powering you for over a fortnight. Make the most of this period and success is yours. You are in line for windfalls. You are in full flow and there is rampant progress in your affairs. The time has come for you to look at new decisions at work and play. You fix new visions of the future and have the chance to share them with people who appreciate you as a person and as a serious professional. Ganesha blesses you.

There is travel on the cards mid-month and you will be meeting many new people and making several profitable associations. There are happy times at home with greater bonding with relatives, family members, parents and children. New enterprises and projects will materialize, but you will have to work hard and see to their completion. This is a wonderful period and Ganesha feels that you should optimize it.

The new moon is in your sign towards the month-end and you should maximize this period. You fix your mind on much higher levels now as you look at vistas far removed from the mundane chores of work and family. Education and research will draw you like a magnet. Travel will be a great education, broadening your horizons. You want to expand your mind and grow as a human being and you will do everything possible to make it happen. This period could also be an emotional one and many maudlin thoughts travel through your mind. But this phase is a great one as there will be gains on many fronts and happiness in love. There will be marvellous results at work too. You are much more sympathetic, warm and caring, and make it a point to understand your own limitations and the other person's point of view. Humanitarian efforts, social reform and spiritual growth will bring out the best in you. There is money to be made and your mood is upbeat and euphoric. Your life is on an upswing and Ganesha is happy for you.

APRIL

In a way, the trend continues and you will be in touch with a complete overhaul of the self. You will look at the world with a wider vision and Ganesha is happy for that. The focus is more on the mind and soul and less on worldly, material considerations. Those interested in business or matters connected with the sea, liquids, medicine, diving and treasure-hunting could find March-April conducive to progress. But consciously try to avoid a tendency towards depression and melancholia. It will be counter-productive, and get you down further. These are definite astrological indications. Your main gain and asset in your birth-month, with ramifications through the year, will be the much-needed fillip to contacts, communication, correspondence, relationships with relatives and family members, trading and commissioning and agency work and publicity. This will hold good for yourself personally and professionally. There will be plenty of activity, mostly good, if you can turn it to your advantage. This will seem a month of conflicts, contrasting pulls, contrary trends, but hectic, nevertheless. There is an underlying similarity, though, says Ganesha, since it is in the meadows and avenues of the mind that your major activities lie, almost through the year. It is going to be a classic case of the superiority of mind over matter. Your spiritual strength will stand you in good stead as you cope with the world. There could be some health challenges and it will be necessary to take adequate rest.

Once again, mid-month, you are in the throes of a lucky spell. You do marvellously well with Mercury, the mighty planet, in your sign. It is very important and occupies a prominent position now for over 20 days. There is new work and your bonds of love are strengthened. You are happy, healthy and joyous. Make the most of this phase as Mercury will help you achieve whatever you want. Towards the month-end, you may be swept off your feet by a potential lover. These are exciting times and you must savour each mouthful to the fullest. There is love, romance, fun and games, partying, socializing, get-togethers. Yes, your plate is full and overflowing. You look towards the future with hope and optimism. You find great satisfaction at work and this joyful spirit adds colour to your life. Ganesha has truly blessed you. You live large and attract many liaisons, some of which can be dangerous. But Ganesha is with you all the way and removes the cobwebs and bottlenecks.

MAY

There are many forces and pressures at play. You will be torn on all sides and will not know what route to take. You look for escape hatches but there are none. Your expenditure will be so high, you will feel oppressed. The good news is this expensive phase is a short one. Relationships are the central theme of this period. Expect sudden windfalls, great wealth or luck, and all kinds of wonderful opportunities. You may also make investments in a second home and take a holiday with the family.

As the month progresses, Ganesha believes that you will reach out consciously and unconsciously and ask more of the world; along with this, you are also prepared to give more of yourself to the world. This trend makes you feel either more demanding or more giving toward others. Additionally, you are also busy with loans, funds, rent, leases, legacies and inheritances. There is also travel on the cards and new ideas and new people to flirt with. There will be new circumstances that give you increased freedom or an opportunity to do something that you have never done before. Sometimes, this influence also brings about financial gains. Towards the end of the month, you have a strong need to express yourself by doing something that is different from your normal routine. It is not that you want to rebel but you definitely do not want the status quo to continue. You need to experience a new kind of freedom in your life and to discover dimensions of living that you have not known before. It all depends on several factors including a personal horoscope reading to be more accurate. These are exciting times and Ganesha is with you all the way.

JUNE

In many ways, the situation heats up for you. It is not just the summer in the sub-continent but also in your life as many issues come to a head. This is the time to figure out how to put your plans in action. Don't be impatient or expect quick results/changes. Play out your hand with forethought and planning. You can't afford to be careless or neglectful of your money or of your health. Make sure that adequate safeguards are in place for both. The purpose of forecasts is to ensure that you are at least forewarned. This is what Ganesha does for you, now. This is full moon time and you should make the most of it. You are much more receptive to new ideas now and that is a good thing. You look for more novelty, more originality. There will be sudden changes or an event that gives you a new chance in some way. There could also be a sudden windfall or promotion or even a sudden chance encounter that works to your advantage. There are many openings and opportunities spread out before you like a buffet. There is travel, expansion and growth as the month moves on. You are in the throes of success. Your partner and you have a holiday together at some exotic location. You love the bonding and take the relationship to the next level if you are not already married. At work you are in line for accolades. There is profitable travel and new business associations. But there could be some trouble on the domestic front. There may be a bitter divorce or the termination of a long and meaningful relationship. You will be in deep stress and it is time to look after your health. Ask Ganesha for help. Once again, these are mere indications. Your personal horoscope will be more accurate.

As June ends, there are many changes happening in your life now and there is an enormous revolution in your consciousness. You are exposed to aspects of life that you never dreamed possible. Many new vistas open up magically and suddenly before you and may include the occult or metaphysics, astrology, magic and altered states of consciousness. You may even contemplate joining extremely idealistic and radical groups. This is a particularly important period for young people on the threshold of life.

JULY

There is suddenly a lot on your plate. You have to work out the details carefully and Ganesha will help you. July is action time for your long-drawn plans. July brings you a large agenda of things to be done – personally, professionally and family-wise. It will lead to several new avenues, beginnings and start-ups. A more objective, pragmatic approach will prove to be a good bet. You will thus be able to prioritize what needs to be done, and also decide how best to cope, especially in the finances and expenses area, but also with your time and effort. July centers and focuses you, gives you grounding, a base, especially on and after the 9th. Ganesha says that there is more stability now but many changes too. There are tremendous new understandings asserting themselves in your life with great force. A new consciousness slowly asserts itself.

There are also many close bonds of genuine love. You have many new psychological insights. There could be many changes in your life and you will have to be fluid to accept them. There will be no permanent structures and a lot will be changing in your life. This is a significant period. There will be many emotional moments and the family will be at centre stage as the month wears on. There will be demands from the spouse, children, in-laws and extended family. Your consciousness will be changing rapidly. There will be new goals and new directions. Charles Darwin said that the species that is receptive to change survives, and not the one that is the strongest, fastest or the fittest. This is the time to be receptive to changes in your life. Towards the end of the month, there is a new intensity and new direction. The period of soul-searching is coming to a close. There are many lucky influences at play now and you could be fortunate in gambling, speculation and at risk taking. You also grasp new ideas quickly. There could be a fortunate discovery or invention and you receive rewards and awards, kudos and applause. You have had many realizations and you grow as a person into a finer and happier human being. Just ask Ganesha for guidance.

AUGUST

The pace increases and you are on fifth gear most of the month. The work scene will be hectic and you make great progress. Of course, there is no free meal in the world and there is a lot to pay for. If you thought July was hectic, August will be nothing short of frenetic. August is also for adventure, enterprise and most certainly romance, children, hobbies and fun, with the second half being particularly stimulating. The first 10 days of August could find you coping with the pending work of July, and as you will realize, it's best to take care of previous assignments and commitments. It will leave you with a free mind to take on new projects. Money and opportunity, says Ganesha, knock at your door and you give them a warm welcome. You are moving ahead and pretty fast too. The start of the month sees a flow of energy that enables you to act effectively and to take initiatives that demand foresight, planning and considerable self-confidence. This is a good time to start any enterprise. You want to grow as a person and will do everything that helps you make it happen.

There is genuine growth after all the soul-searching of the past many weeks. As a result of your self-evaluation, you gain in credibility, popularity, authority and win kudos for your accomplishments. The creative pursuits - cinema, television, the performing arts, hobbies, even speculation and playing the stock market - will yield excellent results.

Towards the middle of the month, you approach life and work with a much more open frame of mind leading to greater ingenuity as well as better, brighter ideas. There will also be new bonds and ties of love which will be much more intense. There is emotional balance leading to success. The gains you make will be long-lasting and pleasing and they will remain so for a long time. Your popularity soars and nothing can come in the way of your steady and sure progress. As the month ends, you are in great spirits and nothing can stop you. Your success with people and your relationships keep you on a high. You want to have fun and enjoy the limelight. You savour the pleasures of good company, good friends and good food. In short, all the good things of life. Finance will be important and activities like leasing, rentals, taxes, funding, bonds will be a major part of the week's theme. There will be a grand fusion of work and pleasure.

SEPTEMBER

There is a lot going for you. Of course, you must be careful that you don't overdo the work bit as other areas of your life may suffer as a result. The energy of the past two months keeps you fired up half-way through September. Employees, co-workers and colleagues will all get taken along as you head for goals, success and achievements. They will co-operate, assist and support you.

Therefore a scintillating, exciting month lies ahead for you. You look for a million outlets, like love, marriage, friendship, trips with a stopover, interacting with people, going places, but, also fighting battles, legal and otherwise, and here, you will have the energy to go all out for it, which is on par for the course. You branch out in different directions like the roots of a giant banyan tree. You fine tune your professional goals and indulge in serious planning to get where you want to be. Your sights are set high and you will need to improve the work environment, streamline office procedures and work on improving inter-personal and intra-personal relationships. You also take a hard look at spirituality and at ways to give back to society.

This month sees you on the fast track to progress and the first priority is to get your act together. You will be doing some serious thinking and changing in your lifestyle and priorities. Even though you are truly into breaking new horizons, do not leave neighbours, relatives and friends behind. Carry them with you. Ganesha believes that you will have the four G's - gains, glory, good times and genuine companions. You make progress and there is an expansion of your horizons. There are new inclinations and predilections, a new focus, a deep gnawing desire for spirituality and the higher issues of life. There is greater intensity and depth in all your interactions. Ganesha blesses you with wonderful times.

The full moon is in your sign towards the end of the month and this is a momentous period. You have made money and earned accolades. Now you look at many other aspects that make life more complete. You are excited by parapsychology, psychic insights, nursing, healing, mantra, tantra, healing, charities and all activities far removed from the regular tenor of life. You have a new mindset now and the full moon phase brings a sense of completion and direction to your growth as an individual. This is a great period and if carefully handled can lead to stupendous success.

OCTOBER

You are sprinting away to glory. There is not a moment to waste; at least that is what you feel. The mountain goat wants to climb to the pinnacle and you literally leave no stone unturned. Another very busy and active phase comes this month. Right from September 28, you have been setting a cracking pace and reaching out to people and places, extending yourself. You will focus this month on the work arena and on your spiritual life. A strange combination, but it makes for an exciting, fulfilling period. There are different commitments of all kinds confronting you now. Work and family will demand not only hard work and effort, but also investments and outlays in finance and time. You will have to cope with several demands on you. There is Venus in your life, and money and honey (my favourite phrase) is the central theme of this period. The highlight now is personal and shared finance, love, passion and romance, and also partnerships and trade. Ganesha says that you have a busy time ahead, both professionally and emotionally. The earth element now balances your fiery temperament and grounds it. You have evolved, developed a vision of the future, worked hard and made all possible efforts to convert your dreams and hopes into reality. There are many possibilities that you will explore.

As the month progresses, it is also a time for consolidation. Finances will keep you busy. The focus will be on property, acquisitions, possessions, buying and selling, stocks, realty, inheritances, wills and so on. There will be genuine gains as you also plan carefully for the future. There is urgent need for peace and harmony and you should work towards that. There will be business issues, acquisitions, capital, funds and other fiscal issues taking up your time. This is also a good time to launch a project, finish pending work, take on new assignments. Lending/borrowing/ investing/ buying/selling/shopping will continue to be very important.

NOVEMBER

This is the time to remember Ganesha as you will have to make many important decisions and will not be able to do with it without divine assistance. Also, there could be many issues at the crossroads. Money will pour in, but you still need to make decisions about how best to utilize it. This trend, ushered in now, will firm up next month and take you to a truly different plane/ level of existence altogether. A wider world view, travel, greater faith, true religious insights come to you. There are equally strong possibilities of conflicts, disappointments, and hindrances – either socially or personally. Perhaps, even both are possible. You continue on the fast track of progress. You feel good about yourself as you follow your heart and your true inclinations. Moonlight and roses, love and storybook romance, leisure and pleasure, fun times and children are what this week has in store for you. You are on a high and will have many affairs of the heart. Ganesha asks you to guard against causing disappointment to a loved one, resentment or impatience with others, and inconsideration in your dealings. You are now able to enjoy life, laughter, love, the good times.

You are happy and turn to prayer, spirituality or meditation. You are drawn to the contemplative life, thinking and looking within, the merging of the lower and higher selves. It is a unique phase when material and spiritual progress will be linked. This is a significant period and you will reap the whirlwind in the days to come. As the month progresses, it could also be a taxing, tiring, demanding time of highs and lows. While there is a probable wish-fulfilment, there is also much anxiety. There will be a lot of work along with a fair amount of socializing. Family life will be good but you may not have much time for home. There will be international travel and those in the media, in particular, will do well. Life is good as you savour many golden moments.

DECEMBER

Despite it all, there is some peace, harmony and accomplishment now. Somehow, it has all worked out well for you, and don't we know that all is well that ends well. You are, finally, happy and I dare say the credit goes to Ganesha for this. Of course, you have worked hard and created the openings, but a lot of life is not in our hands. The year ends on a good note. All the spheres will hum and progress, but the balance will tilt heavily in favour of family and loved ones. You will reach out, every way you can, and at all levels. New orientations, directions will suggest themselves and you will pursue them. You will also be keenly interested in research, spirituality, higher studies. You will, in addition, reach out for fresh new, meaningful collaborations and tie-ups. Another unique indication is of travel, not just for work or pleasure but also mental voyages and philosophical journeys, flights of fancy and thought into the realm of the unknown, seeking hidden meanings. Thus, growth and expansion of the intellectual, mental kind are your major gains. There is a lot of movement now. You meet people, make profitable travel, sign deals and are in the thick of action.

The first part of the month sees a lot of socializing and you gain financially and emotionally. There is greater happiness, peace and contentment. You have all that you desire. You are more relaxed and responsive to others. This phase teaches you, in a fresh new way and very strongly, the joys and methods of getting the most out of life. You meet up with old flames and there is a lot of partying too. You want to end the year in a blaze of glory.

There are many emotional moments with loved ones. You re-examine your life and look at how others view you. You may need to change your perceptions. This has been an interesting year with many life lessons imparted. There are special new bonds of caring, sharing and affection. This is also the time for an engagement or marriage. Gosh, what a year it has been. Even Ganesha is awestruck!

ARIES

THE MONTHS AT A GLANCE

January
You have the vision and perseverance to achieve magical results at work. There is applause and you spruce up your persona. You want to present the world a better image of yourself. This is a great start to the year.

February
You are satisfied with life and there are massive gains in business. You experience great camaraderie, shared dreams, true love and support, and a grand vision of life. Ganesha blesses you as there is visible all-round progress.

March
This is a magical period and Ganesha hopes that you make the most of it. Mercury, the mighty planet, is all-powerful. Mercury, in short, is the ambassador and salesman of the zodiac. It is very important and occupies a prominent position now. Mercury is turbo powering you for over a fortnight. Make the most of this period and success is yours.

April
Once again, mid-month, you are in the throes of a lucky spell. You do marvellously well with Mercury, the mighty planet, in your sign. It is very important and occupies a prominent position now for over twenty days. There is new work and your bonds of love are strengthened. You are happy, healthy and joyous.

May
There will be new circumstances that give you increased freedom

or an opportunity to do something that you have never done before. Sometimes this influence also brings about financial gains. Towards the end of the month, you have a strong need to express yourself by doing something that is different from your normal routine.

June

There could also be a sudden windfall or promotion or even a sudden chance encounter that works to your advantage. There are many openings and opportunities spread out before you like a buffet. There is travel, expansion and growth as the month moves on.

July

Ganesha says that there is more stability now but many changes too. There are tremendous new understandings asserting themselves in your life with great force. A new consciousness slowly asserts itself. There are also many close bonds of genuine love.

August

The start of the month sees a flow of energy that enables you to act effectively and to take initiatives that demand foresight, planning and considerable self-confidence. This is a good time to start any enterprise. You want to grow as a person and will do everything that helps you make it happen.

September

Ganesha believes that you will have the four G's --- gains, glory, good times, genuine companions. You make progress and there is an expansion of your horizons. There are new inclinations and predilections, a new focus, a deep gnawing desire for spirituality and the higher issues of life.

October

As the month progresses, it is also a time for consolidation. Finances will keep you busy. The focus will be on property, acquisitions, possessions, buying and selling, stocks, realty, inheritances, wills and so on. There will be genuine gains as you also plan carefully for the future.

November

You are happy and turn to prayer, spirituality, and meditation. You are drawn to the contemplative life, thinking and looking within, the merging of the lower and higher selves. It is a unique phase when material and spiritual progress will be linked.

December

New orientations and directions will suggest themselves and you will pursue them. You will also be keenly interested in research, spirituality, higher studies. You will, in addition, reach out for fresh new, meaningful collaborations and tie-ups.

ARIES

WEEKLY REVIEW

(By the Phases of the Moon)

January 1 - Moon's first quarter in Aries

You start the year with a bang. Events move at a furious pace and you have to cover a lot of ground. This is a very productive period and you will be busier than ever. You exhibit great skills at work and bond with loved ones. There is travel and mounting costs and many visitors. There may be shortcomings in your plans and a financial crunch. It may be a good idea to be discreet and low-key in your activities, particularly with financial matters. Don't trust others too much or you may end up disclosing secrets, projects or assets that are best kept to yourself. This is the time for new beginnings and focussed effort. The start of the year may also see a new love interest and this can be very significant. There is passion, beautiful bonding and great times. You start the year with the intensity of intimacy. Ganesha wishes you well.

January 9 - Full Moon in Cancer

You pass through several testing emotional moments. The new love interest keeps you on your toes. There is melodrama in your life. From money and material assets, the focus shifts to the domestic set-up. You are keen to enhance and improve your family and social interactions in a big way. There are partnerships, religious ceremonies, meetings and interviews and you come out with flying colours. If interested in any sort of partnership or business/collaborations/connections, this is the right time to go ahead and take it all head on. Journeys, meetings and conferences will produce pleasing results. Future plans, in-laws, disputes about politics, religion and faith - all occupy your thoughts. There could be some trouble with children and teenagers and you should resolve it before it gets out of hand. Ganesha is with you. It is a good time to solve all domestic issues and move ahead.

January 16 - Moon's last quarter in Libra

You come out with guns blazing. There is a lot on your plate and you will have a lot to cope with, especially continued pressure at work. There could be many changes on the domestic scene; what these are likely to be, I am not in a position to say in a general forecast. I will need personal details for that. But there will be growth in parental ties and duties, and a new attitude of pooling, caring and sharing. There will be deep bonding, wonderful family interactions and a happier home environment. You will find time for leisure despite the pressures of work. There are love interests, buying and selling, and expansion on the work front. Ganesha is with you.

January 23 - New Moon in Aquarius

You are in a whirl of new ideas. Having experienced the joys of togetherness and closeness with people, you will focus now on group and shared activities, visits to amusement parks, clubs, even the disco and the races. There will be congenial and pleasant company. Your own changed persona will contribute greatly to the happy atmosphere. You have come a long way emotionally and discarded old opinions and dogmatic attitudes. You have become a much easier person to get along with. You find the time to relax, take a breather, entertain and be amused. The main trend now will deal primarily with how best to make career and business mesh well with home and hearth. You go about creating the necessary atmosphere and environment for it. Ganesha wishes you well.

January 31 - Moon's first quarter in Taurus

You move to more stable ground. You have gained belief in yourself and faith in those you care for. You learn to take setbacks calmly, especially when plans don't quite work out the way you had anticipated and friends don't live up to your hopes and dreams. You have the ability to change the situation with your own efforts and don't allow delays, problems or snags to hold you back. You have the vision and perseverance to achieve magical results at work. There is applause and you spruce up your persona. You want to present to the world a better image of yourself and so take up a gym membership, yoga and meditation and find the time to concentrate on improving your health with proper care, lifestyle changes and fitness. You also attempt to resolve personal problems and are on a rapid growth trajectory. Take Ganesha's blessings and sally forth.

February 7 - Full moon in Leo

Life now is large and fabulous. You think big and plan big. You also execute big. You recently embarked on a programme of self-improvement and now you are ready to claim your treasure chest. There is a great desire to work harder, earn more and build assets. You are satisfied with life and there are massive gains in business. You meet up with old and new friends, and social and family activities will be most pleasurable as both, work and pleasure come together beautifully for you. The chance to be both successful and happy is rare. It happens only to the most fortunate and in this phase you are the chosen one. You experience great camaraderie, shared dreams, true love and support, and a grand vision of life. Ganesha blesses you as there is visible all-round progress. Success comes easily and you are on a good wicket. There is no need to be run-out!

February 14 - Moon's last quarter in Scorpio

There is passion and new liaisons. You play the field as though tomorrow would never come by. You look back in satisfaction at the growth in every sphere of your life and there is a glow of contentment. You experience the pleasure of a bright, new image, feelings of self-worth, gains in money matters and personal assets. You realise that success is valid only if it is apparent and visible.

You revamp your finances and it leads to greater prosperity. You focus strongly on property, gains, friendship and fraternity. Loans and funds also come your way easily. You may join organisations to increase your social status, probably become a member of the Lions or Rotary clubs, and socialise. There is warmth in friendship in all your dealings. There could also be an addition to the family, even an adoption. There may also be a wedding or engagement or some such happy occasion. Ganesha is with you all the way.

February 21 - New Moon in Pisces

There are several soft and emotional moments and deep, intimate bonding with your special partner. If newly married, this will be a blissful period. You realise that life needs the sweet smell of money to enhance and enrich it. Therefore, finances, funding, capital-raising, investments come to the fore and you are aware of the need to handle them imaginatively and well. You will also focus on building strong family ties, bonds of love and caring. You know that both areas can be interdependent and so you turn your attention and efforts to the house, home and property once again. Buying and selling are all important, whether of assets, shares or real estate. Elders, parents, in-laws, siblings and extended family will also be in the picture. Ensure that you do not hurt or neglect dear ones and take care not to burn the candle at both ends. The temptation to overdo things will be very strong as you whole-heartedly pursue your objectives. Your determination and enterprise will ensure that you pull through difficult situations. But Ganesha cautions you about over stretching like a rubber band that may just snap one day.

March 1 - Moon's first quarter in Gemini

This is a period of ideas and growth. There is harmony at home and accolades, rewards and awards at work. You can pull a rabbit out of the hat. This is a magical period and Ganesha hopes that you make the most of it. Mercury, the mighty planet, is all-powerful. It favours travels/ meetings/conferences/ interviews/ trips/

more brain power/ contacts/ communication/correspondence/ contracts. Mercury has a special connection with the circuits of the brain. Chess, crossword and other such games belong to Mercury. Also, short distance runners and spin bowlers are controlled by Mercury. Mercury, in short, is the ambassador and salesman of the zodiac. It occupies a prominent position now. Mercury is turbo powering you for over a fortnight. Make the most of this period and success is yours. You are in line for windfalls.

March 8 - Full Moon in Virgo

You are in full flow and there is rampant progress in your affairs. The time has come for you to look at new decisions at work and play. You realise the necessity of steady work and income and look for new ways to augment earnings. You have a burning desire to achieve at the highest levels and you seriously look at new lines of business, a crash course, higher study and research, even accessing the internet to forge fresh links with the world. You understand well the great uses of technology and social networking and make the most of it. This phase will be very favourable in several ways. You fix new visions of the future and have the chance to share them with people who appreciate you as a person and as a serious professional. Ganesha blesses you. There could be a hike in domestic expenses and elders at home could be a cause for concern.

March 15 - Moon's last quarter in Sagittarius

There is travel on the cards and you will be meeting many new people and making several profitable associations. In your decision-making, you have to focus on determining the right directions for the future. There are happy times at home with greater bonding with relatives, family members, parents and children. New enterprises and projects will materialise, but you will have to work hard and see to their completion. Some relationships and/ or professional interactions could turn sour. People you interact with will blow hot and cold and you could be quite irritated, even outright resentful. It is vital that you deal with and resolve your own complexes and neuroses. Do not lose your natural generosity and understanding of life. Do not tread on toes or treat colleagues and subordinates with arrogance as, buoyed by all the success, you could lose humility. This is a wonderful period and Ganesha feels that you should optimise it.

March 22 - New Moon in Aries

The new moon is in your sign and you should maximise this period. You know quite clearly the activities that will lead you to progress and happiness, and so focus all your attention on them. You fix your mind on much higher levels now as you look at vistas far removed from the mundane chores of work and family. Education and research will draw you like a magnet, and travel will be a great education broadening your horizons literally and figuratively. You want to expand your mind and grow as a human being and you will do everything possible to make it happen. There will be pleasant times with friends and there will be wonderful moments of shared love with your partner or spouse. There are strong ego drives and Ganesha asks you to keep them under wraps. Children will be a source of joy.

March 30 - Moon's first quarter in Cancer

This is an emotional period and many maudlin thoughts travel through your mind. But this phase is a great one as there will be gains on many fronts and happiness in love. There will be marvellous results at work too. You are much more sympathetic, warm and caring, and make it a point to understand your own limitations and the other person's point of view. Humanitarian efforts, social reform and spiritual growth will bring out the best in you. There is money to be made and your mood is upbeat and euphoric. There are many expenses as you soldier on to your lofty goals. Your life is on an upswing and Ganesha is happy for you.

April 6 - Full Moon in Libra

You look for peace of mind amidst all this frenzy. Your spiritual strength will stand you in good stead as you cope with the world. There could be some health challenges and it will be necessary to take adequate rest. You could check out a health resort or yoga, meditation and deep breathing. You have been pushing too hard. Once again, this can be an expensive and demanding phase. There will be postponements and cancellations and delays along with compromises, meetings, negotiations and settlements. Collaborations are also likely, maybe even a marriage or engagement. Ganesha ensures that success is yours despite the odds and the challenges.

April 13 - Moon's last quarter in Capricorn

Once again, you are in the throes of a lucky spell. You do marvellously well with Mercury, the mighty planet, in your sign. Mercury favours travels/ meetings/conferences/ interviews/ trips/ more brain power/ contacts/ communication/correspondence/contracts. As I mentioned earlier, Mercury has a special connection with the circuits of the brain. Chess, crossword and other such games belong to Mercury. Also, short distance runners and spin bowlers are controlled by Mercury. Mercury, in short, is the ambassador and salesman of the zodiac. It is very important and occupies a prominent position now for over 20 days. There is new work and your bonds of love are strengthened. You are happy, healthy and joyous and Ganesha is happy for you. Make the most of this phase as Mercury will help you achieve whatever you want.

April 21 - New Moon in Taurus

These are grand times and you must seize every opportunity. You may be swept off your feet by a potential lover. You are not excited by the person per se but by something within yourself that you are projecting upon him or her. When you finally learn the truth about the other person, you may have difficulty accepting the person and your fatal attraction. But that is how life is with its many mysteries and surprises. They just never seem to stop. These are exciting times and you must savour each mouthful to the fullest. You can have it all. There is love, romance, fun and games, partying, socialising, get-togethers. Yes, your plate is full and overflowing. Relationships, both personal and professional, give you great pleasure and benefit you in manifold ways. You look towards the future with hope and optimism. You find great satisfaction at work and this joyful spirit adds colour to your life. Ganesha has truly blessed you.

April 29 - Moon's first quarter in Leo

You live large and attract many liaisons, some of which can be dangerous. You could be attracted to an unattainable person. You may be setting yourself up for a situation in which you cannot win as the person you have set your sights on appears to be an unrealisable dream. You will be torn by several emotions. Should you continue and push ahead or should you withdraw? You attract attention with your actions and become the source of wonderment and, maybe, even envy. You make many new contacts and have remarkable career growth. There could be overseas travel and an affair with a person from a completely different culture. Of course, like I keep saying, nothing certain can be said until I refer to the personal horoscope. These are all mere generalisations. Ganesha is with you all the way.

May 6 - Full Moon in Scorpio

Relationships are the central theme of this period. You live a lot in a fantasy world. By avoiding confrontations with real people, you also avoid a confrontation with yourself. You do this precisely because you fear that you will be the loser. Yet a real confrontation is just what you need. If you persist in any of these relationships, you will have to confront both yourself and your partner as real individuals. That will be the real test of the relationship. Along with all this, there will also be growth and progress. You can expect sudden windfalls, great wealth or luck, and all kinds of wonderful opportunities. You may also make investments in a second home and take a holiday with the family. Take life as it flows, says Ganesha.

May 12 - Moon's last quarter in Aquarius

There will be many types of meetings that make you wiser and more mature and have a broader understanding of the world. You will reach out consciously and unconsciously and ask more of the world; along with this, you are also prepared to give more of yourself to the world. This trend makes you feel either more demanding or more giving towards others. According to the law of conservation of energy in the universe, you can transform the energies in your life from one form to another, but you cannot create them out of nothing. Additionally, along with all this, you are also busy with loans, funds, rent, leases, legacies and inheritances. Certainly, by all accounts, Ganesha gives you a mixed and sumptuous week. It will take a long time to digest.

May 20 - New Moon in Gemini

There is travel on the cards and new ideas and people to flirt with. Many old flames and friends from the past come into your life. There will be new circumstances that give you increased freedom or an opportunity to do something that you have never done before. There will be opportunities for higher education and travel. Sometimes this influence also brings about financial gains. This is an excellent time to invest or expand in business as long as you are very careful not to overdo it or overextend yourself. Ganesha wishes you well.

May 28 - Moon's first quarter in Virgo

There is stability but along with it are many new influences. You have a strong need to express yourself by doing something that is different from your normal routine. It is not that you want to rebel but you definitely do not want the status quo to continue. You need to experience a new kind of freedom in your life and to discover dimensions of living that you have not known before. You are keen on taking risks but just make sure that they are calculated ones. You may search for higher realities, for inner truth on the metaphysical or philosophical level, or you may just change jobs to experience a new adrenaline rush. It all depends on several factors including a personal horoscope reading to be more accurate. But the indications are that there will be change. These are exciting times and Ganesha is with you all the way.

June 4 - Full Moon in Sagittarius

This is full moon time and you should make the most of it. You are much more receptive to new ideas now. You look for more novelty, more originality, and this is a good move as you are tired of the boring and the mundane which has dominated most of the recent past. You may have got into a rut and this is the time to get out of it and make new forays into the big, wide world. There will be new opportunities or a piece of good luck that seems to have emerged out of the blue and taken you by surprise. There will be sudden changes or an event that gives you a new chance in some way. There could also be a sudden windfall or promotion or even a sudden chance encounter that works to your advantage. There are many openings and opportunities spread out before you, like a buffet. Make the most of it, says Ganesha. There is travel, expansion and growth. You are in the throes of success and that is most certainly a good feeling.

June 11 - Moon's last quarter in Pisces

Your partner and you have a holiday together at some exotic location. You love the bonding and take the relationship to the next level if you are not already married. There is a lot of work too, it is not all love and play, and all your actions are governed by a strong sense of integrity. You are ambitious but also very ethical and set high standards. Loosely translated this means that you will not accept bribes, 'haftas', 'chai paani', baksheesh or under the table 'rewards' that is normally the rule in business in the sub-continent.

This will be noticed by your subordinates and colleagues and there will be rewards, awards and accolades. You want to be a person of renown in the world or in the community you live in, you have a strong desire to make something of yourself in the broadest sense of the term. There is a great drive to succeed, and succeed you will, says Ganesha.

June 19 - New Moon in Gemini

There is profitable travel and new business associations. But there could be some trouble on the domestic front. There may be a bitter divorce or the termination of a long and meaningful relationship. There could be messy litigation and a loss of money and prestige. You will be in deep stress and it is time to look after your health. The domestic scene will take up most of your time. Ask Ganesha for help. In times like this, you just have to hold on and let the bad times pass as they will. Once again, these are mere indications. Your personal horoscope will be more accurate.

June 27 - Moon's first quarter in Libra

You feel trapped and in several minds wondering what to do and how to move ahead and in which direction. There are many changes happening in your life now and there is an enormous revolution in your consciousness. You are exposed to aspects of life that you never dreamed possible. Many new vistas open up magically and suddenly before you and may include the occult or metaphysics, astrology, magic and altered states of consciousness. You may even contemplate joining extremely idealistic and radical groups. This is a particularly important period for young people on the threshold of life. There are many influences beckoning and you will have to choose the right path carefully. Ganesha wishes you well.

July 3 - Full Moon in Capricorn

There is more stability now but many changes too. You will have to watch your step. But this can lead to many new learnings and the period can be very good if used well. There are tremendous new understandings asserting themselves in your life with great force. A new consciousness slowly asserts itself. It all depends on how you handle these changes. The work front is fine but you may be inclined to team up with a guru or god man or join a spiritual organisation. There are many close bonds of genuine love. Many decisions you make now will also depend on your age, circumstances and status because you can embark in any direction. There are many influences acting on you. Ask Ganesha for guidance and choose the right way.

July 11 - Moon's first quarter in Aries

The moon's first quarter is in your sign and this can be a significant period. You have many new psychological insights. There could be many changes in your life and you will have to be fluid to accept them. There will be no permanent structures and a lot will be changing in your life. You will wonder if you want to leave it all, sell out, and move to another place and another life altogether. This can have many meanings: leave urban life and move to an ashram or leave the country and move to a more prosperous environment. Like I said earlier, a lot depends on several factors. This is a significant period. Ganesha blesses you.

July 19 - New Moon in Cancer

There will be many emotional moments and the family will be at centre stage. There will be demands from the spouse, children, in-laws and extended family. This can be a rough time in the sense that you will not have time for yourself. There could be some confusion, doubt and uncertainty. It will be best to let the situation settle before looking for solutions. Try to minimise the elements of your life that require you to make long-range commitments. Your consciousness will be rapidly changing. There will be new goals and new directions in due course. There is a revolution in ideas and consciousness and it would be best to go with the flow and see where it docks. Be open to change. Charles Darwin said that the species that is receptive to change survives, and not the one that is the strongest or fastest. This is the time to be receptive to changes in your life. Ganesha blesses you.

July 26 - Moon's last quarter in Scorpio

There is a new intensity and new directions. The period of soul searching is coming to a close. There are many lucky influences at play now and you could be fortunate in gambling, speculation and at risk taking. If you play the stock market, this could be a good phase. You also grasp new ideas quickly. There could be a fortunate discovery or invention and you receive rewards and awards, kudos and applause. You have had many realisations and you grow as a person into a finer and happier human being. You could be a better parent, son/daughter, colleague or boss. This is a very good period for the evolution of your soul. Ganesha is with you.

August 2 - Full Moon in Aquarius

You are moving ahead and pretty fast too. This week sees a flow of energy that enables you to act effectively and to take initiatives that demand foresight, planning and considerable self-confidence. This is a good time to start any enterprise as chances of something new working out are very good. This is also a good time to mend fences. If you haven't gotten along with someone or have had a temporary dispute, this is the right time to make an effort to settle it. You are in the mood for compromises and quick settlements. Legal affairs, if any, will also be sorted out quickly and fast. Your scope of action increases and there is more freedom of movement and opportunities for new experiences. You look at new options and take on many new challenges. You want to grow as a person and will do everything that helps you make it happen. Ganesha encourages you.

August 9 - Moon's last quarter in Taurus

There is genuine growth after all the soul searching of the past many weeks. As a result of your evaluation of yourself, you gain in credibility, popularity, authority and win kudos for your accomplishments. The creative pursuits - cinema, television, the performing arts, hobbies, even speculation and playing the stock market - will yield excellent results. You approach life and work with a much more open frame of mind leading to greater ingenuity as well as better, brighter ideas. There will also be new bonds and ties of love which will be much more intense and deeper. There is professional and personal recognition as you enjoy greater gains and deeper joy. You face life's challenges with equanimity. There are expenses as well as more earning. This is a great phase to be. Ganesha blesses you.

August 17 - New Moon in Leo

One reason for your success is the way in which you handle people. You take the middle path and win friends easily. You have realised that this is the best way. As a result, all ties, both domestic and professional, are upbeat. There is no room for hurt, acrimony, false expectations or acquisitions in all your interactions. Attachments, friendships, love, romance and other ties are constantly strengthened and reinforced. There is emotional balance leading to success. The gains you make will be long-lasting and pleasing and they will remain for a long time. Your popularity soars and nothing can come in the way of your steady and sure progress. Just believe in Ganesha and go with the flow.

August 24 - Moon's first quarter in Sagittarius

You are in great spirits and nothing can stop you. Your success with people and your relationships keep you on a high. You want to have fun and enjoy the limelight. You savour the pleasures of good company, good friends, good food, in short all the good things of life. You are ready to mingle, socialise and party like there is no tomorrow. You do all this with élan and a touch of class. You have charisma and you charm even the worst critics. You make new acquaintances and renew old friendships. There is domestic bliss as the family draws closer. This is a wonderful period as you get closer to your ideal of the good life. Ganesha is pleased.

August 31 - Full Moon in Pisces

Your two main areas of interest will now be money and the people in your life. You will reinvent old school ties and also focus on work and forming new associations. There will also be a lot of partying as you mix business with pleasure. Finance will be important and activities like leasing, rentals, taxes, funding, bonds will be a major part of the week's theme. There will be a grand fusion of work and pleasure. Ganesha is generous. There will also be great moments of beautiful bonding with a new love. You may escape the routine of everyday life and even shack up in some exotic locale with your new love interest.

September 8 - Moon's first quarter in Gemini

You branch out in different directions like the roots of a giant banyan tree. You will be confronted by certain issues and will have to make important decisions. You don't want your success/ popularity to falter. But you also find the time to help others, to share resources, give charity or monetary help to those in need. You fine tune your professional goals and indulge in serious planning to get where you want to be. Your sights are set high and you will need to improve the work environment, streamline office procedures and work on improving inter-personal and intra-personal relationships. You also take a hard look at spirituality and at ways to give back to society. Ganesha blesses you.

September 16 - New Moon in Virgo

You are on the fast track to progress and the first priority is to get your act together. You will be doing some serious and hard thinking and changing your lifestyle and priorities. You may have to curtail the excessive partying and spending habits. But you know what is best in the circumstances. There could also be unnecessary roadblocks like jealously, animosity from your peer group and your own ego drives. You will have to handle all this with care. Even though you are truly breaking new horizons, do not leave neighbours, relatives and friends behind. Carry them with you. Share your success with others and it will really help. You may also undertake new studies. Ganesha believes that you will have the four G's - gains, glory, good times, genuine companions. Please tell me if there is more needed in life.

September 22 - Moon's first quarter in Capricorn

You make progress and also get into an introspective frame of mind. There is an expansion of your mental horizons and many interests occupy your mind. There are new inclinations and predilections, a new focus, a deep gnawing desire for spirituality and the higher issues of life. You are concerned with justice, law and order, the higher self as you look hard at widening the vistas of your mind. Travel, publicity, visits, interviews, meets, conferences, collaborations and networking within and outside the family add to the quality of life. There is greater intensity and depth in all your interactions. Ganesha blesses you with wonderful times.

September 30 - Full Moon in Aries

The full moon is in your sign and this is a momentous period. You have made money and earned accolades. Now you look at many other aspects that make life more complete. You get deep within yourself and seriously examine the workings of the mind and the meaning behind your actions. You are excited by parapsychology, psychic insights, nursing, healing, mantra, tantra, healing, charities and all activities far removed from the regular tenor of life. You have a new mindset now and the full moon phase brings a sense of completion and direction to your growth as an individual. This is a great period and if carefully handled can lead to stupendous success. Ganesha feels that you are truly blessed.

October 8 - Moon's last quarter in Cancer

There are different commitments of all kinds confronting you now.

Work and family will demand not only hard work and effort, but also investments and outlays in finance and time. You will have to cope with several demands made on you. There could also be an illness in the family, and elders and children will need particular attention. A parent or in-law may need to be hospitalised. You will also have to go slow and look for time to recuperate from the hectic periods of the recent past. Look at yoga, meditation, alternative healing and massages to prevent anything serious from happening in the future. Ganesha is with you.

October 15 - New Moon in Libra

There is Venus in your life, and money and honey (my favourite phrase) is the central theme of this period. The highlight now is personal and shared finance, love, passion and romance, and also partnerships and trade. Ganesha says that you have a busy time ahead, both professionally and emotionally. But you are determined to enjoy it. There could also be journeys, legal issues, and dealings at law courts, even some settlements and compromises. You will be in the midst of negotiations of all kinds. There will be sharing, togetherness, bonding, warmth, love, true accord and harmony.

October 22 - Moon's first quarter in Capricorn

The earth element now balances your fiery temperament and grounds it. You have evolved, developed a vision of the future, worked hard and made all possible efforts to convert your dreams and hopes into reality. There are many possibilities that you will explore. Of course, finance remains a central theme and there will be much buying and selling, signing of lease documents, contracts, instruments of negotiation, promissory notes etc. The other angles that will be both interesting and vibrant will be fashion and food as you keep exploring. You have been striving hard for a long time to achieve all this and now success, happiness and all the goodies of life are firmly in your grasp. This is also a great time for love, adds Ganesha. There will be passion and several intimate moments.

October 29 - Full Moon in Taurus

This is a time for consolidation. Finances will keep you busy. The focus will be on property, acquisitions, possessions, buying and selling, stocks, realty, inheritances, wills and so on. There will be genuine gains as you also plan carefully for the future. It is important in this phase to protect your interests, not to get unethical in your dealings and to prevent others from riding roughshod over your principles. There will be new love too and you could get waylaid. The domestic scene also demands your time and attention. Ganesha asks you to take special care not to be pressurised and exploited. There is urgent need for peace and harmony and you should work towards that. But your desire to have a larger, steadier income will overshadow all other activities and concerns. There will be business issues, acquisitions, capital, funds and other fiscal issues taking up your time. This is also a good time to launch a project, finish pending work, take on new assignments. Lending/borrowing/ investing/buying/selling/ shopping will continue to be very important.

November 7 - Last quarter in Leo

You continue on the fast track of progress. You feel good about yourself as you follow your heart and your true inclinations. Moonlight and roses, love and storybook romance, leisure and pleasure, fun times and children are what this week has in store for you. There is also more money and great luck in dealing with funds and investments. You are ready to take risks but do not treat true love with disdain. You are on a high and will have many affairs of the heart. In the process, do not look down on someone who truly loves you. You have both, the resources and the chutzpah to make a success of whatever you take on. But do not get too overconfident and guard against becoming complacent or too sure of yourself. Ganesha asks you to guard against causing disappointment to a loved one, resentment or impatience with others, and inconsideration in your dealings. You expect too much from friends and colleagues and that can mean trouble. You will have to meet others half way. There is also great danger in breaking hearts as we all know how a woman (if it is one) who has been scorned is!

November 13 - New Moon in Scorpio

In this intense period, there is genuine love, romance and laughter, fun and frolic, the social whirligig, and many bouts of profound happiness. There is respite, relaxation, excitement and glamour and you will revel in it. Your burdens will seem to have fallen away. It will also reflect happily on both your family life and personal interactions. You are now able to enjoy life, laughter, love, the good times. The trends are truly pleasing, something that most people long to experience. There is closeness and warmth in all your relationships. You bond powerfully with loved ones and there will be an addition to the family or a marriage or engagement. You can look forward to happy times, says Ganesha.

November 20 - Moon's first quarter in Aquarius

You are happy and turn to prayer, spirituality or meditation. You are drawn to the contemplative life, thinking and looking within, the merging of the lower and higher selves. But there are also mounting expenses and other domestic issues to deal with. But you tide over all the roadblocks with Ganesha's help. You are well equipped to handle life and turn to the spiritual self for answers. It is a unique phase when material and spiritual progress will be linked. This is a significant period and you will reap the whirlwind in the days to come. Ganesha blesses you. There are also wonderful moments spent with loved ones.

November 28 - Full Moon in Gemini

You are moving in many directions and not all of them are right. This could be a taxing, tiring, demanding time of highs and lows. While there is a probable wish-fulfilment, there is also much anxiety. There will be a lot of work along with a fair amount of socialising. Family life will be good but you may not have much time for the home. There will be international travel and those in the media, in particular, will do well. This will be a busy and demanding week with many pleasant moves and a lot of pleasure. You make contact with old friends and there will be many happy reunions. Life is good as you savour the golden moments. Ganesha is happy.

December 6 - Moon's last quarter in Virgo

You will be busy tending to an ailing relative. The family will be the centre of attention in every way. There will be many demands at the workspace and you are drawn, whether you like it not, into family and property matters, house and home. In your usual friendly manner you will try to resolve differences that may have arisen and also create an atmosphere that is both pleasant and harmonious. Family and work are your twin involvements and you will be drowned in them. But this is not a problem, since you enjoy it and do whatever is expected of you marvellously well. Ganesha blesses you. Children will be a source of joy and you spend many happy moments with them.

December 13 - New Moon in Sagittarius

There is a lot of movement now. You meet people, make profitable travel, sign deals and are in the thick of action. This week sees a lot of socialising and you gain financially and emotionally. The family is better placed and that gives you great satisfaction. There is greater happiness, peace and contentment. You have all that you desire. You are more relaxed and responsive to others. This phase teaches you, in a fresh new way, and very strongly, the joys and methods of getting the most out of life. You manage to use your time and resources to your advantage, and in turn, give the best of yourself. You meet up with old flames and there is a lot of partying too. You want to end the year in a blaze of glory. You will, says Ganesha.

December 20 - Moon's first quarter in Pisces

There are many emotional moments with loved ones. You realise that you need to control your ego drives and relate better to others. You need to get a handle on your pride and egotism and be more tactful and diplomatic, committed and responsible. You re-examine your life and look at how others view you. You may need to change your perceptions and there is a lot of work to be done on yourself. You want to be a better human being and that is the challenge. You go about it with utmost sincerity. In reviewing both your private and public image, you evaluate and assess what you have achieved. You work on all the areas that need improvement and spruce up your physique, wardrobe, manners, make-up, total turnout, and behaviour patterns - the works. Ganesha blesses you.

December 28 - Full Moon in Cancer

This has been an interesting year with many life lessons imparted. There have been material rewards which, most certainly, have been valuable and pleasing. You look for more love and warmth in relationships which will also happen. As you reach out to others and give them love and respect, it comes back to you manifold. You gain love in equal measure, are appreciated, valued and cherished. There are special new bonds of caring, sharing, affection. This is also the time for an engagement or marriage. Who knows, if eligible, it could be yours! Or to someone dear to you, which will not only give you joy and pleasure, but immense satisfaction too. You want to give yourself wings and you look at more meanings of the word 'achievement'. You want to do more than just work mechanically and cope with the nitty-gritty of life. You want more from life and you are on the right track. Ganesha is happy.

ARIES

KEY DATES

January
1, 4-5, 9*-10, 14-15, 19*-20, 23*-24, 27-28.
Possibly the answer to your wishes/hopes, says Ganesha! You get domestic happiness, progress in work and good health, and it is visible now.

February
1*-2, 5*-7, 10-12, 15-16, 19*-20, 23-25, 28.
Romance, marriage, children, speculation, entertainment, new projects, religious ceremonies, functions, arts, and sports. A full plate!

March
1, 5*-6, 10-11, 14-16, 19*-20, 23-24, 27-28.
Romance and finance, work and play make a memorable match. But you must learn to take care of your health and that of your dear ones. *March to May* is for loans and funds, most definitely.

April
1*-2, 6-7, 11*-12, 15*-16, 19*-20, 23-25, 28-30.
Ganesha says, marriage and personal, professional and platonic partnerships, journey, legal cases — all together.

May
1*-5, 8-9, 12*-14 (important), 16-18, 21-22, 25*-27 (important), 30-31.
Loans, funds, joint-finance, insurance, inheritance, investment, moving house or office. Once again, take care of your health.

June
1*, 4*-10 (important week), 13*-14, 17*-18, 22*-23, 24*-28.
There are stars on half the dates simply because June will be most

important — lucky for meeting people, contacting them, finishing pending work, starting new projects, realizing your dreams and aspirations. It is a month for breakthroughs.

July
1-3, 6*-7, 10-12, 14-16, 19*-20, 24-26, 29-30.
Tremendous pressure of work, but the condition at home will improve and make you happy. From 20th July, you have more energy, more vitality, and that reflects on all your activities.

August
2*-3, 4*-8 (important), 11*-12, 15*-17, 20*-23, 25*-26, 30*-31.
Friends help you, your enthusiasm will be seductive and welcome. You will socialize, and have a ball.

September
1-3, *7*-8*, 12*-13, 14-16, 22-23, 26*-27, 29-30.
Expenses, taking care of the sick and the weak, medical check-ups, journeys and spirituality are the highlights.

October
1*-2, 4*-6, 9*-10, 13*-16, 19-20, 21*-27, (important) 29-30.
You will have both, pleasure and profit. Once again, the home will have your attention. Progress at work, too.

November
1-2, 5*-7, 10-12, 18*-19, 22-25, 28-29.
Buying, selling, investing, wining and dining keep you busy!

December
1*-4, 7*-9, 12*-14, 17*-20, 21*-22, 25*-26, 30*-31.
December will be especially important for trips and ties, communication and computers, contacts and contracts.

Taurus

April 20 - May 20

TAURUS

(April 20 – May 20)

ELEMENT AND RULING PLANET: Earth and Venus.

STRENGTHS: Taurus is quite affectionate, patient, stable, determined and practical, stubborn and resistant to change.

WEAKNESS: Rigidity, stubbornness tendency to be overly possessive and materialistic.

SYMBOL: The Bull – Strong, stubborn, plodding, can be both fierce and gentle.

MATCHING SIGN: Scorpio.

MAGICAL BIRTHSTONE: Turquoise and Emerald – I protect against infidelity and deceit, ensure loyalty, and improves the memory.

TAURUS

YEARLY FORECAST

Main Trend

"Perfume is pure seduction. Its ingredients are costly resins like balsam and myrrh, spices like cinnamon and cardamom, and iris root, lotus, saffron and marjoram. Memory and fragrance are intertwined, some biologists insist, because the sense of smell plugs smack into the limbic system, the seat of emotion in the brain. No other sense has such immediate access. It takes 800 pounds of roses to produce a pound of concentrate. The heart of a fragrance lies in the fraction of the nose, shoots up the olfactory bulb, and plucks a chord of delight in the mind. The traditional elements come from animals --- musk (now replaced mostly by synthetics) from a deer, for example, from plants, most notably flowers."

- National Geographic Magazine

Taureans and Librans are the beauty wizards. Therefore they are best at perfumes, music, dance and so on. Ganesha says, astrologically Taureans will have much to do with beauty and utility in 2012 because of the happy influence of Jupiter.

Jupiter will work its magic for you in the following directions:

a) Jupiter helps you in terms of finances, family affairs, using your voice to mesmerise people as only you folks can, budgeting vigorously, paying or taking rentals, taxes, finding out how to improve your property, buy/sell it too. A second marriage is also a possibility. Law suits could end, either by settlement or court decrees.

b) Your personal belongings, say jewellery, watches, clothes, suitcases and bags (personally, I am very fond of suitcases and bags!), will have an added zing to them. Also, you will have to balance your budget. The truth of this prediction will become self-evident by the end of 2012.

c) Taureans will have much to do with shopping, trading, renovating, decorating, agencies and commissions. All this could well be fast and furious.

Luckily, Pluto and Neptune are in a fine position, therefore for you, they will signify:

1. Gains in journey, collaborations;
2. Dollops of pure joy and merriment; and
3. Exceptional, high voltage creativity.

The minor planets Mercury, Venus, and Mars also assert themselves powerfully for you.

Mercury:

Mercury dances and dollies in your sign from 10th to 24th May. Mercury, the messenger, the fleet-footed one, will help you in securing good health, a new or a better job, perks and promotions, better working conditions, or an assurance of it, confidence, skills, intensive courses to sharpen you mentally and physically, superior communication and better contracts, service to others, concern for and involvement with pets and projects. The message should, therefore, be loud and clear. Therefore, it would be best to start ventures and projects then. I have deliberately used 'therefore' consecutively, to draw your attention to this.

Venus:

Venus the planet of wealth, marriage, all the arts (you Taureans are usually artistic, even though you're practical and down-to-earth). Good living is in your sign from 6th March to April. It will help you in your money power, loans, earned income, new projects, pets, colleagues, servants, your employees (if you are an employer), better health. In short, Venus will act as a general tonic for you, especially because the end of its transit comes in your birth phase.

Mars does not enter your sign at all, actually. However, from January to July 3, Mars influences your sign in several ways. Law cases, marriage, divorce, heavy expenses and even immigration are possible. A change of residence or house move, as the Americans say, could also happen. Mars will boost your morale, stir up your sexual appetite, give you good health or at least better health than before, make you aggressive and perhaps even rash, impulsive and impatient. Your other failings - being blunt and argumentative - will be enhanced, but Mars will give you courage in your conviction. Courage and confidence are wonderful assets in the game of life, which is, definitely, a tough game. But you don't have to have the last word, you don't have to always be right and rigid, and you don't have to be outspoken and vocal so as to turn people against you. That is Ganesha's final word for you, Taureans.

"Money is round. It rolls," it has been said, Ganesha points out; in 2012 it will run and roll YOUR way!

Ganesha requests you to pay heed to actor-comedian Vic Oliver's discourse on money: "If a man runs after money, he's money–mad; if he keeps it, he's a capitalist; if he spends it, he's a playboy; if he doesn't get it, he's a ne'er–do-well; if he doesn't try to get it, he's a parasite and if he accumulates it after a lifetime of hard work, people call him a fool who never got anything out of life!"

You are going to get money, lots of it. You are most welcome to come to me to help you spend it! Together with this money trend, another trend almost runs parallel for you. According to the Buddha, "Not to do any evil, to cultivate good, to purify one's mind," is what life is, or should be, all about. This trend will also come into full operation for you Taureans.

Normally, money and spirituality do not go together. Your special duty and dharma will be to reconcile these two. That's what 2012 is all about, points out Ganesha. The results of your activity will start coming in, from a trickle to a stream. Funds and your own vitality will have to be kept intact and protected. Buying and selling, trade and commissions, mutual funds, joint-finances, joint-holdings, rentals, estate duties, taxes - the entire gamut of money matter is to be dealt with.

Romance, sexual powers, physical rather than totally emotional involvements will also hold/attract you. Retirement, a job change, a move away from your regular profession could also happen now. Security, mortgages, home-finances will have to be dealt with too; probably, also a second home.

The year ends with you stretching yourself in many directions, hammering out a new deal for yourself, your loves ones and dependents, committing yourself strongly, forcefully, emphatically. Above all, you believe in yourself, says Ganesha, and that's what makes things happen!

Jupiter will be in your 2nd angle of:

1. Finance;
2. Taxes;
3. Augmentation of income through various sources;
4. Passion and love;
5. Inheritance and unexpected money;
6. Joint-finances;
7. Trusts and funds and use of public money;
8. Taking steps to better your health and your earning potential (these two are very definite)
9. Moving house/office;
10. Looking after the old and infirm in body, mind and spirit - and as we know, it is all in the mind,
11. Vicarious pleasures, necromancy and the use of tantra and mantra are accentuated. A strange assortment. But remember, truth is often stranger than fiction.

The best gift of the year will be a great boost to your self-confidence. I can compare it to the mighty F-17, Night Hawk, fighter aircraft with laser accuracy.

Anything to do with land, building, shop, office, buying, selling, renting, leasing, renovating, decorating will be lucky. An increase or augmentation of income through your earning, loans, savings, taxes, contracts, transactions, inheritance, and lotteries are also indicated. In short it is food, family and finance time. It is also time for fashion, fads and frolic. Just remember the number of F's I have used for you! There will be a few disappointments and even separations in family and friends. Children and grandchildren will give satisfaction. A wish-fulfilment is also possible.

Saturn:

Let me remind my dear readers what I had said about Saturn in my 2010 book. Saturn will be in your 6th angle from October 30, 2009 to October 5, 2012. The 6th angle stands for:

1. Health problems;
2. A big change in the nature and scope of your work;
3. Your efficiency and the services you offer to others.
4. Heavy expenses, your hospitalisation or that of your loved ones, danger of debt and/or thefts, food, diet, exercise, servants, poisons, (example: a slight possibility of food poisoning, Ganesha forbid!) both problems and help from the maternal side of the family, enemies and opposition to plans.

After 5th October 2012, Saturn shifts to your 7th angle. Saturn will there for about two-and-a-half years. There are different opinions on Saturn in your 7th angle but there will be, or rather, could be separation and repression in relationships. Duties and responsibilities on the personal level and the professional front will be very definitely there for you. THAT IS CERTAIN. But we astrologers are not gods. We do go wrong. Therefore, if you folks want to marry, or go in for a business or professional partnership, feel free to do so. If you believe in astrology, you can match the horoscopes. But remember, your Ganesha devotee keeps an open mind. YOU HAVE A RIGHT NOT TO BELIEVE IN ASTROLOGY. One of my favourite signs is Taurus. Therefore, let me assure you that from 27th June 2013 to 15th July 2014, Jupiter and Saturn will be in a beautiful and lucky formation. Technically, we call it trine. This is a good period for any relationship you want to go in for. We will talk much more about it next year. Fair enough?

Neptune:

Romance, entertainment, children, inspiration, love, will catch you by the throat from 4th February, because Neptune will be in your 5th angle of pleasure and joy. I am now 80. I have lived a full and romantic life. Therefore, I think you should take love as a window of opportunity. Artists, poets, painters, musicians, interior designers, mothers, property owners, cooks, chefs, gardeners, should do particularly well.

Pluto continues its power stay in your 9th angle of planning and preparing, the two puissant P's. Puissant means strong and effective. Pilgrimages, education, research and discovery, experiments, parents and in-laws come directly under the orbit of Pluto. Pluto and Neptune are in good formation. And therefore the happy results of Neptune and Pluto will help you to ward off or discard or prevent the bad influence of Saturn.

Uranus:

Uranus continues in your 12th angle of religion, expenses, sudden and often disturbing events. You could feel left out or debarred or discarded or disappointed; these are only possibilities. Except Ganesha and Allah, who can say with certainty?

It is in the collective influence and impact of all the planets that your future will be manifested. But the bottom-line is finance, family, health, slight disturbances in relationships, love and romance, and a possible engagement next year.

There is much to look forward to.

TAURUS

MONTH-BY-MONTH

JANUARY

Taureans are the hard workers or, should I say, sloggers of the zodiac. Once they set their sights on something, they keep persevering to get it. This could be called obstinacy or determination; choose your word! You start 2012 full of determination and conviction. From the word 'go' you decide that your major, if not total, focus will be on your advancement. You will try to not only rid yourself of financial worries but make yourself and your family secure and comfortable, money-wise. Let me stick my neck out a bit --- studies, research, dealing with in-laws, visits and interviews, are undoubtedly emphasized, so you need to keep your PR good. There will be a lot of work and the rewards will justify the effort. There will be many new opportunities but you will have to get out of your comfort zone. The year starts with a bang, assures Ganesha. As the year unfolds, you continue to work hard but there are many emotional issues to be resolved. The home needs attention. The spouse, children, parents, in-laws and many other domestic issues need to be sorted out. Towards mid-month, you make many new purchases. You may invest in real-estate or play the markets or make some astute purchases. There may also be a new relationship in the offing and it may be necessary to be discreet about it or it could blow up in your face. Ganesha urges caution in matters of the heart. I repeat that romantic liaisons, engagements, weddings, strengthening bonds with your loved ones, be it your lover, your children, or even your extended family – will hold centre stage. As the month ends, you enter a hectic work phase. You explore and optimize all the opportunities that come your way. You have learned a few of life's lessons in the past few weeks and the time has come to forge ahead. Ganesha assures you that all the good things in life are yours for the asking. You are on all cylinders and blazing away.

FEBRUARY

If there is a problem with you, it is that sometimes you could have blinkers on and feel that you are right and everyone else is wrong. Watch this attitude and all will be well! This is the time for almost total focus on goals, in your profession and career, perhaps even an obsessive commitment, so great is your desire to get going. Your life becomes expansive and extravagant. There will be many expenses, meetings and travel. You will be reaching out to as many people as possible. There will be progress but it will also take its toll. You will be taking loans and making the necessary changes for the big leap ahead. This is a very intense phase. All the ingredients that make life combustible come to you in a rush. You may be in the throes of a new love affair. If single, this could lead to the altar. It is a romantic time and Taureans are the great lovers of the zodiac. You make the most of this sizzling phase. As the month moves on, a sensitive and thoughtful phase takes over your life. Your love life is at a crucial juncture. If married, you may be lured into extra-marital affairs with dire consequences. Be on your guard. There are monetary gains at work and you do well but affairs of the heart tend to sidetrack you. You look for escape routes and delve into dharma/ karma/ tantra and mantra in search of answers. You explore several possibilities in a quest for peace. The forces pushing you are compulsive, almost demonic, and you need respite. This is a learning process, says Ganesha.

MARCH

Please remember that these are mere generalizations. A deeper and more accurate study depends on a personal horoscope. But Ganesha is my boss and with his help I am able to say many things about people and life. Insights into the nature of truth, reality, work, love and philosophy are the specialties of the month. There will be more money, but more demands on your time too. Adequate rest, health safeguards and, of course, not over-extending yourself financially, will be necessary. New vistas will beckon and there will be meetings and prolonged travel. You may also make contact with old associates from a long time ago and there could be many fun-filled moments. There will be time for leisure and indulging in your favourite hobbies. This is also a great time for the creatively inclined. An interesting period with fun and success, assures Ganesha. There will also be a lot of travel. You will be moving fast and making fruitful contact. Expenses mount and you look seriously at cutting back on non-essentials. There will be partying, new friendships and many fun times. Ganesha's blessings are with you. As the month ends, there is movement and bluster. Expenses mount and there could be domestic worries. Accidents and possible hospitalization may also be a cause for concern. New projects will also get underway and you have your plate full. There will be romantic dinners, overnight trips, exotic travel and shopping. There will be many things to binge on and you may have to watch your weight. You could go overboard with all the drinking and eating. This is a period of indulgence.

APRIL

You will have to be a bit careful here. This is an auspicious month for behind-the-scenes activities. Ganesha suggests caution, since there's a danger of accidents. You will need to use tact and patience in all your dealings, but more so at work, since there is the likelihood of setbacks. There could be likelihood also, of a hurt, a sense of sorrow/ disillusionment or pain. Better times will come, and then your plans and hopes will click smoothly, without your needing to worry too much, says Ganesha. This month will see you pulled in different directions. At one level, work and domestic responsibilities weigh you down. At another level, you want time to indulge your fantasies and fly. You want to dream and be carefree. You are busy with all sorts of things and your energies are diffused. You are caught up in the frenzy of activity. There are also many domestic issues calling your attention. You are walking the tightrope. The tide steadies somewhat as the month wears on. There are important forces at play here and you are pushed into career expansion at full throttle. There may be some travel thrown in too but you emerge the winner in the cauldron of events that try to snare you. Despite everything, your gains are solid and profound. As the month ends and the new moon is in your birth sign, you have many gains. Use the waxing phase of the moon well. Whatever you start now will lead to success. These are grand times and you just want to partake of the miracle of life with gusto. The expansion of last week in several spheres of your life continues unabated. You look at new horizons and new targets and set very high goals for yourself. So, there is a lot happening on all fronts and you are hard pressed.

MAY

This could be a very significant period. Your birth-month phase gives you an extra edge to succeed. Passion overwhelms you. Ganesha asks you to be careful while playing with fire. Put a cap on your famed passion and temper as they are both very inflammable and could only get you into trouble. In your birth month Mercury, the mighty planet, is all-powerful. There is tremendous appreciation for your work and loyalty and your image catapults into the stratosphere. You are basking in the spotlight. The 3 P's – power, pelf and privileges – are yours. There is also a good chance that you could indulge in philanthropy. You cast your net wide. You meet up with friends and extended family and take a break from the mundane and the humdrum. As the month unfolds, the work area intensifies. You slog away and burn the midnight oil. You are in an expansion mode and are making new contacts and connections. There could be a rich haul if all the new contacts are optimized. It is a hectic period.

JUNE

The mood heats up as it does all over the sub-continent in the summer months. Plans and projects will click. However, don't be in a tearing hurry to get things done, and keep your personal equations balanced. You will try to make this a time to consolidate your gains and then try to build further. Ideas, plans, long-term projections for the future will come spontaneously and you will know just how to implement them. As a continuation, Ganesha gives you a truly marvellous month to follow your birth month. You are renewing old contacts and making new ones. There are journeys of all kinds ahead. You go full steam to achieve your goals. You are a great hit with people. Though normally reticent and retiring by nature, you make waves in group activities. Right now, you are riding the crest of the tallest wave and enjoying every delirious moment. The last quarter in Pisces in the middle of the month makes you sensitive and emotional. You look for a super power or a greater consciousness to guide you. Towards mid-June, there will be many changes in your life. You will be on the rollercoaster wondering where you are headed in this wide world. There will be luck escorting you in all your ventures and so you needn't worry. Ganesha's blessings will always be with you. This is also a great time for creative work and you will be well rewarded. Writers, painters, musicians, actors, artists will be in for a windfall as they make money and earn fame. Taureans love the whiff of money and are also sensible enough not to waste hard-earned bucks.

JULY

Ganesha says that you will manage to communicate magnificently, make contacts with new people, gain a stranglehold on new work, new contracts, new assignments, and do it well. You will cultivate the right mindset to deal with people of all kinds. Also, you will be signing important documents and contracts and cheques. Loans and other monetary instruments will occupy your time as you make serious decisions to forge ahead in your business or job. You have the full support of Ganesha. You are charting a new course for your life, giving it a new direction, and are keen to make a mark in the world. You inspire others and meet with success in whatever you undertake. You set new benchmarks and win applause. Towards mid-month, you have other issues to contend with. Elders in the family may need hospitalization, or the spouse and children may meet with emergencies. The new moon is in Cancer and you have many bottled up emotions to deal with. You may also be tempted to think of the glorious past or the good old days. This is a serious phase and you may even want to go on a pilgrimage to propitiate the Gods.

AUGUST

Many domestic issues come to the fore along with travel. This month is meant for bonding with people. You look at work more seriously now. With Sagittarius making its presence felt in your chart towards mid-month, there is more time and room now for travel and meetings. You will meet new people and make profitable contacts. There is money to be earned and to be spent and you are constantly on the move. It is, finally, a happy period with some merrymaking thrown in. There is a lot of work but as the month ends, emotions cloud your judgements. You live in a world of abstractions and get overly sensitive. You look for divine intervention and you try to escape your responsibilities. This is a time when you need to be disciplined to come out on top.

SEPTEMBER

There is good luck coming your way, maybe even a new love affair or greater intimacy with your spouse/partner. This is the month for cultivating a hobby. This period inspires you, and you will perform some mind-boggling feats. It is also a good time for fresh bonding, closer interaction and greater intimacy. Ganesha is definitely generous to you now. You are creative and think out of the box. There is support from family and friends and they understand what you are going through. The world is empathetic. It has seen your struggle and now all the forces at play want you to succeed. There will also be many pleasant moments with the family. As the month moves on, you are in full flow and make rapid progress. During this period you will establish yourself. You earn repute for your formidable skills. Your approach is disciplined and organized. You achieve all that you set out to do.

OCTOBER

You may want to have it your way all the time but please remember that it pays to be flexible. The focus shifts from creativity and interpersonal equations to money matters like your income, taxes, rentals, the signing of important documents and cheques. This will be an important period for joint-finance, loans, funds, earned income, add-ons and extras and how best to generate them. I recommend both health precautions and serious attempts at proper management of both time and resources. Learning to let go, to prioritize, to relax more, will pay dividends. There is money and honey, spiritual growth, the family is well taken care of, and there is domestic bliss. The stage is also well set to display your strengths. You have established yourself in the world and now you have to work harder to remain there. You are ambitious, determined and almost ruthless to get whatever you have set your sights on. In many ways, it represents a period of culmination in your life. With the full moon in Taurus, as the month ends, the tendency is to go after everything that you want in the material world. You want to indulge yourself. You want to get yourself as many possessions as you can. Work with others in a spirit of sharing and mutual growth.

NOVEMBER

Ganesha believes that this is the time for ties, attachments, bonding, love, affection, marriage, partnership. There may also be an addition to the family and many happy moments in the domestic sphere. Romance and love will be both rewarding and pleasing. While you make progress at work, you can also be insufferable to colleagues with your mighty ego issues. You are drained of valuable energy that has been lost in this unnecessary expression of your ego. It will be a good idea to travel or go on a short holiday or take a break. Make time for the three F's – friends, fun and frolic. As the month extends, you throw yourself at work and in the party circuit and make new friends. You are flamboyant in your display of affection that also spills into the work arena. You dream big, larger than life. The season is certainly one for romance with candlelight and roses.

You also feel like doing some quality social work and helping the less fortunate. As the month ends, you are at your creative best and win the applause of all those who hear you out. You are filled with wisdom and brilliant solutions to office problems. You resolve matters that have so far seemed insurmountable. There are happy moments too with family and friends.

DECEMBER

This month has a mixed bag on offer. A rare opportunity to prove yourself has come to you. Not only do you work well, you love even better. A probable home-away-from-home is on the cards as you power your way along. Projects that you had embarked on in the middle of the year need to be completed now. Health is good. Thankfully, you have a strong constitution that you normally take care of. You are busy with the three big C's – computers, correspondence and contacts. Just remember to invoke the blessings of Ganesha! Travel is foretold and you have many new interactions with people. The mood is happy but along with it are many issues that still need solving. The year has had many facets to it and as it ends you are richer and wiser. The next year promises to be even better. As the year ends, it is party time and you go all out. However, despite all the good tidings, your mind is busy conjuring plans for future growth. You combine flair, genius and spirituality to move into the next level.

TAURUS

THE MONTHS AT A GLANCE

January
As the year unfolds, you continue to work hard but there are many emotional issues to be resolved. The home needs attention. The spouse, children, parents, in-laws and many other domestic issues need to be sorted out.

February
This is the time for almost total focus on goals in your profession and career, perhaps even an obsessive commitment. So great is your desire to get going and excel.

March
Adequate rest, health safeguards and, of course, not over-extending yourself financially will be necessary. Insights into the nature of truth, reality, work, love, philosophy are the specialties of the month.

April
This month will see you pulled in different directions. At one level, work and domestic responsibilities weigh you down. At another level, you want time to indulge your fantasies and fly. You want to dream and be carefree. You are busy with all sorts of things and your energies are diffused.

May
Health improves. Love is spectacular, fulfilling, and even intense. There is rapid recovery from the troubling issues of the last month.

June
As a continuation, spin-off, spill-over, Ganesha gives you a truly

marvellous month to follow your birth month. You are renewing old contacts and making new ones. There are journeys of all kinds ahead. You go full steam to achieve your goals.

July
You will manage to communicate magnificently, make contacts with new people, gain a stranglehold on new work, new contracts, new assignments, and do it well. Ganesha says, your success is all about connectivity, connections, links, collaborations, associations and tie-ups.

August
You will meet new people and make profitable contacts. There is money to be earned and to be spent and you are constantly on the move.

September
You are brimming with ideas and win applause for them. You are creative and think out of the box. There is support from family and friends and they understand what you are going through.

October
I recommend both health precautions and serious attempts at proper management of both time and resources. Learning to let go, to prioritize, to relax more, will pay dividends.

November
Ties, attachments, bonding, love, affection, marriage, partnership, is what this month is all about. Romance and love will be both rewarding and pleasing.

December
You are busy with the 3 big C's – computers, correspondence and contacts. Just remember to invoke the blessings of Ganesha! There is travel foretold and you have many new interactions with people. This has certainly been a wonderful year with many new opportunities on the anvil.

TAURUS

WEEKLY REVIEW

(By the Phases of the Moon)

January 1 - Moon's first quarter in Aries

Taurus is generally a lucky sign. It is also a sign that believes in hard work, money and the comforts it can buy. Along with that, Taurus is also creatively gifted. As you can see dear readers, Taurus has a lot going for it. The previous year had been filled with changes and upheavals and Taurus has never been keen on change. However, you have ridden the wave, taken the challenge head on, and come out on top. The year had opened many new vistas for you and you have explored new avenues of work and play. The upswing will continue this year too. There will be a lot of work and the rewards will justify the effort. There will be many new opportunities but you will have to get out of your comfort zone which, I must add, Taureans do with great lethargy and deliberation. The bull doesn't want to be disturbed from his 'happy patch'. But he will most certainly have to move out to explore more fruitful opportunities. It will be worth the effort though as bank balances will swell and new work will occupy you creatively as well. The year starts with a bang and that good start will help you over the course of the year, assures Ganesha. Like in a relay race, the first lap sets the tone; and the year is long with twelve months! Of course, along with the hard work there will be some fatigue. But these are trifles; nothing a strong bull cannot overcome! I must add here that a lot also depends on the individual horoscope like with all the other sun signs. But these can be reasonably accurate generalisations, as Ganesha will vouch.

January 9 - Full Moon in Cancer

You continue to work hard but there are many emotional issues to be resolved. The home needs attention. The spouse, children, parents, in-laws and many other domestic issues need to be sorted out. You will be distracted from routine; may I say, even waylaid. You are kept busy with many distractions that somehow conspire to keep you away from your goals. But do not worry too much about it as Ganesha will set things in order. You will return with renewed focus and energy. Consider this a mere aberration. Remember that domestic matters also play an important part in a person's life and should not be neglected or kept on the back burner for too long or they will just explode in your face when least expected.

January 16 - Moon's last quarter in Libra

You love the good things of life and make many new purchases. You may even be on a spending spree, and why not? You have earned money and you want to decorate your home and get yourself the goodies that money buys. You may invest in real-estate or play the markets or make some astute purchases. There may also be a new relationship in the offing and it may be necessary to be discreet about it or it could blow up in your face. Ganesha urges caution in matters of the heart. This is also a time for the good life – family outings, picnics, get-togethers. Relationships will be of utmost importance and there will be many new realisations from them. I repeat that romantic liaisons, engagements, weddings, strengthening bonds with your loved ones, be it your lover, your children, or even your extended family – will hold centre stage. All this also contributes to your sense of well-being. There is money and honey, says Ganesha.

January 23 - New Moon in Aquarius

Once again, emotional issues swarm you. You are doing well but you look for deeper answers to life's questions. Do not get morbid.

Let life unfold its myriad colours to you when it chooses to. You go deep into yourself seeking solutions to pressing questions. You are in an introspective mode and like the Buddha look for answers to life's disturbing questions. This is a good phase, assures Ganesha, and helps you in becoming a fully rounded personality. Life is not just about work, money and comfort; phases like this help you unravel the mysteries of this great universe. Go with the flow, advises Ganesha.

January 31 - Moon's first quarter in Taurus

You are now back on track and moving ahead with single-minded determination. You enter a hectic work phase. No stone will remain unturned. You make the most of this trend, and explore and optimise all the opportunities that come your way. You have learned a few of life's lessons in the past few weeks and the time has come to forge ahead without a pause. Ganesha assures you that all the good things in life are yours for the asking. There is a caveat though: learn to take short breaks as this constant hard work may drain your energies. There is no need at all to fall sick as health is the only true wealth. Try to find time to relax with loved ones. But you are filled with ambition and are determined to make the most of the situation. You are on all cylinders and blazing away.

February 7 - Full Moon in Leo

Your life becomes expansive and extravagant. There will be many expenses, meetings and travel. You will be reaching out to as many people as possible. There will be progress but it will also take its toll. There is growth in your career but along with it there are also many distracting trifles. You will be making many investments and will be studying the stock market, mutual funds, fixed deposits and other monetary instruments. You will be taking loans and making the necessary changes for the big leap ahead. Ganesha advises you to be cautious but not to duck from the fight. Go with the flow and success is yours.

February 14 - Moon's last quarter in Scorpio

This is a very intense phase. All the ingredients that make life combustible come to you in a rush. You may be in the throes of a new love affair. If single, this could lead to the altar or, at the least, be something serious, much more than a frivolous affair. If married, your spouse and you could share great moments of intimacy. There may also be an addition to the family. It is a romantic time and Taureans are the great lovers of the zodiac. You make the most of this sizzling phase. Work is also going great guns and the intensity of life suddenly picks up without warning. This is a great time of life; seize the moment. Ganesha wishes you well.

February 21 - New Moon in Pisces

Another sensitive and thoughtful phase takes over your life. Your love life is at a crucial juncture. If married, you may be lured into extra-marital affairs with dire consequences. Be on your guard. There are monetary gains at work and you do well but affairs of the heart tend to sidetrack you. You make compromises in moments of weakness which could be a source of regret later. It may impact your work and lead to gossip and other unsavoury situations which you could do well to avoid. You look for escape routes and delve into dharma/karma/tantra and mantra in search of answers. You explore several possibilities in a quest for peace. The forces pushing you are compulsive, almost demonic, and you need respite. This is a learning process, says Ganesha. A sharp and glistening sword has to come through fire and you are being subjected to what could be simply called a purification ritual.

March 1 - Moon's first quarter in Gemini

Different pressures are at play now. New vistas will beckon and there will be meetings and prolonged travel. You may also make contact with old associates from a long time ago and there could be many fun-filled moments. Family members will also take your time and it will all be pleasurable. Your mind will, thankfully, be diverted from the mundane chores of work and home. The focus is not on work and money right now, and this is a good distraction. There will be time for leisure and indulging in your favourite hobbies. This is also a great time for the creatively inclined. Those in the media will bask in the spotlight. An interesting period with fun and success, assures Ganesha.

March 8 - Full Moon in Virgo

Work tightens and you have to look hard at the nitty gritty. You have many responsibilities and duties to attend to. There is hard, unrelenting work to catch up on. There is no respite from paperwork. Bills, documents and balance sheets occupy your time. You look for loans and may even sell assets to have a sustained cash flow. The phase is hectic as you drown yourself in more and more work. You may also be misunderstood but it is not your fault if you don't have time for close family and friends. There are many other demands on your time and you have several things to attend to. This is a period of sustained and concentrated work. Don't lose hope and leave it to Ganesha to steer you home.

March 15 - Moon's last quarter in Sagittarius

There is a lot of travel now. You will be moving fast and making fruitful contact. Expenses mount and you look seriously at cutting back on non- essentials. This is not a troubling phase but you need to get more disciplined and cut down on your extravagant ways. There will be partying, new friendships and many fun times. You let your hair down and enjoy yourself fully despite it all. Ganesha's blessings are with you.

March 22 - New Moon in Aries

Once again, you are pitch forked into a hectic phase. You make plans for expansion. If in a job, you could get a promotion or a better offer elsewhere. There is movement and bluster. Expenses mount and there could be domestic worries. Accidents and possible hospitalisation may also be a cause for concern. But all is not lost. New projects will also get underway and you have your plate full. This is certainly an exciting period with many influences working on you at the same time. Never lose hope, says Ganesha. After the long night is the dawn.

March 30 - Moon's first quarter in Cancer

Domestic issues are at the forefront now. Your time is usurped by family and friends. There is little time for work but then you are not unduly perturbed as your finances are in order and that is a great worry off your chest. You will have to manage time and various commitments as your loved ones will want more of you and it will be difficult to give them the time they demand. There will be romantic dinners, overnight trips, exotic travel and shopping. There will be many binges and you may have to watch your weight. You could go overboard with all the drinking and eating. This is a period of indulgence and you go all out. Enjoy, says Ganesha!

April 6 - Full Moon in Libra

There is a lot to ponder over now. You are being pulled in different directions. At one level, work and domestic responsibilities weigh you down. At another level, you want time to indulge your fantasies and fly. You want to dream and be carefree. You are busy with all sorts of things and your energies are diffused. There are many projects on hand, and repairs, renovations, constructions and additions to property that need to be supervised. There is a lot of buying and selling going on and your mind is in a twirl. You are caught up in the frenzy of activity. There are also many domestic issues calling for your attention. You need to be steadfast now and focus. Take to meditation or yoga to still your mind. You are walking the tightrope and it is necessary to ask Ganesha for help and blessings.

April 13 - Moon's last quarter in Capricorn

The tide steadies itself somewhat in this phase. There are important forces at play here and you are pushed into career expansion at full throttle. Your work grows in leaps and bounds and you win the applause of your peers and bosses. If self-employed, you look at starting new ventures as you are filled with confidence and innovative ideas. Grab the moment by the horns and you will be successful. You have a lot to gain now on the professional front. There will be minor pin-pricks, of course, like family matters to attend to and some legalities that need your presence. There may be some travel thrown in too but you emerge the winner in the cauldron of events that try to snare you. Despite everything, your gains are solid and profound and this is a good period to make substantial headway.

April 21 - New Moon in Taurus

This is a very good phase as the new moon is in your birth sign. Use the waxing phase of the moon well. Whatever you start now will lead to success. There will also be great camaraderie and good vibes with loved ones. You expand your sphere of influence at all levels. There is partying and fun times thrown in and the chances of a new affair in your life. Romance is kindled and you just let go. You throw caution to the winds. While this could be dangerous, you are in no mood to listen to reason. These are grand times and you just want to partake of the miracle of life with gusto. Go for it, says Ganesha, as life is too short for regrets.

April 29 - Moon's first quarter in Leo

The expansion of the last week in several spheres of your life continues unabated. You look at new horizons and new targets and set very high goals for yourself. You also get indulgent and, if not careful, this could lead to medical problems. You will have to exert strong discipline over yourself. Get to a gym or hire a personal trainer. Watch your intake of food and drink too. Taureans can gain weight easily and this is the cause of most of their health issues. So, take special care. You could also visit spas, go for healing massages, and look at preventive alternative treatments. Hard work and no play can be disastrous. There are also several new expenses on both, the work and personal fronts. The family needs more attention and children, in particular, may need medical help. Elders in the family may need hospitalisation too. So, there is a lot happening on all fronts and you are hard pressed. Just hang on, says Ganesha. This too shall pass.

May 6 - Full Moon in Scorpio

There is rapid recovery from the troubling issues of the last week. But this is also an intense phase with more work and more demands on your time. You look closely at more opportunities to make money and also find them. You have a lucky streak, maybe even the Midas touch. There is love, or may I say, more accurately, a lot of lust in the air. You lose yourself in the arms of a new partner. Passion overwhelms you. You neglect work and family duties in this moment of madness. To err is human, what more can I say? Ganesha asks you to be careful while playing with fire. Put a cap on your famed passion and temper as they are both very inflammable and could only get you into trouble. You will also have to pay off loans, possibly take new loans, and strengthen your monetary base. It is a mixed bag with many things happening all at once and Ganesha wants you to slow down and take stock of the situation. You are at the crossroads; please look at both sides and drive carefully.

May 12 - Moon's last quarter in Aquarius

Mercury, the mighty planet, is all-powerful now. It favours travels/ meetings/conferences/ interviews/ trips/ more brain power/ contacts/ communication/correspondence/contracts. Mercury has a special connection with the circuits of the brain. Chess, crossword and other such games belong to Mercury. Also, short distance runners and spin bowlers are controlled by Mercury. Mercury, in short, is the ambassador and salesman of the zodiac. It is very important and occupies a prominent position now. Your birth month has many pulls and pressures. Your sustained hard work over the last many weeks provides results. You haven't buckled down to pressures and you get your due. There is tremendous appreciation for your work and loyalty and your image catapults into the stratosphere. You are basking in the spotlight. The 3 P's – power, pelf and privileges – are yours. It is time for Taureans to have their feet on the ground now as fame can be heady and life has a way of imparting valuable lessons. Is it any wonder that the University of Life is the greatest teacher of all! There is also a good chance that you could indulge in philanthropy. You may visit homes for the destitute and institutions for the challenged and help out. This is a good sign, says Ganesha as it will keep you grounded and prepare you for more important tests in the days to come.

May 20 - New Moon in Gemini

You are reaching out to all corners now. You cast your net wide. You meet with friends and extended family and take a break from the mundane and the humdrum. You also look at new machinery for business expansion. Technology and its uses seem to excite you and you look at new ways of streamlining your work. This is also party time and you seem to be overdoing the bubbly. You will make inroads into many new areas of your life and there will be rapid business expansion. Ganesha urges you to make the most of the period.

May 28 - Moon's first quarter in Virgo

The work area intensifies. You slog away and burn the midnight oil. There is a lot of paperwork and accounts to attend to, and you count the pennies despite making huge profits. It may be wise to loosen the purse strings a bit. You are in expansion mode and are making new contacts and connections. There could be a rich haul if all the new contacts are optimised. You see many opportunities and go all out to seize them. It is a hectic period but Ganesha's blessings are with you.

June 4 - Full Moon in Sagittarius

You are now in travel mode and renewing old contacts and making new ones. There are journeys of all kinds ahead. You go full steam to achieve your goals. You are a great hit with people. Though normally reticent and retiring by nature, you make waves in group activities. This surprises everyone and you are the toast of the party. This a lucky phase and you seem to make one conquest after another. All this invariably makes you happy and fulfilled. You love hard work and when it pays off, nothing can please you more. Right now, you are riding the crest of the tallest wave and enjoying every delirious moment. Ganesha is with you all the way!

June 11 - Moon's last quarter in Pisces

The last quarter in Pisces makes you sensitive and emotional. You get moody and may brood. You think about the past and the mistakes you have committed. This maudlin note is not in your temperament which is normally sunny, and the sooner you snap out of it the better. You are not the party animal and prefer the comfort and sanctuary of the indoors to a romp in the outdoors. But now you spend more and more time alone and with your innermost thoughts. You also seek out the company of family members. You look for a super power or a greater consciousness to guide you. In short, you look for the benevolence of the almighty. You are not God shopping but you are certainly looking for answers and for an inner peace. Ganesha is benevolent and magnanimous and he holds you in his tight embrace.

June 19 - New Moon in Gemini

There will be many changes in your life. You will be on the rollercoaster wondering where you are headed in this wide world. There will be luck escorting you in all your ventures and so you needn't worry. Ganesha's blessings will always be with you. You take special care to secure the future of your loved ones with material assets. This is also a great time for creative work and you will be well rewarded. Writers, painters, musicians, actors, artists will be in for a windfall as they make money and earn fame. There is also romance in the air and it all depends on the individual horoscope if this new alliance is meant to take a serious tinge. Life will display many aspects to you and it will be many splendoured.

June 27 - Moon's first quarter in Libra

The good times continue and you reap name, fame and money. You also make many purchases and spread yourself thin. Taureans love the whiff of money and are also sensible enough not to waste hard earned bucks. So, most of your investments are classy and wise. You work hard now for a secure future. There is also a hint at speculation and you play the markets with abandon. The mood is infectious and you are the soul of the party circuit. You are in great demand and shed your inhibitions and solitary nature. You suddenly become a people's person. You paint the town red as you bask in the joys of achievement and its rewards. You are also in a generous frame of mind and bestow all and sundry with gifts. Money, fame, romance, fun are in the air. Ganesha urges you to enjoy!

July 3 - Full Moon in Capricorn

There is a sudden turnaround and you are full throttle at work. There is a lot to catch up on and you leave no stone unturned. Party time is over and the serious aspects of life take hold of you.

You make plans for expansion and new investments. Loans and other monetary instruments will occupy your time as you make serious decisions to forge ahead in your business or job. There is also intimate bonding with family members and many domestic responsibilities to look into. You cast your net wide and make progress on all fronts. There is seriousness in all your undertakings, and you realise that the time is ripe for you to make more of headway in the world. You have the full support of Ganesha. Don't worry.

July 11 - Moon's first quarter in Aries

You are pushing ahead on all cylinders. You are charting a new course for your life, giving it new direction, and are keen to make a mark in the world. You explore new areas of work and look for unopened territories to push your products and ideas. This is a very profitable phase. You inspire others and meet with success in whatever you undertake. You set new benchmarks and win applause. You lead from the front and are not shy to roll up your sleeves and do the lion's share of the work. You are able to run over all opposition and silence your critics. Make the most of this phase, says Ganesha.

July 19 - New Moon in Cancer

While work is still hectic, you have other issues to contend with. Elders in the family may need hospitalisation or the spouse and children may meet with some emergencies. This takes a lot of your time and energy and you are hard pressed. The new moon is in Cancer and you have many bottled up emotions to deal with. You may also be tempted to think of the glorious past or the good old days that, alas, will never return. There are many expenses too and you cut down on all frivolity. This is a serious phase and you may even want to go on pilgrimage to propitiate the Gods. Believe in existence and it will take care of you, urges Ganesha.

July 26 - Moon's last quarter in Scorpio

You are plagued by many thoughts and you wonder if there is anything at all called true happiness. You look for perfection and you don't find it. You are in a tizzy and ask several searching questions of yourself. In this period, you are inclined to fall hopelessly in love. If already attached, the relationship with your partner will be strengthened. If not, a new love enters your life and it is smouldering. It takes you to new heights of ecstasy and you forget all the cares and worries of the world in the arms of your partner. You look for weekend getaways as your life is consumed by passion. This can be a short-lived relationship but its intensity will be unmatched. You may have met the person at the workplace and it is possible that both of you have several common interests. There is a chance that something more meaningful may also develop from this liaison but there is no doubt that you are now in the arms of sheer joy, living every moment to the hilt. Passion and Taureans are never far apart and your expressions of love are flamboyant, to say the least. Your partner is also besotted with you; it is the stuff that dreams are made of. While you may have lost your head and heart for the moment, let the passions cool off before you decide on taking the relationship to the next level. Ganesha is happy for you.

August 2 - Full Moon in Aquarius

The passion of the last phase continues and you are still lost in love. Nothing else makes sense in the world. It is the type of love story that happens once in a lifetime and you are caught in its web. But, unlike the Tarantula, you have to survive it and live long to savour its aroma. This is an obsession that defies rationale. You have to sort it out and get on board before the fire consumes you in its entirety. There are other aspects of life that you have neglected. You have to make tough choices and sort out your life. You have work to do and many responsibilities at home. You have lost focus and are shirking from the several duties and jobs that have piled up. Your friends wonder what is happening and your family suspects something is not right, particularly if this is just a passing affair. If married, this could be sheer bliss. Ganesha blesses you.

August 9 - Moon's last quarter in Taurus

The sensuous nature of the past week continues but there is, thankfully, some respite. You look at work more seriously now. There are many earthly issues to contend with and your pragmatic nature comes into full play with realty, rentals, leases, insurance and taxation matters taking up your time. There are expenses too and you decide that there is more to do in life than spending time with your partner. This is a period for hard, sustained work. You need to forge ahead and make sound investments and the right career choices. You may look at buying land or property and may also indulge in important work-related travel. There is a lot to do on many fronts, says Ganesha.

August 17 - New Moon in Leo

Expenses mount. There are health concerns too. You have been in an indulgent frame of mind and may now need a medical check-up. You have clearly been overdoing the good life. It is time to check into a spa or healing centre and detoxify. There is no point in falling ill; it is important to discipline yourself. Your agenda is packed and you need to be fully fit to carry it forward. The family is also worried and this period is earmarked for recuperation from the excesses of the recent past. Ganesha advises you to slow down a bit as there is no sense whatsoever in burning the candle at both ends.

August 24 - Moon's first quarter in Sagittarius

With Sagittarius making its presence felt in your chart, there is more time and room now for travel and meetings. There is a lot of upheaval and movement. You will meet new people and make profitable contacts. There is money to be earned and to be spent and you are constantly on the move. There are new trends at work and many changes and not all of it is pleasant. But, with Ganesha's blessings, you come out trumps. It is, finally, a happy period with some merrymaking thrown in. Most of the new contacts will help in your career and you stand to profit from the exchanges.

August 31 - Full Moon in Pisces

There is a lot of work but emotions cloud your judgements. You live in a world of abstractions and get overtly sensitive. You also don't accept criticism easily. You think you are right and are not open to new ideas either. You dig your heels in and refuse to budge. And let me tell you that the bull can really be stubborn! Competitors will try to undermine you by spreading rumours and indulging in unwarranted gossip. This will affect you and you'll sulk. But Ganesha wants you to ignore it all and keep plodding away. The false propaganda will eventually peter off. How long can people get at you when they don't get the expected reactions from you? They will finally stop provoking you and you would have won a major emotional battle. So, you have to be on your toes. Work has piled up and there are many deadlines staring at you down the barrel. You look for divine intervention and try to escape your responsibilities. But please stay away from drinks, recreational drugs and gluttony. This is a time when you need to be disciplined to come out on top. Just remember that when the going gets tough, the tough get going!

September 8 - Moon's first quarter in Gemini

Things are improving at work but you are still not out of the woods. Manoeuvre with caution. You are brimming with ideas and win applause for them. You are creative and think out of the box. Most of the new ideas are also workable. Take rest and try to get yourself a much- needed break. You don't need to burn out at this stage when you are close to the summit. The final heave over Everest awaits you. This is difficult and you have to muster all your strength for the final haul. Once done, you can rest in joy and adulation. There is support from family and friends and they understand what you are going through. The world seems to be empathetic. It has seen your struggle and now all the forces at play want you to succeed. Take Ganesha's blessings and go forth to conquer.

September 16 - New Moon in Virgo

Matters settle down. You are doing well and your sustained efforts are bearing fruit. The brickbats will always be hurled. Do not take any notice of them. This is life. Along with the good is the bad; along with the night is the day. You are blessed with success, and good fortune follows you like a faithful shadow. You also give back to society a portion of your time and earnings and this is not going unnoticed. Ganesha assures you that all will be well. Just have faith in yourself. There will be many pleasant moments with the family.

September 22 - Moon's first quarter in Capricorn

This is a time of serious and even pessimistic thinking. Communication with others becomes more difficult. You take life more seriously than usual and run the risk of losing your sense of perspective. You think over your life thoroughly and decide to embark on a new tack: new ideas and opinions and new ways of communicating. This consumes you. You feel there is a need to root out old ideas and notions that have outlived their usefulness. You want to broaden your scope and look at alternatives at work and play. You set the pattern for new vistas and this proves to be an excellent time for working ideas through. You look for perfection but please remember that you have to work in a team and others may not be able to keep pace. Do not alienate them as you need their support. Do your best and leave the rest to Ganesha.

September 30 - Full Moon in Aries

You are in full flow and make rapid progress. During this period, you will establish yourself. You earn repute for your formidable skills. You have reached a point of equilibrium and your actions and behaviour are consistent. People now rely on you a great deal. Your approach is disciplined and organised. You achieve all that you set out to do. You mix conservatism with new, liberal ideas and the matching works well. This is not the time for relationships and your nose is to the grindstone. Ganesha wishes you well.

October 8 - Moon's last quarter in Cancer

The good times continue. You will come in contact with older, more experienced people and you have a lot to learn from such chance encounters. You may meet someone who becomes your guru and shows you the path to enlightenment. There is money and honey, spiritual growth, the family is well taken care of, and there is domestic bliss. This is an emotional phase and you feel content. You go on a pilgrimage to thank the Gods who have helped you along a tricky trail. You are filled with gratitude. Ganesha's blessings are with you.

October 15 - New Moon in Libra

The stage is well set to display your strengths. You have established yourself in the world and now you have to work harder to remain there. The test may take many forms, but you are the master of all that you survey and you like the look and the thought of being the alpha male/female. Your self-control is tested. You are ambitious, determined and almost ruthless to get whatever you have set your sights on. You know precisely what you need to succeed and after you are satisfied and achieved whatever you wanted, you are willing to compromise and share your success. You must learn to be accommodating. Stand up for your rights but don't overstep your bounds. There will also be happy moments at home, away from the clutter and ambition of the workplace. You will find time to bond intimately with loved ones. Ganesha wishes you luck.

October 22 - Moon's first quarter in Capricorn

This is a very positive period. In many ways it represents a period of culmination in your life, and you will be tempted to expand beyond reasonable limits. You have a good chance for success in any of the new endeavours you are embarking on. However, you should not restrict yourself solely to material growth. It may be time to turn your attention to spiritual needs. Objects that money can buy, even prestige, are all illusory; they are *maya*. You realise this and look for the solutions within yourself. This is the turning point, says Ganesha.

October 29 - Full Moon in Taurus

With the full moon in Taurus, the tendency is to go after everything that you want in the material world. You want to indulge yourself, you want to get yourself as many possessions as you can. But remember that it can leave you empty later. This is not the time for arrogance either. Work with others in a spirit of sharing and mutual growth. Set goals for the benefit of all, and the team backs you. Please remember that we are all selfish in nature even if we pretend we are not. With a little tweak in your efforts, this can be an extremely productive and growth-oriented period. Ganesha showers you with good luck.

November 7 - Last quarter in Leo

You could be tempted to lose your legendary temper. There is nothing worse, no greater nightmare, than a bull that is scorned. So, take care not to lose your cool. Learn to ignore trifles and make that extra effort to keep your cool. While you make progress at work, you can also get insufferable to colleagues with your mighty ego issues. Ganesha warns you to keep it in check. You are drained of valuable energy that has been lost in this unnecessary expression of your ego. It will be a good idea to travel or go on a short holiday or take a break. Make time for the three F's – friends, fun and frolic; do anything to distract you from the intense energy of the moment. Learn to be patient and cool. This is a testing time, says Ganesha.

November 13 - New Moon in Scorpio

You are in a better frame of mind but the intensity of the period still lingers. You throw yourself at work and in the party circuit and make new friends and, I dare say, new lovers as well. You are flamboyant in your display of affection that also spills into the work arena as you scout for mega projects and big money. You dream big, larger than life. If married, you enjoy memorable moments with the spouse. For those with children, family life is most enjoyable; there is great bonding. Ganesha wishes you many happy moments. The season is certainly one for romance with candlelight and roses.

November 20 - Moon's first quarter in Aquarius

You put on your thinking cap and get very serious about life. You feel like doing some quality social work and helping the less fortunate. This is marvellous as it is always good to give back to society. You have many new work ideas too but they don't seem to fit in with the larger plan as they seem too futuristic and idealistic without any practical rationale. Try to work out some ideas that can be followed through with ease, something more realistic. You are a practical person by nature; so look for more workable solutions. Right now, you are zooming far ahead of your contemporaries who fail miserably to comprehend you. But this is a good time, says Ganesha, and there is nothing to worry about. Your health is good and money will finally come your way!

November 28 - Full Moon in Gemini

Ideas flow out of the cupboard in a deluge. You are at your creative best and win the applause of all those who hear you out. You are filled with wisdom and brilliant, zany solutions to office problems. You resolve matters that have so far seemed insurmountable. There are happy moments too with family and friends. You are communicating with all comers and reaching out with a vengeance. You also work well in a team and are able to meet all deadlines and make substantial profit. Your fantasies have takers now and people around you are finally beginning to see sense in whatever you are doing. Ganesha wishes you well. Go with the flow and nothing will block the ideas swarming out of your head.

December 6 - Moon's last quarter in Virgo

There is a lot of fine tuning left and many loose ends to tie up on the personal and professional fronts. Projects that you had embarked on in the middle of the year need to be completed now. You have lobbied hard for them and now you have to go through with them; you have to see that they are completed and deadlines are met. As we all know, what is well begun is half done and so, despite the festivities, you are still working hard. Health is good. Thankfully, you have a strong constitution that you normally take care of. Like last year, you are busy with the 3 big C's – computers, correspondence and contacts and you will be looking at more profitable opportunities with new eyes. Just remember to invoke the blessings of Ganesha!

December 13 - New Moon in Sagittarius

There is travel foretold and you have many new interactions with people. The mood is happy but along with it are many issues that still need solving. You need to prioritise your commitments and take on only those that you feel you can fulfil. Sometimes, you feel that you are over- stretched and may snap like a worn out rubber band. You will have to guard against making enemies as you could be very forthright during this period. Watch your tongue. There will also be enormous expenses and you will shop till you drop buying classy and expensive gifts for loved ones and pampering yourself too in the process. Ganesha wishes you happy times anyway!

December 20 – Moon's first quarter in Pisces

The year has had many facets to it and as it ends you are richer and wiser, thanks to all that you have been through. You have learnt many valuable lessons and are indebted to Ganesha for having protected you and given you so much. You have had a fair share of the happiness pie. You have had work, love, laughter, passion, money, travel and a few discordant notes too but that is a part of the package of life. You are happy. Your cautious and conservative nature has been well fed with success and riches. Since you are ambitious, you make plans for the future. You are a plodder and no work is too small if it pays you well. You thrive on hard, sustained toil that sometimes also becomes your undoing as people take advantage of your temperament and load you with work that you are not really keen on. You have great determination and stamina and look for both material and spiritual goals. The next year promises to be even better. Ganesha asks you to step into 2013 with renewed confidence of having done a job well.

December 28 - Full Moon in Cancer

It is party time and you go all out. You make time for friends and family and all new work is put on the backburner. Now, you just want to have fun. However, despite all the good tidings, your mind is busy conjuring plans for future growth. You are intelligent enough to see where you have faltered and wise enough to make the necessary changes in your life. You want to be a success in life. Everyone wants it, but you, dear Taureans, I dare say, and Ganesha agrees with me, are possessed with a desire to excel. You burn with a scorching light that wants to make the planet a happy place. And that, most certainly, includes you too as you are very much a part of the planet. Sachin Tendulkar is a contemporary Taurean who comes to mind easily with his single-minded dedication. Taureans also have a deep spirituality residing within them; Gautam Buddha is another prime example. You combine the flair and genius of Sachin and the spirituality of the Buddha to move into the next level as 2013 unfolds.

TAURUS

KEY DATES

January
2*-3, 6*-8, 11*-13 (important), 16*18, 21-22, 25-27, 29-31.
The tremendous efforts made in December will pay off now. You will have the power needed to be successful as well as happy. A month of progress as well as travel. Action time, says Ganesha!

February
1-4, 8*-9, 13-14, 17-18, 21*-22, 26-27.
The key is that *November to February* are interconnected, and you should push hard for what you desire in these three months. February is also for anything to do with house, home, shop, property in general, including buying, renovating, selling.

March
2*-4, (important) 7*-9 (important), 12*-13, 17*-18 (important), 21*-22 (most important), 25*-26, 29*-31 (important).
March is the time for taking a chance, testing out new ideas, having new experiences, loving and being loved, earning and spending.

April
1*-5, (important) 8-10, 13-14, I7*-18, 21-22, 26*-27.
Love and passion, sex and salvation, finance, job, servants, earned income and loans are the highlights now.

May
1*-2, 6*-7, 10*-11, 15*-20 (important), 23-24, 28-29.
Be sure of what you want, because you will be meeting a lot of people in May. It is all a question of meeting the right people, at the right place and time. Journeys, collaborations are probable. Take care of your health.

June

1*-3, 7*-8, 11*-16 (important), 19-21, 24-26, 29-30.
Finance, inheritance, gifts, opposition, law cases, and after June 21, journey and ceremony, says Ganesha!

July

1*-5 (important), 8*-9 (important), 12-13, 17*-18, 21*-22, 26-28, 31.
You start with a bang – journey and ceremony, publicity and projects.

August

1, 4*-6 (important), 9-10, 13-14, 18*-19, 23*-29 (important).
Thanks to a quick and fine start in July you succeed in your enterprises in August. It will be very hard work, but well worth it.

September

1*-2 (important), 5*-6, 9*-11 (important), 14*-16 (important), 19*-21, 24*-25 (important), 28*-29 (important).
Take the help of friends, well-wishers, boss/ superiors and loved ones and you will find joy and fulfillment. It is time to work in groups, and also in the social circle.

October

2-3, 7*-8, 9*-13, 16-18, 23-26, 29-31.
A mixed bag for you. Take care of expenses and ill-health of family members and yourself. But you will face all difficulties and triumph. Journeys are possible.

November

1*-4, 8*-9, 13*-14 (important), 18*-19 (important), 22*-23, (important), 26-27, 30.
This is a month for both, finance and romance, work and joy. Go all out for what you want.

December

1-2, 5*-6, 10*-11, 15*-16, 19*-22, 27*-29.
Possessions, selling, investing, restoring of foreign connections, import and export, will be important.

Gemini

May 21 - June 20

GEMINI

(May 21 – June 20)

ELEMENT AND RULING PLANET: Air and Mercury.

STRENGTHS: Gemini is lively, energetic, versatile, and intellectual, lives primarily inthe mind rather than the emotions are extremely adaptable to situations.

WEAKNESS: Gossiping, superficiality, using words to mislead or misinform, hurting others with harsh speech.

SYMBOL: The Twins – Associated with duality, humanism, versatility, communication.

MATCHING SIGN: Sagittarius.

MAGICAL BIRTHSTONE: Emerald and Agate – protect from deception and falsehood, and bestow eloquence, especially in declaration of love.

GEMINI

YEARLY FORECAST

Main Trend

"Health is the greatest possession. Contentment is the greatest treasure. Confidence is the great friend. Non-being is the greatest joy."

- Lao Tzu

Ganesha says you will experience a boost in will-power and mental energy, and will be able to slay the dragon of doubts and misgivings that were bothering you. This is the month when you have the confidence, the savvy and the panache to go out and be a winner. And that's what counts when you need to go out and flatten the opposition. The fields that are especially favoured will be communication, information, research and new inventions and the tinkle of money in the till. You will peak in terms of both credit and productivity.

The patience and tact that you have displayed in the face of adverse circumstances in the past few weeks will be amply rewarded. Some kind of wish-fulfilment may also happen. Remember, this is your birth-phase, which is typically full of heightened activity, for *all* signs. The unique thing is that right now, *you* are the one who *is making* it all happen with your own inspiration, initiative and energy. You will be inventive, even brilliantly creative, making inspired moves.

Your angst and gloomy mood of the past will melt away. Along with August, and certainly along with April, this year emphasises the superior mind, the higher consciousness, and how to improve your menial world-vision. And from this, are bound to come the right motivation as well as the right moves. Personal relationships will therefore prosper. Romance will blossom, under the onslaught of your charismatic appeal to members of the opposite sex, though the appeal will be more of the mind than of physique. All for the good, chuckles Ganesha. It will last!

The sum total of all your qualities make your personality – namely, body, heart, mind, appearance, style and the way you appear to others. Personality is also that extra X factor which you alone have and exude and radiate to others. It is the real you, I have tried to explain it as simply as possible because you will have the courage and the confidence to conquer the world. Jupiter the planet of personality will now be in your sun sign. Jupiter will make the difference.

Ganesha says, the sun's radiance, the sparkle of diamond, the strength of steel and the softness of silk – all combine superbly in you, Geminis, in 2012-13.

Jupiter:

Jupiter, your money planet, your life's blood astrologically, moves in your own sun sign. Astrology is all about timing, that is, the right person, the right place, the RIGHT TIME.

Bhargava says "People have different conceptions about prayer: some think that real prayer lies in worshipping God in the temple, mosque or church. Others believe in fasting, jap and charity. Some believe in going around sacred places and feeding the poor. Many have faith in meditation or yagya and other rituals. Some feel that performing good actions and serving humanity is real prayer. *Those who perform their duty with complete devotion, sincerity and honesty also pray in an indirect manner; and derive the same advantages.*

Real prayer will sharpen intelligence, give proper and timely guidance in day-to-day actions, show the correct path in all directions, restore mind-peace and infuse the power to think correctly and attain achievements with greater speed and efficiency while elevating one to higher levels of consciousness.

The other benefits of Jupiter in your sun sign will be:

a) House, home, land, warehouse, vehicles, and property, all come into focus now, with the emphasis on buying/ selling/ renovation/decoration/alteration/acquisition. You may be laying the foundations not only of a new home, but also of a new project, even a new attitude to your immediate kin (read: family, neighbourhood) and larger environment (read: society, shifting your base of operations). A change of ambience is almost definite around this time;
b) You may also be motivated towards making household and security improvements. Alongside --- and this is important – you'll now place more value on your inner resources, especially the ability to perceive and decide future trends. *In that respect, says Ganesha, you may be close to a launch into a different lifestyle and life cycle – in short, a different stratosphere;*
c) Marriage, alliance, collaborations, journeys with a stopover, advertising and publicity, confirms Ganesha.

From 12th June 2012 to 26th June 2013, Jupiter will be in your sun sign. Ganesha says the main purpose of Jupiter will be to heal you in body, mind and spirit. Jupiter is also called jovial Jove. It will help you with a strongly positive attitude and approach to life. Mainly, it will help you in two definite directions:

a) Contacts, communication, writing, teaching, publishing, interviewing, reporting, corresponding, collaborating, negotiating, signing deeds, documents, contacts, agreements. At meets and conferences and courts of law, you will be at your brilliant best.
b) New ventures, experiences, job environment, home and office, loans and funds, charitable causes, leadership, daring victory,

great ambition, dealing with servants, subordinates, employees, finding personal interests, improving your image, learning to use new skills and methods of improving relationships.

Saturn:

The second big gun is Saturn. Let us see how Saturn booms for you. Saturn will be in your 5th angle this year. Saturn is the planet of restriction, rigidity, discipline, duty, dedication, and limitation. The 5th angle stands for:

a) Official engagement, marriage;
b) Awesome creativity at all levels and planes, and that says it all;
c) New plans and projections;
d) Joint-finance, funds, capital, investment, also augmentation of earned income;
e) Weight (physically it will be your problem and you will also have to deal with weighty issues, including the birth of a child).

Saturn will be in your 5th angle from 30th October 2009 to 5th October 2012, according to western astrology. Please note that Saturn will give ONLY mixed results.

Therefore, Saturn in your 5th angle will teach you how to be responsible and do your duty towards your children, loved ones and also do justice to your creative activities. You will have to take hobbies and recreational pastimes very seriously. In other words, a great effort will have to be made to be happy in any matter connected with love, children, sex and mantras. Disappointments are also possible. Ganesha says life has many different colours. Astrology holds a mirror to life. Therefore, astrology prepares you for the *true realities of life.*

Ganesha concludes by saying that there will be solid achievements, also failures, great interaction with people, and the possibility of marriage. But divorce, pain, separation are also possible. But please remember. This reading is only a general reading based upon your solar scope. It is not an individual reading based upon your personal horoscope.

Saturn, Ganesha says, can show creativity in your 5th angle. Here is a good definition of creativity by George Kneller:
"Creativity, as has been said, consists largely of rearranging what we know in order to find out what we do not know. Hence, to think creatively, we must be able to look afresh at what we normally take for granted."

Ganesha's final comment is that the tentacles of Saturn reach out to hobbies, sports, children, education, romance and speculation.

India is crazy about films and cricket. We have Test cricket, one day cricket, a premier league and so on. Batsmen now use new strokes. You Geminis are very creative, versatile, curious and sharp. Also, Saturn in your 5th angle brings out the best in you in terms of originality. Therefore, especially for you, I am mentioning the different strokes in cricket, to illustrate my point.

a) Slog sweep
b) Reverse sweep
c) Paddle sweep
d) Switch hit
e) Upper cut
f) Paddle scoop.

Who knows, tomorrow they may invent the upright sky shot, or something else? Keep reading my books! Ha, ha!

Nadal, the current tennis champion is a Gemini. INTENSITY, PASSION, BRUTE STRENGTH and EXTREME FITNESS make RAFAEL NADAL. He is left-handed and therefore the ball kicks up high onto the backhand of the right-handed players. It makes it difficult to return his serve.

Uranus:

Uranus will be in excellent formation with Jupiter from June. In practical terms it means, prestige, honour, rewards, promotion, extra income, excellent job prospects, loans and funds. I am sure you understand the power of money and credit cards. There is also a possibility of sudden gains, promotion windfalls. Chance works doubly for you. Let me put it in another way. You will be lucky in money matters. Money will fly to you!

Neptune:

Neptune will be in your 10th angle. It will help you in studies, travel, long-distance connections, spirituality, genuine inspiration and intuition, helping out the unfortunate and the downtrodden, the retarded and miserable. In other words, you will be high up on the ladder of evolution. Anything to do with e-signatures, computers, internet, cartography, aviation, aero-dynamics, electronics, gadgetry, inventions and patents, rocketry and space missions, even UFO's holds great promise.

Venus:

Ganesha says Venus will be in your sign from 11th April to 7th August. This is a long period for Venus. It will be ideal for home, house, office, shop, showroom, contacts, communication and contracts. In short, the more people you meet and the more places you go to, the better for you. Buying and selling will be a special feature.

Mars:

Mars is in control of your work and of the social circuit. By work, I mean a fatter pay packet, job opportunities, promotion and better working conditions. Your circle of friends will widen; you will entertain and be amused. At parties, you will be rocking and happy. The birth of children or grandchildren is a possibility. In short, Mars will activate and energise you.

Mercury:

Mercury fills in your sign from 26th May to 7th June. It will be an excellent time for travel, comforts, children, romance, arts, research, and creativity. Pilgrimages and ceremonies, social work and charity also come within the ambit of Venus. Yes, willy-nilly you will make / get money and enjoy it, too.

FINAL WORD ON SATURN

We have already talked about Saturn. But we are not through yet with Saturn. Saturn will enter the 6th angle for Gemini on October 6, 2012. It will bring about mixed results. Do take care of health, finance, loans, pets and you your relationships with colleagues and subordinates. Saturn is a lame man, therefore, he moves very slowly. The effect and impact of Saturn will be felt in the next two and a half year. This year the impact will not be great. It would be best to repeat this manta 21 times: "Om Praam Preem Proum Sa Sanaye Namah".

The second mantra is "Shri ram jai ram, jai jai ram". Going to the temple of Hanuman on a Saturday will help. Why Saturday? From Saturday, we get the word Saturn. So, there is a complete and direct connection between Saturn and Saturday. I am sure you, my intelligent readers, will understand immediately. Good luck and happy reading.

GEMINI

MONTH-BY-MONTH

JANUARY

There are many things on your mind as the year unfolds. Your personal status, the perks and prestige that are your due, your professional desires and several other issues crowd your mind. There are also many domestic issues that need to be resolved. You start the year well and are capable of taking many risks. Your ego is highly developed and you may think too highly of yourself. Tone down the ego bit, suggests Ganesha. This can be a restless year and you keep moving from one project to another. At least, this phase suggests this trend. The focus will be on money and making your life as secure as possible. Geminis are generally restless and are forever on the lookout for action. Those in the media will do exceptionally well. Your creative outbursts will meet with monetary success. Towards mid-month, you could be lost in the throes of passion. You may also look at spirituality with new eyes and may go guru shopping. There is more stability as the month ends. You will display the fun-loving, generous and passionate side of your personality. There will be improved ties at home and family life will give you great joy and harmony.

FEBRUARY

Your self-belief is immense and you feel that you can do anything, that nothing is impossible. Many ideas crystallize into real-time action. You are inspired to do big things and you get along well with people. Good people-skills are your forte, and you can encash them now, in several ways. You are a natural at communicating with others and also have a strong streak of creativity. What could also be easy, warns Ganesha, are the workings of your conscience. It could make you willing, even eager to turn a blind eye to unorthodox ways of earning, or access to money by some rather unconventional methods. These could spell danger for you, Ganesha says quite sternly. You make many flamboyant career moves. You take risks without caring too much for the consequences. There is love, passion, new assignments and a lot of contacts and correspondence as the month advances. The end of the month sees the new moon in Pisces and there are many emotional moments. You spend quality time with loved ones and may take a relationship to the next level.

MARCH

You may have a problem keeping your word. You often shoot your mouth off and do not follow it up. Watch out for health issues this month. Ganesha suggests you take the necessary precautions. There may also be health problems for parents, elders, in-laws, and friends. But, despite it all, you have the confidence, vitality, even daring, to enjoy life -- grab it. Caution, restraint and moderation should be part of the fine time you're having. All your relationships (from purely personal to professional interactions) will definitely improve. Ganesha promises adding glamour, glitter, a special glow to your family and personal life, emotional equations and interactions. The moon's first quarter in Gemini sees you meeting people and discussing new ideas of expansion. There could be international travel and new interests. There are relationships, new projects and initiatives, renovations to home and office and several fiscal instruments to deal with.

Towards mid-month, the moon's last quarter is in Sagittarius and there is a lot of movement, communication and contacts. The main thrust and focus of your activities will definitely be finances. With the new moon in Aries, there is relentless work. There is also kudos from all quarters for your phenomenal efforts. Your prestige is at an all time high and Ganesha is delighted.

APRIL

There are many domestic issues including intense love and bonding. You relish the warmth in personal interactions and family bonding. You are able to give a lot and so it is no surprise that you are also able to receive a lot. There is comfort, intensity and security in your life and you enjoy yourself to the hilt. This will therefore be a progressive, productive month that helps you to enjoy life to the hilt. You are far more accepting and tolerant, and aware of the many truths that people often ignore in their quest for success. A wish fulfilment is also quite possible. Ganesha shows me the true picture and I interpret it, that's all. Take it or leave it.

The full moon is in Libra at the start and you begin to do well. There is travel, romance, marriage, collaborations, financial gains, family reconciliations. Your plate is filled with opportunity. Glory, achievements and gains stare you in the face. With some effort and risk-taking, some courage and daring, a few brilliant and inspired moves, you will strike gold. The new moon is in Taurus as the month ends. There is more stability and you are grounded. You have the energy and the focus and so there is a very good chance of success. All the P's – pets, projects, pastimes and protégés will keep you occupied. There is travel, more money and a new love.

MAY

You display the caring side to your nature and attract a lot of love too. This month sees you also in a serene mode as you do a lot of self-evaluation. But this is also a month when you make rapid progress on all fronts. You may spend long periods in trying to understand yourself. Ganesha wishes you well of course. Visits to lonely places, hospitals and welfare centers are very probable – they give you solace, even as you make efforts to give it! Mid-month the moon's last quarter is in Aquarius and your mind will give you restless times. You are torn by many thoughts. But this is the beginning of a great period and the next two weeks will be very lucky for you. Make the most of it. Mercury, the mighty planet, is all-powerful. Mercury is with you from 25th May to 7th June. Ganesha encourages you to make the most of this stimulating period.

JUNE

You continue to feel the full impact of Mercury and do exceptionally well. Ganesha points out that after the 18th, in particular, there will be business deals, hectic romance, rendezvous, slight secret activity, journeys and collaborations and enormous opportunities to earn money. You may get it through a million different sources like rentals, legacy, tax rebate, loans, funds, joint-finance and so on. This could well be a superlative month. Ganesha raises your levels of enthusiasm, energy, performance. You attack life with renewed zeal and confidence. You look for more success in all areas of your life. You want material progress and recognition. To make this happen, you will be reconciling different trends and squaring up to your responsibilities. There is hope and promise, optimism and joy, as you move along the path of greater glory. You are in line for peace, plenty and prosperity. There is also time to relax, to laugh and to enjoy yourself with friends. The new moon is in Gemini towards the middle of the month and the theme of this period will be bonding, family ties and relationships. There will be a happy mix of fun and work as the month ends.

JULY

There could be happy moments like a marriage or engagement in the family. There will be domestic bliss. You seem to have a sudden awakening in terms of the joys of family life and you enjoy every moment of it. There is also a lot going on for you in the sphere of finance. You take risks and make investments. Ganesha blesses you. There is a certain joy in life and a huge amount of confidence. Your mind and attitude are all open, expansive, and charismatic. There is a lot on your plate and you could have bitten off more than you can chew. Make space for new spiritual insights and look for rest, relaxation and inner peace. With the moon in the first quarter, there is a lot of upward mobility in your affairs and when the new moon is in Cancer you are filled with confidence. Happy makeovers will definitely be the theme in all spheres of activity. The new moon in cancer will make some beautiful and powerful intimacy happen. As the month ends, there will be an important new trend and your work, projects and plans will move smoothly.

AUGUST

This is a great period. The stars are smiling on you. You will be receptive to ideas, influences, ideals and new suggestions. You are at your creative best. The results could be breathtaking. You invest in people and are immensely popular. Ganesha promises you that whatever you have aspired for could happen. All your efforts now start to yield dividends. There is success, happiness and achievement. You will do well at the workplace and have a contented, fulfilled family life. You will also be very creative and those in the arts, literary fields, even technology, research, the whole of the world of information, will be at their best. The new moon in Leo mid-month will compel you to look purposefully at the coming months and make the necessary plans. You look at links, associations, friendships, popularity, socializing and friendships, even marriage. As the month ends, your schedule will be frenetic. There is socializing, partying, hectic lobbying and networking. Despite hectic schedules, you find time for matters of the heart.

SEPTEMBER

There are many new trends and they pan out slowly starting this month. There is a changed attitude, progress and sustained growth in all areas of your life. You are receptive to new ideas and this helps a lot. The domestic scene occupies you, says Ganesha and you will be drawn closer to home and hearth. There will be many demands on the home front and there could be many expenses too. Keep your head cool, and don't over-react to stressful situations, says Ganesha. This is a period of joyousness. You realize the value of domestic commitments and feel happy and contented when you are able to meet all the demands of family members. But you will have to strive for objectivity. The new moon is in Virgo mid-month. In this period, work, family and filial responsibilities will all be handled with sensitivity and grace. As the month progresses, you are on the fast track to success. There are joys and achievements. The negative aspects of life can also be energized and so you should steer very clear of shady deals.

OCTOBER

Those in the creative fields do well. You will be inspired and brilliant and will look to move into a higher level of consciousness. There will be creativity of the highest order. You will have great intuition and insights into life and all kinds of ties will be forged. You will have the magic touch in forging relationships. I've already said this, but in terms of importance it needs to be said again. It is all about ties and bonds this month. Ganesha bids you to do your best. The moon's last quarter is in Cancer and there will be many sensitive and emotionally charged moments. This is not a particularly low phase but many doubts will assail you. There will be romance in the air and many meets, conferences and family gatherings. There will be fresh achievements and successes. The 5 F's of family, finance, fun, fortune and food hog your attention. A wide spectrum of business and professional transactions, deals and negotiations will have to be handled. As the month ends, you make a lot of progress on the work front. You also look at expanding your consciousness. But with the full moon in Taurus, your mind is more settled and you are at peace. There could be sudden windfalls, great wealth or luck, and all kinds of wonderful opportunities that take you many rungs up the ladder of success.

NOVEMBER

As the year ends, you are pedalling hard. You break all records of endurance and have fun too in the process. There are a few glitches and roadblocks you have to watch out for as you push yourself to limits you didn't know existed. Ganesha is happy that you are putting in your best efforts and ensures that you get the necessary rewards: perks, benefits, accolades and approval are all yours. A tremendous surge in confidence, enthusiasm and energy comes to you now. The theme/trend is definitely huge efforts, and matching results. There is international travel and new love in your life. There will also be new circumstances that give you increased freedom or an opportunity to do something different. With the new moon in Scorpio, you may get enmeshed in an affair. You could even be cheated in some recent deal and so it will be worth your while to scrutinize the fine print with a magnifying glass. But with the full moon in your sign, you manage to remove the roadblocks and somehow surge ahead.

DECEMBER

This is party time. You charm everybody and your popularity soars. Your inherent kindness, caring and generosity take you places. More importantly, you are liked for what you are as a person and not just for what you can do in terms of work and achievement. That is saying a lot, and I mean it. Ganesha points out that partnerships and collaborations and your bonding at family and personal levels reach the high point of achievement. This is a period of hard toil but there are also just rewards and that is the best part of work --- what more do you need when you are well appreciated? You set your sights very clearly on whatever needs to be done and you go ahead and accomplish all your tasks with single-minded zeal. With the new moon in Sagittarius, you are reaching out to everybody. There could be new international associations and overseas projects. Your creative potential is also unleashed and you blaze the marquee. There is inner growth too and Ganesha is happy. The year ends with the full moon in Cancer and there is a feeling of well-being. Ganesha is your helmsman. Be grateful.

GEMINI

THE MONTHS AT A GLANCE

January
Your creative outbursts will meet with monetary success. Towards mid-month, you could be lost in the throes of passion. You will have to make some firm decisions.

February
You make many flamboyant career moves. You take risks without caring too much for the consequences. There is love, passion, new assignments and a lot of contacts and correspondence as the month advances.

March
There could be international travel and new interests. There are relationships, new projects and initiatives, renovations to home and office, and several fiscal instruments to deal with.

April
Glory, achievements and gains just stare you in the face. With some effort and risk taking, some courage and daring, a few brilliant and inspired moves, you will strike gold.

May
Mercury, the mighty planet, is all-powerful. Mercury is with you from May 25 to June 7. Ganesha encourages you to make the most of this stimulating period.

June
You look for more success in all areas of your life. You want material progress and recognition. To make this happen, you

will be reconciling different trends and squaring up to your responsibilities. The beneficial aspects of Mercury help you out.

July

Happy makeovers will definitely be the theme in all spheres of activity. The new moon in cancer will make some very beautiful and powerful intimacy happen.

August

There is success, happiness and achievement. You will do well at the workplace and have a contented, fulfilled family life. You will also be very creative and those in the arts, literary fields, even technology, research, the whole of the world of information, will be at their best. There is success in the offing, says Ganesha.

September

This is a period of joyousness. You realize the value of domestic commitments and feel happy and contented when you are able to meet all the demands of family members.

October

The 5 F's of family, finance, fun, fortune and food hogs your attention. A wide spectrum of business and professional transactions, deals and negotiations will have to be handled.

November

A tremendous surge in confidence, enthusiasm, and energy comes to you now. The theme/trend is definitely huge efforts, and matching results. There is international travel and new love in your life.

December

There could be new international associations and overseas projects. Your creative potential is also unleashed and you blaze the marquee. There is inner growth too, and Ganesha is happy.

GEMINI

WEEKLY REVIEW

(By the Phases of the Moon)

January 1 - Moon's first quarter in Aries

This can be a restless year and you keep moving from one project to another. At least, this phase suggests this trend. If you had been cheated of monies last year, this year could be lucky as far as recoveries are concerned. The focus will be on money and making your life as secure as possible. You need to do it now as you may consider settling down and starting a family. Those in business may do exceptionally well as there will be many international projects. Realty will be an excellent area of profit. There will be happy moments with the family too. There will be recognition of your worth along with all the benefits and add-ons that increased prestige brings. It may not be as easy as it seems. There will be a walk over coals. You will have to resolve personal matters, align fresh priorities, and reassess your own values. You will also have to work hard at maintaining domestic harmony. Financial issues will pan out well and you will be happily buying whatever you fancy. There is a strong possibility of wish-fulfilment. There will be happy times too and so go enjoy, says Ganesha.

January 9 - Full Moon in Cancer

There are many moments spent with the family and you will feel blessed. Geminis are generally restless and are forever on the lookout for action. Those in the media will do exceptionally well. Your creative outbursts will meet with monetary success. Of course, money doesn't stay long with you as friends will ask for treats and you find it very difficult to refuse earnest entreaties for money. You have also lost a lot of money in the past by lending to friends and this may happen again; money always manages to slip out of your fingers. There will be travel and you meet up with old flames; what an exciting start to the year. You will start implementing new plans right from this week. Journeys, travels and mental growth take precedence. You have realised the value and relevance of genuine bonding and are keen to make the most of it. This impacts your relationships and siblings. Relatives and people really close to you will come to mean much more in this phase. You will also be drawn to intellectual activities, education and higher studies, even research and information technology. Ganesha blesses you.

January 16 - Moon's last quarter in Libra

There is new love in your life. You will be lost in the throes of passion. There will also be many expenses as you indulge in hectic shopping and travel. You will be splurging on the latest brands as though a scarcity loomed large. But you will also feel restless and indecisive. You may look for an escape in the usual indulgences. Ganesha asks you to slow down and take care. You may look at spirituality with new eyes and may go guru shopping. You are looking for solace and comfort. You are looking for answers to free you from the demons lurking in your subconscious. You feel as though your soul is torn and you want to steady it.

January 23 - New Moon in Aquarius

Your mind continues to play games. You have to get a grip on it before it overpowers you. As we all know, the mind is a monkey on a stick. Imagine what happens if hundred monkeys danced on the stick! You are in that frame of mind. But there are many professional and personal obligations that need your attention now and you slog away and make your dreams a reality. Thanks to this enforced discipline, your self-belief and confidence have increased and you now feel a surge of power. There is a mixed bag to deal with. There are many things on your plate – from passion and sex to finance and religion. There may be ceremonies and prayers for the living and the dead. There is also a slight risk of ill- health and accidents. Take the necessary precautions. Ganesha blesses you.

January 31 - Moon's first quarter in Taurus

There is some stability now and you make sustained progress. This is also a great time to be with loved ones. There may be a new relationship and you will be spending steamy times with your beloved. You will display the fun-loving, generous and passionate side of your personality. There will be improved ties at home and family life will give you great joy and harmony. You will also show interest in community activities and even volunteer to help. There could be international collaborations, promotions and a hike in your perks. You rise in reputation and prestige. You earn applause, win rewards and awards and are the toast of all. Ganesha is with you.

February 7 - Full Moon in Leo

You make many flamboyant career moves. You take risks without caring too much for the consequences. Finances continue to occupy your attention and you make shrewd calculations resulting in massive profits. There will be domestic happiness and deep bonding with those you care for. There are many influences; work and family occupy your time. From your strong, even single-minded focus on work, you now shift your concentration to your immediate and extended family. There are many trends: weekend outings, a home-away-from-home or a holiday home are likely. Travel is also a definite possibility. There could be renovations at home and the office as you want both to reflect your personality and the aura of success that surrounds you. Ganesha is happy for you.

February 14 - Moon's last quarter in Scorpio

There is a new intensity in all your endeavours. There is love, passion, new assignments and a lot of contacts and correspondence. You are keen on worldly success and take your career/business to the next rung of success. You have stupendous inter-personal skills and are a great success in whatever you do. There may be a need to temper your activities as you could be grossly overindulgent. Ganesha likes to reward genuine effort and he makes this phase a truly pleasing one. There is power, position and pelf. You are raking in all kinds of benefits, and moving from strength to strength. This reflects very positively on family and personal life but also spurs you on to make sustained, new, inspired moves. There is productivity, progress and plenty as you are on a great ride to success. Ganesha's blessings are with you.

February 22 - New Moon in Pisces

There are many emotional moments at home. You spend quality time with loved ones and may take a relationship to the next level. By this I mean there may be marriage on the cards. However, I must make it clear that these are all mere generalisations and a more accurate reading will depend on the personal horoscope. Astrology never compels. So a reading like this depends on several factors. These are trends and can work in different ways depending on your free will and action. But results in this phase can be spectacular at both work and play. There is harmony at home and success at the workplace. What more can Ganesha bless you with? You are filled with confidence and self-belief as you perform really well at tests and interviews. Children will do well at examinations and they bring you great joy. There will also be travel as you reach out to people and places. There will be many new associations and your popularity soars. You are always there when people need you and this is a trait that endears you to many.

March 1 - Moon's first quarter in Gemini

The moon's first quarter in Gemini sees you meeting people and discussing new ideas of expansion. You are able to sort out all misgivings and arguments by sweet talking your way through the situation. There could be international travel and new interests. You may delve into metaphysics and spirituality. You may also take to gardening and nature walks. The money position is strong and so you have time for leisure. Your prestige has risen in the community and you turn your thoughts and efforts to helping others. You reach out to people and places, journeys and relationships, neighbours, the community and society. There are also many flings as new relationships spill out of the woodwork. Your timing is perfect and you are at the right place at the right time. This is a great time for striking new deals. Ganesha wishes you well.

March 8 - Full Moon in Virgo

You manage to steady the boat and fold your sleeves and get down to hard work. If you are the boss, you will lead by example. You will earn the respect of your peers. There are many items on your plate. It is like a giant *thali* - there are relationships, new projects and initiatives, renovations to home and office and several fiscal instruments to deal with. Your interactions with friends and lovers have a new edge thanks to a change in your behaviour, attitude and handling of situations. You will pay great attention to the work front and make tremendous strides. You will accomplish mammoth tasks and achieve targets well within deadlines. Go with the force, says Ganesha. This is a good phase for those working with realty. The trends favour you.

March 15 - Moon's last quarter in Sagittarius

There is a lot of movement, communications and contact. You are networking furiously and are in touch with everyone that matters. You are at the vanguard of some social movement and will have a large following. You also manage to meet up with long lost family and friends. There are many inspired activities this week. The entire gamut of home, family, parents and pets, dependents, work, colleagues, social life, the arts and creative pursuits follow you like a dog following its master. You need phenomenal energy to handle all this and you do your best. The main thrust and focus of your activities will definitely be finances. You are practical enough to realise that nothing in the world moves without money to oil the wheels. You know that there is no free lunch in this material world. You seek movement, growth and progress and Ganesha is with you.

March 22 - New Moon in Aries

There is relentless work in this phase. There is also kudos from all quarters for your phenomenal efforts. Your prestige is at an all time high. You may also be spending recklessly and may have to tighten your purse strings. Keep modest and treat everyone, the big and the small, equally. You want to redefine goals and priorities, think and plan for the future, as you re-assess the manner in which your life is shaping. The pace is hectic and there are many expenses. You are kept on your toes. There is a strong indication of visits to hospitals. You may be attending to sick relatives and, probably, even checking in yourself. This is the time to take stock of the situation and adopt preventive measures. Do not allow the body to break down. Do not ignore the warning signals. Take care, suggests Ganesha. Take special care if you suffer from any chronic illness.

March 30 - Moon's first quarter in Cancer

There are many emotional moments in this phase. You look back at life, at all that you have missed out, and are filled with regret and sadness. You feel that you could have done a much better job of life with better planning. But there is no use crying over spilt milk and living with regrets you can do nothing about. Ganesha suggests that you ensure that mistakes are not repeated. Everyone makes mistakes. Even I have; it is the way of all life. You can't do much in the mood you are in. You may even feel that you have married the wrong person and could end up in a downward and negative spiral of futile thought processes. Make the most of what you have and plan for a better tomorrow. This may be the time to improve your self-image. Change your wardrobe, visit the gym, detox, or maybe get a new hairstyle. Do anything to get out of the box you are in. Self pity is useless, underscores Ganesha. Get a move on.

April 6 - Full Moon in Libra

The full moon is in Libra and you begin to do well. There are many maudlin thoughts though and you look for an escape from the drudgery called life. You get indulgent and obsessive. You cannot make up your mind and yet you listen to no one. There are roadblocks, obstacles and potholes ahead but there are also rewards, returns and revenues. You spend a lot and surround yourself with goodies. You are surrounded by love but you are still searching for it. True love, in that sense of the word, may always remain a mirage. Maybe, you are better off without it. Ganesha wishes you well.

April 13 - Moon's last quarter in Capricorn

Ganesha gives you just about everything you want and yet you don't see it. You are wearing blinkers or your eyes are closed. There is travel, romance, marriage, collaborations, financial gains, family reconciliations. Your plate is filled with opportunity. Glory, achievements and gains just stare you in the face. With some effort and risk taking, some courage and daring, a few brilliant and inspired moves, you will strike gold. Go for it, urges Ganesha. With a little effort, there are amazing results. Colleagues and workmates help out and share the burden. The domestic scene also calls for some effort. This is indeed an interesting period but take care not to burn out.

April 21 - New Moon in Taurus

The new moon is in Taurus. There is more stability and you are grounded. Your mind doesn't play any more games and you get clear and focused. You know what is to be done and you do it. You have the energy and the focus and so there is a very good chance of success. Expenses mount, and the party circuit and new love ensure that your spare time is used well. Finance plays an important role in your life now. Loans, funds, capital formation will all keep your hands full. So will social work, serving others and reaching out to those in need. All the P's – pets, projects, pastimes and protégés will keep you occupied. You will focus on larger, global issues and social concerns that encompass the welfare of others. You realise that the world is one family and you need to share with others. Your performance is high pitched and you are in a position to be large hearted and generous. Ganesha is with you all the way.

April 29 - Moon's first quarter in Leo
You will concern yourself with your own advancement rather than the welfare of others. There is a shift in the wind this week. You realise that you need to get a bit more selfish and do something for yourself before thinking about the world. You are pushed to attain, achieve and show the world your true potential. You are upwardly mobile. There could be a promotion or a raise, a job change or switch, even a new line of work. There will be definite gains but take care not to be too critical of other people or their methods. It won't work. It may, in fact, undermine all that you have gained. You have earned the respect of others. Now don't lose it with arrogance. Keep your temper in check and watch your words. Take deep breaths and count to ten before retaliating. One stray word can make you lose out on all the gains made so far. You also make contact with old friends and share tender moments with your partner. There is travel, more money and a new love. Way to go, says Ganesha.

May 6 - Full Moon in Scorpio
The intensity of the phase gets to you like rising mercury. The summer is on and you can feel the heat. You are now busy with the daily grind, the mundane areas of life. You make superhuman efforts at your job/work/profession. There is little time and scope for entertainment and extravagance. It is time for sincere hard work. You want to do more, achieve more. You could be also plagued by a sense of isolation, of loneliness, of being on your own in a hard and cruel, perhaps even hostile environment. You will have to work hard to change your perceptions. The spiritual path is one way. You may even want to see the world, travel and meet people who share your ideas, beliefs and concerns. You want new stimuli and new experiences. You want new learning. Ganesha wishes you the very best in this search.

May 12 - Moon's last quarter in Aquarius
The mind is still giving you restless times. You are torn by many thoughts. You are also pursuing pleasure and profit. You want to

have fun and also to have funds to keep going. You will go much beyond the call of duty to fulfil your domestic obligations, which will be quite a handful. The health of elders, dependents, and even in-laws could require your prolonged involvement. Children will also be a source of worry. There are many work demands too and you are in a quandary. You want to go solo but you also know that you need the team to help you with all the challenges confronting you. Ganesha feels that the mood will pass and things will settle down in due course. Just hold on a while and the dust will settle. You will then know how and where to steer the boat.

May 20 - New Moon in Gemini

This is the beginning of a great period and the next two weeks will be very lucky for you. Make the most of it. You will be able to achieve miracles in this period. Take risks, speculate if you want to, go for the jugular in all areas of life, both professional and personal. Mercury, the mighty planet, is all-powerful. It favours travels/ meetings/conferences/ interviews/ trips/ more brain power/ contacts/ communication/correspondence/contracts. Mercury has a special connection with the circuits of the brain. Chess, crossword and other such games belong to Mercury. Also, short distance runners and spin bowlers are controlled by Mercury. Mercury, in short, is the ambassador and salesman of the zodiac. It is very important and occupies a prominent position now. Mercury is with you from May 25 to June 7. Ganesha encourages you to make the most of this stimulating period.

May 28 - Moon's first quarter in Virgo

You are on a roll. There is true inspiration, genuine wisdom and insights about how to lead your life. You make a lot of money and branch off into new areas of activity. You do well and are able to win others to your way of life and thought processes. Your convictions will be lofty and noble. You display a true willingness to serve. You will also step up your own efficiency as you are on the treadmill of great achievement. You also spend time at home strengthening family ties which you realise is important for peace and harmony. There are many expenses but all expansion comes with a caveat. You take all the necessary steps to build a strong financial foundation. You also seek out true knowledge and devote time to higher studies, research and new learning. This is a great period and Ganesha wishes you well.

June 4 - Full Moon in Sagittarius

You look for more success in all areas of your life. You want material progress and recognition. To make this happen, you will be reconciling different trends and squaring up to your responsibilities. Your personal and professional life will call for a positive approach and the right mindset. You are on track to make wonders happen. Your plans will focus on both personal advancement and family welfare. Confidence, determination and a sense of sweet satisfaction will be a part and parcel of your week. There is hope and promise, optimism and joy, as you move along the path of greater glory. You look for mastery in your chosen field of work and you get it. There may be higher studies or the quest for additional knowledge or an added qualification. You are filled with gratitude in this wondrous phase. Ganesha blesses you.

June 11 - Moon's last quarter in Pisces

You are in tune with your instincts and intentions in this sensitive phase. There are many opportunities beckoning you as you strive for true happiness. You are in line for peace, plenty and prosperity. There is also time to relax, to laugh and to enjoy yourself with friends. You participate happily in group activities and enlist in many new and novel ventures. All your ventures will be on firm ground and this is a good time to think of the higher values. You ask metaphysical questions and ponder the real meaning of life. A lot of time will also be spent on relationships, especially with your spouse/lover and family which could include children, dependents, parents, siblings, in-laws and even colleagues and co-workers. You will be motivated to extend yourself not just physically but also emotionally. Communications, contracts and collaborations will be important. It is not all smooth sailing though as there is a chance for unexpected events, accidents and losses. Remain alert and flexible. It is important to flow like water. If you cannot frontally break down an obstacle, go around it. Ganesha blesses you.

June 19 - New Moon in Gemini

The theme of this period will be bonding, family ties and relationships. You will be reaching out to all and sundry and getting to know extended family members. Those you love and cherish will really get closer to you. A long-term friendship will be a source of both inspiration and true companionship. There will be successful journeys too. Romance and marriage are the other strong possibilities. Ceremonies, conferences, publicity meets, PR exercises, all add up to a very interesting period. You could also touch the money angle and may look at stocks, shares, mutual funds or government bonds with some intent. But the main theme will be one in which you reach out to others. Deep bonding will be the focus of your life now. Ganesha wishes you well.

June 27 - Moon's first quarter in Libra

There is a lot on your plate in terms of work and social commitments. You realise the need for both effort and ingenious thought to make a go of it. In financial affairs, you will take audacious risks to maximise your profits. There will be a happy mix of fun and work, hectic activity and a lot of hustle and bustle. But it will all be well worth the effort. There are also many expenses and possibly a new love in your life. If single, you could take this to the next level. But astrology never compels and these are mere generalisations. Ganesha will take care of you.

July 3 - Full Moon in Capricorn

There is a lot on your plate and you could have bitten off more than you can chew. There could also be overt and hidden stresses to cope with. There could be a kind of rebellion against you at the workplace. There may be colleagues you have hurt and there could be a lot of hidden resentment. There could be secret transactions, hush-hush deals, surreptitious meetings and tie-ups. It may all sound like a Bond espionage film but this is real life. You could also feel a strong desire to flout social norms in your desire to taste new thrills and experience. You must look for true happiness, says Ganesha. That is the only way. Make space for new spiritual insights and look for rest, relaxation and inner peace. That is most important in these troubled times. Do not squander your gains away through hurtful words and actions. Keep a close watch over your temper. Despite all the roadblocks, you still manage to make headway at work.

July 11 - Moon's first quarter in Aries

There is a lot of upward mobility in your affairs. You are committed, sober, responsible and respectable. You have had your thrills and now want to settle down to a more regular way of life as this is the real you. There will be more happiness this way, you feel more centred. You turn to domestic affairs, to the house and home, family and property matters. Happy makeovers will definitely be the theme this week in all spheres of activity. You will also see success in buying/selling, shopping for goods and assets, even investments on the stock market. Just remember always that Ganesha is with you.

July 19 - New Moon in Cancer

You are filled with confidence. You feel that you have got the knack of accomplishing whatever you have set your sights on. You want a sense of daring or bravado to enter your psyche now and influence your activities and approach to life. The focus will be on finance. You will have to deal with funds, joint-finances and loans, and a fair amount of buying and selling which may also include acquiring property. There may be a house shift, or renovation or redevelopment on the cards. There will be gains of different kinds. You will also see the 3 P's - promotion, position and power. There will also be, quite naturally, added work and accountability. There will also be genuine bonding with loved ones. The new moon in Cancer will make some very beautiful and powerful intimacy happen. Ganesha blesses you as always.

July 26 – Moon's last quarter in Scorpio

In this intense phase you realise that you are smart enough to know what is required and are convinced that you will make your way through all the boulders. You know that your skill at handling people will be vital. You will be doing a lot of public relations work and interacting with distinguished or influential people in the hot seat or in positions of power. This will be an important new trend and your work, projects, plans will move smoothly. You are in the mood to be a really good caregiver. Pets and dependents will also need attention and care along with children, extended family and relatives who look to you for guidance and support. Marital and personal bonding will be stronger and more meaningful and a source of great joy. Ganesha wishes you well.

August 2 - Full Moon in Aquarius

You take stock of your life. You have worked hard and very sincerely to get your professional and personal commitments in order. All your efforts now start to yield dividends. There is success, happiness and achievement. You will do well at the workplace and have a contented, fulfilled family life. There are also monetary gains in addition to love and laughter, good times and romance, marriage, friends, partnerships, companionships and collaborations. You will also be very creative and those in the arts, literary fields, even technology, research, the whole of the world of information, will be at their best. There will be plaudits and kudos, rewards and awards. Those in the electronic and print media will shine. Ganesha blesses you.

August 9 - Moon's last quarter in Taurus

There is more stability now and more progress too. Of course, when more money comes into your hands there are also new expenses. You have marvellous flashes of genuine inspiration that help you accomplish whatever you set your heart on. Getting your heart's desire could well be the theme of this week. It is almost certain that you will realise some long held dream. It could be a wish fulfilment that could be professional or personal. This is a period when you will be re-aligning goals, priorities, embarking on a self-improvement programme, and even an overhaul of your outfits, accessories and image. Your desire to please and achieve success also makes you perform rites and rituals as a part of the grand design to reach out to the world at large. You will work at getting more diplomatic and humble in all your dealings and also pay more attention to your manners. Ganesha is with you as you move ahead in life.

August 17 - New Moon in Leo

Every year is different and yet there are many similarities. Sometimes there is illness or a marriage or an addition to the family or bereavement. There are happy moments and sad ones. Nothing remains stationary as life is a continuous process of movement. One needs to constantly take stock of the situation and assess one's life. This will be one of those periods. You will add up your gains and appreciate the necessity and importance of hard work. You look purposefully at the coming months and make the necessary plans. Your attention shifts to more practical issues like money, loans, funds and projects of various kinds. You look at expansion if you are going solo and a promotion if employed. The domestic scene also occupies your mind. You look at links, associations, friendships, popularity, socialising and friendships, even marriage if I may stretch it a bit. Ganesha suggests that you go with the flow. Your thinking is on the right track.

August 24 - Moon's first quarter in Sagittarius

There is travel and new associations. There is a lot of movement both physically and intellectually in this phase. You will have new experiences and will dabble in everything that is thrown on your plate. Your schedule will be frenetic. Old projects and new ones fall on your lap and you don't want to refuse work. So this can be a crazily busy time. You have taken on a lot and are determined to do justice to it all. There are other demands too. There is socialising, partying, hectic lobbying and networking. Rest and relaxation will be vital. Prayers, meditation, tantra and mantra, religion and rituals will give solace, strength and inspiration. There is also a large dose of love and romance. You manage to sail through it all with Ganesha's help. This trend will continue for a while and you will be at the grindstone. Why complain in these recessionary times? Honour whatever work comes to you now as there could be periods when there may be nothing on your plate. It is the law of life.

August 31 - Full Moon in Pisces

There are family get-togethers. You may meet up with an old flame and share notes. Despite hectic schedules, you find time for matters of the heart. There is love and longing and your thoughts go back to beautiful moments of togetherness when the world was a lot younger and so were you. The focus is on finances and achievements, and also on bonding with those you care for. There will be parties, ceremonies and functions and you will be loving, giving and sharing. This is also a lucrative period and a good time to profit from brokerage, commissions, ties and collaborations. Ganesha wishes you well.

September 8 - Moon's first quarter in Gemini

There is peace, harmony, balance and excellence. This is a period of joyousness. You realise the value of domestic commitments and feel happy and contented when you are able to meet all the demands of family members. But you will have to strive for objectivity and see both sides of the coin if you want your relationships to grow. You will have to pace yourself and find the time for the various demands on you --- work, personal aspirations, career on the one hand and home, family and domestic responsibilities on the other. It is a tough balancing act but you manage to pull it off. There are rewards and awards at work and kudos from family members. Ganesha is happy that you manage all the pulls and pressures so well. You will be fully stretched and may face the possibility of a burn-out.

September 16 - New Moon in Virgo

There is harmony in your life and you are in a position to change direction and focus. Your ties and bonds have been reinforced and you seem to enjoy domestic chores and commitments. In this period, work, family and filial responsibilities will all be handled with sensitivity and grace. You will be all the I's – independent, inventive, innovative, inspirational and ingenious. You will manage to solve problems at home and work and feel happy with the results. You are filled with gratitude for Ganesha.

September 22 - Moon's first quarter in Capricorn

You are on the fast track to success. You pull out all the stops and think and plan ahead. There is a lot to do and you wonder what to prioritise and how to go about it. It could be a slightly confusing phase. There will be both personal and professional issues to address. On some counts, you may need to compromise too and meet the situation halfway. Personal relationships will be the focus now. But, on the whole, there is more positivity, hope and optimism. Children will be a source of joy and you will spend a lot of time pottering around in the garden. Nature walks and the outdoors will be rejuvenating. It may also be a good time to spend in a spa or naturopathy institute. Ganesha blesses you.

September 30 - Full Moon in Aries

This is a week of joys and achievements. Ganesha gives you a lot. In fact, you are inundated with goodies. You manage to achieve a lot but then you have also worked hard for the success. There are no free lunches in life. You will concentrate on increasing your influence and status as well as your bank balance. You handle finances with flair and wisdom. In this period there is flux, movement, new happenings and even a touch of uncertainty. The negative aspects of life can also be energised and so you should steer very clear of shady deals. What goes around comes around. Be ethical in life or you will pay a heavy price. Take care to avoid the law and steer clear of litigation. It is better to settle disputes across the table or they could just get exaggerated. Ganesha advises caution.

October 8 - Moon's last quarter in Cancer

The moon's last quarter is in Cancer and there will be many sensitive and emotionally charged moments. This is not a particularly low phase but many doubts will assail you and you will have to think proactively and let go of the doubts and insecurities plaguing you. You need to charge out of your crease with the right energy, play life on the front foot like Sehwag or Afridi, build bridges and mend fences. This will attract the warmth of others as this mood is always contagious. There will be romance in the air and many meets, conferences and family gatherings. There will be fresh achievements and successes and you will be keen on new goals and targets. You are able to carry everyone with you on this achievement spree. Just believe in Ganesha and go with the flow.

October 15 - New Moon in Libra

You are busy and active on the professional and social fronts. The 5 F's of family, finance, fun, fortune and food hogs your attention. A wide spectrum of business and professional transactions, deals and negotiations will have to be handled well. You will be entertaining, attending or giving parties, being a good host/ hostess, even dealing with dietetics and nutrition. The family will make demands on you but you will be more than willing to help them out. There could be the illness of elders, parents or in-laws that cause you much discomfort. An old and steady relationship may also come to an end. This can be most disconcerting and you will be off the rails for a while. Ganesha wishes you well as always.

October 22 - Moon's first quarter in Capricorn

This is a period when you make a lot of progress on the work front. You set targets and deadlines and go for it big time. In this phase you can also be more demanding or more giving; you will oscillate between extremes. But one thing is for sure: your obsession with mundane material pursuits may come to an end. You look at expanding your consciousness. There will be many events and meetings which will change your life. There will be definite changes in your psyche and you become wiser and more mature and have a broader understanding of the world. You will reach out consciously and unconsciously and ask more of the world. This works well for you as you are also willing to give more to the world. Existence sees this change and blesses you manifold. Ganesha blesses you too. There is always an action and a reaction to it. You get what you give. So give well and truly now.

October 29 - Full Moon in Taurus

You are on the right track. Your mind is more settled and you are at peace. There is money to be made and rewards and awards for the taking. The domestic scene is also more settled and there is intense bonding. You are happy. There are many expenses but that can also be read as wise investments. There is buying and selling. There are many positive influences at play indicating growth and progress. You are also filled with exaggerated expectations. There could be sudden windfalls, great wealth or luck, and all kinds of wonderful opportunities that take you many rungs up the ladder of success. The impact of this period is not at all subtle. You may even be taken aback by the largesse of this period. This is a fortunate time and you should make the most of it, says Ganesha.

November 7 - Last quarter in Leo

Expenses mount but earnings from various sources manage to keep pace. So you don't have to worry too much. There is international travel and new love in your life. There will be many new and fruitful associations too. There will also be new circumstances that give you increased freedom or an opportunity to do something different. You may pursue new courses in education or you may travel to learn more by seeing the world. There is also money to be made in new ventures. You think and act large and your positive approach and vision pay rich dividends. This is a profitable period by all accounts. Go with the flow, says Ganesha.

November 13 - New Moon in Scorpio

As the year ends, the intensity increases. You may also get enmeshed in an affair and this could cause a lot of heartburn. If you are married, this fling will create many unpleasant domestic ripples. Take care or this could result in the breakdown of your marriage. You may also be in an indulgent mood and could be prone to excesses in food and drink. Old liaisons will also appear out of the woodwork to haunt you and you will have to carefully sidestep the repercussions. There could be a lot of emotional tension and your health may suffer. It may be a good idea to cool off, slow down and take it easy. This will also pass but your indiscretions could leave a sour aftertaste. But, like I keep saying, astrology never compels. Ask Ganesha for help. Keep low and the tempest will pass.

November 20 - Moon's first quarter in Aquarius

You are filled with new ideas and find new ways to tackle work and domestic issues. There could also be some despondency and an occasional temper flare-up. You could even be cheated in some recent deal and so it will be worth your while to scrutinise the fine print with a magnifying glass. There could be many mood swings and people close to you will find you difficult to deal with. You look at spirituality, yoga, meditation and other options to still your mind. You are on edge and even the slightest provocation can trigger off an upheaval. You also realise that this is not the way you should be and that you should change in a hurry; this is a new trend as you are generally loving and genial. You are passing around all the wrong vibrations and not doing yourself and others any good in the mood you are in. Ganesha wishes you well.

November 28 - Full Moon in Gemini

The full moon is in your sign and this could be very significant. You have been through a rough patch and are now seeking answers to the complexes nestled deep in your subconscious. There are many new professional relationships and they seem to work well for you. You are not particularly idealistic now, you have learnt your lessons, burnt your fingers, and now you want a clear roadmap. You look at professional and business relationships with seriousness. You sign new contracts and examine the details. You do not want to be deceived again and you are taking all the precautions. Ganesha is happy that you have learnt your lessons. The way forward is clear and you have managed to remove the roadblocks. Now there should be no looking back.

December 6 - Moon's last quarter in Virgo

This is a period of hard toil. You set your sights very clearly on whatever needs to be done and you go ahead and accomplish all your tasks with single-minded zeal. There may also be an unusual new relationship with a much older or younger person. This may not be sexual in nature and could veer towards a parent-child relationship. But it will be a learning process for sure. Both of you should gain in this. You may also begin an exacting and detailed creative project involving media that requires cutting edge technology. This is new and you could be pioneering a trend. There will be many takers for this. There is success staring you in the face. Go grab it, says Ganesha. There are accolades to be won.

December 13 - New Moon in Sagittarius

You are reaching out to everybody. There could be new international associations and overseas projects. All your relationships will also achieve a degree of stability at this time. This really makes you happy. There are many pleasant influences now and you may be inclined to sit back and do nothing. But you also know that this is a very important time in your life in which you can have new and rewarding experiences. Your creative potential is also unleashed and you blaze the marquee. Your inner energies are strong and you are full of self-confidence. The new moon is in Sagittarius and you are enveloped by beneficial energies. Ganesha wishes you well.

December 20 - Moon's first quarter in Pisces

There are many moods to this period. This is an excellent time for all financial matters and you will spend a lot of money on making your surroundings appear more elegant. There is inner growth too and you are very clear in your material acquisition. This is a good sign. There are strong indications of travel, either physically or mentally. You are keen on more knowledge and want to broaden your understanding of the world around you. Your mind expands and you want to embrace all types of ideas. There is a new you and you are filled with positive energy. Ganesha is happy.

December 28 - Full Moon in Cancer

You could be in party mode and having fun. There is good health and a feeling of well-being. You will explore the outdoors and may take a holiday in the hills, mountains, beaches or some wildlife reserve. This is a favourable period and you are in touch with your emotions. You also want to establish empathetic relationships with others. You get into sentimental mode and get very attached to your surroundings and to familiar objects. You think about the past and get emotional about it. Please remember that there is no point at all in drudging up the past. Whatever has happened has happened; nothing can change it. This is the time for healing and new energies. The New Year beckons. Go for it with Ganesha as your helmsman.

GEMINI

KEY DATES

January

1*-3, 5-6, 9-10, 14*-16 (important), 19*-20 (important), 23*-24 (important), 27*-31 (most important).

Ganesha says January stands for finance, family, food, favours, and life's flavours. A month of plenty, in all the F's, and otherwise, too.

February

1*-2, 4*-7, 10*-12 (important), 15*-16, 19*-20, 23*-25, 28.

News and views, meets and conferences, trips and ties, computers and the internet --- all come together.

March

1*, 2*-6, 10*-11, 14*-16 (important), 19-20, 23*-25 (important), 27-28.

Home and journey, money rentals, loans, health, servants, court cases – all keep you on your toes.

April

1*-2 (important), 6*-7 (important), 11*-12 (important), 15*-16, (important), 19*-20, (most important), 23-25, 28-30.

April helps you to be a good parent, cultivate friendship and happiness, entertain lavishly and be amused. Fun and work combine to make April very special.

May

1*-5, 8-9, 12-14, 16*-18, 21-22, 25-27, 30*-31.

April, May, June, July are interconnected regarding house, home, shop, property, health, money, servants, colleagues and work, says Ganesha.

June

1*, 4*-6 (important), 9*-10, 13*-14 (important), 17-18, 22-23, 27*-28.
June is for meeting people, marriage, partnerships of every sort, journeys both short and long; also for the union or clash of minds.

July

1*-3, 6*-7, 10*-11, 14*-16, 19*-20, 24*-25, 26*-31, (important).
You open the account with loans, joint-finance, insurance, taxes, legacy. Shift/ transfer/ house move are also indicated, says Ganesha.

August

2*-3, 7*-8 (important), 11*-12 (important), 15*-17, 20*-22, 25*-26, 30*-31.
Journeys, mobility, pilgrimage, rites, religion, tantra and mantra, inspiration and travel are the possibilities.

September

1*-4 (important) 7*-8, 11*-13, 17*-18, 22*-26 (important), 30*.
You will be working and slogging hard like a soldier, and also enjoying the fruits like a commander.

October

1*, 4*-6, 9*-10, 14*-15, 19*-20, 23*-24 (important), 27*-28.
You will walk your way to fame, success, love, riches, power, promotion. The health of parents, in-laws might be a problem.

November

1*-2, 5-7, 10*-12, 15*-19, 24*-25, 29*-30.
The balance sheet of life will be mixed, that is, profit and loss, income and expense, joy and sorrow in this phase.

December

1*-4, 7*-9, 12*-16 (important) 18, 21*-22 (important), 25*-26, 30*-31. Ganesha says, you will run the race of life, be it honey, money or Indian rice and curry. Jewellery, job, profession, business are energized and you work wonders!

Cancer

June 21 - July 22

CANCER

(June 21 - July 22)

ELEMENT AND RULING PLANET: Water and moon.

STRENGTHS: Cancer is receptive, sensitive and imaginative, sympathetic, kind emotional and active shrewd, and intuitive.

WEAKNESS: Negativity and over – sensitivity. Moody, clingy, self- pitying and self- absorbed.

SYMBOL: The Crab – Possessing and impenetrable exterior, covering soft flesh underneath. At the first sign of danger, it withdraws into its shell and scuttles back to the sea where it feels safe.

MATCHING SIGN: Capricorn.

MAGICAL BIRTHSTONE: Pearl – changes bad fortune into good and discord into harmony. It also brings support from influential people.

CANCER

YEARLY FORECAST

Main Trend

Even if there is much darkness - and this world and the physical nature of man are full of it - yet a ray of the true Light can prevail eventually against tenfold of darkness. Believe that and cleave to it always.

Ganesha gives you a complicated picture. Not a bad phase, just complex and fraught as you cope with several pulls. Let's look at it closely, for its impact will prevail long and deep into the year ahead. Along with June/July, this will be a good time for money matters pertaining to fund-raising, capital-formation, long-range investments, and trusts for public good. Even punishments, limitations, confinement at home are possible. You will be occupied and obsessed with death --- either of a loved one, or with necromancy, life after death, maybe (on a practical level) legacies and wills. Try not to be too confrontational in your approach to all of this, and also, definitely, in your personal and family interactions and relationships. In the emotional sphere you will put your own needs first --- whether purely physical or not. Passion, sensuality, a sexual frenzy may stir up a maelstrom within you. With all this inner turmoil (both favourable and otherwise), there could be definite health problems if you stress yourself too much. And that, says Ganesha, is never a wise thing. It is totally counter-productive and self-defeating. You may feel that you're in the grip of a force beyond your control, since it is a time for great, perhaps even radical or drastic, changes in your material as well as emotional world. Lots of tossing on the high seas of life, but in the final analysis, Ganesha is watching over you. Ultimately, the domestic and familial changes that happen now will provide new hope for the future as well as long term stability.

Spirituality, great INNER POWER, lasting peace and sometimes God's realisation are POSSIBLE.

"O Lord, make my life full of divine inspiration, that it may become productive only of good. Free me from all pettiness and narrowness. Help me to keep my thoughts fixed on that which is vast and majestic. Expand my heart and enlarge my mind that I may be able to contain Thee and give myself up wholly to Thee."

- Swami Paramananda.

Jupiter:

This is the year of spirituality, expenses and possible ill-health, so the above prayer to the Lord will set you free, make you happy, lessen your worries, erase your doubts and anxieties, and keep you relaxed. Jupiter will be in your 12th angle. Visits to holy places, foreign lands, law-cases, accusations, separations and new unions are possible. You may have much to do with hospitals, centres of knowledge, wisdom, yoga, meditation and charity. You could be initiated into secret knowledge and hidden mysteries. But debts and losses are also possible. It is this unusual mix of pleasure and pain which makes the year unique for you!

Do not opt for liaisons, secret links and relationships and please try not to exaggerate your troubles, or health problems. In other words, learn to maintain your balance.

Embracing the world for peace and harmony:
Lokha samastah sukino bhavantu! Om Shanti, Shanti, Shanti....
May all beings in the world be happy Om peace, peace, peace.....

Amma is a beacon of hope in our turbulent times. If charity is giving food to the hungry, drugs to the sick, home to the homeless, education to the unlettered, love to the stricken soul, Amma's words are magic, and her touch is healing. For the poor, she is a rich source of inspiration to live on. For the homeless, she is the final abode of hope. And for the entire humanity, she is the other word for peace.

"True religion is a language forgotten by modern society. We have forgotten the love, compassion and mutual understanding taught by religion."

- Amma

My dear friend Seshadri Iyer has often referred to Amma. Ganesha says, my Bejan has not even met Amma in his life. But he has intuitively felt that for you, Cancerians, Amma will be the right role model. The astrological reason is that Jupiter will be in your 12th angle. Jupiter in your 12th angle stands for secret knowledge, expenses, journeys, an initiation, travel, spiritual and uplifting experiences that dissolve the dark aspects and recesses of life and sorrow, all of which will be yours. Yes, you will overhaul your entire life and make its design grand and complete. It is like a vacuuming from within, and after that, how can there be any looking back? Expenditure, foreign lands, pilgrimages to holy places, property of parents and spirituality are the other possibilities. All of it will not happen. Only a few of these could occur for you. You must learn from your past mistakes. There will be contact with hospitals, the sick, the suffering, the disabled, the weak, and the helpless. Charitable undertakings and causes are probable. Affairs of the heart and liaisons are also indicated for you.

This is your year of spirituality, expenses and possible ill-health. Therefore, the above prayer to the Lord will set you free, make you happy, lessen your worries, erase your doubts and anxieties, and keep you relaxed. Jupiter will be in your 12th angle. Visits to holy places, foreign lands, law-cases, accusations, separations and new unions are possible. You may have much to do with hospitals, centres of knowledge, wisdom, yoga, meditation, charity. You could be initiated into secret knowledge and hidden mysteries. But debts and losses are also possible. It is this unusual mix of pleasure and pain which makes the year unique for you!

Do not opt for liaisons, secret links and relationships, and please try not to exaggerate your troubles, or health problems. In other words, learn to maintain your balance.

You are, as I have always said, completely free to pray to Ganesha/ Allah/Zoroaster/Christ/Buddha or any power you like. Amma is only a powerful illustration which flashed in my mind.

Saturn:

The other key planet, Saturn, will be in your 4th angle from 30th October 2009 to 5th October 2012.

The fourth angle signifies:

a) Home, house, land and buildings;
b) The end part of life, especially if you are a senior citizen;
c) Karma and dharma;
d) Retirements and endings;
e) Renovation and decoration and refurbishing;
f) Elders, parents, guardians;
g) Community matters.

The other important aspects of the fourth house are: near and dear ones, caste and ancestry, mother, relatives from your mother's side, land and houses, agriculture, farming, gardens, orchards, installations, buildings, parliament, favours from the ruler, medicine, education, knowledge of land and geography, hidden treasures, comforts and discomfort, courage, faith, victory and defeat, perfumes, clothes, milk, digging, agricultural produce, vehicles, possession of cattle, horses and elephants.

Unlike with Jupiter, the Saturn impact will not be totally favourable.

Saturn restricts, sets limitations and expects you to perform well within them. Saturn will cramp your working style, or conditions may not be completely suitable, or your surroundings could be uncongenial. Pets could pose problems. Also, and this is the crux, your health might buckle under the strain of your workload. Loans and funds will be an albatross, an encumbrance, and an added burden for you.

Your sense of responsibility to your work will be fully tested and that's what Saturn in the 4th angle will do to all working Cancerians. Everything will not be hunky-dory. The operative phrase will be struggle-to-achieve. In all fairness, those who finally make it will stay at the top of the heap for quite some time to come, for the simple reason that the rewards conferred by Saturn are long-lasting and truly solid.

Parents, in-laws, elders, home, house, retirement, family disputes and property, are also covered by Saturn in your 4th angle. Expect troubles, worries, vexation, and sometimes a permanent separation! The rough with the smooth. As the French say: *C'est la vie* which means, 'That is life'!

This is an extremely important transit of Saturn. At this time you will focus on your innermost personal and domestic life, for this is the area that requires work now. Any problems in your domestic life will become more critical at this time, and anything you have been 'putting up with' but not really handling will have to be dealt with. Consequently, the effects of this transit range from a simple reorganisation of your domestic environment to a total reshuffling of personal relationships and contacts that affect your domestic life.

Elements that used to be important in your life come back into prominence now, especially if they were never resolved in the past. Therefore, this is an especially good time to get in touch with your innermost self through psychotherapy or other consciousness-raising and consciousness-expanding techniques.

During this time, you may have to take on a parental responsibility for someone, not necessarily your own child, or you may seek out someone who will play a parental role for you. If you do find a 'parent', make sure that this situation will ultimately lead you to independence on your part. Be certain that it is a growth relationship for you and not the beginning of a long-term dependency, which would prove detrimental in the years to come.

At this time, a period of several years' preparation is coming to an end. You are ready to emerge from comparative dormancy, at least in terms of outward success, and begin to move upward and forward to achieve your ambitions. But you must start modestly. The fourth house acts as the foundation of your horoscope, and you must pay attention to securing and building up this foundation. This is what lies behind your outward concern with your physical home. It is really the inner house that you are attending to, which is the reason this is such a good time to involve yourself in psychotherapy. Inner problems that you do not clear up now will be the source of most of the problems along your personal road for the next 14 years. The fourth house is opposite the tenth house of career and social status. Any negative factors at work will oppose your successful achievements later. This is a time of new beginnings. So get off to a good start.

Finally, let me make it very clear that the effect of Saturn in your 4th angle will be spread out from 30th October 2009 to 5th October 2012. Saturn in your 4th angle is your Karma and Dharma. Saturn will direct you in your endeavours for the next 12 years. The mantra, "Shri Ram Jai Ram Jai Jai Ram" is best for cancelling, or at least lessening, the negative influence of Saturn.

Mercury:

Mercury speeds up all matters and happenings for you, from June 8-26. Something like a roller coaster ride: we have the recent example of fast bowler Zaheer taking 5 wickets against New Zealand. Letters, calls, emails, fax, ads, poster, computers, the use of the internet should be frequent, and the pace furious. Together with this, paradoxically enough, you will be given to introspection, bouts of tremendous restlessness and sudden impulsive action, and, therefore, may I remind you of the Spanish proverb, *La Almonanda es buen consejo*, meaning, 'It pays to sleep over it'. It pays to take just a little time before deciding. Journeys and yielding to the lure of distant places are a strong probability. You will definitely be on the move.

Mars:

Mars stimulates you mentally, physically, emotionally and even spiritually between 24th August and 6th September. Your energy levels will be touching a high and so also your hormones: passion could have you by the throat. Ganesha assures you of great creativity and moments of intense happiness and exhilaration. You will show mettle like the Cancerian Sunil Gavaskar, and win plaudits. You will be the top gun. What's life worth without some excitement, anyway?

Venus:

Venus swings in your sign from 8th August to 6th September, emphasising your love life, companionships, and your social circle; as we Indians say, 'happy events in the family'. A short sojourn but a pleasant one! There will also be renovation, decoration, alteration, any sort of home and office improvement, since Venus also emphasises the luxuries and the good things in life. And yes, you will pay much attention to fashions and ads, and food. Extramarital connections and flings are possible, if you feel so inclined, as you have the charisma and class, and could thus attract others with a mere glance, a touch or a word. The goodies of life will be yours, in more ways than one.

Neptune:

Neptune will move in your 5th angle from 4th February. It will be all about love, creativity, children and hobbies. The Nobel laureate poet Pablo Neruda sings:

"I love you like the flower-less plant
Carrying inside itself the light of those flowers,
And, graced by your love, a fierce perfume
Risen from earth, is alive, concealed in my flesh.
I love without knowing how, whence, when.
I love you truly, without doubts, without pride,
I love you so, and know, no other way to love."

- Pablo Neruda.

Uranus:

I compare Uranus to a powerful jet which zooms in the sky and finally disappears. Uranus in your 10th angle makes you ambitious, energetic, and enthusiastic, and most certainly an achiever. Uranus motivates you to powers and glory. **Ganesha says use this power wisely and well.**

Pluto:

Pluto will be in your 7th angle of love, marriage, partnerships, travel, contacts and communication. Here, disturbances and upsets are possible. Many times, but not always, matters might be outside your direct control. But you must learn to accept fetters outside your orbit of direct influence. In short, Pluto is both a blessing and a bane. But that is life.

Final Word on Saturn:

From 6th October 2012, Saturn moves in your 5th angle of children, creativity, entertainment, hobbies, pastime, prayers and the element of luck and good fortune, which is so very important for a good life. Astrologers interpret Saturn in the 5th angle in different ways. I believe Saturn in the 5th angle will make you a winner. So, have faith, hope and courage. The next year will be much better. You will win the game of life.

CANCER

MONTH-BY-MONTH

JANUARY

You shed your inhibitions and work your way through heaps of letters and emails. This is the internet age and I know that I should stick to emails, but then Cancerians can be emotional and would love to hear from loved ones in their own handwriting! Communication and contacts will start from this month itself and last through the year, announces Ganesha! Love will definitely also take a front seat and so indeed will finances and money matters. Journeys or plans to travel are probable on and after the 13th. Partnerships, new deals, positive tie-ups are emphasized, so also are collaborations, local and foreign. Try to take a breather and fix priorities. You start the year on an upbeat note. This is a good time to incorporate the fruits of previous successes, analyze them, re-look them over and appreciate them for what they were. This is the theme for the start of the year. There may be some domestic issues including bereavement, but that is all part and parcel of life. As the month moves on, there are many positives. Your outlook on life has reached a point of equilibrium. You have a good understanding of life, and everything is working well for you. Towards mid-month, there could be a crisis in your personal relationships. This is a period of testing old relationships to find out whether they can survive. New relationships are hard to come by. Your emotional state could trigger illness. As the month ends, you look at making sweeping changes not only in your consciousness, but also in the circumstances in which you live. You will have to be flexible and allow the changes to enter your life.

FEBRUARY

Your emotions are at play and many of the decisions you take now may not be too practical. So Ganesha asks you to take care. You realize that all kinds of practical considerations have to be dealt with now. You turn your attention to financial matters. The money planet, Jupiter gives a rocket thrust to your money-related activities from the 4th, inspiring you to give your best. Joint finances for loans and public trusts and charities and philanthropy, buying and selling, investing are all bunched together. You are being pulled in several directions, so once again Ganesha's advice is to prioritize. Your mate/spouse will not want to be side-lined or neglected either. This is also a period of expansion and a heavy interplay of emotions. There are several domestic issues to sort out, including the health of a parent or an ailing relative. There will be problems at work and spiralling expenses. You may be tired and dispirited. Mid-month, the intensity increases. This could also be a time of material and financial adversity. I suggest that you keep a low profile and wait for this period to pass. Conserve your energies for the good times that will soon come knocking. As the month ends, you desperately try to hold on to circumstances, possessions and relationships that no longer have any real value in your life. You are holding on for dear life to illusions. Find time for leisure and hobbies like gardening or working out. There is no point in being emotionally high-strung. Believe in yourself, says Ganesha.

MARCH

You are in a tangle as there are many serious questions that you have to solve. I suggest you take Ganesha's help. This is my earnest and humble request. You may feel that the demands on you are endless. Some conflict situations may also have to be dealt with in the personal/family angle. There could be a measure of disillusionment and hurt in store for you. I have to tell it like it is, insists Ganesha. Therefore my astro-tip is, be reasonable and do not take slights and hurts too much to heart. Journeys, festivities, celebrations, pilgrimages, invitations, functions, research, travel and ties keep you mighty busy. The connectivity and bonding themes of the last two months will not just crystallize but enlarge their scope and vision. In the beginning of the month, you are working at cross-purposes. There are many thoughts dominating your life and you need to sort out your priorities first. You need to get a grip on your affairs. There is a strong tendency to excess. Beware of ego issues and delusions of grandeur. You may be tempted to overestimate your self-importance and this can lead to arrogant behaviour and inflated pride. When you are confronted by others, you will retreat into your shell like the crab and get morbid and morose. As the month moves on, you make many new contacts and there may even be international travel. This is a good period. Your health is much better now and you feel optimistic and capable of taking on a lot. Make the most of this phase. Towards the month end, the trend is that you may be caught in some kind of relationship, maybe a bad marriage or love affair. But the good news is that it won't bother you much longer and it will end soon. Go with the flow of events. The moon's first quarter is in your sign and this can be a significant period. You can be extremely emotional and sensitive about many issues. You also want your space; you are in a dilemma.

APRIL

If you have been unlucky in love or really scared to go for it, put your best foot forward now. Ganesha is with you and will help you in matters of the heart. This month finds you gaining momentum in the publicity and information sectors. You will work like a beaver and also stockpile both assets and goodwill. Discard pride and touchiness. In any case, there is a tremendous moving ahead this month. April will also be important for relationships and the health of parents, in-laws, partners and elders. Social and family give-and-take and meetings help you to see everything clearly. Cooperation and help come to you from several quarters, not least of them being Ganesha. The goodwill you have built up will be reflected in a million different ways. This is a period of good times and expenses and many meetings. There could be love too depending on your personal chart. You have a great need for people and bonds. The stress is on relationships at all levels. There is also the need to put your finances on track. You will carry on with your strong, definite focus on the 3 F's – funds, family and finances. The desire to have genuine material security will dominate you. The month sees familial support for all your ventures. Ganesha rewards you with satisfaction and joy from things that matter to you like pets, creative pursuits, hobbies and, of course, work which fuels everything else in life. As the month ends, you will be in a great hurry to get things done. Delays and impediments will be a nuisance and you will be chancing your luck as you look at new avenues and take risks.

MAY

There is great emphasis on the domestic scene. Ganesha ensures happiness. This is a very comfortable month. Friends help you, your mate will be affectionate and attentive, money pours in, food and fun keep you in high spirits, and the social and professional buzz energizes you. A marvellous time for you in terms of achievement, fulfilment, great times with loved ones, outings and just plain fun. You are motivated and happy. You look for love, romance, happy times and the simple pleasures of life. You fuse work and pleasure and there is no letting up. You will be interacting with people at all levels. The focus is on the 3C's --- contacts, communications and correspondence. You reach out to people and places and your relationships will grow and prosper, enriching you no end. As the month ends, there is a lot of movement in your life both literally and metaphorically. Your relationships are harmonious and smooth and you focus more on work. There will be romance, attachments, love affairs, maybe even an engagement or a wedding. Many things will happen to add to the flavour of the period.

JUNE

This can be the best period of the year by far. Ganesha sums it up well: an unusual June in the sense that while you will be introspective and in a mood to take stock of everything, you will also be reaching out to people. In this month of contradictions, you feel you're moving ahead and yet standing still. In fact, you could even be moving backwards in your attitude, moods and concerns. You are attempting to reconcile conflicting demands, aspirations and commitments. Mercury, the all-powerful planet, is in your sign now. It is very important and occupies a prominent position for a fortnight. This is a golden period and exactly what you have been waiting for. With your confidence restored and enhanced, there will be greater ability to balance work and commitments better. You handle life more positively and look at a suitable job/vocation to express yourself genuinely and with creativity. All this will add quality to your life and depth to your personal interactions. Your heart will rule and you will partake in the splendour of human relationships. Your confidence grows in leaps and bounds and enhances your interactions with people.

As the month ends, there are awards and rewards, plaudits and kudos, and you rise in value and prestige. You are appreciated by one and all and success is well-earned. There is also love and passion and several moments of deep, powerful intimacy.

JULY

There will be a merry pace and gait to whatever you undertake now. Make the most of this period as it is beneficial. It is your birth month, and both Mars and Venus have something to contribute, in order to liven things up for you. You are eager, even keen to meet life head-on, give it your best shot. This is a month to grab what you want and be assertive. Enhanced activity almost always happens in a birth-phase. Do remember, however, that both the good and the bad always get energized so don't make rash moves or take hasty decisions. Ganesha can't always help! This phase will make you energetic, productive, intuitive, charming, and, therefore, an outright success in both the professional and personal spheres. There is visible success and everything you touch turns to gold. In this phase, you rise in your esteem and leave the opposition far behind. You will experience and do full justice to a rare state of exceptional creativity and charisma. There is better health and a much more positive mindset. This will be a period characterized by the love of all that is beautiful. There are new ventures, avenues and interests to expend your recharged energies. Ganesha is happy for you. The new moon is in your sign and this is a significant period for you. You will be tremendously busy and extremely productive as you engage in all kinds of work and leisure activities. You are firing on all cylinders and there could be the danger of a burnout. As the month ends, the domestic angle is highlighted and there will be many demands on your time and resources. You will be terribly stretched.

AUGUST

There is a lot going for you. The happy and positive influences of July continue undiminished in August and I suggest you do not spare the horses! Just believe in me and Ganesha and go for broke! At any rate, the money scene will be good, or at the least, adequate. On the personal and family level, you're eager to give of yourself. A good month, full of gains, fine moments, lots to do and lots to enjoy. You feel challenged to perform in several spheres and will have to deal with mounting expenses. You look for new ways to earn more and at the same time you ask more out of life; you desire a lot more than a humdrum existence. You want a meaningful life. People will play a major role in your life socially, emotionally, and of course, professionally. There is need for less emotion and more objectivity, patience and calm. You interact with siblings, co-workers, neighbours and they all appreciate your concerns. You are a caregiver and are naturally empathetic. Your people skills have not only improved greatly but will now be your strength. Both colleagues and loved ones will support you. You want to project yourself well, and so you work on your public and personal image. You may need to take care of your health and will have to watch your diet and exercise regimen. As the month ends, money will be the theme. Tax and estate problems, marital funds and expenses, mutual profit and gifts, family divisions and other fiscal instruments will dominate your thoughts and influence your actions.

SEPTEMBER

There will be many changes on the work front and this will impact your life significantly. Your interactive skills and good interactions will help ensure that this is an excellent month to win friends as well as influence people and bag contracts, assignments and have tons of affection and caring. Travel and correspondence and communication by all possible media will boost your image. Let me just say that trips, ties, bonds, connectivity are more or less the theme for this month. This phase will bring out the best in you, but in a strange way that may not be evident at first. There is a hike in your self-esteem and self-worth. The focus will be on income and your assets and also partnerships, collaborations and ties. You keep giving your time, energy and resources to others and there are many demands on you. You display great fortitude and determination in the face of all odds and challenges. Health safeguards will be essential as work pressures mount. As the month ends, you get the strange feeling that your opportunities for growth and expansion in life are limited. This period requires patience but you seem to be in a tearing hurry. You need to put down roots and get some stability in your life.

OCTOBER

The mood is overrun by domestic concerns and obligations. Home, family, house and the property scene will definitely predominate, as will your interactions with siblings, children, even extended family. There is no doubt that this will be your major priority. For some time at least, the home could be the base of operations. Yes, a home-away-from-home is also on the cards, or perhaps acquiring a second home or property, if you are so inclined. Ganesha says your family will be of utmost importance to you whether spouse, parents, children, siblings, or all of them. These are emotional times and you could have unrealistic attitudes in personal relationships. There will be many pressing family issues to deal with. The health of an elderly relative will remain a grave cause for concern. The focus is domestic in nature and the attention is riveted on kin, community and family. As the month progresses, the good moves and wise choices of previous weeks start paying off. There is new hope, greater joy in the future and long-term stability. Towards the month-end, you sweat it out, slog away, plough the land in a manner of speaking, and burn the candle at both ends to get all that you want.

NOVEMBER

You should take care not to get into a shell now, says Ganesha. It is all going your way and so do not allow emotions to cloud your life. You will work well, love well, and react well. Family demands and professional concerns will be handled with flair. Once again, it is your capacity to multi-task, to communicate well that will be emphasized. Liberty, joy and creativity in their widest sense form the tripod on which you base your existence. There is rapid progress in all spheres of your life. With a little luck, there will be outstanding success. You are able to rise above petty squabbles, gossip and bickering. Finances are on the upswing and you will enjoy the comforts of life. The interactions with people will be your primary focus. You will be communicating with all types of people and reaching out in different ways. As the month progresses, your success and general happiness could lead to over-confidence. You may excite envy, perhaps even hidden or open rivalry, and people may want to pull you down. On a more down-to-earth plane, increased employment, gifts, a legacy or other benefits come your way. A tremendous sense of aestheticism, of beauty, now grips you.

DECEMBER

You look for a happy ending to the year and I like to be optimistic and so I say clearly that you have all the chances to make the year end on a happy note. The world lives in your mind, in what you conceive it to be. Please remember that. You come to the year-end on a high note, extremely busy because home, family, work and profession, your spouse/ partner will all have major expectations and will need extra attention. This is also a good time to launch a project, finish pending work, take on new assignments.

Lending/borrowing/investing/buying/selling/shopping will be highlighted. Home/house/property affairs also come into sharp focus. It is the last month of the year and you are in deep contemplation: how did the year vanish so fast and where am I headed now? The desire to accomplish more occupies your mind and you look for ways to reconcile your work with your true inner impulses. You are ready to stick your neck out, lead from the front to make change happen. You are ready to take on a leadership role.

There is professional success and you are admired and respected. You have a tremendous will to excel in your chosen field and you put in extra efforts and win respect, status, perks, benefits, awards, rewards, kudos and applause. It is all richly deserved, I must add along with Ganesha. You are confident, pragmatic and determined as you forge ahead to power, glory and accomplishments. As the year ends, your entire persona undergoes a huge change for the better. You are a new person now full of commitment, caring and confidence.

CANCER

THE MONTHS AT A GLANCE

January

Your outlook on life has reached a point of equilibrium. You have a good understanding of life, and everything is working well for you. Towards mid-month, there could be a crisis in your personal relationships. Love seems harder to come by. Watch your moods and do not get into a cocoon, says Ganesha.

February

This could also be a time of material and financial adversity. I suggest that you keep a low profile and wait for this period to pass. Conserve your energies for the good times that will soon come knocking.

March

The moon's first quarter is in your sign and this can be a significant period. You can be extremely emotional and sensitive about many issues.

April

The stress is on relationships at all levels. There is also the need to put your finances on track. You will carry on with your strong, definite focus on the 3 F's – funds, family and finances. The desire to have genuine material security will dominate you.

May

You will be interacting with people at all levels. The focus is on the 3C's - contacts, communications, and correspondence. You reach out to people and places and your relationships will grow and prosper enriching you no end. As the month ends, there is a lot of movement in your life both literally and metaphorically.

June

With your restored and enhanced confidence, there will be greater ability to balance both work and your commitments better. You handle life more positively and look at a suitable job/vocation to express yourself genuinely and with creativity.

July

There is visible success and everything you touch turns to gold. In this phase you rise in your esteem and leave the opposition far behind. You will experience and do full justice to a rare state of exceptional creativity and charisma.

August

You interact with siblings, co-workers, neighbours and they all appreciate your concerns. You are a caregiver and are naturally empathetic. Your people skills have not only improved greatly but will now be your strength. Both colleagues and loved ones will support you.

September

There is a hike in your self-esteem and self-worth. The focus will be on income and your assets and also partnerships, collaborations and ties. You keep giving your time, energy and resources to others and there are many demands on you.

October

The focus is domestic in nature and the attention is riveted on kin, community and family. As the month progresses, the good moves and wise choices of previous weeks start paying off. There is new hope, greater joy in the future and long-term stability.

November

You are able to rise above petty squabbles, gossip and bickering. Finances are on the upswing and you will enjoy the joys and comforts of life. The interactions with people will be your primary focus. You will be communicating with all types of people and reaching out in different ways.

December

There is professional success and you are admired and respected. You have a tremendous will to excel in your chosen field and you put in extra efforts and win respect, status, perks, benefits, awards, rewards, kudos and applause. It is all richly deserved, I must add along with Ganesha.

CANCER

WEEKLY REVIEW

(By the Phases of the Moon)

January 1 - Moon's first quarter in Aries

You start the year on an upbeat note. This is a good time to incorporate the fruits of previous successes, analyze them, re-look them over and appreciate them for what they were. The whole purpose is to get to know yourself better, to understand your life in a more holistic manner and therefore be better able to take conscious control of it. There is more to life than an intellectual understanding of it; you have to understand the essence of life experiences. You have lived through an entire gamut of experiences, there has been an entire road show of life; you should come to grips with it all and move ahead on the basis of that understanding. This is the theme for the start of the year. Ganesha wishes you well as you plough ahead. You should watch out for mood swings and tendencies to go under when the chips are down. Just remember that you are well loved and highly thought of despite your recurring insecurities.

January 9 - Full Moon in Cancer

There is rapid progress despite your emotional plays which will not mar work. You are far ahead of your times and may not fit in with the humdrum demands of everyday work and life. You could easily be misunderstood too. But your business or professional life will run smoothly and employers, superiors and colleagues will appreciate the calm, controlled manner in which you handle your work. Harmonious relationships will also reflect your own inner stability. There may be some domestic issues including bereavement but that is all part and parcel of life. Ganesha wishes you well. There could be many expenses and emotional moments, like the children leaving home.

January 16 - Moon's last quarter in Libra

There are many positives now. Your outlook on life has reached a point of equilibrium. You have a good understanding of life, and everything is working well for you. This is not a time of testing and so you don't know how well your ideas will stand up to future crises. But life is dynamic and many things that have no relevance to past experiences and lessons can happen at a terrific pace. It is imperative to keep your mind open and flexible and be ready to learn all the time. Do not be closed to experiences as they can often catch you in unguarded moments. Continue to examine yourself and see how you can improve your life and times. Ganesha wishes you well.

January 23 - New Moon in Aquarius

There will be all types of thoughts that will hamper your growth. You move around in circles without being able to arrive at the crux of the issue. There could be a crisis in your personal relationships. Love seems harder to come by and you may turn cold with those who have been close to you once upon a time. Or you may want to maintain contact and they may just cool off. This is a period of testing old relationships to find out whether they can survive, are still concerned about you, and if they can contribute to your life. But all this is difficult and messy. New relationships are hard to come by and you are unsure about old relationships. These moods could also hurt your work and health. Take care or you could fall seriously ill. Your emotional state could trigger illness. Ask Ganesha for help.

January 31 - Moon's first quarter in Taurus

There is some stability now and you begin to find your feet. But this is a good time to make sweeping changes, not only in your consciousness, but also in the circumstances in which you live. You have been eyeing changes for a long time now and conditions that have been developing slowly will force major changes upon you now. You may have to start a whole new phase of life. You will have to be flexible and allow the changes to enter your life. Initially, there will be a lot of resistance and you may even detest the idea of a new start in your life. But you will have a new birth of awareness and will be able to deal with your life unhampered by old patterns of thought. You seek to break all barriers and doors to allow the sunlight in, metaphorically speaking. Do not despair. Ganesha will guide you the right way.

February 7 - Full Moon in Leo

This is a period of expansion and also the heavy interplay of emotions. As they say in everyday language, 'you won't know if you are coming or going'. There are several domestic issues to sort out including the health of a parent or an ailing relative. If someone has been unwell for some time, this may be a time for emergency medical aid. Pets will also face distress and the mood will be glum all around. You get into your shell and feel even worse. There will be problems at work and spiralling expenses. You will be busy with loans, funds, and every fiscal instrument you can lay your hands on. You may be tired and dispirited. Of course, all this depends on the personal horoscope and nothing more can be said about this period barring some generalizations. Astrology never compels. Ganesha is with you.

February 14 - Moon's last quarter in Scorpio

This is an intense period but may also be a very discouraging time. Your vital energies are pretty low, and you may feel quite incapable of dealing with the problems that may surface. This could also be a time of material and financial adversity. You may have to re-examine your attitudes toward money. It may be a good idea to cut corners and prune your lifestyle. There will be better times and you will be able to be more eloquent with your spending habits. There will be several work pressures. Employers and those in authority may oppose your plans. I suggest that you keep a low profile and wait for this period to pass. Everything comes to an end and so will adversity. Conserve your energies for the good times that will soon come knocking. Focus on the family and, possibly, enroll in some yoga or meditation programme. Learn to be calm and do some deep breathing before you react to people and situations. Ganesha is with you. One good method is to work at having a maximum of six breaths per minute and slowly calm down. In meditation, focus on the third eye and dissolve all your worries.

February 21 – New Moon in Pisces
One method that is tried and tested is to adapt to situations and be as flexible as you can. This could be a period of great turmoil and stress as you desperately try to hold on to circumstances, possessions and relationships that no longer have any real value in your life. You are holding on for dear life to illusions. Find time for leisure and hobbies like gardening or working out. Please remember that the richness of your life does not come only from your achievements in the outer world of business and society, but also from what you know and understand about life. There are several other factors needed for happiness and that includes love and health. There is no point in being emotionally high strung. Elderly Cancerians will face a crisis of reorientation. This is the time to expand your horizons and turn to your inner values. Look for richness within and stop thinking of times gone by. Nothing lasts, everything passes. There is no use in living in regret. Believe in yourself, says Ganesha.

March 1 - Moon's first quarter in Gemini
You are working at cross-purposes. There are many thoughts dominating your life and you need to sort out your priorities first. There have been upheavals on the job front and those keen on a new assignment will need to get the basics right before taking up something new, or the trend will only repeat. You need to get a grip on your affairs. There is a strong tendency to excess. Be careful about financial matters as you may be spending without a thought in the world. There may be a lot of feel good shopping but please remember that your resources are not infinite. Ensure that you

save for a rainy day. When the going gets tough, the tough have to get going, as they say. Ganesha blesses you.

March 8 - Full Moon in Virgo

Those in the field of teaching and education will get a big boost in their careers. There is money to be made and promotions and perks. But beware of ego issues and delusions of grandeur. You may be tempted to overestimate your self-importance and this can lead to arrogant behaviour and inflated pride. When you are confronted by others, you will retreat into your shell like the crab and get morbid and morose. You can do away with all this. There are family matters to attend to and several new work opportunities too. You may also over commit to projects that demand more time than you really have. Make sure that you have the resources to do what you have set out to do. There is a possibility that you could have overestimated the resources at your disposal. But along with this is also good luck flowing your way and a great power and zeal to achieve a lot. Ganesha watches over you.

March 15 - Moon's last quarter in Sagittarius

You make many new contacts and there may even be international travel. This is a good period. Your health is much better now and you feel optimistic and capable of taking on a lot. Make the most of this phase. This is a good time to initiate new projects and expand your activities so that you can experience life from a broader perspective. You look at new ways to escape the narrowing and inhibiting circumstances of the past that prevented you from realizing your full potential as a human being. You look for more meaning in your life and push ahead to make it more joyous. There will be many changes in your life and you may even consider emigrating. There are many surprises in store. The flow of events will catch you by surprise and not of all it will be bad. In fact, all this will rejuvenate you as you swim with the flow of events. Challenges taken in the right spirit can be morale boosting. Ganesha guides you along the way.

March 22 – New Moon in Aries

As I keep saying in all my columns, these are generalizations and trends. They are not compulsive. Unless I have an individual horoscope, I cannot be completely accurate and even that is left in the hands of Ganesha. I am a mere human being and prone to make mistakes. But the trend now is that you may be caught in some kind of relationship, maybe a bad marriage or love affair. But the good news is that it won't bother you much longer and it will end soon. Go with the flow of events and there will be new beginnings which will be quite happy and fortunate for you. Keep your chin up, do not go under or get discouraged and frustrated. There may also be some issues at work that need resolution. You will have to work around people and circumstances and find a way around roadblocks. Ganesha will help you.

March 30 - Moon's first quarter in Cancer

The moon's first quarter is in your sign and this can be a significant period. You can be extremely emotional and sensitive about many issues. Your desire for relationships is in strong conflict with your need to feel like a distinct, separate and definite individual. You also want your space; you are in a dilemma. There could also be some bitterness at home with family members. You will find it difficult to relate to people and may even feel very lonely with family members and loved ones. Somehow, communication may become a problem. You are hard working and talented but you need some discipline where your emotions are concerned. Ask Ganesha for guidance.

April 6 - Full Moon in Libra

This is a period of good times and expenses and many meetings. There could be love too depending on your personal chart. It will be a good idea to re-examine your relationships and determine with finality your rights, duties and obligations. This will help smoothen the communication between partners. There may be heavy demands on you and you are in a quandary: do you break free or still hang on in the relationship. You can't live without the person and can't live with the person either. You will have to take the call on this. You will also spend time with social work and animal welfare. This will be a much-needed diversion too. There could be a marriage in the family or an addition to it. Ganesha blesses you.

April 13 - Moon's last quarter in Capricorn
You have a great need for people and bonds. The stress is on relationships at all levels. This makes you happy. You are keen to strengthen existing bonds and forge new ones. There is also the need to put your finances on track. A lot of your time will be spent on house, home and property matters. You will carry on with your strong, definite focus on the 3F's – funds, family and finances. The desire to have genuine material security will dominate you. There will be acquisitions, budgeting of household expenses and finances, add-ons, extensions, renovations, new purchases. You will have to be more adaptable and flexible in your dealings as you look at achieving more and more. There will be support from extended family and kin and your colleagues. The immediate family too will pitch in. Just leave it to Ganesha.

April 21 - New Moon in Taurus
There is familial support now for all your ventures and this makes you really happy as you want deep bonds with loved ones and are unhappy when that doesn't happen. You look for more funds. Speculation, gambling and betting will also interest and excite you as you look at all money-making possibilities seriously. Ganesha rewards you with satisfaction and joy from things that matter to you like pets, creative pursuits, hobbies and, of course, work which fuels everything else in life. You look at all new avenues of income and that includes new areas of work too. One has to change with the times and flow like water and find one's level. You need to step out of your comfort zone and look at the world with new eyes. Ganesha is with you.

April 29 - Moon's first quarter in Leo
Events are outpacing you and you will be in a great hurry to get things done at breakneck speed this week. There will be some

restlessness too as you are impatient to get cracking at what you want to do. Delays and impediments will be a nuisance and you will be chancing your luck as you look at new avenues and take risks. It would be a good idea to take precautions, do your homework, read the finer points of contracts and documents and comb the details. Your upbeat mood reflects in whatever you do and there is great enthusiasm for love and passion, spirituality, tantra and mantra. There could also be a shift in your residence or office as you move ahead quickly and efficiently. Along with greater earnings are also many expenses. Ganesha watches over you.

May 6 – Full Moon in Scorpio

This is an intense phase and you push yourself very hard. You are burning the candle at both ends as you also entertain with flair and enjoy time-out at social gatherings. You look at long-term benefits and plan with caution. You are motivated and happy. You look for fun, love, romance, happy times and the simple pleasures of life. You will have a good rapport with all comers both at domestic functions and official gatherings. You fuse work and pleasure and there is no letting up. There could be a new romantic interest but nothing certain can be said of it now. Ganesha asks you to wait and watch.

May 12 – Moon's last quarter in Aquarius

You are in a thoughtful mood and I dare say morbid and dissolute. There is no use getting unnecessarily sentimental and emotional about things from the past that you cannot change nor do anything about. Learn from whatever has happened and move on. Also, one swallow doesn't make a summer and so don't generalize. You will be interacting with people at all levels. The focus is on the 3 C's - contacts, communications, and correspondence. You reach out to people and places and your relationships will grow and prosper enriching you no end. People will matter to you and you will keep your interactions with them vibrant and meaningful. There is travel and a grand reaching out to new experiences. There will be new studies, trips to nearby places, even developing social ties with neighbours. You become a vibrant and fully involved member of the community. You like it that way and Ganesha is happy for you.

May 20 - New Moon in Gemini

There is a lot of movement in your life both literally and metaphorically. Your relationships are harmonious and smooth and you focus more on work. Be positive always and remember that it is contagious as no one wants or likes a whiner. You may consider several new areas of work or specialty: metaphysics, computer and space technology, social reform, electronic media etc. You over-extend yourself both physically and financially and will have to prioritize. This may not be the right time to make vital decisions. So hold on a while. The health of elders will be a problem area although children will be a source of joy. You could also be planning a family holiday this season and meet up with far-flung friends and relatives. Ganesha is beside you.

May 28 - Moon's first quarter in Virgo

You roll up your sleeves and get serious about work. This will be a week of very slow movement, sometimes even none at all. You may feel that you are just marking time, waiting to move into action. There could be feelings of insecurity and a lack of self-belief. There may also be a touch of frustration in your dealings with others. Avoid rash moves and speculation. Try to smoothen the path with colleagues at work. Away from it all will be romance, attachments, love affairs, maybe even an engagement or a wedding. Many things will happen to add to the flavour of the period. Ganesha is with you always.

June 4 – Full Moon in Sagittarius

You are in for a great phase now. You will make rapid progress in all your endeavours. Ganesha advises you to strike while the iron is hot and it is steaming hot now. Mercury, the mighty, all-powerful planet is in your sign now. It favours travels/ meetings/

conferences/ interviews/ trips/ more brain power/ contacts/ communication/correspondence/contracts. Mercury has a special connection with the circuits of the brain. Chess, crossword and other such games belong to Mercury. Also, short distance runners and spin bowlers are controlled by Mercury. Mercury, in short, is the ambassador and salesman of the zodiac. It is very important and occupies a prominent position now for a fortnight. This is a golden period and exactly what you have been waiting for. This is the time you have to take bold steps, leave the past behind and look ahead. Ganesha will give you whatever you want now. Just ask!

June 11 - Moon's last quarter in Pisces

These are sensitive times and the family will play centre stage. You will also reach out to friends and, most surprisingly, foes too become friends. With your restored and enhanced confidence, there will be greater ability to balance both work and commitments better. You handle life more positively and look at a suitable job/ vocation to express your creativity. All this will add quality to your life and depth to your personal interactions. It will also enhance and sharpen your work skills. You now become the true achiever you always wanted to be. There is success in all your endeavours and a good chance for a major wish-fulfilment. The trends favour you, says Ganesha.

June 19 – New Moon in Gemini

The tempo of life increases and you meet many people. It can be both personal and work-related. You continue the great run and will truly appreciate reaching out to both people and places in this emotion-packed period. Your heart will rule and you will partake in the splendour of human relationships. You display a more caring and open attitude to people, to life, to the world, and it comes back to you in shovelfuls. Your confidence grows in leaps and bounds and enhances your interactions with people. There is powerful bonding and fruitful partnerships. You may also find yourself attending a wedding celebration or being part of one yourself if you are single and eligible. There are as many possibilities as there are ideas. Ganesha blesses you. Just ensure that you make the most of all the possibilities thrown your way. Grab every opportunity.

June 27 - Moon's first quarter in Libra

This is a great period and is most certainly a week of confidence and charisma. This feel-good phase finds you enjoying the fruits of your past endeavours and making new inroads. There are awards and rewards, plaudits and kudos, and you rise in value and prestige. You are appreciated by one all and success is not only well earned but also very sweet. There will be promotions, more perks, career advancement and several gains. You deserve all the applause, says Ganesha. You have worked hard for it. These are just dessert for someone who truly deserves it. You make serious gains in all your endeavours and are sensible enough to make the right investments too. There is love and passion and several moments of deep, powerful intimacy. There could also be an addition to the family. Ganesha smiles with satisfaction.

July 3 – Full Moon in Capricorn

You make rapid progress. There is visible success and everything you touch turns to gold. In this phase you rise in your esteem and leave the opposition far behind. You will experience and do full justice to a rare state of exceptional creativity and charisma. There is better health and a much more positive mindset. You are ready to take on the world and its challenges and come out trumps. There will be nothing that you feel is difficult to achieve or is impossible to surmount. You dig deep and draw on your resources. You display an iron will and an impressive capacity for sheer and sustained hard work. You will excel in all areas of life. Ganesha blesses you.

July 11 - Moon's first quarter in Aries

You continue with rapid progress in whatever you do. The bold and beautiful side of you will rule this week. This will be a period characterized by the love of all that is beautiful, by all that appeals to your aesthetic senses. There will also be a lot of hard work. You will find time for hobbies, sports and leisure activities and may be drawn to higher study and research. You have worked hard and now is the time for rewards, as you immerse yourself in pleasurable activities. There are new ventures, avenues and interests to expend your recharged energies. This bountiful trend will continue for a while. Ganesha is happy for you.

July 19 - New Moon in Cancer

The new moon is in your sign and this is a very significant period for you. You will be tremendously busy and extremely productive as you engage in all kinds of work and leisure activities. You are firing on all cylinders and there could be the danger of a burnout. Take the necessary precautions or you might just undo all that you have set out to achieve if you don't take care of yourself. You may need a change of lifestyle, more organized eating habits and regular hours to sustain yourself as you relentlessly forge ahead on all fronts. You are in a brilliant phase as far as the ingenuity and quality of your work is concerned. You make shrewd, inspired moves that get you places. Ganesha is watching over you.

July 26 - Moon's last quarter in Scorpio

The intensity of the phase takes you by surprise. The domestic angle is highlighted and there will be many demands on your time and resources. There will be hospital expenses and issues with children and teenagers that need to be dealt with firmly. You will be terribly stretched in this period. Expenses soar and you could be at your wit's end. In a bid to escape the pressures, you do a lot of feel-good shopping. To feel and look better and to present a more impressive image to the world, you get yourself a new image/ wardrobe/persona. New acquisitions or refurbishing your old possessions will renew your zest for life which has taken a beating in recent times. There is intense bonding and many new alliances and partnerships. There is joy in relationships and many happy moments with loved ones. This can be a crazy and confusing period, says Ganesha. You will be pushed and torn in different directions.

August 2 - Full Moon in Aquarius

You are plagued by several thoughts and indecisions and may be running around in circles for answers. You feel challenged to perform in several spheres and will have to deal with mounting expenses. You look for new ways to earn more and at the same time you ask more out of life; you desire a lot more than a humdrum existence. You want a meaningful life. There will be journeys for business or pleasure, or both. You try to leverage your knowledge and personality to become more successful. People will play a major role in your life socially, emotionally, and of course, professionally. You will reach out to others and be fully involved with contacts, contracts and communications, all of which will lead to progress and material gains. You will also deal with deeds and documents for both, personal and business purposes. You will meet new people, socialize, accept invitations, attend many parties and outings and live a bit daringly and dangerously. In the midst of it all, you will also enjoy life. Ganesha watches over you.

August 9 - Moon's last quarter in Taurus

You turn your efforts and energies homewards. There are many domestic responsibilities and you plunge into taking care of children, parents, elders and in-laws. There is need for less emotion and more objectivity, patience and calm. You interact with siblings, co-workers, neighbours and they all appreciate your concerns. They recognize your worth and you are delighted by all the effusive praise showered on you. The work front is on stable ground as of now, you have sewn up the loose ends, and so you feel that it is time to concentrate on domestic and family commitments. You are a caregiver and are naturally empathetic. You like looking after people and will be a great asset in a world of suffering and despair. Ganesha blesses you. You are like Florence Nightingale; always there for those who need you.

August 17 - New Moon in Leo

The main thrusts of this period are finance and romance, or money and honey, as I like to call it. While you are naturally romantic, money matters will include joint accounts, loans and funds, insurance, realty, bonds and every other fiscal instrument. You will also be looking at wills and there could be a windfall from an inheritance. There could be profitable travel, maybe a pilgrimage or visits to tourist spots. There are expenses of all kinds and more earning too but you will also be having a lot of fun. You think large and get expansive and look at life in its several macro dimensions. Ganesha is with you right through.

August 24 - Moon's first quarter in Sagittarius

You will be moving fast and furious and making several new and profitable contacts. Your people skills have not only improved greatly but will now be your strength. Both colleagues and loved ones will support you. They will form an important part of your support system and will contribute positively in several ways. You want to project yourself well and so you work on your public and personal image. Avoid rivalries and legal contests. It will help to remain calm and more objective. Work on compromises on the work and personal fronts for greater harmony. You may also need to take care of your health and will have to watch your diet and exercise regimen. A health check may be a good idea. You could check in to a naturopathy centre if so inclined. Of course, like I always say, these are generalizations and a personal horoscope will provide more details. Trust in Ganesha and go with the flow.

August 31 - Full Moon in Pisces

Finances occupy your life now. Money will be the theme of this period. Tax and estate problems, marital funds and expenses, mutual profit and gifts, family divisions and other fiscal instruments will dominate your thoughts and influence your actions. Money will be the core of all your ties and interactions. There could also be partnerships and marriage, contacts, professional and business associations. This is a mixed bag of several disparate influences. There could also be a new romance or an old flame will enter your life and cause disruption. Tread carefully, says Ganesha.

September 8 – Moon's first quarter in Gemini

You are shooting off in many areas and moving rapidly in several tangents. This phase will bring out the best in you, but in a strange way that may not be evident or visible at first. There is a hike in your self-esteem and self-worth. The focus will be on income and your assets and also partnerships, collaborations and ties. Household and family matters will also have to be handled, issues and problems addressed, and every roadblock squarely and frontally faced. There will be expenses on renovation, decoration and beautification, the buying, selling and development of land, assets and property. You will also spend time in the care of elders, parents, in-laws and siblings which you do willingly and graciously. Life is looking good and you are happy. There are many surprises in store, says Ganesha.

September 16 - New Moon in Virgo

You keep giving your time, energy and resources to others and there are many demands on you from everyone - at the office and at home. They know that you will never refuse a genuine call. But you are only human and have only two hands and how long can you overextend yourself? You display great fortitude and determination in the face of all odds and challenges. There may be a few nagging worries and fears that could escalate but you work hard and optimize your time. You get through all challenges and manage to turn enemies into friends. But despite it all there will be delays and snafus, postponements and setbacks. There may also be an aborted journey. Health safeguards will be essential as work pressures mount. All these preoccupations will distract you from work and they will need to be resolved or sorted out. You must not neglect to build up reserve funds as there may be some time in the future when you may have to dip into your savings. You are faced with many demands and commitments and you walk the tightrope. You will have to master time management and the delegation of authority. Ganesha blesses you.

September 22 - Moon's first quarter in Capricorn

You will have to make many changes in your life. This is a period of readjustment after a period of rapid expansion. Do not be discouraged by recent setbacks as they may be blessings in disguise as you will realize in a while. This is the right time to make your life more secure and stable. Be cautious and do not start any new projects now. If your expectations are too high, you may be disappointed. There will be a reality check in your work area and you will understand where to cut down on non-essentials. This could also be a testing time for personal relationships which will go through a period of trial. You often feel as if your personal freedom is controlled by others. There could be separations, even a breakdown in marriage. Ganesha tells you not to worry too much as this may be a much better way to be in the long run. It may be the only way to achieve the freedom that you truly want.

September 30 - Full Moon in Aries

You get the strange feeling that your opportunities for growth and expansion in life are limited. You may feel that you are not moving ahead with any sense of purpose. You may be moving sideways, if not actually in reverse gear. There could be financial problems to be sorted out and restlessness and impatience with restrictions imposed upon you. This period requires patience but you seem to be in a tearing hurry. You need to put down roots and get some stability in your life. This is not a time for growth and expansion. You have to make plans on a more solid basis and keep away from the pressure of circumstances and people. This influence teaches you a lot about life. Believe in Ganesha and move on.

October 8 - Moon's last quarter in Cancer

These are emotional times and you could have unrealistic attitudes in personal relationships; your expectations are out of proportion. There is no connect with reality as you live in a fantasy land. There will be disruptions and disappointments in your domestic life. You tend to avoid the truth about yourself and about your relationships; your reluctance to deal with reality could hurt you a great deal. It will undermine your self-confidence and your sense of reality in relationships. You should take care not to get too trusting and, if bitten, you should also see to it that you are reborn to love and cherish again. Don't let an odd experience mar you forever. There will be many pressing family issues to deal with. The health of an elderly relative will remain a grave cause for concern. Ganesha is with you.

October 15 - New Moon in Libra

You have many challenges to deal with. The focus is still domestic in nature and the attention is riveted on kin, community and family. Look for compromises and solutions. Take a conciliatory approach but do not allow it to be interpreted as a sign of weakness. Do not let others infringe upon your rights. Make sure that you put yourself first or no one else will. You will have to be a bit selfish here. Direct your energies to improving the domestic situation as you busy yourself setting the house and property in order. There is buying and selling and you make it a point to be surrounded by beauty. You may spend long hours in beauty treatments or at exclusive spas to de-stress. You also indulge in bouts of mood elevating shopping. Ganesha is with you.

October 22 - Moon's first quarter in Capricorn

The scenario changes a bit now. There is more focus on work and professional growth. You realize the need to make inner revisions to your personal foundations and attitudes and you let go of old dependency needs, or at least you try your utmost to. A burst of self-belief will see you through. The good moves and wise choices of previous weeks start paying off and your domestic scene is fully charged and revitalized. There is new hope, greater joy in the future and long-term stability. You also look for a second home, a home-away-from-home as you make steady and sustained personal progress. There is domestic peace now and you are happy. So is Ganesha.

October 29 - Full Moon in Taurus

There is stability and growth on all fronts and you have put the past behind you and are singing a new, upbeat tune. You realise that you want recognition as well as security. Both these needs are best addressed by having more money. Your need to have a higher income is intense and you work harder and also follow-up new job leads. You sweat it out, slog away, plough the land in a manner of speaking, and burn the candle at both ends to get all that you want. You make new acquisitions and you do everything in your command to feel secure in your own right. The wish to stand on your own feet motivates you and you leave no stone unturned. The whole idea is to change your mindset and drop old enemities and prejudices which have been clouding you. Ganesha is with you in this endeavour.

November 7 – Last quarter in Leo

There is rapid progress in all spheres of your life. You have managed to resolve your doubts and have adopted a positive attitude. Now your optimism and vision shines through and influences all your activities. It will reflect strongly at work and in your family and personal interactions. This week gives you just the right combination, the perfect mix of determination and imagination. With a little luck, there will be outstanding success. You are able to rise above petty squabbles, gossip and bickering. You are a better person now, much more confident and more integrated as a human being. Your people skills are better and you meet up with compatible and like-minded people who will help you in reinforcing your beliefs. Finances are on the upswing and you will enjoy the joys and comforts of life. Like Dhoni you are on a good wicket and like Sehwag you are batting on the front foot. Ganesha is happy for you.

November 13 – New Moon in Scorpio

There are many new aspects to this phase of growth. The interactions with people will be your primary focus. This may also be a good time to fall in love, dally over romantic alliances. You may travel, meet new and interesting people and profit from the interactions. You will be communicating with all types of people and reaching out in different ways. You will be sure of your own capabilities but people will also be your strength and asset. There could be many special, beautiful and stolen moments with a loved one. You could be in the arms of passion and loving every moment of it. Go with the flow, says Ganesha. You deserve the happiness.

November 20 - Moon's first quarter in Aquarius

You spend a lot of time thinking about the lovely moments that have suddenly happened in your life. Your success and general happiness could lead to over-confidence and you need to exercise caution. Watch your step or you could fall into a manhole. Of course, please do not take this in the literal sense. You may excite envy, perhaps even hidden or open rivalry, and people may want to pull you down. So there is great need to be both vigilant and tactful. Take care of your health and take the necessary precautions while travelling. Expenses will mount but there are more good tidings than bad and your interactions with people remain pleasant. All this contributes to happy and loving moments with progress and prosperity as the key words. Ganesha asks you to step on it as the time is good for you.

November 28 - Full Moon in Gemini

You are filled with new ideas; they seem to be bursting out of your skull. In this phase your creative instincts blossom. This can be a mildly pleasant, somewhat strange, even esoteric week. On a more down-to-earth plane, increased employment, gifts, a legacy or other benefits come your way. There will be more perks and recognition on the job front too. You plod away looking for more rewards both monetarily and aesthetically. A tremendous sense of aestheticism, of beauty, now grips you. Trust in Ganesha and move on.

December 6 – Moon's last quarter in Virgo

It is the last month of the year and you are in deep contemplation: how did the year vanish so fast and where am I headed now? The desire to accomplish more occupies your mind and you look for ways to reconcile your work with your true inner impulses. You are ready to stick your neck out, lead from the front to make change happen. You are ready to take on a leadership role. You will find time for religion and spirituality, travel and education. Issues revolving around your career, identity and home absorb your thoughts and plans. You also make projections for the future. You understand the need to build harmony in the home and family as you realize that social interactions are vital not only for growth but as a security blanket when the chips are down, with no warning balls to announce their arrival. Ganesha blesses you.

December 13 - New Moon in Sagittarius

There is professional success and you are admired and respected everywhere. You have a tremendous will to excel in your chosen field and you put in extra efforts and win respect, status, perks, benefits, awards, rewards, kudos and applause. It is all richly deserved, I must add along with Ganesha. There will be monetary gains and chances of enhanced income. There is also room for passion and romance, legacies and inheritance, loans, funds, bonds, parties and the whirl of social activities. You are in an ebullient and enthusiastic mood as you resolve many pending issues and make waves.

December 20 - Moon's first quarter in Pisces

These are soft and emotional moments. It is time to let your hair down. Cancerian women, in particular, are very feminine and romantic and will be in great demand. You will be in the throes of love and having a wild and wonderful time. You are confident, pragmatic and determined as you forge ahead to power, glory and accomplishments. Name and fame, popularity and plaudits, come your way along with outright competition and jealousy which are, as we all know, part and parcel of life. However, you will turn your attention to money matters and strike out in new areas of money making. You want to grow and to develop as an evolved human being. There have been several attitudinal and occupational swings to cope with. Now you will attempt to reconcile them all gainfully and harmoniously. Ganesha is happy that you have found your way.

December 28 -Full Moon in Cancer

As the year ends, your entire persona undergoes a huge change for the better. You have seen a lot including true success. You resolve to continue with your efforts at both work and play. There is a great intensity in your approach as you plan ahead. There could be some disruptions in your creative endeavours but you surmount all roadblocks. You also manage to make time for social work and bond well with everyone you meet. Your professional and personal successes have really empowered you and you look at the future with confidence and charisma. You rely solely on your sense of personal satisfaction and do not care too much about the good opinion of others or a desire for recognition. You work quietly and steadily, avoiding fanfare and publicity. Your interactions with parents, siblings, extended family and in-laws could also be demanding. You look at new ideas of income generation and look at yourself with new eyes. You are a new person now, full of commitment, caring and confidence. You are alert and active and you experience the sweet satisfaction of achievement. Ganesha guarantees that!

CANCER

KEY DATES

January

2*-3, 8-9, 12-13, 16*-18, 21*-23, 25*-26, 29*-31.

Ganesha says, January will bring you the horn of plenty. Both power and pelf (money) will be yours. You will be amused, entertained, delighted.

February

1-2, 3-4, 8-9, 13-14*, 16-18, 21-22*, 26*-28.

Insurance, heavy expenses, gifts, taxes, wining and dining, buying and selling, lots of fun and frolic make this month a happy one.

March

2*-4, 7*-9, 12*-13, 16*-18, 21*-22, 25*-26, 29*-31.

A great reaching out to people and places. Your work will be done and your dreams realized. Friends and well-wishers make you happy and proud.

April

1*-5, 8*-10, 13-14, 17-18, 21*-22, 26*-29.

Home, house, renovation, decoration, good news, domestic happiness, joy. Harmony and merry-making for you, says Ganesha!

May

1*-2, 6*-7, 10-11, 15-16, 19*-20, 23*-24, 28-29.

A time for revelry, ceremony, functions, children, romance, hobbies, socializing, making and spending money. Both will give you happiness, says Ganesha!

June

1*-3, 7*-8, 11-12, 15*-16, 19*-21, 24*-26, 29*-30.

You will get your due awards and rewards, promotions and inspiration. Health will improve. Funds and loans will be available. Servants and colleagues will love and respect you.

July

1-2, 4*-5, 8*-9, 12*-13, 17*-18, 21*-23, 26*-28, 31*.

Marriage, companionship, travel, trade, foreign affairs, meetings give you publicity and fame, says Ganesha!

August

1*, 4*-6, 9*-10, 13*-14, 18-19, 23*-24, 27-29.

Inheritance, joint-finance, loans, investments, windfalls, litigation, buying and selling, a second marriage, if that's the way the wind blows, says Ganesha!

September

1*-2, 5*-6, 9*-10, 14-16, 19*-20, 24*-25, 28*-30.

Pilgrimage, ceremony, name and fame, publicity, foreign connections, all spell out success and victory for you.

October

2*-3, 7*-8, 11*-13, 16*-18, 21-22, 23-24, 25*-26, 29*-31.

You will be working hard and long for success, changes in your work are possible. You will be recognized, appreciated, rewarded, says Ganesha!

November

3*-4, 8*-9, 13*-14, 18*-19, 22*-23, 26*-27, 30.

You will be at your best. Love, money, attention and praise should make you happy. You look back at a good and productive year.

December

1, 7-9, 10*-11, 15*-16, 19-22, 23*-24, 27-28.

Secret work, meets and conferences and travel. Expenses and visits to hospitals or distant places. Be positive, advises Ganesha, you have much to be grateful for!

Leo

July 23 - August 22

LEO

(July 23 - August 22)

ELEMENT AND RULING PLANET: Fire and Sun.

STRENGTHS: Leo is enthusiastic, powerful, expansive and creative, generous and extravagant.

WEAKNESS: Dogmatic and fixed in opinion, melodramatic, domineering, vain, stubborn and pretentious.

SYMBOL: The Lion – Regal, brave, dominating, sometimes indolent. Possessing nobility and pride.

MATCHING SIGN: Aquarius.

MAGICAL BIRTHSTONE: Ruby – protects against physical injury and ensures faithfulness. It also brings its wearer serenity of mind.

LEO

YEARLY FORECAST

Main Trend

"May I be like the Sun in seeing; like Fire in brilliance; like Wind in power; like Soma in fragrance; like Lord Brihaspati in intellect; like the Asvins in beauty; like Indra-Agni in strength."

- Sama Veda Mantra: Brahmana

Ganesha says your soaring confidence and self-esteem lead you to learn to do things much better, if not perfectly. You can be a leader, an innovator by the sheer force of your personality, convictions and ideas. It's a wonderful time for bonding - in marriage, friendship, personal relationships, affairs and attachments. A tremendous time for socialising, group activities, non-material gains as well as profit in business. You realise there is no need to go it alone and learn how to work with others for maximum benefit/gain - and not just your own. Guard against going to extremes in your emotions or being a little eccentric, careless or uncooperative. In short, as they say these days, don't wear your attitude. Much more is achieved with charm and tact, and caring. Your attitudes, worldview, outlook on life and the environment you live/ work at will. It is for you to wrest success and joy out of these changes. The way to do it, says Ganesha, is to approach everything in a positive manner without being stubborn or pig-headed, or by ignoring the interests and welfare of others. You will find that what you give to others comes back to you - in spades!

"Ambition is like sex and power. You never have enough of it"

- Bejan Daruwalla

Ganesha says on your marks, get set go. The main trend and tenor of 2012 is very definitely trips, ties, travel, foreign affairs, higher education, finding a guru, prophetic visions, intuition and inspiration as never or seldom before, ceremonies for the dead, felicitations, fabulous fancies and creativity. By Ganesha, what a list!

The timing for it will be January 23, 2011 to June 4, 2011.
After that what? From June 5, 2011 to June 12, 2012 you will be at peak power, at full throttle, at breakneck speed. To use a cliché, you will be at your brilliant best.

Let me put it differently. You will be able to achieve your goals and targets, whether physical, material, intellectual, emotional or spiritual. In these very simple words, I have said much.

This is only part of the story. From, October 6, 2012 to December 23, 2014 you may have problems connected with your health, and/ the health of your parents, elders, in-laws. Retirement is foreseen from October 6, 2012 to December 23, 2014. In other words, this is the downside. The reason is very simple. Saturn will be in your 4th angle of house, home, family, property, shop, godown, warehouse, office, land, building, construction, farming, health resorts, gymnasium, and hotels and so on.

There is another side to it. If you are into joint-finances, mutual funds, equities, loans, trusts, debentures, public ventures, banking, Ganesha advises you to proceed with caution. This is only a general reading. It is not a reading by your horoscope, because I do not have your time of birth. Even if I did a horoscopic reading there is no guarantee. Therefore do not worry, do not fret and fume but caution is advised.

Mercury the messenger will be in your sun sign from June 27, 2012 to September 16, 2012. This is an unusually long time for Mercury to be in one sign. Push with all you have for news, views, messages, opinions, ideas, finance, sales, social gatherings and parties, friends and laughter.

Venus:

Venus will be in your sun sign from September 7, 2012 to October 3, 2012. It is an excellent period for cooing and wooing, starting a project or venture, having fun and also making money, secret links and ties, rendezvous. In short, it is a time for love, life and laughter.

Mars:

This year, Mars does not enter your sun sign by Western astrology. Mars is the warrior, the muscleman of the zodiac. This does not mean that you will not have energy. From April 4, 2012 to May 14, 2012, Mars will be in your angle of friends, camaraderie, promotion, perks, all group activities, especially wish-fulfilment, children, entertainment and good cheer. It is a time to be happy. I have given you this hint. I know very well that Leos can live life to the hilt. They can live life King Size, to use a cliché. We Indians often use a cliché.

Saturn:

As I have been explaining all along, Saturn will be in your 3rd angle till October 5, 2012. This transit of Saturn will allow you to go in for enterprise, entrepreneurship, journeys, trips and ties. You will be in a mood and position to communicate feverishly, wonderfully, efficiently. You will have much to do with your neighbours, brothers and sisters, relatives and cousins. My advice to you is very simple. Try something new and different especially if it is based upon relationships and experiments. You will have much to do with public and mass relationships be it circulars, faxes, iPods, mobile, internet or even writing messages in the sky. Why do I say messages in the sky? The reason is that till October 5, 2012, Saturn will be in Libra. Libra is the king of the airy signs. Therefore, planes and air travel could excite you.

From October 6, 2012 to September 18, 2015, Saturn will be in the next sign Scorpio. Saturn is a slow moving planet. Therefore in 2012 Saturn will not hit you or affect you much. But take care of your parents, in-laws, elderly people, home, office, shop, godown, vehicles, land, building, property. Older Leos could face retirement.

But it is not all downhill. Buying/ selling/ leasing/ resting/ renovating/ decorating/ installing of a flat, factory, shop is also a possibility. So also chemicals, agriculture, mining, fisheries, oil drilling, minerals are other areas for you to consider.
In other words, Saturn gives mixed results. Do not be afraid of Saturn.
Here are the mantras for Saturn.
1: Shri Ram, Jai Ram, Jai Jai Ram.
2: Om Praam Preem Prum Sa Sanaye Namah.
The word Sanaye means Saturn. You have to do both the mantras 11 times or 21 times or 108 times. It will help. You can go to the temple of Hanuman or Shani and give oil to the Pandit, and let him anoint the idol with it. It will help. But it should be done with complete faith.

Uranus:

Uranus will be in your 9th angle in 2012. This is an excellent augury for ceremonies, rituals, pilgrimage, VERY PARTICULARLY NEW ENTERPRISE, BE IT ART, INDUSTRY, COMMERCE, COMMUNICATION, ELECTRONICS, AVIATION, DESIGNING, INTERNET, INVENTIONS AND SO ON. The excellent impact of Uranus will be felt in April, more certainly in June, August (lucky month) and December. Uranus in your 9th angle means imagination, instincts, intuition - the three I's.

Neptune:

From February 4, Neptune will hover in your 12th angle of salvation, hospitalisation, loss, social welfare, deception and also inspiration; this is the paradox of Neptune. You must avoid drugs and drinks.

Conspiracies can be hatched against you. I don't want you to feel disturbed and hassled. Neptune, I must say, in the name of Ganesha also represents inspiration and salvation for you especially. Also trips and ties. Therefore, do not be totally upset and disturbed.

Professionally it is a good year. You should do splendidly. But from October 5, 2012 to September 18, 2015 Saturn in your fourth angle could upset the domestic and the home front. The health of parents and in-laws could cause serious concern. Ganesha says nobody can have everything in life; but confidence in yourself.

LEO

MONTH-BY-MONTH

JANUARY

The lion has it going well right away. Ganesha assures you money and honey. There is a lot going for you in this exceptional Mars-Jupiter combination. The mood is upbeat and there is a hike in finances and more than just a touch of romance too. Sheer effort, and perhaps a touch of bravado, will be what works best for you, and you do it in style. Of course, there is no free meal in life and you will have to slog away. But Ganesha ensures success. Your contacts will definitely help you, both socially and professionally, leading to concrete gains. But it's not going to be a walk-over. After an interesting and reasonably profitable 2011, you brace yourself for the great leap forward this year. Your projects are always gigantic. You travel and have many new experiences. This is also a time when there is a rapid growth in consciousness. This is a good time to achieve the right perspective in all possible senses of the word. It is also a good time for education, for getting in touch with yourself through self-awareness studies, or for seeing the larger picture. Life is smooth with beautiful moments with loved ones and, I must add here, some powerfully passionate moments too.

FEBRUARY

You are busy with the 3C's - contacts, communication and contracts. There will also be the frenzy of reaching out with trips, ties, collaborations and new associations on the cards. You will look to establish long lasting and profound bonds. It is important in this period that you relate well to others. How you relate to people will be vital as it will play a huge role in determining your progress and your happiness levels. Ganesha warns you to think well, think carefully, and not rush into action. I also feel that you should bide your time and make the right choices. The full moon is in your sign and this is a very good period. You plough away with serious, single-minded determination. This is a lucky phase and everything will fall easily on your lap. You could feel a bit stretched with the various demands on you. There could be some domestic problems too. As the month ends, the emphasis is on social service, work performance, your relationship with your boss, colleagues and subordinates and on extending a helping hand to those who need it. You are preoccupied with kin, neighbours, near and dear ones, as well as your own immediate family. There is progress but replace egotism with balance. Please exert some control over hasty, belligerent reactions.

MARCH

There are domestic issues that make you sit up and think. There are many family issues that you need to solve first before making sure of your professional moves. You look at your roots, your family and your work with new eyes. You look at security for loved ones and will work towards it very seriously. This could be a month of strange impulses and ideas, and some unusual events too. But Ganesha says that the money is pleasingly stable, if not good, since your sources of income will multiply and that's always important. This is an excellent time to achieve real stability in your relationships. There will be harmony as your personal needs will not conflict with the demands of the relationships. Towards mid-month, you are on a weeding out and pruning process and are busy getting rid of all associations that were inappropriate or didn't quite fit in. This is a good time for collaborations and new projects. As the month ends, various aspects of your life will be transformed. You will be shown many dimensions that can broaden your life and experience and make a totally new person out of you. This is a period of many positive energies. You feel emotionally secure and in touch with your feelings.

APRIL

You will be seriously looking at growth in all areas of life. There are many influences working on you. Ganesha feels that this month is a fine time to study, improve your mind and to be receptive to ideas and opinions different from yours. There is a much wider canvas for you to paint on. Do not get bogged down in old fashioned ideas and ego hassles. Change is the only truth and you have to accept it. You strive to improve your skills, knowledge, wisdom, and acquire new techniques and improve the vistas of your mind. The life of the intellect will hold promise and excitement. Ganesha assures you of success in your efforts. This is a good month for contemplation and meditation too. This is also the time for social networking as near and dear ones from all over the world tweet in to say 'hi'. Take care not to get too indulgent and try to bring about some discipline into your life. Towards mid-month, there is stability and progress. You are energetic, optimistic and confident and the mood is upbeat. As the month ends, there is sustained growth.

MAY

You will be very busy with many tasks. Ganesha ensures that you have a very busy period ahead. Issues of prestige, power and pelf will take top priority. Renovation/ decoration/ buying/ selling of property or office are possibilities. Loans and investments are emphasized. Trying to get things done is what keeps you involved. You are ruled by the sun and will outshine your rivals. If there is a problem, it is that your ego issues may sometimes just flare up. But Leos are achievers. But please always remember that all these are generalizations and unless I have a personal chart, accurate predictions cannot be made. There is love and passion in the air. You and your partner will help each other grow in every which way and make it a very profitable alliance. Towards mid-month, there will be fireworks and celebrations. You are more ambitious than ever and you re-examine your image. There will be global expansion at work and, possibly, a new romantic interest. This is a valuable period in life when you learn a lot of lessons and grow as a human being.

JUNE

There are many roadblocks but you manage to get past them with skill. Boulders are thrown in your path. You will know instantly how to make the right moves, say and do the right things! It's a good idea, cautions Ganesha, once again, to keep your arrogance and impatience under control. Your social skills bring you a time of respite from your demanding lifestyle this month – fun and frolic galore. Saturn ensures that you are back to work. There is a lot on your plate and you slog away. It may be a bit of a struggle at times, but you rise to the occasion. You strive to conquer many new peaks. Your self-appraisal of last week sets you on the path to true creativity. Those in the media make their presence felt with an extra dollop of creativity, dash and josh! The moon's last quarter is in Pisces mid-month and there could be emotional, sentimental and maudlin moments in this soft phase. You will express deep feelings of love. The new moon in Gemini then shows you a period of innovation, creativity and original ideating. Your soul-searching has set you well and truly on a deep spiritual and fulfilling path. But as the month ends, one of the best phases for Leos begins. You will make rapid progress and scale new heights. This period will continue for at least another two months and you should make the most of it. Mercury, the mighty planet, is all-powerful. There are material, spiritual and emotional gains. I feel that this is a purple patch and you should make the most of it.

JULY

You are in the throes of success. As I mentioned earlier, the Mercury effect is profound. Expenses will hit the ceiling. There could be a few problems if you are travelling, moving house, buying/ selling, but the end result will be positive. The sun and Jupiter come together to ensure that things ultimately work out favourably for you, especially as your birth month approaches. The health of parents, elders and in-laws will cause anxiety. But Mercury makes its presence felt and you continue making progress. All your ties will be joyous and filled with hope. There is bonding, romance and passion. In addition to your job/ business/ profession, there will also be room for research and philosophy, justice, law and order. You display rare insights along with determination, creativity, imagination and style. The growth trajectory continues. You are aware that this is the right time to make the world your oyster. With Cancer predominant mid-month, the mood is softer. It is one of conciliation, a willingness to meet people more than halfway.

AUGUST

You continue to be on a roll. It is a great way to be. You pursue success and all doors open to your magic touch. The luck of the draw will be with you, and that's half the battle won! You will find yourself quite convinced of the need to project your personality, the image of your company, forcefully and effectively. In this birth-month phase, you seek out and improve on the flaws you perceive not only in your persona and personality, but also in your environment. It ensures a marvellous month of joy and achievements and a high happiness quotient. You are giving off your best at work and socially. Now you will be totally absorbed in the domestic scene, the house and home, along with working at a punishing pace. There is a lot on your plate. Try not to go under with this monumental burden. Learn to make time to relax, to pursue hobbies, pleasure activities, sports and exercise. You may get carried away with excesses. There is a kind of careless rapture pervading your life and pursuits.

Mid-month, there will be many propitious new beginnings as the new moon is in your sign. Everything you embark on now will lead to success. Ganesha blesses you and encourages you to spend more time with your loved ones. As the month ends, there could be international travel and you make several profitable contacts.

SEPTEMBER

Ganesha says that the health of loved ones may cause some concern but it is all going well for you on the work front. You may even be looking at entirely new vistas of work and employment. New assignments should fall into your lap, aiding your progress. You are also determined to give off your best. In the midst of all this work is also love, passion, and affection. You're still on the upward spiral of life, and determined to make the most of it, professionally and financially. September finds you pursuing your goals aggressively and confidently. Mars in your sign gives you just that amount of energy and enthusiasm to conquer all obstacles. Mid-month sees many domestic demands. Ganesha walks with you on the stormy path. As the month ends, you look for more freedom in whatever you do. But this is a significant period because you can reach out to people and taste new areas of life and have several varied and rewarding experiences.

OCTOBER

This is a period that will be important for contacts, contracts, communication and hi-tech computerization; you could be looking at new trends in technology for both personal and professional benefit. There could be a bonding on the personal level too. There will be a fine-tuning of existing ties and relationships, especially marital and emotional ones. You will also be wining, dining and hosting parties. The end of the year mood may have set in early. This is an excellent time for all financial matters and you plunge into them. You will feel like making your surroundings appear more elegant, and you may spend quite a lot of money too. Expenses soar but along with this concern with material acquisition, there are also some very real possibilities for inner growth. By mid-month, understanding yourself is vital, whatever the circumstances. And this period of self-inquiry will stand in good stead in the long run. There will be opposition and many challenges and roadblocks. But you manage to surmount it all and grow in many ways.

NOVEMBER

The mood is good and you are seriously planning ahead. You have the heart to take on both extra work and some calculated risks that may pay off soon. Follow your hunches, says Ganesha, but do not go overboard. You may be making big plans and signing documents. Watch your intuition and go with the flow. The last quarter of the moon is in your sign. This will be a significant period. Do not get obsessive and keep away fanatical thought processes. There are maudlin and soft moments mid-month and you meet with family and friends. You could get very emotional too as you bask in the love, warmth, admiration and care of loved ones. As the month ends, you are restless and go hunting for even bigger projects.

DECEMBER

You are in party mode and will have a great time. The Venus-Saturn combination helps you to be popular, have a relationship, travel, communicate superbly, and generally have a great time. Ganesha blesses you with all the goodies of life. Children, hobbies, games of chance and holidaying delight and captivate you. There are many pleasurable moments with the family. You've done a lot and it's time to take life a little easy. You earn well but also spend enormously. Plug all the holes in the bucket! No rash moves, or giving in to wild impulses, cautions Ganesha. There are several inhibiting factors at work and you will have to plough through them which you will with Ganesha's help. There could be marital troubles and you may have to terminate a long association. Of course, like I always say, it all depends on the personal horoscope. Towards mid-month, you are on a growth trajectory and your life is bullish. It is the time to initiate new projects, expand your activities and broaden your perspective. As the month ends, you overreach yourself. But you end the year on an upbeat note. This is an exuberant time, with high energies at play.

LEO

THE MONTHS AT A GLANCE

January
Your projects are always gigantic. You travel and have many new experiences. This is also a time when there is a rapid growth in consciousness. You earn well and spend too.

February
The full moon is in your sign and this is a very good period and you plough away with serious, single-minded determination. This is a lucky phase and everything will fall easily on your lap.

March
This is an excellent time to achieve real stability in your relationships. There will be harmony as your personal needs will not conflict with the demands of the relationships. This is a good time for collaborations and new projects.

April
You are energetic, optimistic and confident and the mood is upbeat. As the month ends, there is sustained growth. The mid-year trends are favourable.

May
There is love and passion in the air. You and your partner will help each other grow in every which way and make it a very profitable alliance. Towards mid-month, there will be fireworks and celebrations.

June
Your self-appraisal of last week sets you on the path of true

creativity. Those in the media make their presence felt with an extra dollop of creativity, dash and josh!

July

There is bonding, romance and passion. In addition to your job/ business/profession there will also be room for research and philosophy, justice, law and order.

August

There is a kind of careless rapture pervading your life and pursuits. Mid-month, there will be many propitious new beginnings as the new moon is in your sign. Everything you embark on now will lead to success.

September

You pursue your goals very aggressively and confidently. Mars in your sign gives you just that amount of energy and enthusiasm to conquer all obstacles. This can be a very successful period.

October

Expenses soar but along with this concern with material acquisition, there are also some very real possibilities for inner growth. By mid-month, understanding yourself is vital whatever the circumstances.

November

The last quarter of the moon is in your sign. This will be a significant period. Do not get obsessive and keep away fanatical thought processes.

December

There could be marital troubles and you may have to terminate a long association. Of course, like I always say, it all depends on the personal horoscope. Towards mid-month, you are on a growth trajectory and your life is bullish. Learn to rein in your temper and your authoritarian temperament.

LEO

WEEKLY REVIEW

(By the Phases of the Moon)

January 1 - Moon's first quarter in Aries

After an interesting and reasonably profitable 2011, you brace yourself for the great leap forward this year. You like to be dominant, in command and in control and you think big. You are not one for the tiny details. You think and believe king and queen size and aim for the stars. Your projects are always gigantic and you spend and live dangerously. You walk on coals, on ice and the tightrope. There are many projects and dangerous liaisons in your life. But that is the way you are unless your personal horoscope says otherwise. The tendency now is to go after everything that you want in the material world, without caring about what or who is in your way. You conquer, acquire and indulge yourself. But then you also begin to feel empty after all the mammoth efforts. It may be necessary to be more humble and more humane and realise that you can be insufferable even if others don't tell you that to your face. Ganesha urges you to keep your ego, anger, impatience and delusions of grandeur in check before you embark on new projects. You are buzzing away and if these words of caution are well taken, you have nothing to fear.

January 9 - Full Moon in Cancer

Many emotions are at play now. There will be time spent with family and loved ones and you will love every moment of it. But it is important that you are not arrogant toward others or assume that you have everything right. You have meaningful encounters with others, especially intimate one-to-one moments. Look for mutual growth at work. By trying to achieve goals set by the team you not only achieve more but are also more conscious of what you are as an individual. There are many new meanings and stimulating influences in your life now and this can be an extremely productive and growth-oriented period packed with meaning and genuine intent. Ganesha is with you. But do not misuse your power and always remain rooted to the ground.

January 16 - Moon's last quarter in Libra

You travel and have many new experiences. But this movement will be work related and not for pleasure. The direct experience of new people, places, events and happenings will be a great learning experience. You may also take time out to help with the disadvantaged sections of society. You have a strong feeling of social equity and, at this juncture in your life, you feel that justice should be tempered with mercy and compassion. You make rapid expansion and sign many new deals. There could be new love interests and you happily play the field. You are a charmer with a voracious appetite and Ganesha loves your lust for life. There will also be hectic partying and many bouts of excesses. It may be a good idea to slow down.

January 23 - New Moon in Aquarius

After all the indulgence, you settle for some balance and equilibrium in your life. Your affairs are also running smoothly and without much effort on your part. It is a time when you can relax and take it easy for a while as your plans are working out well and your life is in good order. This is also a time when there is rapid growth in consciousness, in your profession, in your social life, and wherever you feel that personal growth is important. You enjoy yourself and also examine your life to see what needs to be done to make it better. There is equilibrium in your life and you look inside of yourself with calm and detachment. There is balance in your affairs and this is a good time to give your life some perspective. Ganesha blesses you and, as always, wishes you well.

January 31 - Moon's first quarter in Taurus

There is stability and rapid growth as you make ferocious progress in all areas of your life. This is a good time to achieve perspective in all possible senses of the word. It is also a good time for education, for getting in touch with yourself through self-awareness studies, or for seeing the larger picture. You don't want to be a frog in the well and you want the macro picture. You want to be respected, admired and thought well of. You want to be a person of consequence and someone to reckon with. This is a great time to plan business expansion and various types of negotiations. Life is smooth and as you like it with beautiful moments with loved ones and, I must add here, some powerfully passionate moments too. If there are court cases, disputes or long- standing and chronic medical problems, they will find a solution. Ganesha is with you.

February 7 - Full Moon in Leo

The full moon is in your sign and this is a good time to go whole hog in whatever you do. You are in expansion mode and there are many expenses as you buy and sell furiously. This is a very good period and you plough away with serious, single-minded determination. The emphasis is on property, land, realty, construction and joint investments. There will be solid gains, acquisitions, assets. This is a lucky phase and everything will fall easily on your lap. The right choices will come easily to you, and inspired moves will be the result. You make progress without difficulty. There could be travel and many new agreements to be inked. You think big and plan big and earn big. There could also be beautiful moments with loved ones. Ganesha blesses you.

February 14 - Moon's last quarter in Scorpio

You are in the throes of passion. There will be many new relationships and if you are committed to one partner there will be several engrossing and beautiful moments that will be cherished for a long time to come. The focus now is on partnerships of all kinds. You will feel the need to re-evaluate your attitudes and perceptions so that you can do justice not only to your own hopes/aspirations but also to other people's expectations of you. You could feel a bit stretched with the various demands on you. There could be some domestic problems too. Children, especially teenagers, could be very troublesome and you may have a tough time disciplining them. There could be other problems too with the spouse or partner, depending on your personal horoscope. There could also be illness in the family and elders may need to be hospitalised. Ganesha wishes you good luck while you grapple with whatever is thrown at you.

February 21 - New Moon in Pisces

The focus is on people now. Your relation to and interactions with others will be of great significance. The emphasis is on social service, work, performance, your relationship with your boss, colleagues and subordinates and on extending a helping hand to those who need it. You are preoccupied with kin, neighbours, near and dear ones, as well as your own immediate family. Loans and other fiscal instruments will work out in your favour and you may now find yourself more comfortable financially than in the recent past. There is progress but replace egotism with balance. Please exert some control over hasty, belligerent reactions. Ganesha blesses you as you go about setting your house in order.

March 1 - Moon's first quarter in Gemini

You will be meeting people from all walks of life and there will be many new relationships formed. This is an excellent time to achieve real stability in your relationships. There will be harmony as your personal needs will not conflict with the demands of the relationships. You know who you are and what others need from you. Your vision is clear, you know what you want and what to expect from others, and you are not likely to enter a relationship under the spell of romantic illusions. It will not be mere infatuation. There will be romance if you are so inclined and through it you will understand yourself more clearly. When you understand your emotions and drives, you get to know yourself much better. All relationships now will provide a window to your soul. Ganesha is with you.

March 8 - Full Moon in Virgo

You are on a weeding out and pruning process and busy getting rid of all associations that were inappropriate or didn't quite fit in. You are looking for quality and real value and will settle for nothing less than that. All this helps you to understand yourself in relation to others as you want to tune in to the real you. This is a time when you attract only those people who help you expand your awareness. So there will be many interesting encounters for you to savour and learn from. This, of course, doesn't in any way mean that all your relationships will be strictly personal. The dynamics of the relationships will be complicated, will lead to a more realistic view of the world, and will also be connected to business and your profession. This is a good time for collaborations and new projects. Your negotiations are more solid, you know your real needs, are able to appreciate the other person's requirements better, and whatever you decide on can be mutually profitable. There is creativity and discipline as you embark on new vistas at work and play. You may even examine difficult and exacting techniques as long as they are practical or useful; the bottom-line is that you are sincerely looking for solutions. Ganesha is with you all the way.

March 15 - Moon's last quarter in Sagittarius

You will be meeting different people as the trend has already begun and various aspects of your life will be transformed. You will travel and may even settle down in a foreign land. You could meet up with someone from a totally different culture and get hitched or you could simply get a promotion or take up a new job on another continent. Try to go with the flow, says Ganesha as there will be many disruptions and you will try to resist them in the beginning. It will be much later that you will understand the true import of all the changes. There will be expenses and a lot of soul searching too. You will go through the whirlwind but come out trumps. Nothing comes easy in life all the time and you have been gifted the luck of the draw anyway.

March 22 - New Moon in Aries

There will be rapid progress on all fronts as you move from one level to another in a tearing hurry. You will be shown many dimensions that can broaden your life and experience and make a totally new person out of you. You are growing at several levels – from the spiritual to the physical if one considers the changes in geography that can accompany this period. You have to be careful and patient too as there could be deceit or some form of betrayal. While you rush headlong into situations and people, it will be well worth your while if you can adopt a waiting attitude and commit yourself to as little as possible. Think twice before signing on the dotted line. Ganesha wants you to be cautious.

March 30 - Moon's first quarter in Cancer

This is a period of many positive energies. There is deep bonding with the family and many happy moments. You feel emotionally secure and in touch with your feelings. Children will be a source of joy and there will be many outings with friends, loved ones and even with distant relatives who will flock to meet you from far and near. I don't have to add here that you will enjoy every moment of it as you love the spotlight. You enjoy yourself immensely and there is great purity in every expression of love and friendship. You are also very generous and are able to give freely without feeling diminished or encumbered in any way. You are able to nurture, protect, care, help and support without being troubled by such feelings or gestures which is truly remarkable. Ganesha is happy for you.

April 6 - Full Moon in Libra

There are many expenses on the home front. There is a lot of buying and selling too. You have decided to make your home and personal life as positive as possible. You may take to Feng Shui and Vaastu seriously and make the necessary alterations and changes or simply make your home more comfortable and elegant. Many people will drop in too and this is the time for festivities. You may also go away on holiday. You think of the past and all its happy times. School friends drop in or connect with you on the net. This is the time for social networking as near and dear ones from all over the world tweet in to say 'hi'. You love all the camaraderie and bonhomie. Ganesha is happy for you.

April 13 - Moon's last quarter in Capricorn

Your mind shifts to work-related issues and you ink new projects. You are in luck and receive assistance from a lot of people. You are more self-sufficient now and slog away. There is some tension too and you will have to watch your health. Take care not to get too indulgent and try to bring about some discipline into your life. You are burning the candle at both ends. The right diet, work-outs, maybe even a short stint at a spa or health resort can work its magic. There is restructuring and progress in all your endeavours. Ganesha wishes you well.

April 21 - New Moon in Taurus

There is stability and progress now. You are energetic, optimistic and confident and the mood is upbeat. You are all geared up to take on new challenges and work wonders. You are filled with enthusiasm and zeal as several time-consuming projects may be coming to a head at the same time. You may be pushed and you have your back to all but you come out firing with all guns blazing like a shootout at the OK Corral. This can also be a time of restlessness; you want to do big things and feel that you are not being given the opportunity. Your success may breed enemies and there will be roadblocks placed on your path. Ganesha wants you to compromise and take a middle path and to not get arrogant. In the long run, this is the best method. I would even add that it is the only method.

April 29 - Moon's first quarter in Leo

This is a good time for expansion. With a little fine-tuning and a little care and restraint, you can convert this into an excellent period. You can be very successful professionally. There is sustained growth and many fruitful contacts made. This is a particularly good time for dropping the solo moves and to get into partnership mode which will be mutually beneficial. In your personal life, you may become romantically involved with a business associate or colleague. This is a good phase to solve all pending domestic and work-related issues. Litigation, if any, will be in your favour and old medical problems may find a solution. If not cured, the problem will be arrested and you will have to learn to live with it. Just remember that what cannot be cured will have to be endured. This is the motto for life too. Ganesha is with you.

May 6 - Full Moon in Scorpio

There is love and passion in the air. You will fall headlong for someone you have just met. A marriage or intimate relationship should work better than usual now. You and your partner will help each other grow in every way and will make it a profitable alliance. This will be a beautiful relationship with great scope for self-expression and individual freedom. You grow in leaps and bounds and revel in the unique bonding it offers so effortlessly and marvellously. You are romantic and charming, with dollops of sex appeal. Conquests are easy. But this time there will also be a new, spiritual dimension to the relationship which will be altogether different from all that you have ever experienced in the past. You feel, see and experience a new side to you altogether. Ganesha blesses you.

May 12 - Moon's last quarter in Aquarius

Your mind wanders off in different directions like a puppy that has lost its leash. You may become involved in unrealistic schemes as you could be blinded by extreme optimism. You may want to gamble and take risks but please remember that wild speculations could leave you bankrupt. This is a huge risk; gambling can also lead to major profits and you know it. You are goaded on by the profit motive. Ask Ganesha for help if you may! If you are really keen on this, go ahead and take bold steps with calculated risks. You may also find it difficult to distinguish between the real and the ideal. This is an extremely spiritual influence and you look for escapes from the real world. Some discipline now will be important lest you seek an escape through drugs or alcohol. You could also get obsessed with abstract speculations or high ideals that are difficult to actualise. You live in fantasy, in a dream world. This is okay once in a while as long as the implications are not detrimental. There will soon be a reality check and you will get back to good old terra firma. Ganesha will ensure that. It is also not in your temperament to be far removed from reality for too long.

May 20 - New Moon in Gemini

There are many influences beckoning you now. This can usher the beginning of a very idealistic kind of relationship, one in which you look to your partner as a kind of emissary from the lords or a spiritual guide. This can be a very interesting influence as it is not easy, under normal circumstances, to idealise a person beyond all reason. There could also be deception and betrayals and it will be good to temper your judgement with an extra dose of caution. You will be meeting many different people and romancing many new ideas. Life will most certainly be interesting, to say the least, assures Ganesha.

May 28 - Moon's first quarter in Virgo

There will be fireworks and celebrations; anyway the summer has set in and the heat is on. You are more ambitious than ever and you re-examine your own image, your global self-image and your public image. You carefully study and evaluate them as you want to put your best foot forward. You want to realise your true potential. There will be global expansion at work and, possibly, a new romance. There may be a marriage or an addition to the family even as you soldier on with your manifold duties. You learn the value of building relationships and dazzle your superiors with your talent and intellect. If you are an entrepreneur, the world can be your oyster as you are determined to make your dreams come true. This is a valuable period in life when you learn a lot of lessons and grow as a human being. Ganesha is happy.

June 4 - Full Moon in Sagittarius

You are flying high and how! You strive to conquer many new peaks. Your self-appraisal of last week sets you on the path of true creativity. The focus is on family, children, pets, hobbies and interests, romance and thrills. Those in the media make their presence felt with an extra dollop of creativity, dash and josh! You are innovative and original in your approach and may come up with some winning ideas, true brilliance and ingenuity. You will have to exhibit different people-skills and will have to be diplomatic; do not offend anyone with unnecessary bravado. This phase will throw up a mosaic of many colours and there will be new partnerships and tie-ups, new and old bonds, and several great and profitable associations. Ganesha is with you laying the foundation for solid growth ahead.

June 11 - Moon's last quarter in Pisces

There could be emotional, sentimental and maudlin moments in this soft phase. You will express deep feelings of love. There will be deep bonding and many intimate moments with loved ones. Old friends will appear out of the woodwork too. At work, you should guard against letting communications deteriorate. You need to be gentler and more understanding with colleagues. Your communication and interactive skills will be severely tested. There will be many emotional gains in this period. Warm and fulfilling relationships will be a source of comfort and will motivate you to greater productivity. Ganesha blesses you.

June 19 - New Moon in Gemini

This is a period of innovation, creativity and original ideating. Your soul-searching has set you well and truly on a deeply spiritual and fulfilling path. You find yourself getting more out of life as you make waves socially and are amiable, even-tempered and calm. You have enormous self-confidence, energy, enthusiasm, determination and the courage to face life squarely. You will be focused and efficient and will be able to achieve a lot. This is a fine, pleasant week that helps restore your spirits and boost your confidence. You display panache, a touch of class in all that you undertake. You have proved your worth and can expect rewards and recognition. Ganesha is preparing you for greater challenges and triumphs.

June 27 - Moon's first quarter in Libra

This is one of the best phases for Leos in a long time. You will make rapid progress and scale new heights. This period will continue for at least another two months and you should make the most of it. Take all the chances you wouldn't otherwise take as the luck of the draw is in your favour. Mercury, the mighty planet, is all-powerful. It favours travels/ meetings/conferences/ Interviews/ trips/ more brain power/ contacts/ communication/Correspondence/ contracts. Mercury has a special connection with the circuits of the brain. Chess, crossword and other such games belong to Mercury. Also, short distance runners and spin bowlers are controlled by Mercury. Mercury, in short, is the ambassador and salesman of the zodiac. It is very important and occupies a prominent position now. There are material, spiritual and emotional gains. You build your assets and will be at the receiving end of a windfall. There are many unexpected gains as Ganesha prepares you for a great leap forward.

July 3 - Full Moon in Capricorn

You continue making progress. A fine blend of work and pleasure will be spontaneously attained. There is both progress and pleasure as you will have many profitable journeys and associations. Relationships/public relations/ interactions will be the main thrust now. There will be some fresh, new bonding and partnerships;

perhaps even an engagement leading to marriage. All your ties will be joyous and filled with hope. You also display keen business instincts. There is bonding, romance and passion. The changes within you are both genuine and deep-rooted as you work with efficiency and understanding. The results will be nothing short of pleasing to use a mild word and you are encouraged to push ahead full throttle. In addition to your job/business/profession, there will also be room for research and philosophy, justice, law and order. Your life is humming happily away. Ganesha blesses you.

July 11 - Moon's first quarter in Aries

The good times continue and you make rapid progress. This is a hectic and demanding week. You know what is required and are determined to deliver the goods. Decisive, positive, action is the main thrust. Your approach to life is positive and you spruce up your image and your self-confidence. You display rare insights along with determination, creativity, imagination and style. The growth trajectory continues. You are aware that this is the right time to make the world your oyster and you experience a strong desire to put in that extra effort. New projects/ventures are taken up in this spirit and handled with flair. You are full of renewed spirit and vigour, sure of yourself, ready to go at full strength, all set to hit the pinnacle of glory. Ganesha is happy for you.

July 19 - New Moon in Cancer

The mood now is softer. It is one of conciliation, a willingness to meet people more than halfway, as you work your magic in the world of business and high finance. A whole new mindset finds you caring and sharing, working, helping others, bonding in various ways, affecting major shake-ups in the office and/workplace. This new persona has become a part of your psyche. Your humane and caring approach is well received and appreciated. There will be some domestic issues to deal with, including the health of elders at home; children will also be an area of concern. Ganesha is with you.

July 26 - Moon's last quarter in Scorpio

There is great intensity in your life now. You are passionate, excited and excitable. There is a dramatic shift in your perspective as loans and funds, sex and passion, create a volatility and restlessness within you. Minor health problems are also likely. Prayer and the right use of tantra, mantra and meditation will help. There will be exciting, even fascinating times as you are galvanised into a creative pursuit of goals. All this work may find you over-extended as you cope with increased pressures. You need to pace yourself; strive for streamlining and greater efficiency in your affairs. Learn to delegate so that you can take time off. Leisure is also important and you should learn the joys of simply goofing off. Ganesha wishes you well.

August 2 - Full Moon in Aquarius

You are doing many things at the same time. You are giving off your best at work and socially. Now you will be totally absorbed in the domestic scene, the house and home, along with working at a punishing pace. There is a lot on your plate; try not to go under with this monumental burden. Learn to make time to relax, to pursue hobbies, pleasure activities, sport and exercise. The numerous demands of family/ domestic life/extended family, though demanding, will also be immensely pleasurable. You feel that you have got your affairs in order and now you want to enjoy the fruit of your labours. You have worked hard to achieve whatever you have and are now determined to enjoy a taste of luxury, passion, comforts, and the good life. You are on a high and the good times roll by without too much effort; almost every goodie seems to fall on your lap. Ganesha blesses you. Those in finance and insurance have a great time and, of course, those in the print and electronic media simply sizzle with genius.

August 9 - Moon's last quarter in Taurus

There is urgent need for moderation in whatever you do. You may get carried away with excesses. There is a kind of careless rapture pervading your life and pursuits now. You are prepared to relax, have fun and indulge in the pleasures of the flesh. You have a certain standing in society and you are justifiably proud of it. You want to savour your success fully and enjoy every bit of life. There are expenses and many expansion plans too. You lay the groundwork for an assault at the highest level. If you are in the corporate world, this could be a good time to go global. You can become a corporate giant with a global following. Ganesha is with you.

August 17 - New Moon in Leo

There will be many propitious new beginnings as the new moon is in your sign. Everything you embark on now will lead to success. You have had your moments of fun and now the material world and money matters assume enormous significance. Property, family affairs, taxes, revenues, stepping up of income are your major concerns as you busy yourself handling practicalities. Along with all this, you will also be mending fences and clearing up misunderstandings and misconceptions. There will be demands of the family on your time and resources. You realise that it doesn't help to neglect loved ones or to let your relationships suffer or falter in any way. Ganesha blesses you and encourages you to spend more time with your loved ones. It has been a long time since you met your siblings and extended family and spent quality time with them. What are you waiting for?

August 24 - Moon's first quarter in Sagittarius

There could be international travel and you make several profitable contacts. Intense and intensive intellectual activities are your main pursuits. You will be busy with higher studies, crash courses, self-improvement, and enhancement of your knowledge, expertise and new skills. All this will be geared to increased earning. There will be intellectual advancement, greater creativity and more knowledge. You are driven and determined to succeed. Ganesha cautions you not to get too self-absorbed and to remain humble with your feet on the ground. Unfortunately, it is only hard times that impart valuable life lessons.

August 31 - Full Moon in Pisces

You are a bit tired now and need a break to get your breath back. All the demands on you right from family, home, relationships, work have been heavy. Your patience is running thin but you will have to remain calm and maintain poise. Do not ride roughshod over others. Avoid extreme mood swings lest you damage your own image in the eyes of others. You need the support of everyone to make true progress. You will seek out new pursuits like occult and psychic phenomena, spirits and witches, necromancy and magic, to name a few. You are aiming for an escape from stress and are seeking a balance between the material and spiritual worlds. A lot of time and energy is spent in funds, investments, raising capital, loans, selling and buying. Ganesha wishes you well.

September 8 - Moon's first quarter in Gemini

There has been so much happening in your life the past couple of months that you desperately need a break. You look for a quieter phase in your life which ushers a period of introspection. You may take a second and hard look at alternative medicine, healing, social work and other such diversions. You are not naturally inclined to social work and philanthropy but this can be a much-needed change. You have been on a huge ego trip and have been boastful and arrogant, but now a sense of completion is on the cards. You come full circle. Ganesha approves. You are learning valuable lessons.

September 16 - New Moon in Virgo

You continue with your work but there are many domestic demands. There could be problems in your marriage and trouble with teenaged children. You like to be the boss at home and your commands obeyed but there could be a revolt brewing. You will be put in your place and not listened to at all, and when this comes from family, from your own flesh and blood, it will be very difficult to take. You will have to manoeuvre the situation with delicacy. If you are not careful, there may be repercussions like children running away from home and an elopement. The situation could get even worse as youngsters these days have access to several modes of communication and have many influences acting on them. However, I must add that these are mere generalisations. I do not have your personal horoscope and so cannot be specific. Plus, please also remember that though I have been accurate on several occasions, I can also be wrong. I am not God and have all the frailties of a human being! The focus now is on relationships because they will be the key to your happiness and progress. You will have to compromise to resolve differences at work and at play. Please remember that the stress should be on teamwork and co-operation both at home and the workplace. You need to look at innovations at work and at home as well as come up with new strategies for cohesion and harmony. If you manage to rework basic concepts, harmony is ensured. Ganesha walks with you on the stormy path.

September 22 - Moon's first quarter in Capricorn

You look for more freedom in whatever you do. This can be a very critical time particularly for those in their late twenties. You want to break out of all the structures imposed on you. You seek independence and are serious about establishing your presence in the world. You break away from old groups and branch out on your own. You make significant changes in your life which could include liberating yourself from an existing relationship and looking for another one that will suit you better. For the seniors though there will be stability and progress. There will be challenges thrown at you and you will have to wade through murky waters. There could even be moments of sadness and despair and you may seem distraught at time. You could be sullen and moody but this is all a part of the package of life. You can't have it your way all the time. There will be quiet moments of bonding away from the madding crowd. Ganesha is with you.

September 30 - Full Moon in Aries

This is an energetic and pleasant influence and you may be inclined to sit back and bask in it. But this is a very significant period because you can reach out to people and taste new areas of life and have several varied and rewarding experiences. Your creative potential is enormous, your drives are very strong, and you can very easily accomplish a great deal. You are full of self-confidence and believe that you can do wonders. Usually this is also a time when you enjoy good health and a feeling of well-being. You will be charged to join the gym or will take to the outdoors in a big way. You could be hiking, cycling, running or just walking depending on where you stay and how much time you have at your disposal. Since you will be overconfident and will overestimate your energies, do not take foolish risks. It hurts no one to be a little slow and cautious. Circumstances always play a huge role in such predictions. There is also new romance and it all depends on what you want to do with it. Ganesha wishes you well.

October 8 - Moon's last quarter in Cancer

You look seriously and hard at new money-making ventures. This is an excellent time for all financial matters and you plunge into it. You will feel like making your surroundings appear more elegant, and you may spend quite a lot of money too. Expenses soar but along with this concern with material acquisition, there are also some very real possibilities for inner growth. You may also feel like travelling to broaden your understanding of the world around you. You want to know about new ideas and different ways of living. You want to check out all that life has to offer away from home and work and the usual mundane demands of life. You begin to appreciate life in all its colours. Ganesha is happy.

October 15 - New Moon in Libra

There are many influences at play now. You want to do too many things and there is a danger of misjudgement. You are putting all your energies in different directions. You are caught between caution and optimism. You are not sure how much to push, whether you should expand or retrench. You could have overextended yourself in the past and bitter memories thankfully put the brakes on you. You are pulled between the desire for greater freedom and opportunity and the need to hold on to the safe and predictable. You are tempted to break away from everything and start all over again from scratch without the weight of the past holding you back. All this restlessness can result in many chops and churns and you will make many significant changes in your life. You will opt for casual relationships and friendships as you are busy finding your way and do not have the time to invest in deeper liaisons. Ganesha encourages you on this quest for personal understanding.

October 22 - Moon's first quarter in Capricorn

By no account is the tempo of your life downhill. In fact, it is still on an upward curve. Understanding yourself is vital whatever the circumstances, and this period of self-inquiry will stand in good stead in the long run; please remember that it is a life investment. The positive aspects to this period are also considerable and this is the right time to grow, to expand. There will be new business plans and new responsibilities. There will be many profitable associations too. Ganesha blesses you all the way.

October 29 - Full Moon in Taurus

This is an interesting period and can represent the culmination of a long drive for success or power. There will be opposition and many challenges and roadblocks. But you manage to surmount it all. You grow in many ways and could get a promotion and acquire prestige and power. You are able to impact a lot of people and it all depends on several factors and what you do with your position. You could be driven ruthlessly to get ahead. Do not cut corners or get unethical though the temptations may be very strong. There could be unfortunate consequences with the law or with higher authorities as you will be found out. Control your drives and go slow. There is no harm in it, assures Ganesha.

November 7 - Last quarter in Leo

The last quarter of the moon is in your sign. This will be a significant period. Do not get obsessive and keep away fanatical thought processes. Try to work in a team and hear out even the most disparate thought processes. Shun all self-righteousness and do not try to force your views upon others. Look for compromises and midway meeting points. Your ideas may be great but your style of functioning can come in for improvement. You should be open to negotiation. Ganesha believes that this is not a time when you should resort to coercion of any kind. With a little bit of humility coupled with intelligence, you can enlarge your personal goals to encompass the groups. You love being the top dog, the team leader, and the lion in the ring. But in the real world, every disparate entity has to be taken along with you for success to be achieved. You may have to carry several passengers too.

November 13 - New Moon in Scorpio

An intense and passionate phase when you are filled with genuine warmth and the desire to give and express love. You may have many liaisons and enjoy them all as you will be walking the tightrope and playing with fire to share your passions equally among all. You are like Valentino with an insatiable appetite. You are charismatic and will attract many to your web. There could be a significant relationship too in the midst of it all, but even if nothing emerges from it, you will definitely gain from the wisdom and maturity it offers. The feelings now are compulsive and overwhelming. Your freedom will be curtailed and you will also curtail the other person's freedom and it will be a great challenge to make the relationship a creative one that will be both pleasant and constructive. There could also be domestic issues to handle as a result of your shenanigans. There could be problems at home; don't say you weren't warned! Ganesha wishes you well.

November 20 - Moon's first quarter in Aquarius

There are maudlin and soft moments. You meet with family and friends and spend time in helping others. You could get very emotional too as you bask in the love, warmth, admiration and care of loved ones. This influence stimulates your love of beauty. You make every effort to surround yourself with beauty. You make beautiful purchases and want to be in pleasant surroundings and surrounded by art objects and beautiful people. You could get extravagant in this period and spend on objects that you may not need later. This is a passing phase. The intensity of the moment and its moods seduce you as for now. Seize the moment and go with the flow as tomorrow is always another day, another time, another chance. Ganesha's blessings are with you.

November 28 - Full Moon in Gemini

You are doing well and your plans are on the fast track to success. You are on top of the world and have the confidence to handle just about anything that is thrown at you. You have taken on a lot and it all depends on how you delegate and manage time to accomplish it all. But it is better to be busy than have nothing to do. You are also restless and go hunting for even bigger projects. You will have to micromanage it all but you do it well. There will be new areas of study and accomplishment. You expand, grow and reach for the moon. Ganesha smiles in approval.

December 6 - Moon's last quarter in Virgo

The year is coming to an end and a lot has been accomplished. You could be tired and discouraged as your vital energies are low. You are pushing away at executing your plans but there could be unwarranted opposition to them. You may feel physically distressed as if the burdens of your life are too much to handle. There may be a feeling of world-weariness and it may be a good time to go for a medical check-up as it is in your interest to conserve your energies. There are several inhibiting factors at work and you will have to plough through them, which you will with Ganesha's help. There could be marital troubles and you may have to terminate a long association. Of course, like I always say, it all depends on the personal horoscope and these are mere generalisations. Astrology never compels. Life has a natural cycle and it is best to go with the flow. There will be new beginnings and many new opportunities as you climb new peaks of achievement. Life is never stagnant; every moment differs from the next.

December 13 - New Moon in Sagittarius

This can be marvellous period and you feel good. Your health is fine, you are optimistic and all your plans are falling into place. This is the time to enjoy the rewards of sustained and hard labour. You are on a growth trajectory and your life is bullish. It is the time to initiate new projects, expand your activities and broaden your perspective. You realise your full potential as a human being. There is travel and new contacts as you soar ahead into the stratosphere. You look at new areas of study and try to raise your consciousness and expand your world view. All new associations will influence you positively and there will be freedom and substantial growth. Ganesha is happy for you.

December 20 -Moon's first quarter in Pisces

You are joyous, energetic and exuberant and want to overdo or overreach yourself. It will be good to exercise a certain amount of restraint. You may also be in a spending frenzy. Be careful with your purse strings if you are a sole proprietor as you might leave yourself vulnerable to the more difficult times that will eventually come. Make sure that all expansion is carefully planned and that you have built safeguards against future times of difficulty. You also crave more recognition and may feel cheated. But, away from all this, are glorious moments with the family and a home away from home. There may be travel, even an overseas holiday. There are many tasty dishes on your plate, assures Ganesha. Get hungry for them.

December 28 - Full Moon in Cancer

You end the year on an upbeat note. This is an exuberant time, with high energies at play. You feel physically strong and fit and you manage to accomplish more than usual. Almost anything that you direct your energies to will lead to success. The only real danger is that you overwork and push yourself over the hill. This is a good time to begin a new project, as long as you know your limits. You have great initiative and can accomplish a great deal by yourself; your pace will be scorching and others will not be able to match you. You will display a magnificent sense of timing or planning. All projects begun now will pay great dividends in the future. Ganesha watches over you.

LEO

KEY DATES

January

1*-5, 9-10, 19*-20, 23-24, 27-28, 31.

House-move, office, expenses, spirituality, parents and family nursing keep you even more busy this month than you were last year.

February

1*-2, 5*-7, 10-12, 15*-16, 19-20, 23-25, 28*.

Your own hard work, efforts, success, charisma, leadership – favours will be granted, says Ganesha!

March

1*, 4-6, 10*-11, 14*-16, 19-20, 23-24, 27*-28.

Food, finance, family – some of the F's as well as buying and selling and new projects.

April

1-2, 6-7, 11-12, 15*-16, 19-20, 23*-25, 28*-30.

Travel, neighbours, fine communication, and an even finer reaching out. You will be loved and respected.

May

1-5, 8*-9, 12-14, 16-18, 21*-22, 25-27, 30*-31.

Renovation, decoration, buying and selling (of property and assets) therefore, achievements.

June

1, 4*-6, 9-10, 13*-14, 17*-18, 21*-23, 27*-28.

A wish-fulfilment for you, says Ganesha! That says it all. The exact nature of your wishes cannot be forecast.

July

1*-3, 6-7, 10*-11, 14*-16, 19*-20, 24, 27*-30.

Loans, income, pets, projects are highlighted. Therefore, finances are exhausted. Extra pressures at work could cause bad health, low vitality.

August

2-3, 7*-8, 11-12, 15*-17, 20-22, 25*-26, 30-31.

Success, partnerships, opposition, marriage, journeys with a stopover. Lots of activity this month.

September

3*-4, 7*-8, 9*-13, 17*-18, 22*-23, 26-27, 30.

Funds, buying, selling, property, investment, passion and sex are all spotlighted. Therefore, finance and passion in an intoxicating mix of activity.

October

4*-6, 9*-10, 14-15, 19*-20, 23-24, 27-28.

Contacts, contracts, children, joy, romance are all there for you. Go out and win on all these counts now.

November

1*-2, 5-7, 10-12, 15*-17, 20-21, 24*-25, 28*-29.

Profession, money from the family and father; progress as well as competition. The health of parents, in-laws may not be up to mark. You're more than busy!

December

1-4, 7*-9, 12*-14, 17-18, 21*-22, 25*-26, 30*-31.

Entertainment, socializing, group activities, hobbies and functions make you happy and keep you busy, too, once again. You enjoy it and are full of hope!

Virgo

August 23 - September 22

VIRGO

(August 22 – September 22)

ELEMENT AND RULING PLANET: Earth and Mercury.

STRENGTHS: Virgo is reserved, modest, practical, discriminating and industrious, analytical and painstaking, seeking to know and understanding.

WEAKNESS: Sceptical, fussy, inflexible, unemotional, interfering and cold.

SYMBOL: The Virgo – Representing purity, modesty, industriousness, service to fellow workers.

MATCHING SIGN: Pisces.

MAGICAL BIRTHSTONE: Emerald and Sapphire – bring tranquillity of mind and protect against illness and injury while travelling.

VIRGO

YEARLY FORECAST

"You are now at the hard and solid centre of life."

- John le Carré

Main Trend

Ganesha grants, right from the very beginning, a splendid year - both personally and professionally.

Your hopes, aspirations, profession, your status in the eyes of the world are all favoured and focused in a pleasing display of glory. **By glory is implied not only success but also the achievement of personal milestones you've set yourself in other spheres - things that you have long wanted to do**. And here we're painting a truly broad spectrum; in fact, I seriously doubt if it could get any wider! There is personal status, the 3 P's of prestige, power and position, but there is also fulfilment of no mean order in all the relationships that are dearest to you. So there are F's of friends and family as well, to round off this grand repast.

Love is manifested in all its hues - care and concern for parents, older relatives, your children, intense emotional bonding with your spouse/lover/mate/live-in companion, and total commitment and dedication to your vocation/profession. I would even be prepared to stick out my short, fat neck and say that at this juncture, at least, it is your first love and your major concern. You do not only give it all you've got but also feel it's the only way to go about it. That actually says it all, but I need to add a little note of warning from

Ganesha - the pressures at work will mount, but there is very little danger that you might let them preoccupy your mind to such an extent that personal relationships you value could be in serious jeopardy. You need to keep your priorities clear! And you have both the wisdom and the common sense to ensure that it is so.

A good start is half the battle won, people always say, and it was never truer than your forecast for this year. To mix metaphors a bit, you start by firing in all cylinders, i.e. home, family, parents and in-laws as I said in the context of relationships, but above them all, your own self.

Jupiter:

Ganesha points out that Lady Luck, Dame Fortune, Fate and Chance smile upon you. This makes you fortune's favourite child. Enjoy your good fortune, your year in the sun and share it with others. I know well that you Geminis are generous and helpful.

Why has your astrologer gone ga-ga over you? The reason is that Jupiter and Saturn, the two great stalwarts and champions of astrology, will be in your favours. Let me put it differently, it is a win-win situation. My congratulations to you in advance!

We watch the entry of the first champion, namely Jupiter. Jupiter will be in your 10th angle. Jupiter is Father Christmas; prosperity, God's plenty, golden harvest, all rolled into one. I am sure intelligent, sharp; fast-on-the-draw Geminis will get it.

Ganesha says, it's action time! Time to do a ***relevé***, i.e. a classical ballet dance step in which you have to rise sharply on your toes in a mighty but smooth effort. Let me leaven this description of scintillating success with humour by saying you will have to work enough to earn more money than your wife can spend! As the Bible says, "In the sweat of thy face shalt thou eat bread".

Have I laid it on a bit too thick? NO, dear readers! It is just that the slot, or angle or sector of work is heavily tilted, emphasised. How come? The 10th angle deals with work, whether it's a business or a profession. The spin-offs of having Jupiter in your 10th angle will be:

a) Funds, investments, joint-finance, buying/ selling/ investment opportunities, real-estate deals, success in gas and chemicals and heavy industry.

b) You will enlist in clubs, organisations, and socialise till you almost drop dead! You will have friends and well-wishers to help you along. That's a big blessing, because you learn and grow even while having fun.

c) You will receive gifts, perhaps some inheritance, or unexpected money, or bonus; and one of your wishes might come true. I am truly happy for you.

d) Jupiter, the planet of good luck and also the planet of 'wisdom through plenty" will be totally and absolutely on your side. It will certainly act as ballast, a counterweight to the lash of Saturn. Also, it will make you confident, moneyed and a lover of the good things of life.

e) The two sectors or frontiers that Jupiter will galvanise will be work and foreign connections. That's for sure, says Ganesha, and so shall it be,

f) Journey, festivities, celebration, invitations, functions, pilgrimages, research, travel and ties in an interlink will keep you mighty busy. Yes, you will widen the vistas of your horizon in a million different ways, say, reading, TV, having a guru, cultivating rare insights, and so on. My astro-tip is, be reasonable and do not take slights and hurts too personally. Besides gaining in popularity, you gain materially, too.

g) It will give you the tremendous enthusiasm and power to set the wheels of any project rolling in the right direction, very specially if you worship your own god or deity. And secondly worship Ganesha. Jupiter also connotes (implies and means) ACTION TIME. Whether it is a simple thing like activating the internet, the "mother of all communications", or any other enterprise, activity, campaign, you will be able to execute it splendidly and make a smashing success of it.

Yes, you will be in the right place at the right time! That's why I have motivated you.

Here are the other effects of Jupiter for you:

The six-sigma business philosophy uses the steps:

1. Define the problem,
2. Measure the variables (possible changes and difference)
3. Analyse
4. Control
5. Improve
6. You are the supremo here! That's your forte. AND THIS YEAR, THANKS TO JUPITER, YOU WILL BEAT PEAK PERFORMANCE.

With regard to the wealth and money of any individual, the astrologer must bear in mind the contradictions/ conflicts/ contrast existing in the position of the planets concerned with or affecting the 2nd house, directly or indirectly, and then come to a final conclusion. Chances of a windfall/sudden loss should not be lost sight of.

Every individual relation (parents, brothers/ sisters, grandparents) is basically governed by his or her own stars and another person's stars have side-effects only.

Mercury, Venus and Mars pull you in the tug of war of life. Many of you know that mercury is your major or ruling planet.

Mercury will be in your sign from 2nd to 16th September. Mercury will hone your already sharp intellect, giving editors, writers, teachers, preachers, an advantage over others; it will work at a hectic pace and spur you into further achievements and wins. Yes, you will also be interacting one-to-one with your boss, friends, parents, in-laws, and relatives as never before. This, I understand, could be a slight exaggeration; nevertheless valid, for the most part. Travels and ties are confidently predicted. The more people you meet and interact with, the better, since mercury is your key planet. Mercury is also in superb positioning with the good luck planet Jupiter. Obviously, Ganesha willing, this means that your work will be done, to your complete satisfaction.
From 4th to 28th October, Venus, the bestower of gifts, life and love, slides into your sign according to western astrology. Finances flow in, the family is pleased with you, friends show their appreciation; the three F's will be rocking! Group activities and socializing give not only comfort but also positive joy. The message of Venus is, if you want to earn more money you must circulate and have a great social circle. Friends, your boss, women and well wishers help you to make great money.

From 12th November 2011 to 3rd June 2012, Mars the warrior planet swoops into your sun sign. Ganesha says, Mars will help you in food, family, invitations, parties, and functions and most certainly in journeys, collaborations, publicity, ceremony, religious rites and taking chances. Mars is a great ally for you. The astro-tip is to get away to a great start; it will be difficult for others to catch up with you. Ganesha gives you a hot tip. Between August and September, expect the goodies of life, because all the three planets will be in your sun sign. They will be in a TRINE with the planet of prosperity, Jupiter. Give it your best shot then, dear Virgos, and watch the results.

Neptune in your 7th angle will make you romantic and daring in partnerships, marriages, collaborations, ties, journeys, legal matters. The good part is that it will be a great time for fine adventure and explorations. It is definite that visits, interviews, connections, meeting people, and even neighbourly ties could be very exciting. The bad part is that you could be deceived, cheated, be under an illusion or hallucination. You could wear the rose-tinted glasses of optimism and later on suffer for it. However, you Virgos are normally extremely rational, controlled and cautious. Hopefully you might not fall into such a trap.

Uranus will be in your 8th angle, which means money will roll in your pocket/ purse/ wallet/ bank. Yes, a lottery is possible. Also, there is a distinct possibility of inheritance. You also gain by joint finance, insurance and treasures. Sometimes, passion will hold you entirely. There is also a probability of a major house move or a home-away-from-home. You may find a guru and learn yoga, tantra and mantra. Truly an exciting life ahead!

Saturn

Saturn will be in your 2nd angle of food, family, finance, the 3Fs. It means:

- Personal belongings and money
- Gifts, bonuses, profits
- Economic interests
- Financial matters

YOU ACHIEVE THE GREATEST SUCCESS BY

- Seeking financial favours and recognition
- Making possessions more attractive
- Giving private enterprise a push
- Curbing extravagance

AVOID

- Pursuing impractical sales methods
- Overlooking opportunities for gain
- Spending on unworthy causes
- Handling valuables carelessly (Dell Magazine).

Yes, I always acknowledge the source.

Saturn changes signs from 6th October 2012. Saturn is a slow moving planet. It stays in one sign for roughly two-and-a-half years. What will be the impact of Saturn?

Saturn in the third house of the composite chart indicates that the two of you must be careful not to fall into set patterns of thought in the relationship. This applies to the ways in which you think as a couple as well as the ways you think about each other. For example, it can indicate that there is a real barrier to communication between you, because each of you is so locked into certain ways of thinking and communicating that you cannot loosen up and listen to what your partner is saying, Remember that it is always necessary to talk in the other person's language; no matter how successfully you can communicate in your own language, it will do no good unless your partner understands you.

Unfortunately, a communication gap is precisely the problem that Saturn in the third house is likely to create. You must abandon any tendency to believe that your way of thinking is superior to your partner's, because that will only make communication more difficult.

Saturn in the third house also makes the two of you fond of structuring your immediate environment, a tendency that arises from the mental habits just discussed. Mental orderliness is reflected in the way you organise your world. You dislike disorder and will do everything in your powers to prevent it.

In a personal relationship, Saturn in the third can also give difficulty with relatives. Here again, the best solution is to alter your ways of thinking and try to communicate in the same terms as the people you are talking to.

VIRGO

MONTH-BY-MONTH

JANUARY

This is a month of power plus work and pleasure. You begin the year well and this is a fiery start to the year. You will be moving fast and getting things done in a trice. You also have a spiritual bent of mind and Ganesha will protect you no matter what happens. As the month moves on, emotions will boil over. Watch out for impulsive actions and rash decisions that may have sudden, unexpected consequences and undesirable results. You may also get into disputes with colleagues over trifles. Authority figures, who limit your freedom of movement and self-expression, are likely targets for your rebellion. But there are many beautiful moments with close family and friends in this period. As the month ends, there are inflated expectations, excessive and impractical idealism and sudden disappointments. You need to make a concerted effort to keep your feet on the ground. You are looking for profound answers to life's disturbing questions.

FEBRUARY

Ganesha says there could be tough times. Health needs extra safeguards. From the 16th, your main trend of ties and links, marriage and bonding, will start. This is a good time to enter new relationships, strengthen existing ties and reach out afresh. There are many expenses and travel is also on the cards. Your heartstrings are also pulled. You are filled with compassion for others. This is an intense phase and you may fall madly in love. As the month progresses, you get very sensitive and emotional and your soul is cut into several slices. You may need to make many changes in your life. There are several obstacles preventing you from doing what you have to do and you rebel.

MARCH

Jupiter is now firmly in your angle of relationships. Your people-skills will determine your material and emotional successes. This is a favourable time for ties and bonds. You are busy with new travel plans. There are meetings and new sponsors for your ideas. Your job could be progressing perfectly well and your personal life may be fulfilling, but there could be an unexpected incident that forces you to analyze your life and work. You may have to re-evaluate your relationships to the various groups you belong to and to the workplace and, most importantly, to the person who loves you. Take Ganesha's blessings. The full moon is in your sign mid-month and you will be sorting out your life. You will withstand all the disruptive events that have been plaguing you. You are looking at new directions. You will break free of all restrictions to enlarge your scope of activity. This is a very significant period and what you do now will impact your life for a long time to come. You will seize every opportunity to build new structures.

APRIL

This is a busy period for money and relationships. Be careful as medical emergencies are possible. You make many purchases and are consumed by love for yourself and for the world. You may suddenly become involved in relationships that are quite different from what you would normally expect. This is a very interesting phase and Ganesha asks you to go with the flow. As the month moves on, there is optimism and positive thinking. You seem more balanced and this is the right time to make long-range plans and to reorganize. You will now find psychological and physical equilibrium. If you have been ill recently, the healing process will have begun.

MAY

There is fame, publicity campaigns, journeys and collaborations. April will have a huge gamut of activities. There is popularity, success and you win applause. You will be filled with a feeling of balance and will be unusually peaceful and relaxed. This is also a good time to travel for both, work and relaxation. This period has many hidden energies. It is fundamentally an opportunity to grow and explore the world and also see where and how you fit in. Ganesha's blessings are with you and he urges you to move on with the exploration. This month sees you on the threshold of a new cycle of ideas and opinions, of communicating in new ways. This is an excellent time for working a single idea right through to the end. Plan carefully as what you embark on now can have significant consequences. You have reached a point of equilibrium and your actions are reliable and consistent.

JUNE

June is the culmination of a series of changes in your life. There will be ambition, money, intuition, moments of inspiration and you do remarkably well. No power on earth can suppress you now. You are flamboyant and ambitious and make substantial progress. New people enter your life and assist you in your work as you branch out to new areas of activity. You have stayed in touch with friends from the past, and this networking will help you now. As the month progresses, your ambition is stimulated and your desire for power grows. If there is a ruthless side to your personality, it will show itself now. There is love in your life too and you enjoy yourself no end. On the work front, there could be power struggles, quite possibly with someone in authority. Ganesha urges you to stay calm.

JULY

You make rapid progress and there is a tremendous spurt in your creativity, imagination, ideas and impulses. There could also be love, marriage, collaborations, partnerships and new associations. This is a period of culmination in your life. The old order will end and there will be new beginnings. There is a very good chance of success in whatever you undertake. You have made enough money and it is time to divert your attention to spiritual needs. Ganesha believes that as the month progresses, you are in the spotlight and just love it. If you are a performer, like a dancer for example, there may be stage shows and many plaudits. You make big plans that will be the culmination of many ideas that have taken root over a period of time. You keep redefining goals and priorities and the pace of life accelerates.

AUGUST

There are many trends at play now. Your expenses will skyrocket, there will be delays and setbacks and you will need to be careful while travelling. A certain momentum has been generated over the last three months and you maintain the progress you have made. Saturn slows things down a bit but you still manage to find a way through the maze. Truth is very important in your life now; you are keen to know how the universe works. You look to gain insights through the study of philosophy, metaphysics and the occult. You want to expand your consciousness and want to experience every facet of the world. As the month moves on, you are galloping ahead and this is a period of culmination in your professional and personal lives. There are tangible results, and you bask in accomplishment and applause. Ganesha ensures that all your new interactions will broaden your outlook tremendously.

SEPTEMBER

This is a great period for sure. Your popularity and productivity will be at an all-time high. Ganesha promises a lot of frenetic activity in this birth month phase. You will be inventive, assertive, inspirational and ingenious as Mercury, the mighty planet, is all-powerful. You get whatever you set your sights on, and what more is there to say now? As the month advances, the new moon raises your sensitivities to a sharp, cutting edge. You enter a lucky phase and are helped by strangers and friends. You make significant gains in your personal and domestic life. This is an excellent time to embark on new projects or to conclude any kind of transaction. You move ahead full throttle and nothing can stop you now. This is a lucky phase and I urge you to make the most of it. As I always say, there will be money and honey for the asking.

OCTOBER

There is a lot going for you this month. This is action time and you make rapid progress on all fronts. There is success and many domestic obligations to consider too. The continued impact of Mercury makes life even more pleasing. There is also great love and passion in store for you. Make the right choices as your plate could be overflowing. Ganesha ensures that you have the strength of mind to think clearly and make the right choices. As the month moves on, you realize that a lot of what you had thought of situations and persons in the past does not hold good anymore and you are willing to change and see the brighter side of things. There is no room for negativity and you need to operate from a higher consciousness. There will be many collaborations and meetings and reunions with old friends. There will also be family gatherings and you will be in celebratory mode.

NOVEMBER

There is a lot on your plate. Ganesha insists that travel, trade, commission, brokerage, higher studies, journeys and relationships, a grand reaching out to people and places, great mental astuteness and alertness, neighbourly ties, community service and social interactions of all kinds will hold forth. There is international travel and you make connections that will play a vital role in the years to come. The focus is on family matters: children's health and education, relations with the spouse or partner and the health of elders. You are filled with revolutionary ideas which will force a transformation of some kind in your life. You learn a lot in this period, says Ganesha. This is also an excellent time for writers, filmmakers, artists and photographers. You delve deep into the creativity within you and make masterpieces come alive.

DECEMBER

Ganesha says that December is the focal point from the professional front. The focus shifts to the more personal arena of house, home and property. Pay extra attention to personal well-being and family investments. The last quarter of the month is in your sign and you come into your own. There is stability in your affairs and you move ahead with big plans. This is an excellent time for all kinds of mental work as you are especially decisive and firm. You are brimming with confidence and new ideas, and will surprise everyone with your brilliance. You are reaching out to the stars, if I may say so. There is money and honey and several other inducements. Live with gratitude and peace, urges Ganesha. As the year ends, you are particularly sensitive and emotional. But this is also an excellent time for new business deals and to sign new contracts. With a little foresight and wisdom, you will do wonders.

VIRGO

THE MONTHS AT A GLANCE

January

As the month moves on, emotions will boil over. Watch out for impulsive actions and rash decisions that may have sudden, unexpected consequences and undesirable results.

February

There are many influences at play. As the month progresses, you get very sensitive and emotional and your soul is cut into several slices. You may need to make many changes in your life.

March

You will withstand all the disruptive events that have been plaguing you. This is a very significant period and what you do now will impact your life for a long time to come. You will break free of all restrictions to enlarge your scope of activity.

April

This is a very interesting phase and Ganesha asks you to go with the flow. As the weeks pass, there is optimism and positive thinking. You seem more balanced and this is the right time to make long-range plans and to reorganize.

May

This period has many hidden energies. It is fundamentally an opportunity to grow and explore the world and also see where and how you fit in. Ganesha's blessings are with you.

June

New people enter your life and assist you in your work as you branch out to new areas of activity. You have kept contact with friends from the past and this networking will help you now.

July

This is a period of culmination in your life. The old order will end and there will be new beginnings. There is a very good chance of success in whatever you undertake.

August

Truth is very important in your life now. You are keen to know how the universe works. You look to gain insights through the study of philosophy, metaphysics and the occult.

September

Mercury, the mighty planet, is all-powerful. You get whatever you set your sights on, and what more is there to say now? As the month advances, the new moon raises your sensitivities to a sharp, cutting edge.

October

The continued impact of Mercury makes life even more pleasing. There is also great love and passion in store for you. Make the right choices as your plate could be overflowing with plenty. This is a very profitable period in your life.

November

The focus is on family matters: children's health and education, relations with the spouse or partner and the health of elders. Domestic issues overwhelm you.

December

You are brimming with confidence and new ideas, and will surprise everyone with your brilliance. You are reaching out to the stars, if I may say so. There is money and honey and several other inducements.

VIRGO

WEEKLY REVIEW

(By the Phases of the Moon)

January 1 - Moon's first quarter in Aries

You begin the year well. You are filled with caution and prudence and take careful baby steps. You are ambitious but if you are not careful your life can be drab and boring. Please remember that life is many splendoured and is not just about work and deadlines which is what you have made it out to be. You have many insecurities and can be difficult to get along with; ask your near and dear ones and they will tell you the truth. You need to open your heart and mind to the limitless possibilities existing in the world. Learn to be less critical and less fastidious. Learn to love and be loved; try to loosen up a bit. Be less suspicious of others. If you have been unwell the previous year, you will show signs of recovery now. Stick to the doctor's orders, which I am sure you will. But, whatever said and done, this is a fiery start to the year. You will be moving fast and getting things done in a trice. Money is a major preoccupation in your life, whether you like it or not. You need to be stable and like your larder well stocked. You will make rapid progress and earn well. You also have a spiritual bent of mind and Ganesha will protect you no matter what happens.

January 9 - Full Moon in Cancer

This is a period for emotions to boil over. Watch out for impulsive actions and rash decisions that may have sudden, unexpected consequences and undesirable results. Your ego gets in the way and superimposes itself over commonsense despite your rational mind telling you to let go of it. There may be tense moments with others who seem to be getting in your way all the time. You may also get into disputes with colleagues over trifles. There will be misunderstandings that can be avoided. This influence challenges your sense of security. The more insecure you are, the more likely you are to do something rash. Authority figures, who limit your freedom of movement and self-expression, are likely targets for your rebellion. Act with discretion or you could end up harming yourself more than others. There is a lot of work on your plate but you need to prioritize. You need to brush up on people management skills. Ganesha urges you to show more restraint.

January 16 - Moon's last quarter in Libra

There are many beautiful moments with close family and friends in this period. Make the most of it. The effects of this influence are unconscious and could lead to eruptions of energy which you are not quite sure what to do with. It is not really disruptive, but it can get out of hand if you don't keep a close watch over it. You need to get more secure in who you are and what you are doing. Then there won't be this crazed need to break free and take ill-considered actions. You may still feel like doing something that is significantly different from your normal routine. You have a great desire to buck the trend. The family is fine and work continues as usual. But you need to get a hold on your mood swings. Ganesha is with you despite it all.

January 23 - New Moon in Aquarius

Your thought processes are in turmoil. You live in the mind now and there is a hint of chaos. There are inflated expectations, excessive and impractical idealism and sudden disappointments. You need to make a concerted effort to keep your feet on the ground. You are also ego driven and ready to take foolish risks. But this is certainly no time for any form of speculation or gambling. You should avoid any sort of overconfidence that could possibly trip you. You will make money and new investments but do not overextend yourself financially. Ganesha admits that despite all this, you work hard and achieve a lot. There will be vigorous growth in job prospects and you will be happy in the end. All's well that ends well.

January 31 - Moon's first quarter in Taurus

A very practical phase sets in and you count pennies. Your intrinsic idealism is also aroused. You feel that the world should be a better place and you may get involved with some extreme religious, spiritual or mystical sect. Although it may be a perfectly good idea, you may not reap many benefits from it. The study of religion or mysticism is one thing but the real world and its challenges are another piece of cake altogether. You must learn to cope without props. You look for freedom but you first have to define the word in your context and then find fitting solutions. You are looking for profound answers to life's disturbing questions. The answers will come in due course, says Ganesha. Don't be in a hurry as everything has a time and a plan. Learn to be calm and patient.

February 7 - Full Moon in Leo

There are many expenses and travel is also on the cards. You are firing away on all cylinders and making waves. Your heartstrings are also pulled. You are filled with compassion for others. You want to help people, particularly the less fortunate, and share whatever good fortune you have. But make sure that the people you are assisting will get some real benefit as you are very likely to be preyed on by people who want to take advantage of your generosity. This will leave you feeling bitter in the end and so be wary of such a feeling and the action it promotes in you. Despite all this, you aim for the stars. Success is yours, says Ganesha.

February 14 - Moon's last quarter in Scorpio

This is an intense phase and you fall madly in love. There is a new partner in your life and you spend quality time with this person who has emerged out of the blue. This distracts you tremendously and throws routine into the bin. There may also be sudden, unexpected events that will test your ability to withstand change. You ask yourself searching questions. Your work and life is under a cloud. You wonder if your romantic escapade is just that - an escapade. There are challenges from the outside world and even from psychological forces within. Despite the questions and self-doubts, there is travel on the cards and many collaborations. This new relationship may also give you luck. It may be worth investing in. Let it flow and reach its natural conclusion. Ganesha promises you good times.

February 21 - New Moon in Pisces

You get very sensitive and emotional and your soul is cut into several slices. You may need to make many changes in your life. It may be necessary to break free from circumstances that you encounter in your work. There may even be limiting circumstances in your personal life. There are several obstacles preventing you from doing what you have to do and you rebel. There is expansion at work but your mind is torn and you cannot focus. There may be illness in the family and court cases. You may lose money and your life could be in some disarray. It is by no means a dangerous period, but it can be very stressful. Hold tight, says Ganesha.

March 1 - Moon's first quarter in Gemini

You are busy with new travel plans. There are meetings and new sponsors for your ideas. But your mind needs to be sorted out before you zoom ahead. Your job could be progressing perfectly well and your personal life may be fulfilling, but there could be some unexpected incident that forces you to analyze your life and work. You may have to re-evaluate your relationships to the various groups you belong to and to the workplace and, most importantly, to the person who loves you. You risk losing recently found stability. You are torn by emotions. You can't think straight and your mind is a swamp. You are on edge. You look for new openings and are fickle and fastidious. You also find deficiencies in your mate/spouse/partner and there could be unhappy times because of this. You seem to be on a fault-finding spree with everything. This mood is contagious and your colleagues and family don't like it one bit. You stick to nothing; commitment seems such an alien word right now. Take Ganesha's blessings and continue with sustained, committed efforts in what your conscience tells you is the right thing to do.

March 8 - Full Moon in Virgo

The full moon is in your sign and you should be sorting out your life. You will withstand all the disruptive events that have been plaguing you. You will look within for answers and if you find the energies of this period too destructive, consider necessary changes to minimize their effects or to turn them into positive ones. You are challenged but you also come out triumphant. This is a very positive period and you do well. Unless you ask searching questions, you will not get the right answers. Ganesha applauds you and wishes you well. You will come out of this with flying colours.

March 15 - Moon's last quarter in Sagittarius

You are looking at new directions. You will confront your inhibitions and self-restrictions, as well as the restrictions placed upon you by circumstances. You will break free of them in order to enlarge your scope of activity. You may also choose to grow within the structure of restriction in your life and use the restricting circumstances to enlarge your life. There are many choices. It can go either way, depending on your temperament. But there will most certainly be more clarity as you are taking your life in your hands and making emphatic changes where required. Ganesha blesses you; with his blessings you can be sure to turn the corner. This is a very significant period and what you do now will impact your life for a long time to come.

March 22 - New Moon in Aries

You are brimming with ideas and workable plans. You break free from your shackles and begin to feel very restless. Events and circumstances will make it clear that you have neglected many areas of your life and now they seem intolerable. You are in a hurry to break free from the established order. You could be on the threshold of a new freedom, a new way of life. There could be a change of job or residence or the break-up of relationships. All this may seem catastrophic at first, but these changes are fortunate and allow everything to work out for the best. Please remember that change is the only constant. I paraphrase Charles Darwin who said that the species that accepts change survives, and not the fastest or the strongest of the creatures the Lord made. Ganesha urges you to slow down and accept the changes as it will be good for you in the long run.

March 30 - Moon's first quarter in Cancer

Your emotions and self-doubts may level off somewhat now. You are sure of rapid progress in whatever you do. The ghosts of the past will be laid to rest. You will seek to expand your life and find new freedom. You will seize every opportunity to build new structures and expand the already existing order. If in business, you might use this time to grow in a careful and cautious way. You will not overextend yourself, and whatever you build up now, either in yourself or in the outer world, will be lasting. All the confusion has helped you to come up with lasting solutions. You have been baptized by fire and have emerged much stronger. This is the best way, assures Ganesha. There is no other way to go from now on but forward.

April 6 - Full Moon in Libra

You make many purchases and are consumed by love for yourself and for the world. But your love life and relationships in general could be unpredictable and difficult during this time. You may suddenly become involved in relationships that are quite different from what you would normally expect. You are looking for more excitement as the old relationships have become boring. You may be attracted to people who are quite different in age, class, background or personality. These relationships will also give you more freedom and this is what you really want. You want commitment and look for it. You are ready to give it too but your subconscious mind is looking for something unpredictable and unreliable. This is a very interesting phase and Ganesha asks you to go with the flow. On the domestic front, there may be an addition to the family, even a new pet!

April 13 - Moon's last quarter in Capricorn

There are many expenses now and ill health becomes an issue to contend with.

There may be hospitalization for you or loved ones; so make provisions. On the work front, you are saturated. You have done enough within the circumstances and can't push further. On the personal front, a stable long-term relationship may also go through a period of readjustment. This is a good time to start afresh. Domestic boredom can be very destructive and so try and infuse new life into mundane household chores. Ganesha asks you to get creative with the smaller things of life that finally always impact the bigger aspects.

April 21 – New Moon in Taurus

This is a time to set roots and get more organized. This is a period of optimism and positive thinking. You seem more balanced and this is the right time to make long-range plans and to reorganize. You may find new perspectives in education or travel or by participating in some consciousness-raising activities. You will now find psychological and physical equilibrium. If you have been recently ill, the healing process will have begun. This is also the right time to examine your ideals and goals, for it may be possible to actualize them. You may also be involved in some movement for reform or get more involved in religion or philosophy. All these, says Ganesha, are indicators of an upward swing in your affairs.

April 29 - Moon's first quarter in Leo

There are many issues at play now. While work is on the upswing, you are also in the throes of domestic responsibilities. There are many expenses, and travel is also thrown in. You make many profitable contacts. There is a possibility of a new relationship that enters your radar. It may not last but there will be new excitement for sure. You may indulge it as an expression of rebellion but that is not a good enough reason for a relationship to last. Your peer group will also disapprove of the relationship. On another note, you may begin collecting unusual and beautiful objects for your home. You will enjoy decorating your castle; your home and your workspace may be subjected to renovation. You may even look at purchasing new property. You will also seek out new and different kinds of amusement. You will be in an indulgent and offbeat mood and will want to be entertained. There is money at hand and you splurge. Ganesha warns you not to go overboard. The mood will pass soon, just hang on, and you will be on stable ground.

May 6 - Full Moon in Scorpio

The intensity of the phase may surprise you. But it will not be upsetting as it is quite possible that you will do nothing during this time. You will be filled with a feeling of balance and will be unusually peaceful and relaxed now. This is also a good time to travel, both for work and relaxation. This period has many hidden energies. It is fundamentally an opportunity to grow and explore the world and also see where and how you fit in. Take the initiative and make the most of this time. It can lead to several possibilities opening up in your life, many of which will surprise you no end. Ganesha's blessings are with you and he urges you to move on with the exploration.

May 12 - Moon's last quarter in Aquarius

Your mind is wrapped in strange ideas, even illusions and delusions. You get suspicious and think of strange, even bizarre, happenings all the time. Try not to get bogged down by heavy, pessimistic thinking. Communication with others becomes more difficult and you run the risk of losing your sense of perspective. Your viewpoints get narrowed by this influence. You are on the threshold of a new cycle of ideas and opinions, of communicating in new ways. You now look at rooting out old ideas and notions that have outlived their usefulness. Ganesha urges you to use your creativity as there is a danger of thinking too narrowly. Look for alternatives. Don't fall into depression. Look at the macro picture, the larger aspects of life. Try and get a bit idealistic, maybe even take a few risks. It will be worth it.

May 20 - New Moon in Gemini

You are thinking fast and furious; your thought processes are on a treadmill. You are working out all the alternatives and looking for the right focus to steer ahead. This is an excellent time for working on a single idea right through to the end. Plan carefully as what you embark on now can have significant consequences. Do not be preoccupied with perfection. It doesn't exist even in nature. If you are too exacting and critical, you run the risk of alienating others as there will be none who will meet your exacting standards; not even you. Learn to accept what you cannot do and go with the flow. There is a higher power overseeing all life. Live with faith and confidence. Ganesha is with you right through.

May 28 - Moon's first quarter in Virgo

There are positive trends at play here. You work hard and establish yourself. You win acclaim and respect. After all the soul-searching, you have reached a point of equilibrium and your actions are reliable and consistent. Your affairs are running smoothly and on schedule. Your approach to work and life is well planned and disciplined. You win accolades and are the toast of the town. There may even be awards. This is a good time for those in the areas of realty and the stock markets. This is a good time for speculation. Ganesha blesses you.

June 4 - Full Moon in Sagittarius

There is a lot of movement now. You meet up with old friends and old flames. No power on earth can suppress you as you move about like an India rubber ball.

You are flamboyant and not at all conservative. Your responses may be inappropriate to the situation. You may be pig headed and not very flexible. But you make headway as you gain valuable experience, particularly in your profession. You are ambitious and make substantial progress. Many people assist you now as though the forces of nature want you to be a success. You will be a success without a doubt and will be self-sufficient; if you have borrowed money you will be able to clear your debts. If you have been indebted to anyone, all accounts will be sorted out. Mortgages and bank loans will be cleared. Ganesha is with you.

June 11 - Moon's last quarter in Pisces

There could be many expenses on the domestic front. Your health may need attention and there could be some troubling domestic issues in the form of elders being hospitalized. There may also be problems with the spouse. All this is, no doubt, worrying. This impacts your life and you will be more reserved than usual and wary about forming new relationships. New people enter your life and assist you in your work as you branch out to new areas of activity. You have kept contact with friends from the past and this networking will help you now when you most need it. Do not be unduly worried. There is a support system in place. Ganesha's blessings are with you.

June 19 - New Moon in Gemini

You make steady progress and there is no obstacle that you can't conquer. You will make giant strides in establishing yourself in the world. This is a period when you know who and what you are. Your ambition is stimulated and your desire for power grows. If there is a ruthless side to your personality, it will show itself now. You know precisely what you need to do to succeed. You will go after it doggedly and share your success with others. You are also shrewd enough to make compromises and carry the team along to share the success. You display a rare, accommodating spirit that takes you where you want to be. You strike hard and the iron is hot. Ganesha is with you.

June 27 - Moon's first quarter in Libra

There is love in your life and you enjoy yourself no end. There will be stolen moments with a new friend and a lot of bliss to savour for those who are married. On the work front, there could be competition as you will face opposition from someone who is on a power trip. You may have to stand up for your rights. There could be power struggles, quite possibly with someone in authority. There may be some rebellion to what you see around you as you cannot stand injustice of any kind. But, whatever the provocation, keep away from physical violence. Avoid conflicts with others at all cost as it will be futile and you will only emerge the loser. Ganesha urges you to stay calm.

July 3 - Full Moon in Capricorn

Despite it all, you make steady progress. This is a very positive time. But it all depends on how you handle it, on what shape you give it. This is a period of culmination in your life. The old order will end and there will be new beginnings. There is very good chance of success in whatever you undertake. You have made enough money and it is time to divert your attention to spiritual needs. You must look for the solutions within yourself. Ganesha believes it is the best way.

July 11 - Moon's first quarter in Aries

You may be on a buying spree. You indulge yourself and then feel empty. You go after everything that you want in the material world and when you have acquired it all, you feel empty. You have ego issues with people and are arrogant as you assume that you are always right. You need more meaningful encounters where you focus more on mutual growth. If you soften your temperament and slow down a bit, this can be an extremely productive and growth-oriented phase. There is a lot to be done and you are filled with energy. How you use it depends on your personal evolution, says Ganesha.

July 19 - New Moon in Cancer

Emotions ride high. There are domestic issues to attend to. There may be a welcome addition to the family and happy times with birthdays, anniversaries and other group activities. You are in the spotlight and just love it. If you are a performer, like a dancer for example, there may be stage shows and many plaudits. You make big plans which will be the culmination of many ideas that have taken root over a period of time. You think big and attempt what could be termed grandiose and impractical. But this is also an excellent time to sign contracts or to conclude any kind of commercial transaction. But Ganesha cautions you not to overlook the minute details; this helps you avoid deceit and deception which may be on the cards. It is best to see the overall patterns and to plan with foresight and wisdom to avoid any unforeseen incident. You keep redefining goals and priorities which is a good thing.

July 26 - Moon's last quarter in Scorpio

The pace of life accelerates. Old projects or plans come to fruition now. It is in your hands to work out the details and leave as little as possible to chance. You must also deal with others tactfully and recognize the fact that it is not proper to be high-handed. There is a danger of alienating people by being self-righteous or arrogant. You need to be more tolerant and generous. Ganesha tells you to remember that you need to carry the team along. Tempers are running high and it may be a good idea to cool off.

August 2 - Full Moon in Aquarius

There is a lot going on in your life right now. You feel optimistic and hopeful about the future. You gain insights that can make your life much better. You feel very idealistic. Truth is very important in your life now; you are keen to know how the universe works. You look to gain insights through the study of philosophy, metaphysics and the occult. With more optimism and self-confidence in your life, you are willing to take risks. You may take to gambling or speculation, or you may drop the normal props that have kept you secure all along. You want to expand your consciousness and to experience every facet of the world. You may take to yoga and meditation or go guru-shopping to get more clarity. You feel the time has come to understand yourself better with regard to the world. Ganesha blesses you.

August 9 - Moon's last quarter in Taurus

This is a stable phase and you make substantial progress. You also want a change from the rut. You need to move away from the mundane world of work and achievement and may decide to travel. You want to take a long trip for a direct experience of life. You also want to help the less fortunate in society. You want to help the underdog. You are filled with mercy and compassion. Your life has many turns but they are all profitable. You want to grow into a well-rounded personality and Ganesha says that you are on the right track. You try everything all at once. You are restless for results.

August 17 - New Moon in Leo

The impact of this influence is significant. Various aspects of your life will be transformed. You will encounter new friends and experiences and will be richer for it. There will be positive energy in your life and you will be shown the mirror and made to face yourself. In the beginning you will resist it but the less you resist facing yourself, the better for you. All these new experiences will broaden your life and you grow exponentially as a person who matters. You will have arrived at a very significant juncture in life. The work front continues to expand with new ties and collaborations. There is money to be made and expenses also soar. Plug the bucket or you may end up spending more than you earn. All in all, a good phase says Ganesha.

August 24 - Moon's first quarter in Sagittarius

You are galloping ahead and this is a period of culmination in your professional and personal life. There are tangible results and you feel good as you bask in accomplishment and applause. You are confident about handling any challenge thrown your way. You do too many things at the same time and could face the danger of overextending yourself. Plan your moves well so that you are not cornered later. There is new love too and you spend happy moments with your paramour without a care in the world. This is a great time to be, says Ganesha.

August 31 - Full Moon in Pisces

While your work runs smoothly, you sometimes feel that you do not get the recognition that you deserve. Remain humble with your feet placed firmly on the ground. Life has many lessons to teach; do not act arrogant and smug. It may create negative energy that could lead to your downfall. You will be involved in many different aspects of work and will be meeting people from all over the world. These new interactions will broaden your outlook tremendously. You may also travel overseas on a new assignment. The future looks bright with unlimited potential. Ganesha is with you.

September 8 - Moon's first quarter in Gemini

Mercury, the mighty planet, is all-powerful. It favours travels/ meetings/conferences/ interviews/ trips/ more brain power/ contacts/ communication/correspondence/contracts. Mercury has a special connection with the circuits of the brain. Chess, crossword and other such games belong to Mercury. Also, short distance runners and spin bowlers are controlled by Mercury. Mercury, in short, is the ambassador and salesman of the zodiac. It is very important and occupies a prominent position now. You are reaching out in all directions and growing as a person. This is an excellent time for most kinds of relationships. While you meet new people, you also keep in touch with old friends. Be humble and grateful for existence is throwing a number of opportunities your way. Ganesha says that you have the potential to become a truly better person as all influences favour you and help you grow. You will learn new techniques of yoga and meditation and will take to alternative healing as a therapy of choice. But do not be obsessed with health issues. They will sort out on their own. Do not become a hypochondriac.

September 16 - New Moon in Virgo

The new moon raises your sensitivities to a sharp, cutting edge. You enter a lucky phase and are helped by strangers and friends alike. You are also constantly looking for opportunities that can benefit you. Your sense of timing is acute and your sensitivity to others is greater than usual. You do well and reap benefits as a result of all this. You make significant gains in your personal and domestic life. You spend lavishly on home improvements and there is a decided upswing in your affairs. You meet new people all the time and if you are less arrogant or ego driven you will learn a lot. This can be a very profitable period but it is all up to you, says Ganesha. If you can change your perspective, you will surmount many roadblocks.

September 22 - Moon's first quarter in Capricorn

This is a steadying influence. At this time, you are able to combine breadth of vision with sharp perception and intellect and see very clearly where you are headed. With foresight and long-range planning, you will be able to map out your future. You are filled with optimism and believe that everything will work out exactly as you want it to. Your normally grandiose plans have a practical touch to them. This is an excellent time to embark on new projects or to conclude any kind of transaction. It is also a superb time to buy or sell because you will be in the driver's seat and will profit from a rich bargain. Your ambitions are at their peak and you will do well, asserts Ganesha. A tip: keep your feet on the ground at all times.

September 30 - Full Moon in Aries

You move ahead full throttle and nothing can stop you now. You obliterate all opposition with brute force and élan. You want to learn more and more, and may even enroll in some education programme. The focus in this period will be on communication with others and it will be exceedingly fortunate. You are optimistic and positive about life. People like you because you say nice things and reinforce their belief in themselves. You are the soul of the party and will win any popularity poll hands down. This is a lucky phase, so make the most of it, advises Ganesha. If you stand for elections, the chances of winning are high.

October 8 - Moon's last quarter in Cancer

Emotions are at a peak now. There are many domestic issues to deal with; you may have neglected them thanks to your desire to get ahead. You feel good now and have the confidence to handle just about anything life throws at you. Optimism runs in your blood now but it may be a good idea not to get too overconfident and bite more than you can chew, though you are quite tempted to take on much more than you can handle. There will be work pressures and you will be tested a great deal. Learn to prioritize; it may also be a good idea to use the team and see that you don't take on too much. There is no harm in delegating work; you can do the overall management of the assignment. You may also feel restless for new experiences and may want to enlarge your scope of activities. But, Ganesha says, please do not over reach or it may be difficult to cope. You have to draw the line and know your limits.

October 15 - New Moon in Libra

There are fun times in store for you, including a touch of romance. The mood sizzles and you may think that you are in love. Go for it and let the mystery unravel itself. Leave your over ambitious nature behind and just enjoy these beautiful moments to the hilt. With a little care and restraint, you can convert this period into an excellent time. As I always say, there will be money and honey for the asking. Go for it. You may also spend a lot and make many purchases. You feel good about yourself and there is no harm at all in basking in all the glory. You have earned it after months of toil. Ganesha wishes you well.

October 22 - Moon's first quarter in Capricorn

While you continue to make sustained progress on the work front, feelings and emotions play an important part in your life. Your relationships get more intense. You are generous and giving and people come into your life from the past. You may even have multiple partners. I am not saying this in finality; it is a mere suggestion. I am also not suggesting multiple love relationships. I must underscore this point. You will have to separate the grain from the chaff and some relationships will be of greater significance than others. But you will also have to be wary of self-indulgence and indiscipline. You may feel that the world owes you a living and you may not really deserve it. You may also become selfish and demanding in personal relationships. There is a touch of arrogance now and you feel that others should make the first move, that they should make the first approach while you bask in supreme arrogance. Ganesha's wishes are with you, but this attitude won't help if you want to make the most of this period. As I have said earlier, you may need to change your attitude.

October 29 - Full Moon in Taurus

There is a steadying influence now in your affairs. You realize that it is best to get off the high horse. It is not a pedestal that works for you and you see that quite clearly. Your love relationships can be very intense in this phase. It all depends on how you handle it. There will be feelings of warmth, love, generosity and erotica and you will have many encounters with the opposite sex. They may become associates at work or even your lovers. It all depends on how you work it out. Ganesha blesses you. Use your discretion and do not go overboard. Life is all about people and the connections you make. What goes around comes around. In life, everyone gets their dessert some time or the other. So it is a good idea to keep your slate clean and go about the business of life with a clean conscience.

November 7 - Last quarter in Leo

You are in an expansive mode. There is international travel and you make connections that will play a vital role in the years to come. You are driven to succeed and will leave no stone unturned. There are chances of domestic squabbles; there may be a divorce in your life or in the extended family. There could be litigation which could be messy. There are mixed trends and you will have to steer the course carefully. The focus is on family matters: children's health and education, relations with the spouse or partner and the health of elders. There will be medical bills to pay off and many expenses. You will be at your wit's end. Pray to Ganesha for guidance.

November 13 - New Moon in Scorpio

The new moon will drive you to attain success or pre-eminence in the world. But please don't get arrogant in the process and feel that you are above the law. You may get too domineering and this is something you have to be wary about. Try not to force your views on others. It may be wise and in your own interests to help others along the way. This is an inflammable period and you will have to guard against excesses and becoming a law unto yourself. Do not also get into arguments. This is not the right time for any sort of discord as it could lead to more complications. Small issues can escalate and get blown out of proportion. Be calm and let the moment pass, advises Ganesha. You do not need the police or the courts to sort out your life, do you?

November 20 - Moon's first quarter in Aquarius

You are filled with revolutionary ideas which will force a transformation of some kind in your life. You may encounter someone who has a powerful effect upon you and shows you a good reason to change. This person is so convincing that you even listen to whatever is said; you may follow orders to the letter. In a marriage or love relationship, the two of you may disagree strongly on the management of money. Do not waste precious time fighting over joint resources. It is not worth it. Do not make money the central theme of your existence, however important it is to your daily life. You learn a lot in this period, says Ganesha. It may be the right time to assert yourself in the world.

November 28 - Full Moon in Gemini

You think of several ideas to forge ahead. But there could be some distress too. Hurts of the past begin to bother you and you feel very sensitive and vulnerable. There may be new and related pinpricks. You are distressed, hurt, and you distance yourself from the incident as quickly as possible. But there is a silver lining to this moment. If you move away and observe this hurt from a distance, you have an outstanding opportunity to gain new strength and confidence. This is also an excellent time for writers, filmmakers, artists and photographers. You delve deep into the creativity within you and make masterpieces come alive. You work from the soul; there is truth and honesty and no compromise. Ganesha blesses you.

December 6 - Moon's last quarter in Virgo

The last quarter is in your sign and you come into your own. There is stability in your affairs and you move ahead with big plans. There may be a wedding in the family or an addition to it; even both. This is an excellent time for all kinds of mental work as you are especially decisive and firm. You will be in an upbeat mood and will make a positive impression on those you meet. This influence also favours cooperative ventures and team work. You are good at negotiations and sorting out differences of opinion. There could be work-related travel too and you make many new plans for next year as you could be signing many new deals. You are hyper-active, your energy level is high, and you are restless to get going. You are brimming with confidence and new ideas, and will surprise everyone with your brilliance. The year is ending well and Ganesha is happy.

December 13 - New Moon in Sagittarius

The travel continues. You are reaching out to the stars, if I may say so. There is money and honey and several other inducements to keep slogging away. There is love in the air and the hint of a new romance. You check your balance sheets and realize that you are sitting pretty despite having a volcanic year. You may visit a health spa for treatment and recuperation. If you have been going to one in the past, it may be a good idea to check out another one. Holistic treatments are similar in a sense but different health resorts will provide new experiences. Ganesha says that all will be well and health will not be a troublesome issue. If it has been a source of worry, you will find a cure. Prolonged skin disorders will also find remission. All chronic diseases will find a cure or will stabilize. It may also be a good time to go on a pilgrimage with the family in tow. Live with gratitude and peace. Go for it, urges Ganesha.

December 20 - Moon's first quarter in Pisces

You are very sensitive and emotional now. There may be bereavement in the family and you put the blame squarely on yourself. You are not to blame; don't let the guilt eat you up. This is part and parcel of life and the grim reaper can't be kept away; he will arrive at any time in everyone's life. You spend time in prayer and with friends and in reflection. Work is not on your mind now. The family is the most important thing on your mind. You spend long moments in solitude and reflection. This too shall pass, says Ganesha.

December 28 - Full Moon in Cancer

You slowly get back to the good mood of celebrations and big plans. It is possible now to make your ideas become a reality. This is an excellent time for new business deals and to sign new contracts. You will do wonders with a little foresight and wisdom. Once again, I repeat, don't be on a solo trip. Bring the team into your plans, at least a confidante. Let others whet your plans too. It will help in the execution. This is the last week of the year and it is best to spend it on an upbeat note. Ganesha understands your situation like no one else and wishes you well.

VIRGO

KEY DATES

January

2-3, 6*-8, 11*-12, 16*-17, 21*-22, 25-26, 29-31.

Ganesha says, you will be fulfilled, in more ways than one, and that's a fine way to start the year. Hope, courage, resolution come to you, along with achievements.

February

1*-2, 3*-4, 8-9, 13*-14, 17*-18, 21-22, 26*-27.

Expenses, hospitals, spirituality, new beginnings are all highlighted. January was a forerunner, helping you to cope.

March

2*-4, 7-9, 12*-13, 17*-18, 21*-26, 29*-31.

Confidence, contacts, communications, contracts – all the C's and they spell victory, says Ganesha! Your patience is rewarded. It's more so in your birth-phase.

April

3-6*, 7-9, 13*-14, 17*-18, 21-22, 26*-27.

Family purchases and possessions, bargains, dinners, parties. So, the social and family scenes are energized! You're on a roll, in many ways.

May

1-2 (important), 6-7, 10*-11, 15-16, 19*-20, 23*-25, 28*-29.

Thanks to friends and well-wishers, you get marvellous opportunities. Go out and make the most of them, says Ganesha, but no rash/hasty moves.

June

1-3, 7*-8, 11-12, 15-16, 19*-21, 24-26, 29*-30.

House and home and the outside world all come together and keep you busy and happy. Changes in the home or buying and selling of property are very possible, says Ganesha!

July

1*, 4*-5, 8*-9, 12*-13, 17*-18, 21*-22, 26*-28, 31*

You will be off and away to a grand start and this will help you, obviously, to be successful. Both home affairs and professional matters are favoured.

August

1*, 4*-6, 9*-10, 11*-12, 13*-14, 18-19, 23*-29 (important)

Hard work, getting organized, taking health precautions will be helpful. Work comes first now.

September

1*-2, 6*-7, 9*-11, 14*16, 19*-21, 24*-25, 28-29

You find the right person, in the right place, at the right time. So, success comes to you. It could be in love, romance, friendship or business, but not all, obviously. But, Ganesha says, you never know!

October

2-3, 7*-8, 11-13, 16-18, 20-23, 24, 25-26, 29-31.

It's finance time, in terms of investing, buying and selling, raising funds. Money is important, if you want success.

November

3*-4, 8*-9, 13*-14, 18-19, 22*-24 (important), 26-27, 30.

An excellent month for the launch of any project. The financial build-up started last month. Your friends, journeys, campaigns will give you great satisfaction.

December

1*, 5-6, 10*-11, 15*-16, 19*-22 (important), 23-24, 27*-29.

You will be working hard, but do not neglect parents and in-laws. Rest will help you to work better. Ganesha says, good rewards for good efforts sum it all up, but no overdoing things!

Libra

September 23 - October 22

LIBRA

(September 23 – October 22)

ELEMENT AND RULING PLANET: Air and Venus.

STRENGTHS: Libra is active, artistic, easygoing, peaceable prises beauty and harmony, is diplomatic, polished , and very socially inclined.

WEAKNESS: Superficial, vain, indecisive and unreliable.

SYMBOL: The Scales – signifying balance, equilibrium, order and justices.

MATCHING SIGN: Aries.

MAGICAL BIRTHSTONE: Opal – brings financial success, frees its wearer from jealousy and greed and imparts clear insights.

LIBRA

YEARLY FORECAST

Main Trend

"Philosophy tells us that the mind decides not merely the goodness or badness of a thing or experience. Without the mind, there can be no object or feeling or emotion. No mind, no matter! Mental pictures have concretised themselves as objects and as ideas; so, the Shrutis declare, "Yad bhavan, tad bhavathi- as the mind operates, so the matter is decided".

- Sathya Sai Baba.

Ganesha says, the above suggestions are particularly applicable to you, since you fritter and waste your energies in various, and often needless, pursuits. Concentration is the key!

From spirituality often comes enlightenment that influences your life, work, attitudes. And that's what you see now. Ganesha grants you flashes of brilliance and intuition in your personal relationships. In fact, this extends into your professional life as well. Spiritualism, idealism, a certain psychic and intuitive awareness, and on the practical level, contacts, communication by all means known to man from correspondence to the internet, will keep you on your toes. Those in advertising (both print and electronic media) and/or foreign trade will do particularly well. You're more than usually good with people and display both flair and innovation at work. It reflects in your personal/emotional life too. Love is more ethereal, more a meeting of minds than of bodies for you at this time. Warmth in family ties, particularly in interactions with parents, older people and those who depend on you, is an added bonus. Your sign also has the reputation of being impractical, fickle, perhaps, even uncaring, but right now, it is not that way. You are loyal, committed, and sincere. Your genuineness shines through even as you function in the mundane world. Your emotions, ideals and leanings continue to be your major preoccupation and concern. It is ever so with Librans. Right now that's the main thrust and you're doing pretty well at it, anyway.

Both the major planets, Jupiter and Saturn, huff and puff for you. First, let us take Jupiter, the planet of progress, expansion and good luck that will be in your 9th angle in 2012.

The great Napolean believed in recruiting 'lucky soldiers' for his famous 'Old Guard'. Microsoft founder Bill Gates, the richest man in the world, said, "Success is a mixture of work, belief in what you are doing, and a bit of luck." In cricket, a catch may make all the difference between losing and winning. Sometimes, a tennis ball or a shuttlecock totters unsteadily at the net before falling on one side or the other, thus, deciding the fate of the match. We all know there is many a slip between the cup and the lip, and that slip, we call luck!

In Indian astrology, luck is called 'bhagya', meaning fortune and fate. The 9th sector or angle in the horoscope controls and connotes it. Ganesha says you have Jupiter, the planet of good luck, in the 9th angle of 'bhagya' or good fortune. IT IS LIKE A DOUBLE THRUST OF THE POWER OF GOOD FORTUNE!

Jupiter will remain in your 9th slot. Therefore, you will have to take the bull by the horns, wrest control of the initiative, make things happen. As they say, "Well begun is half-done." You will be quick to grasp the opportunities that come your way, and come your way they will. Finish pending work and get set to start a new one. Make that all-important journey. Education, toying with information fill-ups, for example, the digital versatile discs mentioned earlier, meeting parents, in-laws and relatives, all adding up to improve your status, mind and general state of affairs will take top priority.

A year of great progress and power.

Having defined goals and objectives and realigned priorities, you now pursue these goals with single-minded dedication, shooting straight past the goalkeeper in real international di Baggio or Ronaldinho style. The presence of Jupiter in your 9th angle also energises you, imbuing you with renewed zest and enthusiasm. All this makes for great power and the determination to overcome all the obstacles that are bound to be there in your path. To put it in another way, the irresistible force (you) wins over the immovable object. This is a basic law of physics and of life!

Uranus and Neptune:

"Uranus and Neptune will work wonders for you. Both will help you in:

a) Computers, communication, aviation and aerodynamics, science, warfare, rockets;
b) The phrase, 'to cascade their input to a discussion,' which means to feed a debate with dribbles of information, is very much in your style!
c) Higher education, crash courses, blueprints for action, research, relationships with in-laws and parents, practising religion, are the characteristics/events/features which will be highlighted for you;
d) Consolidation of position, recognition, happier relationships, calmer nerves, greater latitude and the freedom to enjoy life;
e) Your social circle will embrace/cover at least twice the number of people it did previously. That, in itself, speaks volumes;
f) Your surroundings will do you proud, says Ganesha. A fond hope will be fulfilled and that's great going! My congratulations to you well in advance;
g) Matters pertaining to insurance, finances, buying/selling/ representation could be important and successful. You could even start up a new venture. The theme is opportunities for business - tenders, contracts, hypothecation, and loans can all go in your favour. Taxes may need to be paid and expenses

met. Joint-finances, securities, shares, debentures, instruments of negotiation, wills, money for house-moving, pujas, tantra and mantra, pilgrimages, havans and offerings are all included in the orbit of the 8th angle of Jupiter, starting from August 28, this year.

h) Installation of machinery, gadgets, a housewarming, launch of projects, huge chemical plants, food factories, purifying liquids, manufacturing containers, software, computers, electronics, ancillary industries, making multiple package deals, are the other operative areas. Therefore, new beginnings, to sum it all up.

Ganesha says Venus, Mars and Mercury play a very positive role in your life.

Venus:

Venus rules over your sign. She is possibly your most important planet. Thanks to Venus, you are charming, affable, diplomatic and wonderfully effective in dealing with people. Venus makes you an expert at human relationships. Music, the fine arts, joint-finances all come under Venus too. In addition, Venus stands for harmony and duty. This planet will be in your own sign, by western astrology, from 29th October to 22nd November. It will give you relief from financial constraints, debts, while making you charismatic and attractive to others. Favours will be granted, suggestions will be followed, and therefore, your work will be done. Use this period to the maximum, advises Ganesha.

Mars:

Mars, the energy planet, will be in your sign from 4th July to 23rd August. Mars relates to your marriage and your finances (money and honey). Also, you will have boundless energy and enthusiasm, will work in a fine frenzy and thus be truly creative and dynamic. Astrology is about timing, I always say, and here the timing is right: remember that one of the greatest batsmen of the world, Sehwag, is also a Libran.

Mercury:

Zooms in and zooms out in your sun sign, by western astrology from 17th September to 5th October. Mercury, the messenger, the fleet-footed one, will help you in securing a job, promotion, better working conditions, or an assurance of it, good health, confidence, skill, crash courses to sharpen you mentally and physically, superior communication and better contracts, service to others, pets and projects. The message is loud and clear. It would be best to start ventures and projects then. It would be better to take a chance then. It would be better to move ahead then. I have deliberately used 'then' thrice, to grasp your attention!

SPECIAL NOTE

Dear readers, I have pointed out again and again that usually, but not always, you will be at your best around your birth month. Why? Many times the planets, Mercury, Mars and Venus will be in your sun sign then. They will give you money, energy, influence, charm and good luck. The obvious result will be that you will be happy. That's what life is all about, after all, isn't it?

Saturn:

Let us now be up, nice and easy with Saturn. For Saturn, I am referring you to my favourite author, Robert Hand. He comments:
"This transit represents a new beginning of internal growth. The period when Saturn crossed your ascendant was a time of shearing away those aspects of your life that no longer had a valid role, a time when projects were completed. As Saturn continues to transit your first house, your responsibilities will continue to be heavy, but your accomplishments may also be great. During this transit it is not a good idea to start any new, long range projects that will take years to complete. Obviously, you should proceed with anything that has to be done in a shorter time span. Don't use this transit as an excuse for sitting around and waiting for a more favourable time."

Now is the time to turn your attention inward. You have just completed a 14-year period in which your attention was focused primarily on interactions with others, your social life. While you have built up a very elaborate external world, you may be quite unaware of what is going on inside yourself. Now is the time to turn inward and restructure yourself wherever necessary. This restructuring will take several years; so don't be in a hurry. You have learned a great deal about the world, now learn about yourself. What do you really want and need? What have you learned about yourself over the last several years? You have to understand what you are in your own terms, not in other people's terms.

Regardless of what type of person you are, this is a time of introversion and introspection. The more you get in touch with yourself during the next few years, the more successful you will be in the future.

Saturn has a way of forcing you to deal with the appropriate issues. Since this is a time for looking inward, it will obviously present difficulties if you have elaborate commitments in the outer world. If those commitments get in the way of investing energy within yourself, you will begin to have trouble with them. You may feel that you just don't have the energy to cope; you may feel withdrawn and tired. If you are naturally introspective, you may become more so. Often people experience significant failures in their work at this time, because the work is distracting them from an encounter with themselves.

"This is an excellent time for any kind of psychotherapy, human potential work or consciousness-raising. You need to unlearn all of the incorrect and inaccurate ways of thinking about yourself that you have learned from others. You need to know who you are. Then you can properly lay the foundation for restructuring your inner life. This must precede the restructuring of your outer life, which will happen about 14 years from now."

Ganesha explains step by step how Saturn will have its impact on you. One thing is certain. You will be very introspective and you will examine your own self. You will know who you really are. There will be internal growth. Also you will have to cope with heavy responsibilities. Ganesha says you will be able to do so. But if you are thinking of a plan or venture which will take quite a few years to complete, weigh all the options very carefully. Cut away all the fat. You must restructure yourself. This is the real key to your happiness.

There is a possibility of sorrow, delays, difficulties, disappointments in relationships. In relationships, I include husband/ wife, business partner, corporations, lovers and so on. You may also feel lonely and lost though you will be respected by society. This is the strange paradox of Saturn in Libra. Be careful of the company you keep. You may have to change partners before you find happiness.

Please remember, dear readers, that this is only a general reading. It may not come true. Therefore do not worry or panic. The greatest astrologer is God. And what God decides is final. It would be wise to pray to Hanuman, if you have faith in Him. You are also most welcome to pray to your own god and deity.

Final Word on Saturn

Ganesha says there is a pot of gold for you at the end of the rainbow. Why? Saturn, your tormentor, moves out of your sun sign, by western astrology, on 6th October 2012. It will bring relief, rest, relaxation, and recreation - the four R's. Saturn will be there for about two and a half years. We will discuss Saturn at length and leisure the next year. Happiness lies ahead of you.

LIBRA

MONTH-BY-MONTH

JANUARY

You will be busy with several creative pursuits. There is also success, says Ganesha. You will also be busy with domestic chores like children, the spouse, in-laws and other such matters. It is a busy period and in addition to it all will be new hobbies and friends. Your plate is full and overflowing. Guard against losing your cool, says Ganesha. Try not to be too brusque, impatient or irritable. Ganesha says you must overcome this to get the best out of this phase. Home, family, parents and in-laws will continue to demand attention. Be careful of the health of elders and family members as well, and you must also safeguard your own. The mental stress could wear you down, if allowed to grow.

There is a lot of movement in every sphere in the early part of the year. You move ahead with speed and purpose. Domestic issues hog centre stage. As the month progresses, you turn your attention to work and set fresh goals and get your priorities well-aligned. You will concentrate on investments, lending, borrowing, funds, to generate greater income. This is also the time for love, beauty and the great joys of life. There is great bonding and many beautiful moments with loved ones. Towards the month end, there will be some confusion as many new thoughts jostle for space. There is a tendency to look for escape routes in food, drink and indiscreet liaisons. Take care, says Ganesha. Librans are ruled by Venus and love the good life. As the month ends, there is more stability and you focus on work.

FEBRUARY

You have luck on your side as Jupiter influences your slot of work and projects. Make the most of the high tide in your life. This is an excellent time for a change of job or promotion or even new collaborations or branching out. There will be both ideas and opportunities that could lead to very definite and pleasing gains. Plus you are charged and will do whatever it takes to ensure success. There will be domestic bliss as children and the home will be a source of happiness. You also manage to do the juggling act between work and play with efficiency. Ganesha says it will be a busy, hectic and rewarding period for you. No two ways about that. You live life king (or queen size). There is no obstacle that you cannot surmount as you display truly awesome skills at negotiations. You will rise in prestige and power. But please remember that control over your temper, and emotional balance, are necessary ingredients for growth.

MARCH

You are galloping ahead as the New Year firmly takes root. You immerse yourself in several activities. You may find yourself engaged in more than one activity, or doing several things simultaneously. You are keen to do justice to all that's coming your way. But all this can be both demanding and exhausting. There is a lot on your plate, assures Ganesha and you will be frantically looking for time to complete it all. You push hard to meet deadlines. Find time for relaxation, meditation, contemplation, yoga, community welfare and so on. You are now concerned with love, passion, the pleasures of sex. You are also firmly entrenched in the more pragmatic pursuits of funds and loans, legacies and money matters. This is a very pronounced trend. You will be brimming with ideas and will win kudos. There will be a rise in prestige. You are happiest when in love, when you register your greatest and most pleasing gains. Loved ones, your spouse or partner provide you exhilarating moments. There is a lot of anxiety too as there could be illness in the family and many hospital bills to be paid. The phase improves mid-month. This is an action-packed time. There will be many productive and lucrative new associations. Ganesha ensures that in the midst of all the frenetic activity you also have some happy times. In the midst of it all, you also seek spiritual solace, metaphysical truths, deeper insights into life.

APRIL

Several issues confront you almost simultaneously. You will be hard pressed to find the time and resolve to sort it all out. April will be a fraught, somewhat anxious, month that may bring some tussles, conflicts or hassles. These will be more profession or job-related than personal. From mid-April, the money scenario improves greatly and will reach a high point by the end of the month. But, Ganesha says, so is the fact that some animosity/ rivalry/ resentment could also become greatly activated. There may be people jealous of your guts and they will spell it out in no uncertain terms. So, also, could health-related problems; not just your own, but other people's as well. Mars moves out of your opposition angle, giving you relief by the month-end. Believe in the higher powers and ask them for guidance whenever you are faced with a tricky situation. The full moon is in your sign and there is love, luck, passion, harmony and the good things of life. You enjoy your interactions with people and there will be all kinds of bonds and ties, family, domestic bliss, and satisfaction in bonding. You turn back to your roots, maybe return home. Towards mid-month, there is money and honey, romance, partnerships and trade. There is a lot to learn and you are on the right track. There is stability and solidity to your life now. As the month ends, you try to live life in the grandest manner possible. Your most important achievement will be the sense of satisfaction with the direction that you have given your life.

MAY

The summer sets in more ways than one. This promises to be a very busy month. Money will be important for you and you will look at making some important financial transactions. Matters related to legacy, joint-finance, insurance, real estate, buying/ selling/ shopping/ investing/ capital formation take on an extra dimension and importance. May is a pivotal month astrologically. There will be better health and more opportunities to job-switch, start a business, get a promotion or have a spin at games of chance. Quick gains are more than likely, says Ganesha. There will be many new developments as your money worries get resolved. There is passion and deep bonding as you soar with the ecstasy of the moment. You will also indulge in strange esoteric pursuits, to flights of fancy, the supernatural, interest in spirits, witches, life-after-death, and occult phenomena. As the month ends, the focus shifts to the family. You also meet old friends and spend great moments in fond memories of wonderful times gone by.

JUNE

There are many expenses as you love to splurge on the good life. You may look at a new home or even expansion of the office, at renovation or redevelopment. The trend of loans and funds, investment and buying/selling of the last month continues. It is also a fine time for travel and transport, trade, ties, telecommunication - the 5 T's. The high-activity phase will carry on. Ganesha says it will also ensure a hectic social whirl as well as professional and business interactions that could prove very good. You manifest the charm, social skills and charisma of your sign in plenty and could feel on top of the world. You will be a human dynamo, a powerhouse of energy, ready to attain targets. There is a renewed zest for life, lots of vigour and energy, as you work exceptionally hard. Your success will be the envy of all. Children bring joy and you will spend a lot of time with them. Towards mid-month, there is travel on the cards and you make many new friends. There is also personal evolution and you grow in credibility, popularity and authority.

JULY

This is a period of achievement and consolidation. July is a good month to achieve, that's for sure. But what you need to think about, warns Ganesha, is the manner in which you go about it. It will impact you personally and individually. But, definitely, you will catapult to new heights of excellence. Just make that extra effort, says Ganesha so that your relationships, reputation, regard are not put at risk. Do not do anything that you don't believe in and do not look for a quick buck, however tempting the offers. You will have the necessary money to go ahead with plans, projects, assignments and commitments. Prestige, status, position, power will be the attributes which will concern you very deeply this month. The gains of this period will be long-lasting, pleasing, profound and deep-rooted. You find the time to delve into the spiritual and meditative aspects of life. You are oozing with confidence by mid-month. You push ahead in all areas of work and make money and also powerful professional links. You are filled with self-belief and hope for the future. As the month ends, the intensity of the phase increases.

AUGUST

There is love in your life and you could be torched by it as it may not be just a fleeting romance. Love and entertainment bring welcome relief from money and professional concerns. There is a chance that you may even lose all reason and logic. Friends, sweethearts and fraternizing lead to great happiness, especially in the second half of the month. The momentum of the last month, Ganesha predicts, gathers force in August. This month, Ganesha decides generously to give you several things you have long been craving for. There are rewards, returns, recognition and romance. This is a period when Venus is powerful and your sexuality and charisma are expressed easily. You look pleasing to the eye too and may win beauty contests if you enter any. You also fall prey to indulgences and the good life. Those in films, fashion and media do well for themselves and win rewards and awards. In mid-month, the new moon is in Leo and the good times roll without a break. There is grand success and accomplishment waiting for you. Mercury, the mighty planet, is all-powerful. Work and play will be enhanced in this period. Your life is moving the way you want it to and this pleases you no end. This is the time for expansion in thought processes and a new focus.

SEPTEMBER

The effects of Mercury are felt and you manage to do exceedingly well. But, in the midst of it all, you could find yourself falling prey to moods of angst, depression or ennui all of a sudden. It could well be caused by a desire to assess, take stock of your life, aspirations and orientation. You will seek deeper insight, greater meaning or just plain consolation, as you feel that there is a certain futility in your life. Material success alone does not fulfil you or nourish the higher self. Ganesha says, you could be into healing, nursing, helping people. A certain restlessness caused by anxiety or even nervousness is a distinct possibility. This is a common occurrence, astrologically, before a birth-month phase. You are looking at genuine, physical, mental and emotional expansion. You need wider horizons and a broader canvas for your ambitions. There are many sources of income and inspiration as you grow financially, emotionally and spiritually. Deals, mergers, joint-finances, collaborations may prove money-spinners; along with it will also be spiritual pursuits, tantra, mantra and meditation. You look for new experiences to understand life and its meaning.

OCTOBER

As the latter period of the year emerges, there will be some fresh, new deals, hectic romance, rendezvous, slightly cloak and dagger stuff, journeys and collaborations. Around the 13th of the month many new money making opportunities will open up through a variety of ways like rentals, legacy, tax rebates, loans, funds, joint-finance, inheritance to name a few. You could be very lucky here with money; just cross your fingers and hope for the best. Ganesha also helps you to gain favours from friends, well-wishers, the boss, rank outsiders, and to win at races and games of chance. This is also an emotional phase and you recollect all the good times with tears in your eyes. You are introspective and contemplative. The new moon is in your sign and this could be a significant period. You want to go full steam ahead and could be looking for a change of scenario in your work/ career/ employment/ profession. All this could lead to spectacular results. The month ends with greater stability. You are enthusiastic and energized and will be a powerhouse of energy. Even though expenses soar, more money will also be earned. There will be pleasing times with your significant other.

NOVEMBER

This could be another outstanding period. The outstanding characteristic of the month is the speed and slickness with which you will be getting into the gravy called money! It is a trend which did gather momentum in the last month. A month of glamour, gains, getting ahead - all the fulfilling G's, as you will see, says Ganesha. You will also have many moments of bliss with loved ones. What more does one need? Love will knock at your door, making everything worthwhile. Good family bonding will add to your sense of fulfilment as the year approaches its end. The family rallies around you and you feel wanted. Love is the mood of the season and you just revel in it. As the year draws to an end, the phase has an intense pitch to it. There is more work and a lot of love; in all probability there will be many loves to contend with. The primary focus will be on relationships, bonds, ties of love and affection. Your focus will widen to include extended family and kin, the community and the neighbourhood, perhaps even the world at large. You may have to take extra care of your health though since you have been in an indulgent mood for long and will need discipline. Those in the creative fields will be honoured for their outstanding contributions.

DECEMBER

You look back on the year with deep satisfaction. There is a lot going for you. Professionally and in terms of new skills, expertise and knowledge, too, this a fine phase that catapults you into true success in terms of both great achievements and greater benefits. Mars in your sign gives you the ability and the luck to make money, go in for partnerships, collaborations and new affiliations. It energizes several aspects of your life and also creates a true desire for self-improvement. There will be collaborations and ties, maybe even romantic and/ or marital relationships, a fair amount of risk-taking and also substantial travelling. There are many family gatherings and you bond with relatives whom you haven't met for ages. Ganesha says that both professional networking and personal bonding will be equally important in this phase. Towards the end of the year, there are wonderful moments spent with your beloved. The softer side of your personality will prevail.

LIBRA

THE MONTHS AT A GLANCE

January
There is a lot of movement in every sphere in the early part of the year. You move ahead with speed and purpose. Domestic issues hog centre stage. Children and the spouse occupy your time.

February
You live life king or queen size. There is no obstacle that you cannot surmount as you display truly awesome skills at negotiations.

March
You are happiest when in love, when you register your greatest and most pleasing gains. Loved ones, your spouse or partner provide you exhilarating moments.

April
You enjoy your interactions with people and there will be all kinds of bonds and ties, family, domestic bliss, and satisfaction in bonding. You turn back to your roots, maybe return home. Towards mid-month, there is money and honey, romance, partnerships and trade.

May
There is passion and deep bonding as you soar with the ecstasy of the moment. You will also indulge in strange esoteric pursuits, to flights of fancy, the supernatural, interest in spirits, witches, life-after-death, and occult phenomena.

June
There is a renewed zest for life, lots of vigour and energy, as you

work exceptionally hard. Your success will be the envy of all. There are many rewards.

July

The gains of this period will be long-lasting, pleasing, profound and deep-rooted. You find the time to delve into the spiritual and meditative aspects of life. You are oozing with confidence by mid-month.

August

Those in films, fashion and media do well for themselves and win rewards and awards. In mid-month, the new moon is in Leo and the good times roll without a break.

September

You are looking at genuine, physical, mental, emotional expansion. You need wider horizons and a broader canvas for your ambitions. There are many sources of income and inspiration as you grow financially, emotionally and spiritually.

October

You are introspective and contemplative. The new moon is in your sign and this could be a significant period. You want to go full steam ahead and could be looking for a change of scenario in your work/career/employment/profession.

November

There is more work and a lot of love; in all probability there will be many loves to contend with. The primary focus will be on relationships, bonds, ties of love and affection. It is a great time, but do not go overboard.

December

There are many family gatherings and you bond with relatives whom you haven't met for ages. Ganesha says that both professional networking and personal bonding will be equally important.

LIBRA

WEEKLY REVIEW

(By the Phases of the Moon)

January 1 - Moon's first quarter in Aries

There is a lot of movement in every sphere in the early part of the year. You move ahead with speed and purpose. You will concentrate definitely and strongly on the family. Domestic issues hog centre stage. There is need for harmony in your life. You desire peace which is such a vital part of your mental make-up. To bring about the necessary changes in your life, you work hard striving not only for position and power but also for total freedom and independence. At the core, you want to be free of all kinds of demands. You also make all the adjustments to make this happen. You want to rid yourself of shackles and bindings. It is also a time for hard work; you burn the candle at both ends. This is not what you set out to do in the first place – you wanted total freedom and not hard work -- but this is the process of life and we don't get whatever we want all the time. So we need to make the necessary compromises and wait for the right moments. There is more domestic peace as relations with parents, children, extended family and siblings gets better. Your own attitude, personality, interactions will be both pleasant and gentle. There is harmony in whatever you do. Ganesha wishes you well.

January 9 – Full Moon in Cancer

Emotions run high and there are tough moments with the family. You try your best to make the most of the situation. You do everything to make peace. There is a lot on your plate and you don't want niggles to upset you. This week you turn your attention to work and will be setting fresh goals and getting your priorities well-aligned. You will concentrate on investments, lending, borrowing, funds, to generate greater income. You will look at improvements/ adjustments wherever possible. There is a possibility of unnecessary showdowns with loved ones, friends and colleagues and you should try to avoid making changes that may prove unsettling for others as this could boomerang. You don't want to be dominated either and do not like others dictating terms. So you have to walk the tightrope. You are not looking at confrontations and your focus is entirely on peace and harmony. Take care not to end up making too many compromises or you will be the loser. In the process, you will be walked over; you will end up pleasing no one and also cause yourself and the family unnecessary stress, angst and worry. Ganesha wants you to hang in there.

January 16 – Moon's last quarter in Libra

This is the time for love, beauty and the great joys of life. There is harmony restored and you feel good with yourself and with life. You pass all the tests very comfortably. You pull out all the stops at work in terms of both fresh ideas and their execution. At home and in the area of love, as a whole, you are generous. There is great bonding and many beautiful moments with loved ones. There may be some health concerns as you are in an indulgent mood. You will therefore need to take care of yourself. There is a strong, decided emphasis on social service and the larger issues of life. Your undoubted social skills, charm and your genuine ability to put people at ease will be great assets. You will accomplish all your goals and targets with little or no acrimony. You somehow manage to get your way across even in the most daunting situations. Loans and funds come through, and your relationships with boss, colleagues, co-workers and/or subordinates will be both pleasant and productive. You will involve yourself deeply with those who depend on you. The best part is that you will achieve much without any acrimony and bickering. Ganesha is with you all the way.

January 23 – New Moon in Aquarius

There will be some confusion as many new thoughts jostle for space. Your thought processes are in a state of flux and you will have to sort them out. There is a tendency to look for escape routes in food, drink and indiscreet liaisons. Take care, says Ganesha. There is genuine love, romance and laughter in your life but somehow you are also depressed and do not appreciate all that you have been blessed with. You will have to sort these mood swings first. Maybe, spend time alone or with spiritual masters to get a handle on yourself. Librans are ruled by Venus and love the good life. They like to be surrounded by people and hate being alone. Very often, this tendency can see them hang on for ever in marriages or relationships that have lost meaning and value ages ago. You will have to think these issues out in this phase. Ask Ganesha for help.

January 31 – Moon's first quarter in Taurus

Luckily, there is some stability now and you focus on work. You are more calm and composed and spend long hours at the work front slogging away. You do well and earn plaudits from your peer group. There are also many expenses, and buying and selling. You look at new investment options and survey the realty market among other financial sectors. You are now on the fast track to success and roaring away. Your worries have subsided and your prowess at making money comes to the fore. You focus on this side of your personality which is much more pleasing. This is a phase of great material progress. You buy many goodies for the family and there is joy all around. You are happy. Ganesha is too.

February 7 - Full Moon in Leo

You live king or queen size. You earn and spend as though there is no tomorrow. There are many responsibilities towards family and you may need to keep a close watch on expenses. You get down to the nitty-gritty of everyday life this week. You may find it to be a bit of a grind, but you manage to handle it gracefully and graciously. Along with this, you are also drawn to spiritual pursuits, meditation, the higher truths. You will seek a deeper meaning to life as you realize that life is not just toil from morn to eve. There are many pressures on your schedule: there are the demands of family, work and your own inner life and growing spiritual awareness. In addition, there could also be travel and short journeys which could be both productive and a form of relaxation. You do well and climb the ladder of success. There is no obstacle that you cannot surmount as you display truly awesome skills at negotiations. You win accolades and Ganesha is distinctly happy.

February 14 – Moon's last quarter in Scorpio

There is an intensity to this phase that matches your pace. You will be learning a lot about yourself and the world you live in. You will rise in prestige and power. You realize that though your personal progress is more or less assured, self-restraint will go a long way towards integrating yourself in the community. Confrontations and slowdowns will be counter-productive, if not actually dangerous or troublesome. Personal relationships, in particular, will have to be handled with care. You will not find it easy going all the time, but please remember that control over your temper and emotional balance are necessary ingredients for growth. An attitude of calm, restraint and a preparedness to meet people halfway will work best. You will also have to guard against betrayals and let-downs. People will go back on their word and it will hurt badly. It is a time to be wary, to watch your back. All that glitters will not be gold. There will be many love liaisons and you could be cheated or sold promises that will never be kept. Take care, says Ganesha.

February 21 – New Moon in Pisces

You get extra sensitive now. Many demands are being made on your time and resources and you look for ways to escape the routine. You are not cracking up but the boredom is getting to you in a big way. You are surrounded by a sea of mediocrity and you can't take it any longer. There could be a mid-life crisis. The young will find escape routes through sex, drugs and music and the older Librans will look at travel and holidays. You have learnt, over the past few weeks, to assign realistic goals and priorities. There will be a lot you need to do now as you also have to provide domestic comfort, security and protection to the family. Once again, maybe thankfully, your focus is back to the material plane of existence - house and home, land and property, building/construction/ renovation and family matters. You will tread slowly, reconcile conflicts and yet handle people gently even while you assert yourself and get your own way. There will be domestic arguments, strife and turmoil. You could feel hurt, being undervalued or just taken for granted. But this must not be allowed to develop and grow. Look for solutions, learn to work around it. There could also be a divorce or break-up of a long relationship. All this makes the going arduous. Ganesha wishes you luck.

March 1 – Moon's first quarter in Gemini

You look for answers and solutions. There are many in the box but you have to choose one that suits you the best. You are now concerned with love, passion, the pleasures of sex. You are also firmly entrenched in the more pragmatic pursuits of funds and loans, legacies and money matters. This is a very pronounced trend. Along with this, you will also be entranced and captivated by meditation, religious and spiritual practices. There will be many new associations and get-togethers. Travel is also indicated. You will be brimming with ideas and will win kudos. There will be a rise in prestige. Ganesha blesses you. But, in the midst of it all, there will be a gnawing feeling of discontent. You will have to come to terms with it and move on.

March 8 – Full Moon in Virgo

You roll up your sleeves and begin the hard slog. You look for spare time to pursue what you love the most. You are happiest when in love, when you register your greatest and most pleasing gains. Loved ones, your spouse or partner provide you exhilarating moments. You look for a sense of balance and joy. But there are many highs and lows and you are taxed. There is a lot of anxiety too. There could be illness in the family and many hospital bills to be paid. There could be emergencies too but it all depends on the personal horoscope; these are mere generalizations as I keep saying. Astrology also never compels. You are extremely sensitive to vibrations and undercurrents and if things don't go the way you want them to you will disappear into a shell. Just trust in Ganesha.

March 15 – Moon's last quarter in Sagittarius

There is a better phase now and you get more positive and look outwards. You feel better too. Ganesha blesses you and wishes you well. You are on the right track finally. You have fruitful interactions with people as a whole. You will focus on your profession/work and will do well. If you are in the electronic media, the joys of computers in all their applications, perhaps even all of cyberspace, you will become obsessive. There is a lot on your plate and this is a good time to launch a venture, promote a campaign, and take up a new project or enterprise. You will also be busy revamping and re-organizing office procedures. You want to be more organized and efficient to focus on the expansion and growth that you have recently envisaged. You are serious about this and will leave nothing unturned until you achieve your goals.

March 22 – New Moon in Aries

You are filled with fire and decide that you have to come to grips with reality; enough is enough. You can't live in a fantasyland all your life. You make the most of all your powers and skills. The focus is on research, discoveries, inventions, new fields of study, meetings, conferences, interviews and committees. This is an action-packed time. Journeys are rewarding as you travel for both business and pleasure. There will be many productive and lucrative new associations. You work hard to convert your dreams into reality. There will also be a lot of time spent on fiscal instruments. You will be busy with taxes, loans, funds, investments, insurance and other financial transactions. There is buying and selling, the signing of lease documents, contracts, instruments of negotiation, promissory notes and so on. You will be stretched and will be running from pillar to post. Ganesha is with you.

March 30 - Moon's first quarter in Cancer

The hectic times continue, but there are beautiful bonding moments too. Ganesha ensures that in the midst of all the frenetic activity you also have some happy times. You are still busy with financial affairs and this takes up most of your time. In the midst of it all, you also seek spiritual solace, metaphysical truths, and deeper insights into life. The mood is different --- quieter, perhaps even meditative, as there is more introspection and self-assessment. You are interested in forming genuine and very close bonds with others. It will be in your interests to be flexible and keep an open mind. This will be much better than being stubborn or hard. Perhaps you have stretched yourself too far and in too many directions. You may feel somewhat worn out. You look for solace and visit places of worship. There could be overseas trips too as well as foreign collaborations. Ganesha is with you all the way.

April 6 – Full Moon in Libra

The full moon is in your sign and there is love, luck, passion, harmony and the good things of life. You make many grand purchases and feel good. Children bring great joy and you spend a lot of time with the family. You enjoy your interactions with people and there will be all kinds of bonds and ties, family, domestic bliss, and satisfaction in bonding with loved ones and relatives, even of an older generation. They will be your strength, solace, comfort and your inspiration to get ahead in life. In this period, your heredity and your family will be the theme. You turn back to your roots, maybe return home if you have been away for long and spend time with domestic issues. Family matters do get resolved, but with the usual strife and turmoil. Normally, this would have bothered you but you smile it off and the mood is contagious. All is well, says Ganesha happily.

April 13 - Moon's last quarter in Capricorn

There is a lot of work ahead and a lot of your time could be spent away from the home. As I always insist, these are mere generalizations and astrology never compels. Ganesha knows that. Specifics will depend on personal horoscopes. In this phase you will also concern yourself with appraisals of your own limitations. You look at improving your own assets, both material and non-material, and are keen on expanding your role in the community, society, your environment. You are in the throes of self-analysis as you want to grow into a better human being. Along with all this, work continues without a halt. There is money and honey, romance, partnerships and trade. There is a lot to learn and you are on the right track, most certainly.

April 21 – New Moon in Taurus

There is stability and solidity to your life now. You slog away and may even be away on an overseas visit. Most of the time spent away from home will be for professional reasons. This is a period in which you can do a lot and make solid progress. This is also a mixed week in which you feel that you may have been pursuing wrong goals all along. This could be a taxing period. There is also passion and sex, some neuroses, anxiety, minor ailments and an unsettled feeling to contend with. You turn to prayer, meditation, chants. All this will help re-activate, energize and strengthen the spiritual side of your nature. You will regain a sense of peace and calm. You will choose serenity over concrete material gains. Ganesha is happy for you.

April 29 – Moon's first quarter in Leo

As the heat and the dust gather over the sub-continent, you try to live life in the grandest manner possible. Your most important gain, triumph, achievement, will be the sense of satisfaction with the direction that you have given your life. You have also been ethical and that is saying a lot in these times! This is a joyous phase with many good tidings. There is travel, journeys for fun or for work, partnerships and ties, whether new or old, greater joy in matrimony. There will be new pursuits, new interests, and a new slant on life as newer vistas open up all the time. You have been through all the challenges and now are well prepared to taste the fruits of your hard work. Success on these terms is indeed sweet. Ganesha is pleased.

May 6 – Full Moon in Scorpio

The intensity of the week takes you by surprise. There will be many new developments as your money worries get resolved and you look at fun times with new eyes. You are in an indulgent frame of mind and there is non-stop partying on the cards. There could also be many new alliances and it will make sense to be discreet about them. There is passion and deep bonding as you soar with the ecstasy of the moment. There are many unusual aspects now as you also assess the months that have gone by. You will also indulge in strange esoteric pursuits, to flights of fancy, the supernatural, interest in spirits, witches, life-after-death, and occult phenomena. Ganesha wishes you well.

May 12 - Moon's last quarter in Aquarius

You are in a quandary: there are many roads before you and you don't know which one to take. At one level, you want to focus on work and on another level you want to get away from it all and holiday far away in the hills. So what should you do? But this may be a good time to reap the benefits of your efforts and the grinding hard work you have put in. The sweet sound of money in the bank, and the social standing and perquisites that come so easily to you are symbols of success. You enjoy them and revel in the joy they bring you and your family. Once again, you survey the rewards and seek to extend them further. But there are other concerns too. The health of someone really close to you, possibly someone older like parents or in-laws, causes you concern. Along with these pulls and pressures, there are also snatches of contentment and tranquillity in your life. You will also be enthused by meditation and an assortment of spiritual practices. Ganesha wishes you well.

May 20 - New Moon in Gemini

There are many pressures again. Your mind is in a twirl. At one level, you are enthused and rejuvenated. This can be a time of joy. There is positive thinking as you brush up your image, spruce up your life, look at the brighter side, shop for a new wardrobe, and generally project an attitude that spells out the material success you have achieved and also your sense of inner worth. All this will create a hugely improved attitude. There is love and laughter finally. You feel happy and secure. There is also genuine and strong bonding. There could be travel too and you may sign many profitable deals. Ganesha blesses you.

May 28 - Moon's first quarter in Virgo

The focus shifts to the family. There will be beautiful interactions and associations that you will cherish forever. You also meet up with old friends and spend great moments in fond memories of wonderful times gone by. At another level, you are also slogging away like someone possessed. You feel happy and reach out to all that is important and desirable. Ganesha asks you to take chances, take a few calculated risks, but also plan for the future. It is important that you read the fine print while signing documents. There could be hidden clauses or conditions that could prove to be less than favourable in the long run. Your introspective, withdrawn mood will end now and you are raring to go. You display positive thinking and matching action. The results will speak for themselves. They do not need any elaboration.

June 4 - Full Moon in Sagittarius

There is a lot of travel and new associations. You will be drawn into family and property matters and there will be expenses; there is also the risk of someone very close falling seriously sick. You will also be the conciliatory factor between erring factions. There is also an unusual hum in your life and everyone around you joins in. You naturally feel greatly energized, optimistic and very enthusiastic. You will be a human dynamo, a powerhouse of energy ready to attain targets. Many new ideas will emerge as you make glorious plans for future success leading to joy. There is a renewed zest for life, lots of vigour and energy, as you work exceptionally hard. Your success will be the envy of all. Ganesha is with you.

June 11 - Moon's last quarter in Pisces

There are great moments with the family. Children bring joy and you will spend a lot of time with them. There could also be an addition to the family, even the adoption of a girl child. I cannot be accurate here as I do not have personal details but these are the trends. This is an action-packed time without a doubt and you will be making the most of whatever falls on your lap. You will have a strong inclination to indulge in all kinds of mental activity. You look at new avenues of self expression and explore new areas of knowledge. The family and work angles are energized, bringing power, money, joy and glory, but there is a certain restlessness that might prove dangerous if it is not channelized properly. Do not give in to the urge to neglect either your commitments or the people who matter to you. It will be a grand strategy if you could turn enemies into friends. Ganesha advises you to use the energies of this period well.

June 19 - New Moon in Gemini

There is travel on the cards and you make many new friends. You could be furiously networking and may be a huge success in multilevel marketing, if you are involved in it. But you also need more tact and diplomacy in your dealings. This is not difficult but it doesn't ever harm to lay on the charm big time. Librans, generally speaking, are all good looking and that helps with first impressions. Everyone loves something pleasing to the eye. In this phase you have decided to come to grips with life. The domestic scene, with all its joys and sorrows, squabbles and bonds, completely engulfs you. What you need to guard against, however, is NOT to make the world's problems your concern. There is a need for detachment. The health/emotional situation of someone in the family is cause for concern. But the benefits of power and position come your way and you compensate for all the troubles hampering you. Ganesha is with you all the way.

June 27 – Moon's first quarter in Libra

This is a great period with many significant trends. You make many new purchases and maybe even invest in a new home. The family is growing and you look for a bigger and brighter place to accommodate the new additions. There is also personal evolution and you grow in credibility, popularity and authority. There is new love too and the unattached could take it to the next level. There will be professional and personal success. Ganesha urges you to make the most of this phase. Your energy levels are at a peak. You also attain a sense of fulfilment and self-realization as marital and other bonds of love are honoured. You have done a lot of soul-searching and the results are visible. You progress at work and earn plaudits. Nothing seems unattainable with the kind of mindset and attitude you have created within you. Ganesha is truly pleased.

July 3 - Full Moon in Capricorn

You make steady progress and burn the track on all cylinders. The gains of this period will be long-lasting, pleasing, profound and deep-rooted. You find the time to delve into the spiritual and meditative aspects of life. Life's meaning, law, research, philosophical pursuits and questions of justice will keep you busy and on the go. You may find your dormant energies and your spiritual powers awakening. But, despite this metaphysical path, you still mesh beautifully with others. There is mutual affection, love, respect and regard from your peer group. You have achieved true mental balance and poise and this is visible. This is an exciting week. Your ingenuity and fresh approach will inspire truly stupendous work. Ganesha blesses you.

July 11 - Moon's first quarter in Aries

You are oozing with confidence. You push ahead in all areas of work and make money and also powerful professional links.

You manage to optimize your resources and make tremendous headway in all your undertakings. Your confidence and caring will be at an all-time high and this lends that extra quality to your interactions with friends, colleagues and family. Having achieved your targets, you look at the lighter, more pleasant side of life. You decide to have fun, relax. Along with pleasure and recreation, you also network with serious intent. Those in the electronic media and in creative pursuits win applause for their originality. Ganesha blesses you.

July 19 - New Moon in Cancer

There are emotional issues to be wrestled with as you find the time to spend with the family. You love the family and cannot bear being away for any length of time. There is a lot of socializing with family members, loved ones and friends. You are filled with self-belief and hope for the future. You will be bold, creative and assertive. There is profound material and spiritual progress. You have many supportive relationships as you exercise your characteristic Libran flair and charm to win the cooperation of others and execute your plans to their best potential. This can be a spectacular period and a harbinger of things to come. Both socially and professionally, you are at full strength. Ganesha wishes you more happiness.

July 26 - Moon's last quarter in Scorpio

The intensity of the phase increases. You are surrounded by people and if you are in films or politics you can make the most of the situation. Your popularity soars like an American eagle. There are new developments, true growth, and a larger role in the community. You look inwards, there is self-analysis and introspection, and also great financial gains. If in business, this could be a great period. You grow and make substantial progress. The only hitch could be the illness of a parent or an elder relative. You will be called out to assist and you enjoy helping others, particularly family, but all this can be hugely taxing. Take care not to get drained out. Nurture your stamina with the right diet, exercise, antioxidants and massage. Ganesha is watching over you.

August 2 - Full Moon in Aquarius

There will be several challenges facing you this week. I have never spoken about this in the past but times have changed and maybe it is time to speak about changing lifestyles. There is no need to behave like an ostrich in such matters. People are different with different orientations and no one has the right to judge another's lifestyle. Ganesha blesses you whatever you are. Those with a proclivity for alternate sexuality will come out in the open about their feelings for someone they have been attracted to for a long time. This will most certainly be tough as we know how narrow society's moral stance is. The focus will be on communication, understandings and misunderstandings, passion and sex. There will be fears of being misunderstood or wrongly judged. But you have to go with your gut feel. Try out prayer and meditation and ask your soul for answers. There could be many twists here and I do not want to make further generalizations as individual horoscopes can be like chalk and cheese - very different. This is an interesting period. Watch it closely.

August 9 - Moon's last quarter in Taurus

You are in a better frame of mind now. There is more stability in your affairs and your thought processes. There is success at work and you have fun too. You enjoy the good life and seek out happy times with loved ones. This is a period when Venus is powerful and your sexuality and charisma are expressed easily. Those in films, fashion and media do well for themselves and win rewards and awards. You are the toast of the town and accolades pour in. There could be travel and many new friendships that suddenly blossom out of thin air. You are delighted with all this, and why not? Ganesha is happy for you.

August 17 - New Moon in Leo

The new moon is in Leo and the good times roll without a break. You are on a high and this is the time to capitalize on the good tidings of the period. There is grand success and accomplishment waiting for you. Mercury, the mighty planet, is all-powerful. It favours travels/ meetings/conferences/ interviews/ trips/ more brain power/ contacts/ communication/correspondence/contracts. Mercury has a special connection with the circuits of the brain. Chess, crossword and other such games belong to Mercury. Also, short distance runners and spin bowlers are controlled by Mercury. Mercury, in short, is the ambassador and salesman of the zodiac. It is very important and occupies a prominent position now. Work and play will be enhanced in this period and so will the rewards. Ganesha asks you not to spare the horses!

August 24 - Moon's first quarter in Sagittarius

You are on the fast track to success. Your life is moving the way you want it to and this pleases you no end. You are happy and it shows. The mood is also contagious. There is travel, partnerships, attachments, romance and many new and fulfilling bonds. There is a new momentum powering you. This is indeed a great time to be and you are enjoying every moment of it. You thrive on work, which you like, and you deliver the goods. There is domestic harmony too and many intimate moments with loved ones. If there is a significant other in your life, you will have a whale of a time together. You work hard to make the future as secure as possible. You are sensible enough to realize that even the best of relationships can break down when it is not manured well. And money makes for great manure! Ganesha nods in agreement.

August 31 - Full Moon in Pisces

You look at new ideas and get extra creative. Those in the media do exceptionally well. This is the time for expansion in thought processes and a new focus. There is intimate bonding and a deep quest for a higher consciousness. Like Osho declared, you look to move from sex to super consciousness, from the root charka to the higher ones. You have lofty ambitions and do not want to be bogged down with just work and family. You look to widen the limits of your mind.

There is a new intensity to your life. There could be power, status, and prestige. You will be worldly and yet detached or otherworldly. There will also be international travel and many new associations. Ganesha blesses you.

September 8 - Moon's first quarter in Gemini

You are filled with new ideas and are raring to go like a greyhound chasing a rabbit. You activate old friendships and are networking with frenzy. You also streamline office procedures and relationships with those you work with. You are looking at genuine, physical, mental, emotional expansion. You need wider horizons and a broader canvas for your ambitions. Finances will be more than adequate for all that you set out to do. Your own growth will be the most vital and you put all your energies into it. You also manage to take your work to the next level. If you are an artist, painter or writer, the accolades will flow like confetti. There are many sources of income and inspiration as you grow financially, emotionally and spiritually. This is a great week with growth and development in all aspects of life. Ganesha blesses you.

September 16 - New Moon in Virgo

You will worry about the tiniest details and keep bothering about trifles. This can become an irritating habit. Women, in particular, will be at their nagging worst. There may also be indiscretions in affairs of the heart as you sow your oats without caution. There are good times in store and it all depends on how you handle it. You can go overboard or go with the flow; it all depends on you. There is the true realization of your work potential and there is applause for all the hard work that you have put in over the last few months. Your professional skills and performance will be awesome. New projects/ventures/collaborations will be launched and successfully completed. You will find new ways to augment your income; there could be moonlighting and freelance ventures. Ganesha is happy for you as you realize your dreams.

September 22 - Moon's first quarter in Capricorn

This is a period of progress and also some negativity. You can get ruthless which is not in your nature in the normal course. But you exhibit a determination and resolve rarely seen. You spend time in reflection and are interested in metaphysical matters. But, along with these diversions, you also busy yourself with the money angle. Both money and spirituality will hold your interest and attention. Deals, mergers, joint-finances, collaborations may prove money-spinners; along with it will also be spiritual pursuits, tantra, mantra, meditation. As you can see, it is a mixed bag. There will be radical changes like relocating, moving house or changing jobs. You look for new experiences to understand life and its meaning. You seek change, novelty, different experiences and want to share your knowledge with all and sundry, most importantly with loved ones. Ganesha blesses you.

September 30 - Full Moon in Aries

There is great movement in your life now. You reap the whirlwind. There is money in the bank and more prestige at work. What more do you need? This has been an interesting year by all accounts and you have no regrets as it comes to a close. There will be domestic expenses; the health of children will be a particular cause for worry. But you are on the treadmill of achievement. There will be better income, perks, and benefits. You acquire a sparklingly bright image at the office and will shine professionally. There will also be travel for pleasure; possibly with a loved one, a secret rendezvous or love nest. Ganesha chuckles happily.

October 8 - Moon's last quarter in Cancer

This is a period when you are filled with love for the family and close friends. There will be many party times as you bond with everyone. This is an emotional phase and you recollect all the good times with tears in your eyes. You are introspective and contemplative. You also look at social work and help out with some charity organization. You may join an NGO working with disability or with the underprivileged or the less fortunate. Or you may just fund organizations or donate to relief funds. The pall of gloom that envelopes life distresses you greatly and you want to change the situation of the downtrodden. Towards this, you do your best. This is a period of new directions as you look to give your life more meaning and quality. Ganesha wishes you well.

October 15 - New Moon in Libra

The new moon is in your sign and this could be a significant period. You have the right mindset and attitude for great progress and advancement. You want to go full steam ahead and could be looking for a change of scenario in your work/career/employment/profession. Job-hopping, promotions, or even a new business could be some of the possibilities this month. There is a tremendous rush of energy and power and you feel a tremendous need to do full justice to your potential and talent. All this could lead to spectacular results. There are also family and work commitments to be kept. The results of your endeavours will be fruitful. This is a special time and many favours come your way. This is an ideal phase for getting things done. The fruits of your efforts will be tangible. Enjoy the moment, says Ganesha.

October 22 – Moon's first quarter in Capricorn

You keep slogging away. There is no respite in your desire to achieve as you make many plans for the future. Your domestic commitments may have taken a back seat in recent times as you concentrated on work and its many dimensions. The family will now make great demands on your time and attention. You will have to unravel the tangled web of family issues, domestic wrangles and problems. This is going to be a tough task. There is also another aspect at play: the adventure of high finance, of raking in lots of money, of daring and ambitious business transactions. But now the thrust is strongly on family life. Ganesha agrees with the change in focus.

October 29 - Full Moon in Taurus

This is a period of stability. You put your nose to the grindstone and go for it. You are enthusiastic and energized and will be a powerhouse of energy. This is a time of genuine achievements, progress and success. Even though expenses will soar, more money will also be earned. Family and professional life will not only blossom but also bear fruit. You will make all the right moves as you get more streamlined and efficient. There will be many purchases and expenses will mount. You look at realty as a good option and may buy a new home or office. There will be pleasing times with your significant other. The temptations of love will be great and you will have to reign yourself in. Life is good and you thank Ganesha for all the blessings. You live in gratitude.

November 7 – Last quarter in Leo

You make big plans and have the will power to carry them through. You look at every opportunity to make the most of the situation. You look for experiences that can improve your knowledge as you firmly believe that knowledge is power. Librans love beauty and aesthetic surroundings and this will be the time when you splurge on all the comforts of life. You buy goodies and surround yourself with them. You will focus on the future and work and home will be a major priority. You plan ahead with expertise and innovation as you hope to make all your dreams/hopes/ambitions come true. There is a tendency to overdo things now and you may over-extend yourself at work. Take heed of the 3 R's --- Rest, regular hours, relaxation, and you will quite automatically, of course with some luck thrown in, also get the fourth R – results. Ganesha wishes you well.

November 13 – New Moon in Scorpio

Another year draws to an end and the phase has an intense pitch to it. The trends are encouraging. There is more work and a lot of love; in all probability there will be many loves to contend with. You will be playing the field. The primary focus of the week will be on relationships, bonds, ties of love and affection. There will be some upheavals at home and your interactions at work will also be vastly different. You will earn good money and there will also be a lot of entertaining; much of it will be official and you gain from it too. Your children will be a source of joy and the interactions with the elderly at home will be more meaningful, warm, and empathetic. You reach out to others and your focus will widen to include extended family and kin, the community and the neighbourhood, perhaps even the world at large. This is a week of many pleasures and you are greatly enriched. Ganesha smiles in joy.

November 20 – Moon's first quarter in Aquarius

You look at new ideas to get better results. You are looking at every way to maximize your output. You are on the go breathing fire. The family is happy as all misunderstandings have been sorted out and work has a new momentum. You may have to take extra care of your health though as you have been in an indulgent mood for long and will need discipline. It will be a good time to get cracking on a new diet or exercise regimen. You may need to slow down; a short stint at a healing centre or health spa may not be a bad idea at all. Do this as a preventive measure. It is better to be safe than sorry. There could be times when you feel a bit depressed or think differently or out of the box. Do not let this bother you as much as it bothers your loved ones. These things will pass. Ganesha assures you of that.

November 28 - Full Moon in Gemini

New ideas take you by storm. You look at meditation and yoga and try to change your lifestyle. You need to lose weight, and the party scene also beckons. There will be marriages in the family and friend circles and, of course, you have to attend. Those in the creative fields will be honoured for their outstanding contributions. Despite all the distractions, you shine at the workplace. There is no stopping you. You are inspired and hard working. You not only look for new ways to progress but will also try to identify, improve and streamline your efforts. Ganesha is with you.

December 6 – Moon's last quarter in Virgo

You do not let go. It is the last month of the year but you are still at it. If employed, your prospects are bright. If on your own, you will be in the throes of major expansion. Here I must mention that it is not all work. You also give expression to your fun side. You want to let your hair down and join your friends for a good time. But you also know that this is the time to look ahead. All your future ambitions, plans and projects will necessitate a load of work to make them happen. There will be collaborations and ties, may be even romantic and/or marital relationships, a fair amount of risk-taking and also substantial travelling. There will be many partnerships as you move ahead with Ganesha's blessings.

December 13 - New Moon in Sagittarius

There are so many things happening in your life and you are caught up in it like a pigeon in a storm. This period has many challenges and you do well to handle them with purpose and élan. Finance and family are well looked after and there could also be an addition to the family. There are many family gatherings and you bond with relatives whom you haven't met for ages. Journeys, relationships and acquisitions all conspire to come together, and you are both enthused and happy as you cope well despite your hectic schedule. There will be travel, loans, sex, passion, funds, buying/selling/shopping and reaching out to people. Ganesha says that both professional networking and personal bonding will be equally important in this phase.

December 20 - Moon's first quarter in Pisces

There are wonderful moments spent with your beloved. This is a great way to end the year. Those who are single may think of taking the plunge. Those already married will have a second or third honeymoon. Those who have recently broken up will find new love. Love is in the air and you enjoy every moment of it. There may be a family holiday too to some exotic locale. The potential is endless. It all depends on what you do with it. There are many sensitive and emotional moments, and you want to share them with those who matter. Ganesha blesses you.

December 28 - Full Moon in Cancer

Your world is in order and you are relaxed and happy. You decide to have fun and join the party. You are in the mood to wine and dine with your friends, be a happy host, enjoy life, live well and love well. You realize in moments of contemplation that you need love and the warmth of companionship. It is far more important than success, money and material progress. Your attitudes have changed and you firmly believe that marriage, romance, the joys of wedded bliss are much more your scene than being a high achiever. You have lived for yourself long enough and have had professional success in this material world. Now you look for the embroidery that will embellish your life. The softer side of your personality will prevail. Ganesha blesses you as you step into another year.

LIBRA

KEY DATES

January

Ganesha says 4-5, 9*-10, 14-15, 19*-20, 23-24, 27-28 .

Great work, glorious results. You've worked hard to make it all happen, now you reap just rewards.

February

1*-2, 5*-7, 10*-12, 15*16, 19*-20, 23*-25, 28*.

Excellent for 2 P's of progress and plenty, says Ganesha! The fine phase continues this month, too.

March

1*, 5*-6, 10*-11, 14*-16, 17*-20, 23-28 (important).

March running into April will be truly terrific and hectic, and I am not being falsely dramatic! Trust me on this.

April

1*-2, 6-7, 11*-12, 14*16, 19*-20, 23*-25, 28*-30.

You will be a real champion and win in the game of love and of life.

May

1*- 2, 3-5, 8*-9, 12-14, 16-18, 20-22, 25*-27, 30-31.

Finance, buying and selling, investment, property; therefore, merry-making as well as money-making activities.

June

1*, 4*-6, (important) 9-10, 13*-14, (important) 17-18, 22*-23, 24*-26, 27*-29 .

4-6, important for gaining an entry, 9-10, joy and children, 17-18, before the public, 22*-23, friends help you, 24-26, work will be done, 27-28, happiness. The month speaks for itself - I've spelt out some of the details, though.

July

1*-3, (important) 5-6, 10-11, 14*-16, 19*-21, 24-25, 29*-30.
House and home and all therein keep you busy and happy. You enjoy it all tremendously.

August

1-3, 7*-8, 11*-12, 15*-17, 20*-22, 25*-26, 28-31.
Money and honey, or in other words both financial matters and love sum it all up!

September

3*-4, 7-8, 9*-13, (important) 17-18, 21*-23, 24-25, 30.
Hard work, good rewards, change of staff - people are truly important for you this month, in different ways.

October

1, 4*-6, 9*-10, 13*-15, 19*-20, 23*-25, (important) 27-28.

November

1-3, 5*-7, 10-12, 15*-17, 20*-25,(important) 28-29.
Loans and funds, love, as well as new beginnings are emphasized. You could have made a start in April, itself but many things come to fruition now.

December

1*-4, 7*-9, 11-15, 16-17, 21*-22, 25*-26, (important) 30-31 (most important, says Ganesha!).
Gains, glamour, goodies all come to you in a fine burst of glory. A fine way to end a glorious year!

Scorpio

October 23 - November 21

SCORPIO

(October 23 – November 21)

ELEMENT AND RULING PLANET: Water and Pluto.

STRENGTHS: Scorpio is imaginative, passionate and emotional, subtle, persistent, intense, obstinate and unyielding.

WEAKNESS: Selfishness, disrespectful, dictating, envois, cunning, sarcastic, merciless and arrogant.

SYMBOL: The Scorpion – A secretive, deadly creature that can poison its enemy. It sting its often fatal.

MATCHING SIGN: Taurus.

MAGICAL BIRTHSTONE: Coral and Topaz:- release occult powers and ring serenity of mind. They also protect from enemies and illness.

SCORPIO

YEARLY FORECAST

Main Trend

Creativity, ingenuity, personal charisma --- all make you truly successful. The astro-advice, courtesy Ganesha, of course, is to let your own personality shine forth. Harmony comes from sharing ideas. At this time, in any case, you're happily involved with friends, neighbours, even work-mates, in a spate of glorious activity. Some aspirations, desire or even secret wishes known only to you so far may blossom and be realised --- fulfilment, friendship, finances are the 3F's that will most certainly come to you from Ganesha. I can tell you I am pretty sure about this particular forecast!

Ganesha has something else to add --- you have to curb a tendency to want your own way, your own ideas to prevail. Astrologically, this is a trait you share with other signs, Leo and Capricorn, for example. In any case, no one can hope to get away with it all the time, and nor to be fair, do you.

My advice is to tread softly and attempt to get ahead without causing hurt or offence. Love is felt deeply and wonderful ideas shared in mutual affection, which seems to be ever increasing. You are conscious of a sense of well-being, security from older relatives, and peace of mind. Only a fool would not want to hold on to it, and that, you're far from being!

There will be a pleasurable widening in both your interests and pursuits, creatively speaking. In fact, in that sphere, this month should actually be clubbed with March. There will be a kind of continuum, a flow in this spurt of creativity that you experience. Long cherished hopes, dreams and plans now seem ready to be realised.

Travel and home come together and that could also mean a home-away-from-home. You will communicate and act brilliantly and courageously, and that assures both success and satisfaction.

Jupiter:

Ganesha says Jupiter revolves in your 8th angle now. There are two very apt quotations:

'If we could see the miracle of a single flower clearly, our whole life would change.'

- Gautama Buddha

'Blessed is the night when souls unfold with dreams and whispers.'

- Anonymous

Jupiter represents money. But we are talking about flowers and dreams. Why? Jupiter in the 8th angle also shows poetry, imagination and everything that is mysterious.

Honey, it's all about money
Be it alimony, hundi, parsimony.
Yes, it's quite funny-
Like taking out of a hat, a bunny!

- Bejan Daruwalla.

Ganesha roars with laughter, as He is the lord of both wisdom and wealth (now you know why I worship Him!). At least, He appreciates my verse!

The 8th angle signifies several things:

a) Loans;
b) Funds;
c) Joint-finance;
d) Insurance;
e) Legacy and legal matters;
f) Money from different sources, such as rents, rentals;
g) Lottery;
h) Hidden treasure;
i) Tantra and mantra;
j) High passion and sizzling sex;
k) Taxes, real estate issues;
l) Keeping your mouth shut (otherwise there's trouble); and religious rites.

Jupiter helps you to get money. That's important. This period will also be mighty important for: a) buying/selling/godown/ warehouse/ office and so on. Let me know, dear readers, how right I am on these counts. Matters to do with inheritances, wills, codicils, estate and taxes, hundis, taking care of both health and money, cooperating with other workers, finding new sources of money and profit, maintaining secrets and confidentiality, learning to use your energies carefully and not wasting or draining them away. Finally, it is most important that you should use your talents and imagination completely. In short, Jupiter in your 8th angle stands for pleasure (sex, tantra, passion, love, stimulation, drugs) and treasure (money and jewellery) in full measure (quantity).

Strange encounters, bizarre meetings and love affairs are not ruled out. Your sources of income do multiply, one way or the other, and that's important. It will increase the cash-flow and also give you greater peace of mind Vis a vis finances.

This is what Robert Hand, one of my favourite astrologers, has to say about Jupiter in your 8th angle:
"Traditionally, this transit indicates an inheritance. This is a good

time to enter into a relationship in which you and another person have to pool your resources, such as a business partnership. This is also a good time to request a loan from a bank, unless there is another transit at the same time that negates this reading. In general, other people are more than usually willing to help you out in some way."

"On another level, there will be many powerful but fortunate changes in your life at this time. It may not always be obvious, but any sweeping change that happens now will be for the best, and will make your life richer and more rewarding in the long run. It wills your life. If you have recently been through a time of psychological stress or are encountering one now, this transit will help the healing process within you."

This same time-span will also be mighty important for: a) buying; b) selling; c) renovation; d) decoration of house, home, shop, godown, warehouse, office. Co-operating with co-workers, finding new sources of money and profit, maintaining secrets and confidentiality, learning to use your energies carefully, and not wasting or draining them away will all be in focus. Finally, it is most important that you use your talents and imagination completely.

I am writing this forecast on 11th April 2011. Just two days ago Anna Hazare summoned the whole of India to fight against corruption. In the same style, I am summoning the three minor planets Mercury, Venus and Mars.

Mercury:

Mercury will be in your sign from 6th October to 29th October. Like Yusuf Pathan, a Scorpion, Mercury will help you to be fast and furious, hitting mighty sixers. Journey, ceremony, money, and honey (which, to me, means God's plenty), travel and trade, family and friends, the ability to put your message across, will be the important features. I know this is quite a list and we have only a few days for it to happen. But you will gain and make progress in several ways.

Venus:

Venus swings into your sign from 22nd November to 16th December. You may use this period for attending to health, personal appearance and character analysis, using your undoubted charm to good purpose, whether in romance / finance / socialising, projecting your point of view, making your presence felt and leading from the front. Good news in your work areas, say, promotion and perks could await you. Loans and funds will be available. This is also an ideal time to ask for favours and obligations. There are more chances of getting them, despite delays and possible setbacks. Ganesha wants you to go right ahead if you have a project, a marriage proposal, or even a health problem which has to be resolved.

Mercury:

Mercury does a devastating Malinga bowling spell in your sun sign, skittling out the opposition from 6th to 29th October. Journey, ceremony, money and honey (which, to me, means God's plenty), travel and trade, family and friends, the ability to put your message across, will be the important features. I know this is quite a list and we have only a few days for it to happen. But you will gain and make progress in several ways and that's what really matters.

Pluto:

Pluto in your 3rd house shows the importance of contacts, communication, contracts and concord. Luckily, Pluto forms a fine juxtaposition with Neptune from 4th February. It will help you to put your message across, with vim and vigour.
I am sorry that in my 2011 annual, I said Pluto was in your 11th angle. My mistake.

Neptune:

Neptune helps you to be mightily creative. You will be romantic, sing mushy songs, win the hearts of your friends and beloved, and, in the bargain, be extremely popular with one and all. I call it a win-win situation. Alas in love and friendship all of us could be cheated and hurt. THIS IS THE BEAUTY AND CONTRADICTION OF LOVE AND LIFE. I accept it completely; Scorpios, very particularly, should exercise moderation in drugs and drinks.

Uranus:

From 13th March 2011 to 6th March 2019, Uranus will be in your 6th angle. The 6th angle symbolises

1) Health
2) Work habits and ability
3) Social connections
4) Community service
5) Pets (most certainly)
6) Servants and members of the staff
7) Loans and debts
8) Intestines
9) Accidents
10) Great wealth acquired by hard work and/or inheritance.

Scorpio is a mysterious sign of life, death, and regeneration. My personal opinion is that Saturn in the 12th angle will make you intuitive, perceptive and you MAY be able to recall your past birth. Travel to different places for love, business, religion, spirituality, business collaboration, pilgrimage, and social welfare is a possibility.

Saturn:

Saturn in the 12th house also shows imprisonment, hospitals, secret enemies, mystical experiences, liaisons, secret meetings, conspiracies, expenses. It may bring about the ill health of your husband/wife. According to Vedic astrology, it is definitely the house of karma, dharma and final moksha or salvation.

Saturn in your 12th house can make you a victim of your own utterances and return statements and actions of commission and omission, anywhere and everywhere. You may incur losses in industrial ventures, manufacturing units and income-generation factories. (Pandit-Parsai)

Important tips for you:

You must find out your limitations and your strengths, in the sense that you must know how far you can go in life without overdoing it. This applies to practically all aspects of life. I admit that this is a contradiction, because while talking of Jupiter I have praised your tremendous push, creative abilities and power.

My answer is that in real life, you will have to strike a balance. My second answer is that in 2012, you will be learning more about yourself, and your responsibilities. Saturn may not restrict you to the point of acute and awful frustration and disappointment. The lesson of Saturn will be spread out from 13th October 2009 to 5th October 5 2012.

Saturn will help you to revise and even control your plans and learn from past mistakes. THIS WILL HELP YOU IMMENSELY IN THE FUTURE. Changes in your life pattern are absolutely certain, says Ganesha. Be ready for it. Do not be adamant, stubborn, and rigid. I am hammering this point, because you Scorpios are tough and stubborn people. Learn to adapt. Try to be flexible. It will be to your advantage and happiness. Why be your own enemy!

Luckily, you Scorpions can be exceptionally charming and pleasing. Turn on your charm and win others to your side. Believe me, this is the master key to success. I suggest the following mantras:

1) Om Praam Preem Proun Sa Sanaye Namah
2) Om Shri Hanumate Namah
3) Shri Ram Jai Ram Jai Jai Ram

These are the three mantras for Saturn. Do the mantras 21 times, each, if possible.

From 6th October 2012, Saturn will move in your sun sign by western astrology. It is possible that circumstances might make it difficult for you to give yourself completely to others, though you may love them very much. You will feel restricted and limited, without really knowing why. At the same time, if you can handle your energies rightly and control yourself it will finally make a better and superior person out of you. Saturn is therefore a double-edged sword. Also, you must take good care of your health. Saturn in your sun sign will make you moody, introspective, and internally strong. Saturn will test and prepare you for the path of your life. The key is in successful communication. Saturn will be in your sun sign till 22nd December 2014, by western astrology, as your constant companion and shadow.

SCORPIO

MONTH-BY-MONTH

JANUARY

A good start to the year is half the battle, and you have already put your best foot forward. Ganesha says that those in research and dramatics, the media, travel, tourism and trade, do wonderfully well. Scorpios make a great start to the year and make this a most definite look-ahead, get-ahead phase. This is a hectic phase and you are on the go from the start. You make rapid progress. There is also an inner peace and contentment. There is great energy, enthusiasm, ideas, true inspiration and the desire to move mountains. Ganesha is with you as you enter the New Year with optimism, hope, dynamism and freedom. Towards mid-month, with the moon's last quarter in Libra, there will be buying and selling and many different forces at work. You will also be dealing with funds, finances, investments. There may be health niggles too. Believe in a higher power, says Ganesha. As the month progresses, your higher self will assert itself quite strongly and forcefully. But with the moon's first quarter in Taurus, there will be stability and growth. You sign new deals and make acquisitions.

FEBRUARY

The path to glory continues unabated. There will be two major trends, says Ganesha. You will be busy with property deals and parental influences. But Jupiter exercises its influence to your advantage and there are gains and prosperity. Finances, work and promotions come to the fore. You are in luck as financially and professionally, without your having to fight for them, money and awards land on your lap. Mid-month, the moon's last quarter is in Scorpio, and there could be an overdose of love, lust and passion. It is a frenetic, action-packed time and success crowns you.

MARCH

There is a lot going for you and you should consider yourself very lucky. Ganesha says that from the 10th there will be new beginnings, new ideas and new inspirations. The getting ahead theme is in full swing and you could start new enterprises in this phase. You make new plans to acquire comforts, luxuries and the finer things that make a home. You are also keen to improve the quality, depth, intensity of your emotional bonds and ties. You may also embark on international travel and may make plans for a home-away-from-home. There is new restraint, self-control and willingness to compromise and sacrifice. You explore and exploit all potential for growth. Towards mid-month, the pace of work is fast and lively and you accomplish a lot. Scorpio is a powerful sign and can move mountains but it also depends on several factors, the least of which is your personal horoscope. Towards the month-end, you are burning the track and moving ahead with great speed. The moon's first quarter in Cancer, as the month ends, makes you concentrate heavily on funds, finances. Power is the name of the game and you will wish to experience it in all its forms and dimensions.

APRIL

Now there are a few issues that you need to sort out. I am sure you will resolve them amicably. There could be bottlenecks in your work. There could also be many domestic issues to resolve. Ganesha's advice is unequivocal. You need to just carry on to the best of your ability. The slow, steadying influence of Saturn will make you work hard and long and usefully. Once more, finance hogs the limelight in your life. Mutual and marital funds, profits, shares, gifts, legacies, estate issues and other fiscal instruments keep you on your toes. Your prospects at work, personal relationships and communicating with people will be the central theme of this period. The new moon is in Taurus mid-month and this can be a very profitable period indeed. You are greatly energized and full of strength, vigour and determination. As the month ends, the influence of Leo makes you storm ahead, mowing down all opposition.

MAY

There are many things on your plate but you manage to handle it all well. According to Ganesha, May is for taking chances in the game of life. Ganesha rewards your patience/ endurance/ fortitude generously. Along with ambition, perseverance and drive, you appreciate and recognize the value of money. So, great planning and thought is put into financial issues as you study and research funds, loans, buying, selling, investments and stocks. The full moon is in your sign and your passions are ignited. Alongside your preoccupation with finances, there is also deep introspection. In a few cases, there may even be real enlightenment or possibly God-realization. Mid-month will be more about the 3 C's - contacts, communication and correspondence. And as May exits, you expand your circle of activities and go all out making this a time for decisive, definite action.

JUNE

Domestic issues will be paramount. There will be many pressures now. An operation, an accident or illness is not completely ruled out. Health safeguards are a must, says Ganesha. You may also have to deal with health issues of elders at home. A lot is happening in your life. You are pushed into several corners and manage to wriggle out of tight situations. This is a good time to assess your aspirations, realign your focus and start afresh. Towards mid-month, your possessions and investments are most important as you build a strong financial base. As the month ends, you may feel like relaxing. Entertainment, amusement, games, hobbies, warm interactions with children, and love and romance will excite you. There may be a long holiday with the family and there is a good possibility of overseas travel. There is also great family bonding and a grand time with children.

JULY

There is travel on the cards and also many new associations and collaborations. Ganesha says that people will matter to you as will your spiritual/ religious inclinations. Therefore, collaborations, rites, religious ceremonies, looking after parents and in-laws, house and home, etc will all keep you deeply involved. The main focus could be summed up in the 3 T's - trade, ties and travel. Your inter-personal skills are tested and the key to achievements and success will depend on how you relate to people. A sense of joy and fulfilment is a strong possibility. Towards mid-month, the new moon is in Cancer and you spend quality time with loved ones. There are many fun times and several disparate and different influences at play. As the month ends and Scorpio's influence descends, there is an edge to this phase and a new intensity. There could be correspondence, trips for both recreation and work, and several new profitable contacts.

AUGUST

Scorpios are winners in every way. Of course, I can be more accurate in a personal prediction and this is a generalization. There is a point to be noted: Ganesha always rewards genuine and sincere effort and hard work. Mars and Jupiter now come into a great formation, giving a thrust to all that you do. So, you win plaudits. Money and power are at your fingertips. What more do you want? This is an excellent time for working a single idea through completely. This is an important period and if you do the requisite planning and go through the details with a comb the consequences can be very significant. Around mid-month, you make considerable progress. You get rewards and awards and earn the respect of peers and superiors. As the month ends, with Sagittarius' influence, there is rapid movement in all spheres of activity. You are driven and ambitious.

SEPTEMBER

The good times continue to roll despite the hitches. But then life can never be rosy all the time. This is a favourable month thanks to the good placing of Saturn and Venus. You are the master in the ring. You are in a highly competitive frame of mind and emerge triumphant at work. This influence stimulates your ambition and desire for power out of all proportion. You could get ruthless and can create enemies. Away from the professional confrontations, there will be time spent with the family. An elder relative may need hospitalization and there will be other domestic demands. Towards the end of the month, you find your way out of tight situations. You may be surrounded by conditions of breakdown and decay and you prepare to rebuild. The full moon is in Aries and you have a very positive time. This is a period of culmination in your life, and you will be tempted to expand beyond reasonable limits. There is no question that you have a good chance of success.

OCTOBER

You realize that you are spending without a care in the world and it may be wise to cap this unnecessary expenditure. This is a month of expenses, secret meets and conferences, maybe a visit to hospitals, clinics, welfare centres, places of worship and healing, and health resorts. Ganesha warns you of the danger of neglecting loved ones. But, whatever said and done, this is probably the best phase of the year on several fronts. Mercury, the mighty planet, is all-powerful now. Mercury, in short, is the ambassador and salesman of the zodiac and occupies a prominent position now for over 20 days. Seize the moment, suggests Ganesha. Work has never been better and you are deeply in love in a beautiful, powerful and deeply bonding way. You may shift to a new house or buy a fancy new car. There could be foreign travel, a marriage or a birth in the family. There is love, achievement, contentment and peace. It is a time for the big P's -- position, pelf, perks and privileges. The areas of profit will include trade, partnerships, law courts, legal issues and journeys for business and pleasure. There will be progress and many new plans. Your health is fine, the mood is upbeat and you feel positive, energetic and enthusiastic.

NOVEMBER

You are in luck as the powerful and beneficial influences of Mercury continue to work wonders. Ganesha says that there will be no matching your enthusiasm and inspired interactions, and your birth month proves earth-shaking. You give the term 'king size' a new meaning altogether. A truly wonderful phase packed with fun, frolic and pleasure. There is spiritual growth, emotional balance and the sweet fragrance of success permeating your life. There is a lot on your plate to choose from. Mutual funds, shares, stocks, capital-raising and all other money matters come to the fore. Your esteem in the community gets a huge lift, which satisfies your ego drive immensely. You end the year with spectacular fireworks. Mercury, the mighty planet, is once again in your chart. It is very important and occupies a prominent position now for over a fortnight. Need I say more?

DECEMBER

What a year it has been! Ganesha has certainly given you a sizzling time in the sun. This is a great way to end the year. Finances and family values rule supreme. A time of truly creative achievements comes now. But you also need a break to prevent burnout after the frenzied, almost manic state of affairs of the last few weeks. You are in gratitude and in a contemplative mood. But as the month progresses, the frenzy of year-end festivities grab you by the collar and you give a good account of yourself in both the work area and party circuit. Health may need some attention, particularly the health of elders. There is money and honey and festivity in the air and you can't be left out of the party. It will be a good idea to thank Ganesha for this wonderful year. Of course, a lot will depend on the personal horoscope. As the year ends, you feel optimistic and hopeful about the future. You feel that everything is going to be just great and this is not a delusion.

SCORPIO

THE MONTHS AT A GLANCE

January
This is a hectic phase and you are on the go from the start. You make rapid progress. You manage to meet all deadlines and challenges head on.

February
Finances, work and promotions come to the fore. You are in luck as financially and professionally, without your having to fight for them, money and awards just land on your lap.

March
There is new restraint, self-control and willingness to compromise and sacrifice. You explore and exploit all potential for growth. Towards mid-month, the pace of work is fast and lively and you accomplish a lot.

April
Mutual funds, profits, shares, gifts, legacies, estate issues and other fiscal instruments keep you on your toes. Your prospects at work, personal relationships and communicating with people will be the central theme of this period.

May
Alongside your preoccupation with finances, there is also deep introspection. In a few cases, there may even be real enlightenment or possibly God-realization.

June
This is a good time to assess your aspirations, realign your focus and

start afresh. Towards mid-month, your possessions and investments are most important as you build a strong financial base.

July

The main focus could be summed up in the 3 T's - trade, ties and travel. Your inter-personal skills are tested and the key to achievements and success will depend on how you relate to people.

August

This is an excellent time for working a single idea through completely. This is an important period and if you do the requisite planning and go through the details with a comb, the consequences can be very significant.

September

Away from the professional confrontations, there will be time spent with family. An elder relative may need hospitalization and there will be other domestic demands.

October

This is probably the best phase of the year on several fronts. Mercury, the mighty planet, is all-powerful now. Mercury occupies a prominent position now for over twenty days. Seize the moment, suggests Ganesha. Work has never been better and you are also deeply in love in a beautiful, powerful and deeply bonding way.

November

A truly wonderful phase packed with fun, frolic and pleasure. There is spiritual growth, emotional balance and the sweet fragrance of success permeating your life.

December

Health may need some attention, particularly the health of elders. There is money and honey and festivity in the air and you can't be left out of the party. It will be a good idea to thank Ganesha for this wonderful year.

SCORPIO

WEEKLY REVIEW

(By the Phases of the Moon)

January 1 - Moon's first quarter in Aries
This is a hectic phase and you are on the go from the start. You make rapid progress. There is also an inner peace and contentment. There will be joy as well as great charm and appreciation of beauty. You enter the hurly-burly of life with renewed zest and vigour. Your decisions for the future will be vital. You are calm, firm and focused. You are also content to take a back seat, allow others to take the lead, and are keen to avoid tensions and fights. Your happiness quotient is high. You still have a great desire for recognition in the world. There is great energy, enthusiasm, ideas, true inspiration and the desire to move mountains. Ganesha is with you as you enter the New Year with optimism, hope, dynamism and freedom from preconceived notions. You plan to usher a new creativity to your life.

January 9 - Full Moon in Cancer
While the year starts well, there is also some emotional upheaval, which only you can conquer or solve. There may be slight discontent, restlessness, being cynical and disillusioned with life. You begin to wonder if there is any point in making so much effort – financially, socially, emotionally. Everything is going well for you and there are new projects and a great family life with powerful bonding on the cards. Yet you feel somewhat disillusioned. Prayer and meditation will help. There are many demands on you and you need to be in the right frame of mind to meet them headlong. Ganesha blesses you.

January 16 - Moon's last quarter in Libra

There is buying and selling and many different forces at work. You will concentrate now on deciding the future course of action and how best you can optimise your life. It can be a strange, mixed period but it yields surprisingly good results. You will be divided in your mind about whether it's family bonding or material success that you want more. You will also be dealing with funds, finances and investments. There may be health niggles, and another bout of restlessness grips you. There could be psychosomatic problems and you may need medical attention. You will turn to tantra and mantra, meditation, religion, even esoteric practices. There could also be passion and new relationships. You grapple with two worlds - the material and the spiritual. Despite the many forces at work, there is also love and bonding. Believe in a higher power, says Ganesha. The real world is quite often a difficult place to be and you see that quite clearly.

January 23 - New Moon in Aquarius

You are in deep thought and your higher self will assert itself quite strongly and forcefully. Introspection, psychic ability, philosophical questionings, deep insights and serious contemplation will keep you occupied. This is a time of repose, ease and calm as you inculcate new thoughts, peace and quiet into your life. You are looking for a balance in your personal and professional life. There is also more passion and it will be wise not to get too indiscreet. This is also an emotional phase and many old wounds may re-open. But Ganesha is with you. It is best not to dwell on the past but to move on. I don't have to tell you this as you understand it yourself.

January 31 - Moon's first quarter in Taurus

This is a period of stability and growth. You look to give full expression to your creative talents. You want to live a life that you consider meaningful and rewarding. You may even indulge in charity and philanthropy. You may spend time with homes for the aged or work with children. You will be less concerned with material success and social visibility. But let me add here that you still make rapid progress. You sign new deals and make acquisitions. Passion lingers for a long time in your chart unless dictated otherwise by the personal horoscope. There are happy moments with the family and deep bonding with loved ones. There is also travel and new associations. Ganesha blesses you.

February 7 - Full Moon in Leo

There may be some restlessness and you may want to change jobs or location, even residence. Finances, work and promotions come to the fore. You are in luck as financially and professionally, without your having to fight for them, money and awards just land on your lap. The recent upheaval and turmoil will gradually decrease in intensity as you brush aside the cobwebs. Put the brakes on your feelings and try not to offend people by thinking and speaking hastily. Others may seem too slow for you but people are made differently and you must include everyone in your grand plans. You may sometimes feel scattered, undisciplined and nervous but use these stimulants to grow and seek out new vistas. You are interested in new kinds of experiences and will meet people who will challenge your way of thinking. Even your long-time associates will reveal aspects of themselves that you never knew existed. There will also be new expenses as you make solid expansion plans and reach out to the future with both hands. Ganesha wishes you well.

February 14 - Moon's last quarter in Scorpio

You are in for an overdose of love, lust and passion. You throw caution to the winds and make room for a roll in the hay come what may. Cupid is certainly making inroads into your life. You also strive to get ahead and are prepared to work hard. This period can represent the culmination of successful effort, or it can be a time when the opposition becomes too fierce. You may try to gain control over others which is your nature and your energies are explosive during this time. You should also guard against extravagance as you could be on a spending spree. Depending on the personal chart, you have also been striving to live by the higher self. Family, neighbours, socialising, partying, office/home decoration and renovation are all rewarding. You are valued and appreciated for your abilities. There are interviews, meets, collaborations, conferences, ceremonies, publicity, higher studies and research. It is a frenetic, action-packed time and success crowns you. Ganesha blesses you.

February 21 - New Moon in Pisces

Get a grip on your emotions. They are bubbling over and can hurt if not capped fast. But you are also in action mode. Over the coming weeks you will be positive, alert and optimistic as you look on the brighter side of life. You will work on your self-image and persona. You will be much more focused and proactive in your approach and are determined to improve your public and private image. There is bonding and socialising. You meet up with old friends and spend quality time with the extended family. Ganesha is happy for you.

March 1 - Moon's first quarter in Gemini

You make new plans to acquire comforts, luxuries and the finer things that make a home. You are also keen to improve the quality, depth, intensity of your emotional bonds and ties. You work at making the home happier and more secure, both emotionally and financially. You are not scared to take chances, to stick your neck out, to go that extra mile that makes life such a joyous celebration. You attend marriages, anniversaries and other social functions. You may also travel internationally and make plans for a home away from home. You think of love and the beautiful moments of life in a burst of introspection. You think of what you have lost and gained and how you could have improved your life. Ganesha is with you. Such moments of questioning are vital for the evolution of the soul.

March 8 - Full Moon in Virgo

Family and kith and kin are topmost on your agenda. Your pursuits, interests, even work will centre around the home and your spouse/mate/partner. You will be willing to give a lot and be more forgiving and caring to get closer to those you love. There is new restraint, self-control and willingness to compromise and sacrifice. This week is a warm, caring phase in which you will try to deal in far greater depth with bonds, ties, attachments to home, family, loved ones, older people. Parents, siblings and children will enjoy your presence and caring. You explore and exploit all potential for growth. You look for harmony and balance and Ganesha is happy.

March 15 - Moon's last quarter in Sagittarius

The cricket World Cup is on as I write this. You are in the slog or power play overs and are bruising the cricket ball like Virendra Sehwag or Yusuf Pathan. The pace of work is fast and lively and you accomplish a lot. You earn applause and get the cooperation of those who matter! Bosses, superiors and colleagues interact well with you and all financial issues are sorted out. Scorpio is a powerful sign and can move mountains but it also depends on what type of Scorpio you are – the scorpion, lizard or the eagle. A lot also depends on several factors the least of which is your personal horoscope. Remember that a knife can be used to butter a slice of bread and also slice a throat! Circumstances play a large role in shaping our actions. Believe in a higher power and go with the flow. Ganesha blesses you.

March 22 - New Moon in Aries

You are burning the track and moving ahead with great speed. You are on your toes. You will be well and truly challenged and will be hard at work building your image, contacts, communicating with others, taking time off for travel, ceremonies and family interactions. In several ways, the tempo of life suddenly gets a leg up. New opportunities keep knocking and there will be many demands on your time. There could be many tense moments too. The focus on your work has been strong and definite for some time. There will be new projects and ventures, and even partnerships and collaborations will need to be revamped as obsolete methodologies will need to be jettisoned. You will have to take firm decisions which are not always popular. You also make sincere efforts to strengthen ties and bonds. Believe in Ganesha and push ahead. The way ahead is not paved with gold and you have to struggle a bit.

March 30 - Moon's first quarter in Cancer

The focus is on money issues. The moon's first quarter in Cancer makes you concentrate heavily on funds, finances. Power is the name of the game and you will wish to experience it in all its forms and dimensions. Loans, funds, joint-finances, leasing and buying/ selling will all keep you mighty busy. You are full of zest and you take life head on. You recharge your batteries and there is a lowering of stress and tension as you make time for parties and some fun. Your health and general wellbeing responds well to this shift. You are drawn strongly to thoughts of love and romance, and if already married, to greater bonding with loved ones. This is a productive, busy and rewarding period with many different facets making themselves felt. Ganesha assures you that all will be well.

April 6 - Full Moon in Libra

While expenses soar, you realise the need for a regular and enhanced income. Once more, finance hogs the limelight in your life. Mutual and marital funds, profits, shares, gifts, legacies, estate issues and other fiscal instruments keep you on your toes. Don't push too hard though as it makes sense to maintain a semblance of balance. You need to focus on teamwork and take everyone along with you. You must be objective, impartial and fair and major differences will soon get resolved. Compromise and conciliation will be a good way forward. This is the time for cordial interactions which will not only be important but will actively influence your own progress, gains and contentment. Ganesha blesses you.

April 13 - Moon's last quarter in Capricorn

This is an upbeat period that will have you concentrating on cementing both personal and professional relationships/ties/ partnerships. In fact, this has been a recurrent theme for a while. Your prospects at work, personal relationships and communicating with people will be the central theme of this period. Your social position, status, prestige register a tremendous upswing and will contribute to making you happier than you have been for a while. Those in the media make tremendous progress and you win accolades. There could also be international travel and several new and profitable associations. Ganesha blesses you with happiness and success.

April 21 - New Moon in Taurus

The new moon is in Taurus and this can be a very profitable period indeed. You are greatly energised and full of strength, vigour and determination. You feel absolutely sure of yourself and your self-belief is awesome. Luck is also on your side as all your efforts meet with success. You are charged with passion to do well in whatever you undertake. There will be official travel and a lot of upward mobility in your chosen career. There will also be frenetic contacts, communications and correspondence. You will also dabble in new technology and will upgrade your cyber skills. There could also be an addition to the family and several group outings as you bond well with everyone. You have learnt not to get too aggressive. There will be a lot of indulgences too and Ganesha wants you to go slow on that extra pie.

April 29 - Moon's first quarter in Leo

Your temperament is fiery and feisty as you storm ahead, mowing down all opposition. You are in a crazed rush to get things done your way, and fast. You are a leader, not a camp follower, an initiator, and do not generally thrive in subordinate roles. You take on a lot and are stretching yourself in many directions, aiming at achievements on both the home and work fronts. There will be expenses and some losses too but you make up lost ground like a long distance train. You make huge gains and find solutions to difficult issues. Ganesha sees to it that you get your way most of the time.

May 6 - Full Moon in Scorpio
Along with ambition, perseverance and drive, you appreciate and recognise the value of money; you are also able to handle it well. You know how to use money without allowing money to use you. You also know that it is time to make your work more lucrative. You know full well that money is power and you love the hold it has over others when your pockets are juggling with currency. So great planning and thought is put into financial issues as you study and research funds, loans, buying, selling, investments and stocks. The full moon is in your sign and your passions are ignited. There could be new romance and even if there is no love you may just settle for a roll in the hay. Once again, you should be careful of over exertion and doing too much of a good thing. The temptations are too great but it may all just backfire if you don't exert some discipline. Ganesha wants you to slow down.

May 12 - Moon's last quarter in Aquarius
You are in deep thought. Both this world and the next will become hugely important for you. Alongside your preoccupation with finances, there is deep introspection. In a few cases, there may even be real enlightenment or possibly God-realisation. You build your spiritual and financial assets as you realise now that both are important. You make it a point to improve relationships at the workplace and with those you interact with professionally. The results are immediate as you share the goodies and realise that with just a little tweak in one's habits and behaviour the possibilities are infinite. There is genuine progress and recognition. Ganesha wishes you well.

May 20 - New Moon in Gemini
This is definitely a time to reach out and make waves, make your presence not just felt but truly appreciated. This phase will be more about the 3 C's - contacts, communication correspondence. Relationships will be strengthened including work and new contracts. There will be happy times with the family and many profitable interactions. It is action time as you snap out of any lethargy and zero in, instead, on decisive action. You make waves

professionally and also indulge in a few romantic relationships without a care in the world. There are beautiful moments with loved ones, family gatherings, get-togethers, and all the comforts of home. The domestic scene turns lively as you have fun and share leisure pursuits. Ganesha blesses you.

May 28 - Moon's first quarter in Virgo

You expand your circle of activities and go all out, making this a time for decisive, definite action. God is truly in the details. There is profitable travel and a fresh influx of ideas, energy and ingenuity. You broaden your horizons and parents, elders and even in-laws are a source of joy and happiness. You try to reconcile the divergent demands on your time and energy and make space in your life for all that you want to accomplish. At work, too, you streamline office procedures aiming for greater efficiency and productivity. You are very systematic and professional in your approach and manage to achieve a lot. Your planning is meticulous and every tiny detail is worked through with a comb. Ganesha is watching over your every move as you begin the slow march to substantial progress.

June 4 - Full Moon in Sagittarius

A lot is happening in your life. You are pushed into several corners and manage to wriggle out of tight situations. You will focus on professional interests now, put everything else in your life on hold, and get the best possible results. There is personal satisfaction and recognition too. Once this is achieved, there is time for deep bonding. At the same time, despite many other commitments, your family involvement does not lessen. This is a good time to assess your aspirations, realign your focus and start afresh. This is a time when you will factor in domestic responsibilities as they will play a major role in your life. You will also be meeting new people, travelling and incurring huge expenses. This is a good period and Ganesha hopes that you make the most of it.

June 11 - Moon's last quarter in Pisces

A new love enters your life and there are many stolen moments. You forget work, the family and the rest of the world and may even take off to some holiday destination for deep, passionate and intimate moments. This person could also be someone from the past and it is possible that you are finishing some unfinished strands of a hastily ended relationship from not so long ago. You are evolving into another dimension and if there are unfinished matters to attend to please complete them as it will help the soul journey. You are on a quest to know yourself, to understand yourself, to complete yourself, to fulfil your destiny. There are many parts to the full moon and it is all a part of the quest for perfection or what can come close to it. Ganesha is happy.

June 19 - New Moon in Gemini

You will be pre-occupied with assets of all kinds. Your possessions and investments are most important in this period as you build a strong financial base. The focus is clearly on finances and its management. You look at all types of investments, realty, stocks, gold and silver, and drive your portfolio manager relentlessly. You feel that this is the time to prepare a nest's egg and secure your family. You are driven by this thought and nothing else makes sense. You look closely at inheritance, wills, deeds, mutual funds and every instrument of finance in your possession. You know that once this issue is settled and locked up you can focus on family affairs without hindrance. Ganesha wishes you well. You love being in control of a situation and know well that money in the pocket affords freedom. It also helps, in a way, to control your destiny. Money can buy dignity and opportunity and that makes life happen. Under all the altruism and philanthropy rests a keen, razor sharp and shrewd mind.

June 27 - Moon's first quarter in Libra

For the better part of the year, you have concentrated on work, serious issues and money-making ventures. It is time now to relax, having set your house in order. Entertainment, amusement, games, hobbies, warm interactions with children, and love and romance will excite you, please you, and fulfil you. There may be a long holiday with the family and there is a good possibility of overseas travel.

There could also be a marriage in the family or an addition to it. You may even look at adoption seriously and those having difficulty conceiving may visit infertility clinics; as you can see the mood is different! It is time for something new. There is also great family bonding and a grand time with children. Ganesha blesses you.

July 3 - Full Moon in Capricorn

You are back to work and ambition. You look at ways of earning more. Those in the media do particularly well. The main focus could be summed up in the 3 T's - trade, ties and travel. Your inter-personal skills are tested and the key to achievements and success will depend on how you relate to people. You realise that it is the time for contacts and communication, journeys and mobility, gaining in alertness and awareness, a certain sense of values and goals. You make the right contacts and sign profitable contracts. You are shrewd and have developed the right mindset to do full justice to whatever you have undertaken. You are on your toes and there is never a dull moment. This is a period of stability and growth and Ganesha is happy for you.

July 11 - Moon's first quarter in Aries

You make steady progress. You are introspective and thoughtful but there is also a lot of socialising and interaction, making waves in the party scene and making your presence felt in domestic circles. A sense of joy and fulfilment is a strong possibility. Your moods and feelings reign supreme and colour all your actions and interactions. Love and hate come to you in equal measure. There are new challenges in every sphere of life and you work hard to set your house in order. Ganesha is with you.

July 19 - New Moon in Cancer

You spend quality time with loved ones. You are in a sober mood and many thoughts plague your mind. You want to be homebound and yet you also want to go out into the world and make waves, make money and earn fame. You are driven by power and can work relentlessly to get it. You are determined to find ways to concretise your achievements improve property, acquire belongings, and try to deal pragmatically and sensibly with the material concerns of your family, loved ones and your own self. Personal happiness will depend largely on these factors. You are aware of what needs to be done and build on it to consolidate your affairs. The emphasis shifts to several areas of life - from trade, travel, matters relating to spirituality, concern for the entire human race, and to world peace, social justice, law and order. Your spiritual inclinations too are really strong but too much idealism may be misplaced. You bond well with the family and have many special moments like a holiday together or a second honeymoon with your spouse. Ganesha watches over you. There are many fun times and several disparate and different influences at play.

July 26 - Moon's last quarter in Scorpio

There is an edge to this phase and a new intensity. You are moving ahead with gusto. Fresh new concerns/projects may either be planned or initiated. You need to utilise your several talents productively. There could be correspondence, trips for both recreation and work, and several new profitable contacts. You realise that it is not how learned or knowledgeable you are that matters but who you know. The real world operates on an old school network. This is an important realisation and you brush up your PR skills. There is no point being a daffodil flowering in the desert. Even the beautiful Aishwarya Rai was noticed in Mumbai, the fashion and media capital of India. You fully realise how important it is to be in the right place at the right time. I paraphrase Ayn Rand who stated that profitable realty depends on three factors – location, location and location. You understand the full import of all this. Go with your conscience, says Ganesha.

August 2 - Full Moon in Aquarius

Your thoughts are in a whirl. This is a time of serious, even pessimistic thinking. Communication with others becomes not only more significant but also more difficult. If you get too serious, you could run the risk of losing your sense of perspective. Your mental and intellectual viewpoint narrows as you look at new ideas, opinions and methods of communication. This consumes you as you embark on a personal campaign to root out old ideas and notions that have outlived their usefulness. You need also to look at important alternatives that may, at first, seem too idealistic or risky. There is a different type of intensity this week. You drop old relationships without a thought and enter new ones also without a thought. You are a bit reckless. You are attempting to revamp your life. There are dangers in such moves. Tread carefully, says Ganesha.

August 9 - Moon's last quarter in Taurus

You reach a stable point in your life and dealings. This is an excellent time for working a single idea through completely. This is an important period and if you do the requisite planning and go through the details with a comb the consequences can be very significant. Do not look for perfection as it doesn't exist even in nature. When dealing with yourself and colleagues, friends and family be careful not to become too concerned with such trivia. I use the word trivia deliberately because perfection is unattainable and in seeking it you will miss the wood for the trees. If you get too exacting and critical, you will alienate others and all your attempts at doing good and meaning well will backfire. Ganesha blesses you.

August 17 - New Moon in Leo

You make considerable progress in all your ventures and establish yourself. You get rewards and awards and earn the respect of peers and superiors. There are promotions and perks and people rally around you as you assume a leadership role. You have reached a point of equilibrium and your actions are reliable and consistent; all the soul searching has worked well for you. Your whole objective is to ensure that your affairs are running smoothly and on schedule. Your approach is disciplined, well ordered and mature. There is definite progress. There are also new expenses and love affairs. Do not get haughty or impertinent or too domineering and demanding which is often the case with you. You will sparkle, says Ganesha. This is a good phase.

August 24 - Moon's first quarter in Sagittarius

There is rapid movement in all spheres of activity. The only problem is that you find it difficult to make changes conservatively. It will help if you are more flexible and bend a little or take time out to see the other person's point of view. You are driven and ambitious and stop at nothing to get ahead in life. People help you and there is all-round growth. Ganesha goads you on.

August 31 - Full Moon in Pisces

You could be more reserved than usual in forming new relationships. But there is no need to be too cautious. You will meet with many new people and learn a lot from interacting with them. These new interactions will be a learning process and you gain tremendously. If you watch this period closely, you will realise much later that it played a very significant role in your life. There could be a new relationship with a much older person, maybe a teacher or a guru, and your spiritual grounding will be further strengthened. Ganesha blesses you. While you busy yourself with work and play, it will be wise to remember that the great seer Sri Aurobindo said that all life is yoga. So everything you do is a type of yoga!

September 8 - Moon's first quarter in Gemini

You are moving in several directions at once like a headless chicken. You are checking out several openings and playing the field. You test your potential with others and come out with flying colours. You are the master in the ring. You are in a highly competitive frame of mind and emerge triumphant at work. Your word will be law but do not get too authoritarian. This influence stimulates your ambition and desire for power out of all proportion. You could get ruthless and can create enemies. It may be a better idea to slow down and compromise and be willing to enjoy the success of others. You need to carry the team along with you. Ganesha insists that you develop an accommodating spirit and learn not to run roughshod over others. This is the only way to succeed. The planet is a large family and compromise and letting go sometimes can be a good, tactical move.

September 16 - New Moon in Virgo

While matters seem more settled and life is on a more even keel, the tables turn a bit as you encounter another person on a power trip. You both square off like rutting rams. It makes no sense and it is imperative that you back off before someone gets hurt in the process. Determine your rights as an individual and stand up for them. But leave it at that. Do not overstep your bounds as this power struggle could well be with someone in authority in your own profession. Away from the professional confrontations, there will be time spent with family. An elder relative may need hospitalisation and there will be other domestic demands. Go with the flow, says Ganesha. Also, go slow on the confrontation part.

September 22 - Moon's first quarter in Capricorn

You find your way out of tight situations. You may be surrounded by conditions of breakdown and decay and you prepare to rebuild. Many energies are at play, and you must use them cautiously. Do not be in an aggressive mode and become insufferable. I repeat that you need to show the softer side of you too. Under extreme conditions, aggression can lead to highly inflammable behaviour. It may be a good idea to take time off and visit a shrine or go on a pilgrimage. Take a break and try out yoga and meditation or anything that can soothe your frayed nerves. Ganesha asks you to delve within and optimise your powerful, regenerative energies.

September 30 - Full Moon in Aries

You move ahead now and this can be a very positive time. This is a period of culmination in your life, and you will be tempted to expand beyond any reasonable limit. There is no question that you have a good chance for success. However, you should not restrict yourself solely to material and physical growth now. You can look seriously at spiritual growth which is the need of the hour. This is what will make you truly happy. Objects that you acquire like possessions, money and even social prestige are all hollow in the final analysis. They are not the state of satisfaction itself; they are merely a means to an end, they are methods to make you feel happy, however superficial and fleeting the feeling may be. Look for solutions and answers within yourself. This is a critical juncture in your life and could well be a turning point depending on what course of action you decide to take. Ganesha guides you all the way.

October 8 - Moon's last quarter in Cancer

This is probably the best phase of the year on several fronts. You move rapidly ahead and zoom past the finish line. All your problems will be resolved and the periods of strife come to an end. You understand your mistakes and learn from them. You win accolades, promotions and perks and climb the mightiest peaks. You are the talk of the town, the cock of the walk, you talk the talk and walk the walk. You will be honoured and heard and people will look up to you. You will chair high-powered meetings in the fanciest locales of the world. Mercury, the mighty planet, is all-powerful now. It favours travels/ meetings/conferences/ interviews/ trips/ more brain power/ contacts/ communication/ correspondence/contracts. Mercury has a special connection with the circuits of the brain. Chess, crossword and other such games belong to Mercury. Also, short distance runners and spin bowlers are controlled by Mercury. Mercury, in short, is the ambassador and salesman of the zodiac. It is very important and occupies a prominent position now for over 20 days. Seize the moment, suggests Ganesha, and make it count.

October 15 - New Moon in Libra

You are doing fabulously well. The influence of Mercury continues. Work has never been better and you are deeply in love in a beautiful, powerful and deeply bonding way. You may shift to a new house or buy a fancy new car. There could be foreign travel, a marriage or a birth in the family. All debts, if any, have been cleared. You have made enormous profits too and you are at a high, flying away with all trophies. It is a great time for media folk and those in banking, insurance and finance. There is love, achievement, contentment and peace. You take on new ventures, projects, collaborations and partnerships, spend money, make money, and are the soul of the party circuit. Way to go, says Ganesha. There is very little that you can do wrong in the mood that you are in. it is a lucky streak and has come at the right time too. The heavens have opened up for you. What are you waiting for?

October 22 - Moon's first quarter in Capricorn

The good run continues. You have worked hard very conscientiously, sincerely and mostly selflessly. You richly deserve the rewards that are now coming to you. You are in one of the best periods of your life. It is a time for the big P's - position, pelf, perks and privileges. But please don't allow all this to go to your head. There is no need for arrogance or over-confidence, or you will just spoil the party. There will be family commitments too and elder relatives may give you some anxious moments. There will be a lot to excite you. The areas of profit will include trade, partnerships, law courts, legal issues and journeys for business and pleasure. There will be progress and many new plans. The results are spectacular as you grow by leaps and bounds on all fronts. You have fingers in several pies and do not burn any of them. Ganesha blesses you as you reap a rich harvest.

October 29 - Full Moon in Taurus

You are on the fast track of growth and progress. It is definitely money and material gains that will be the focus and theme of this period. All instruments of finance, the signing of contracts, promissory notes, lease or rent agreements for house or office will take centre stage. You also focus on fashion, clothes, dieting, your personal image and how you project yourself. There will be expenses on pedigreed and tasteful acquisitions. You will go in for a complete makeover and become a new person altogether. Your health is fine, the mood is upbeat and you feel positive, energetic and enthusiastic. You come up with new, innovative or even quirky ideas and they all work well. You are creative and successful too. Ganesha watches over you.

November 7 - Last quarter in Leo

You give the term 'king size' a new meaning altogether. A truly wonderful phase in your birth period that is packed with fun, frolic and pleasure. You have been busy with more serious concerns, you have achieved a lot and now you are more than ready to relax, have a ball. You seek enjoyment and thrills from life. Your children and hobbies, leisure pursuits, fun-time activities that provide entertainment, amusement and romance - pictures, parties, theatricals, all the fine arts, will be both, attractive and lucrative.

You display creativity and energy and direct it into earning well. Money and honey are yours, says Ganesha. You have all the ingredients for happiness. There is spiritual growth, emotional balance and the sweet fragrance of success permeating your life. You are well on the road to many further triumphs in life.

November 13 - New Moon in Scorpio

Action stations have been activated. You are on the speedboat to success. There is a lot on your plate to choose from. Mutual funds, shares, stocks, capital-raising and all other money matters come to the fore. Your esteem in the community gets a huge lift which satisfies your ego drives immensely. You also turn to prayer and meditation for guidance. That is sensible and is an indication that you are still grounded. There is also romance blooming and this could well lead to the next level. But Ganesha is with you and the latter half of the year is particularly rewarding. All that you embark on in this phase leads to success.

November 20 - Moon's first quarter in Aquarius

You end the year with spectacular fireworks. Mercury, the mighty planet, is once again in your chart. As I mentioned earlier, it is all-powerful and favours travels/meetings/conferences/ interviews/ trips/more brain power/contacts/communication/ correspondence/contracts. It occupies a prominent position now for over a fortnight. Need I say more? Ganesha has blessed you and the stars are in your favour. You continue living the good life. You make money and rapid progress. Health is good and you bond well with loved ones. What more would one ask of life?

November 28 - Full Moon in Gemini

The good run continues. There could be international travel and you may attend or even chair high-powered conferences and meetings. Your prestige soars and there could be rewards galore. Those in banking and insurance do particularly well. This is a truly exciting and exhilarating time for you. Strive to get the maximum out of life in every which way you can. You enjoy life to the hilt. There is new love and several profitable bonds, ties, relationships.

You are in great demand and you give off yourself with ease and generosity. Ganesha insists that you seize the moment and live it fully. You will be attending all sorts of functions including marriages and anniversaries. There is a good chance that you may even be hosting some of these!

December 6 - Moon's last quarter in Virgo

You finally find time for a break. These moments are necessary to prevent a breakdown. It has all been too rushed and chaotic and you have managed to achieve a lot in no time. You look for a moment to retire, to take a break from the madding crowd. It is a time for introspection. You look for a welcome interlude after the frenzied, almost manic state of affairs of the last few weeks. You are in gratitude and in a contemplative mood. You visit places of healing and check into a resort or spa to rejuvenate. It will also be a good time to plan the next year. They say 2013 will usher a new consciousness, and even much more than that, possibly even the end of the world as we know it. You are curious and if there is a higher consciousness at work, you most certainly want to be a part of it. You want to be included in what Sri Aurobindo called the 'supramental man'. I must insist that I use the male gender only for convenience and women are, of course, included as they are the true and real *shakti* and the *yin* of all life. Ganesha blesses you.

December 13 - New Moon in Sagittarius

The frenzy of year-end festivities grabs you by the collar and you give a good account of yourself in both the work area and the party circuit. You handle the work scene well and also find the time to party. So business and pleasure are well mixed. You are a star and everyone is impressed with your accomplishments. You run through the opposition and also do it in style. Health may need some attention, particularly the health of elders. There is money and honey and festivity in the air and you can't be left out of the party. It will be a good idea to thank Ganesha for this wonderful year. Of course, I must always add that these are mere generalisations and an accurate prediction will depend on the individual horoscope. Also, astrology impels and doesn't compel. There are many factors influencing one's life including one's circumstances, the family, the country, and one's free will. Additionally, please remember that though I am correct more often than not, I am merely human and prone to error too.

December 20 - Moon's first quarter in Pisces

You are delighted that it has all gone your way, particularly towards the year-end. You are fulfilled and happy, but not ready to rest on your laurels. You are not one to idle away time and focus now on the 3 C's -- contacts, communications and computers. You want the whole world to be accessible to you and you are itching to get cracking in 2013. You invest in technology and get adept in the use of the latest innovations. You know only too well that technology shrinks the world and you try to master the e-universe. You want to be in control and in command. Ganesha wishes you well.

December 28 - Full Moon in Cancer

You feel optimistic and hopeful about the future. You feel that everything is going to be just great and this is not a delusion. You know well how to tweak success in your life and you are smart enough to learn from your mistakes. You will feel very idealistic. You look for higher realities, and truth is very important in your life now. You want to know how the universe works. This is a good journey and you will gain many insights through the study of philosophy, metaphysics and the occult. Your energies, optimism and self-confidence are high and you are willing to take risks that you would not ordinarily take. You may indulge in speculation or just get rid of the elements in your life that you have always depended on for security. You now feel that they could have limited the expansion of your consciousness. You want to experience all aspects of the world that you live in and there may be some pruning necessary as you go about cutting down on some material needs and ambitions. You have seen it all and now want to simplify your life. Ganesha welcomes the move.

SCORPIO

KEY DATES

January
2*-3, 6*-8, 11*-12, 16*-18, 21*-22, 25*-26, 29*-31.
Foreign and home affairs prove lucky. Gains and gaiety, says Ganesha!

February
1-4, 8*-9, 13*-14, 17-18, 21-22, 26-27.
Work at full speed, full throttle, and from it, status and power, richly deserved.

March
2-4, 7*-9, 12-13, 17*-18, 21-22, 25*-26, 29*-31.
Friends and fulfilment are the 2 F's. Therefore, lots of socializing for you and you revel in it.

April
1-5, 8-10, 13*-14, 17*18, 21*22, 26-27.
Trips and travel are an outlet for your restlessness and energy. Keep some impulses in check, though.

May
1*-2, (important) 6*-7, (important) 10-11, 15, 19*-20, (important) 23-24, 28*-29.
Full power and energy as you play to win, to impress, to dazzle.

June
1-3, 7-8. 11*-12, 15-16, 19*-21, 24*-26, 29*-30.
Finance, family, food, - all the 3F's of marvelous progress, of impressive performance, too!

July
1*, 4*-5, 8*-9, 12*-13, 17-18, 21*-22, (important) 26-28, 31.
Trips, ties, romance - all come together to keep you busy.

August
1,4*-6, 9-11, 13-14, 18*-19, 23-24, 27*-29.
Lots of ideas and plans come into play as you seek a direction, a new meaning, not just to your life but to your actions.

September
1*-2, 5*-6, 9*-11, 14*- 16, 19-21, 25-26, 28*-29.
Creativity, children, joy, all light your fire. Lots of emotions and excitement, both professionally and personally.

October
2*-3, 7-8, 11*-13, 16-18, 23*-26, 29-31.
A bitter sweet time as you forge new links, partnerships. Obviously old ones are broken or fade away.

November
2*-3, 8*-9, 13*-14, 18-19, 22*-23, 26-27, 30*.
Relationships once again; meeting people, marriage, partnerships, all these will be important.

December
1, 5*-6, 9-11, 15*-16, 19*-20, 23-24, 27-29.
Your mood, your attitude, your confidence will all soar upwards, as you have a firm sense of direction.

Sagittarius

November 22 - December 21

SAGITTARIUS

(November 22 - December 21)

ELEMENT AND RULING PLANET: Fire and Jupiter.

STRENGTHS: Energetic, ambitious, generous, freedom loving, a seeker of challenges, open to new ideas and exploration.

WEAKNESS: Jealous, possessive rude, can be over optimistic, and can exaggerate.

SYMBOL: The Archer – represents directness, high aims, love for outdoor activates, and the chase.

MATCHING SIGN: Sagittarius and Gemini.

MAGICAL BIRTHSTONE: Topaz and Turquoise – attract love, protects from harm and give the wearer, ability to see the future.

SAGITTARIUS

YEARLY FORECAST

Main Trend

Friends, acquaintances, closer family ties, new bonds - all these and more are what make this year special. There can be a whiff of fresh romance blowing into your life, or greater bonding/ caring/ closeness in marriage. The reason is clear: Communication, imagination, cleverness will be an intrinsic part of you, adding greatly to your relationship, in particular. I say this despite frustrating holdups/ conflicts with relatives/ siblings/ associates who can't catch up with you. Travelling, too, is important but not entirely smooth. Impediments to growth, one might call them, but you take them in your stride. Trips, holidays, will give you a change, a fresher outlook. In any case, there's also your hugely exciting sense of adventure. Ceremony and your public image all make for luck, liveliness and, above all, a sense of joyous fulfilment. It could also come from lots of partying, entertaining, companionship, good times with friends. But that's really not the entire picture for you. Work concerns are not pushed out of your mind. Love and marriage, children and creativity at work, all register gains this year, too; though work brings added responsibilities that you take over willingly.

Ganesha says, great good news for Sagittarians on two fronts:

a) If you have been suffering from hallucinations, disorganised speech and behaviour (like dressing inappropriately, crying frequently), delusions, social withdrawal, and cognitive deficits, you will see the end of it. In other words, your mental, physical, emotional health will improve this year.

b) **Thanks to Jupiter in your 7th angle, the emphasis will be on marriage and partnership at all levels.**

To whet your appetite for what lies ahead in this forecast, here are a few quotes on marriage:

'Wedlock, a padlock'

– English proverb

'Man's best possession is a sympathetic wife.'

- Euripides, Antigone (5th century BC)

'The bachelor is a peacock, the engaged man a lion, and the married man a jackass.'

- German proverb

'When an old man marries, death laughs.'

- German proverb

'How marriage ruins a man! It's as demoralising as cigarettes, and far more expensive.'

– Oscar Wilde, Lady Windermere's Fan (1892)

Here is what Pandit Parsai says about Jupiter in the 7th house or angle: The 7th house is yet another house wherein Jupiter showers favours on the individual in money matters, in income, in earnings, in enhancing prestige and power, granting success in a love affair, getting a suitable matrimonial match, also in granting success in buying and selling. Jupiter helps in marriage at the right or desired age.

Jupiter gives the capacity to gain an upper hand over enemies or adversaries on the civil side (but not on the criminal side), in matrimonial disputes, in matters of arbitration, in managing the property and assets and even business or office affairs of the house. It helps in quick recovery from physical injuries, provided it's a bleeding injury.

It also helps in securing loans from banking and other similar financing institutions for any kind of business venture or enterprise.

The individual can, himself or herself, become a successful banker or insurer. Jupiter in the 7th house provides scope for money lending against mortgage of gold and jewellery, or earning a livelihood from running a hotel, motel, restaurant, furniture and furnishing trade. Some readers might question how the 7th house is concerned with livelihood. The answer is that the 7th house is directly and importantly concerned with the buying and selling of goods for business and the gains therefore.

One unique point regarding Jupiter in the 7th house is that these individuals have a remarkably good memory and they are able to express their thoughts and ideas very clearly and impressively in writing but often it is seen that they are not very impressive speakers.

If readers were to investigate minutely they would find that some of the judges on the benches of the higher and lower courts may have Jupiter in the 7th house and they preferred service in judiciary instead of functioning as a lawyer because they considered themselves less proficient in speaking. The same is the case with some chartered accountants, who prefer to prepare returns, representations, notes for submission and appeals but send their colleagues and juniors to argue the cases before taxation authorities. Cases are not rare where a great author is not so impressive while speaking in public. Some actors and actresses are good at acting, but not equally at dialogue delivery.

One major advantage of Jupiter in the 7th house is that whenever there is any problem, which might involve, besides other things, a monetary angle, the family of the spouse comes forward to extend some monetary help and all other kinds of support to the individual.

By Vedic astrology, the 7th angle or house stands for the spouse, sex partner, marriage, adultery, lust or passion, nature and character of spouse, sexual union, secret love affairs, journeys, deviation from one's path, partnership in business, overt enemies, quarrels, theft, loss of memory, recovery of lost wealth, progress, attainment of status, the grandfather, the brother's son and death.

In medical astrology: lower urinary tract, anal canal, semen, seminal vesicles, urethra, prostate, the sexual act. (Elements of Vedic Astrology by Dr. KS Charak)

Ganesha says, the F's of fame, fortune, fancies, and freebies will be yours. You will be in the news as well as make news! "Fame is the perfume of heroic deeds," said the great philosopher, Socrates. And who are we to dispute him? Fame is the magnifying glass of life itself!

Why have I accentuated the fame angle? For two reasons. First, it is the time, the right time, for you to be popular and as I always say, astrology is all about timing. You deserve it. Secondly, Jupiter, the planet of prosperity and pelf, will be in your 7th angle of RELATIONSHIPS at every level. I might add that modern astrology is all about relationships and behaviour patterns, since we have realised their value, relevance and importance as never before.

How come this paean of praise and prediction? Jupiter, the planet of plenty, prosperity and wisdom (a rare mix) whirls away in your 7th angle of achievements and approbation. The 7th angle signifies:

a) Connections, contacts, reaching out to people and places;
b) Journeys, ceremonies, legal matters;
c) Public relationships and competitions, change of locale/ surroundings;
d) Collaborations and co-operation, wedding/ engagement;
e) Blowing hot and cold in relationships.

Jupiter in 7th angle means it could be a live-in relationship, a permanent attachment, a mighty bonding. That wedlock could be a padlock is, of course, a different matter, as I frequently say. Anyway, why not try it out and find out yourself?

Ganesha says, now you know the real impact of Jupiter in your 7th angle. The 7th angle stands for people at large, that is crowds, population, and so on. Therefore, it, in a way, also stands for your opposite number, be it a friend or lover, partner or enemy. The strongest, emotional partnership is marriage, since against it, enemies go to a court of law, or engage in fist fights, the tearing out and pulling of hair, or a shootout, as the Americans say.

The other significant features of Jupiter in your 7th angle will cover:

1) Change of locale,
2) Contests,
3) Sales and PR,
4) Marketing and distribution,
5) Opening of new branches,
6) Expansion at all levels,
7) Being flexible, accommodating, more accepting of views other than your own, and yes, Sagittarians are tenacious but understanding and sympathetic.

Jupiter:

Jupiter, your chief planet, is positioned happily with Pluto till 11th June. The effect will be acquisition of property, be it a shop, house, factory or godown. Let me know how right or wrong I am on this prediction. Rentals, leases also come within the range of my prediction. I am not a god. I admit openly that sometimes I go wrong, but that's the likelihood I see.

Neptune:

Neptune will be in a superb placing with Saturn after 6th October.

You will meet strange people (we call them "characters"), who will keep you busy and thrilled. You will laugh and cry with them. Journeys, possibly with a stop-over, are also foretold. Gains are possible, maybe in February, June and August.

Mercury:

Mercury is in charge of your sectors of publicity, alliance, marriage and journey. From 30th October to 14th November, Mercury performs headers, resulting in goals and victories. You will create a fusion of work and pleasure in just the right proportion. And yes, there is a chance of wedlock, an engagement, a major contract or business deal, or even a great publicity campaign coming through. You will gatecrash headlong into the corridors of fame. Travel and collaborations are likely. Yes, you can start a project. This is a time when you will have renewed vigour and verve and feel at your optimistic, ebullient best. 'Attitude spells attainment' is an original quote, coined by me, which you can shamelessly borrow and use, if you wish to.

Venus:

Venus will move in your sun sign from 17th December 2012 to 9th January 2013. You will have a chance to marry, love well, if not wisely (you can never have both) and, an opportunity to 'warm your hands and heart in the fireplace of love in winter'. Relationships of all kinds will be in strong focus. Ties and collaborations, travel and publicity, on the one hand, but also rivalry and competition, legal cases and confrontations, ventures and adventures, are the other noteworthy features. You sporty Sagittarians usually like to take chances.

Mars:

Mars moves in your sun sign from 8th October to 17th November. And this planet helps you in different ways. It will give you the speed, energy and luck to finish the year in a great blaze of glory.

Ganesha agrees. If married, your spouse could have a minor or major wish-fulfilment, your children and you might be in for a major move, there could be important changes in your work area. You will have to work that much harder, really put your shoulder to the wheel, which though an old world phrase, is still in use because it conveys the meaning so picturesquely and aptly. Agreed?

Saturn will continue his slow marathon run in your 11th angle till 5th October 2012. You can hope for a wish fulfilment. But very surprisingly a loss of wealth is also possible. Why? Saturn often gives mixed reasons. Saturn means delays and disappointments. The 11th angle means gains and good things; therefore I have to combine the bad qualities of Saturn with the fine qualities of the 11th angle. You my readers are clever and sharp. So, I am sure you understand. Saturn also refers to uncle, mother, elder brother, learning and property.

From 6th October Saturn will move in your 12th angle. The 12th angle means expenses, losses, religion, godliness, salvation, limitation, sometimes even imprisonment. In 2012, Saturn will only start his slow but sure run of about two and a half years in your 12th angle. You will feel the heat and the impact in 2013 and 2014.

Take care of expenses, finances, relationships with family and close associates. IN ANY SORT OF CONTACTS, CONTRACTS, COMMUNICATION, MESSAGES, TAXES, FOOD AND FLAVOURS, BE VERY CAREFUL AND CAUTIOUS. You are often quite generous and trusting. As your astrologer, I do not want others to take advantage of your good nature. Be smart. It pays. Good Luck!

SAGITTARIUS

MONTH-BY-MONTH

JANUARY

You are more than willing to take risks and gamble. But please a close tab on greed, if any. In the long run, it will not work in your favour. Financial matters remain at the forefront throughout this month. There will be a financial opportunity in the first half of the year, says Ganesha. You are firing on all cylinders and blazing the turf. Please remember that the choices you make now will significantly impact your future. There will be tricky domestic problems to handle. But this apart, in general, the circumstances of your life and your inner energies are working quite well together. Without stretching yourself, you are able to make significant progress. There is love in your life and you will be on cloud nine.

You will face many critical developments as you will be challenged by a slew of factors. You love your freedom and hate being tied down but now you will have to make compromises and adjustments. Go with the flow; better times will follow. As the month proceeds, your burning ambitions may be thwarted temporarily. Do not squander valuable resources. Do not overstretch; know your limits. This is Ganesha's warning and mine too. So please take heed.

FEBRUARY

Ganesha charges this period with creativity. Of course, this is not a personal chart reading and it is merely a general observation. Writers, artists, actors, TV directors will be in fine fettle. February, in short, favours creativity. It will also be a good time to appear for a test, competition and interview. From February, the main trend will be domestic for a while. With the full moon in Leo, you are moving ahead fast and in a very flamboyant manner. Do not succumb to ego drives and excessive pride. Take care not to act in an overbearing manner as there will be opposition to your plans and you will gather more enemies than you need to.

This is a period of love, joy, eros and merriment. You will be surrounded with love and, I dare say, what a way to be! The period will be sizzling. There are also emotional moments and you remember the past with fondness. This is a good time to go home and meet old friends and loved ones. If you haven't met your parents for a while, spend time with them. It will be well worth it.

MARCH

Jupiter is vital now and favours you in games of chance. Ganesha says this is also the right month to make travel plans or go on a journey. Once you know for sure where you are headed, you Sagittarians are hard to beat in the pursuit of goals. Ganesha says, there will be a sense of adventure and daring. You will also be outspoken and may ruffle feathers in the process. New people will enter your life and there may be a woman – regardless of your gender - who suddenly comes into your life to help you out. This will be a windfall; so accept it happily. There will be many experiences now which will be difficult to fathom. Just believe that it is all Ganesha's blessings. You are in a period of incorporation and assimilation; the universe throws many things at you and you accept whatever can nourish and support you. Towards mid-month, there is a semblance of stability in your affairs and you forge ahead. You feel happy and optimistic and manage to achieve a lot. The mood is also contagious and colleagues rally around you. The last quarter of the month is in your sign. This is a splendid period, so make the most of it. You forge ahead; nothing can stop you. The world is your oyster. This is a time of preparation for the events that will possibly follow. Use this period well to make your world strong and secure.

APRIL

Ganesha blesses you with a fine time to live and love and laugh, easing some of the pressures you have been prey to over the last few weeks. All this will definitely add to the quality of life that you are striving for. You reach out, interact, and enjoy congenial company. There is recognition for your achievements. Employers and your peer group will be impressed with your diligence. You have many new offers coming your way and it is a good time to go flat out, which you do. You feel optimistic and generous. Without a doubt, there is a lot of progress. You are moving ahead at breakneck speed. Along with the hard work, new gains and the money you make, you may also be excited by a new interest in religious and spiritual thought. Ganesha is happy for you. Towards mid-month, there is balance and equilibrium in your life. There is growth at many levels - in consciousness, in your profession, in your social life, and in all personal matters. Under Leo's influence towards the month-end, you can look at yourself, your work, your family and the world with reasonable calm and detachment. This is also a good time for higher knowledge, self-awareness, occult studies and travel.

MAY

The tough get going when the going gets tough. You will have to push yourself really hard now. This is the month to work hard. Ganesha says it is also a month not to attempt to go it alone. Hone your people skills, curb your impatience, and be more tolerant and giving in your attitude. Ganesha says that it would be a good idea to reduce your stress levels, perhaps even the intensity of your work. This period is very intense. You will also need to be very flexible now. Towards mid-month, with the influence of Aquarius, you are filled with new thoughts and make many changes to your life. You may also get a bit morbid or melancholic, but it is a passing phase. As the month ends, you will break free from restrictions and obligations. There is new freedom, with travel thrown in and you make contact with people in a big way. You open the higher chakras and wear the mantle of nobility with ease and pride.

JUNE

There will be a lot of movement and you will be everywhere all at once. Journeys and affection are emphasized in this month. Collaborations are also highlighted. The human element will be what makes the difference. You will be on a quest to acquire true knowledge and wisdom. You will be motivated by new learning and will seek knowledge, not merely for gain but out of the sheer love of it. Ganesha blesses you as you forge ahead with the full moon in your sign. This is also a period of new beginnings. You are networking well and are super-charged. You will widen both your personal horizons and the scope of your activities. Towards the month-end, the moon's first quarter is in Libra and the possibilities are endless. You will get what you truly deserve.

JULY

This is the period of gains and profits. Ganesha sums this month up simply: money will befriend you. As simple as that; nothing more, nothing less. There will be spills and thrills. You have courage, confidence and charisma to get the desired results. This is a very ambitious period when you push ahead on all cylinders. This is a phase of hard, sustained work. The full moon in Capricorn makes you want to climb to the top rung of the ladder. You make serious connections with extended family, colleagues, subordinates, peers and superiors. The new moon is in Cancer mid-month and many domestic issues take over your space. It is this theme that makes you love, provide for and nurture your family, children, and elder relatives. As the month ends, the intensity of the phase takes you by surprise. It is the influence of Scorpio. The money angle is well covered. It is steady, secure, if not spectacular.

AUGUST

While you make progress, there is a chance that you could have bitten off more than you can chew. You seem to be stuffing yourself with goodies. Ganesha says this month will be spectacular for travel, trade, ties, telecommunication and transport, the 5T's. From the 10th, you will sail along comfortably and make rapid headway in your activities. A very strong and definite indication is of overseas trade and business dealings. You may also plough deep into spiritual pursuits. You are a mix of several influences now: you are exceptionally creative, and also willing to help the needy and the downtrodden. You will be far more composed, caring and calm. You manage to invest wisely and find yourself entertaining lavishly. The new moon is in Leo mid-month and there will be new bonds, a touch of romance, of glorious passion and sex. As the month ends, with the moon's first quarter in your sign, it is a period of hope and promise. This phase is a valuable learning experience, says Ganesha.

SEPTEMBER

Many things that you had embarked on earlier finally lead to success and fruition. Popularity and publicity, status and honour, hard work and rapid advancement in your profession/business/job/career are indicated, says Ganesha. September is a power-packed month and gives a thrust to all that you do. There is tremendous movement in all directions. You are obsessed with reaching out to people who matter to you. You also win applause at work and find recognition.

The new moon ushers new trends: hospitality, guests and visitors, developing social interactions. As I have mentioned many times, a lot depends on the individual horoscope and this holds true for all signs. These are, at best, generalizations. As the month ends, you bask in the limelight. The new, the unique, even the mysterious, will attract you. It will add a new twist and dimension to your life.

OCTOBER

Ganesha is with you right through and you can feel the divine presence all around you in all your dealings. There is a lot of affection this month and you relish the warmth in personal interactions and family bonding. This will be a progressive, productive month that helps you to enjoy life to the hilt. Valuable time is spent with domestic issues that hog your time and attention. The health of elders may need attention. There may also be some sort of domestic happiness in the form of an addition to the family. While you work hard, you also pay close attention to your inner voice for guidance. Towards mid-month, with the influence of Capricorn, there is rapid progress. Your self-confidence grows in leaps and bounds. You delve into discoveries, inventions, research, astrology, New Age living, metaphysics, space travel, Scientology and so on. Mercury, the mighty planet, is all-powerful now. You will be zooming ahead like a spacecraft, says Ganesha. Success is yours; nothing can take it away from you.

NOVEMBER

You seem to be in a greedy mood and do not know where and how to stop. A certain restlessness, caused by anxiety or even nervousness, is a distinct possibility. Your loving interactions, warm inter-personal relations take on wider ramifications. The larger community and global humanitarian concerns will grip you. The influence of Mercury continues for a while and you will be in the throes of communication and expansion. You display a tremendous ability to make friends, socialize, give and receive love. Success comes to you both at work and in your personal life. Apart from work, home/ house/ property affairs come into sharp focus. All the P's that matter - power, promotion, perks, position, pelf and progress show a steady upward climb.

DECEMBER

The good times do not stop. Ganesha announces business deals, hectic romance, journeys and collaborations on and after the 18th. It is almost definite that December will prove to be a superlative month. Ganesha raises your levels of enthusiasm, energy, performance. From December, Venus and Jupiter help you a great deal. Your positive approach and energy will be sustained and further enhanced, leading to happiness in relationships and better focus on your work and profession. The new moon in your birth sign ensures all-round growth, advancement and betterment of your life. There is a wondrously pleasing influx of money. There may be an addition to the family too (another form of wealth, I dare say). As the year ends, Mercury is powerful again. Its influence will spill into the New Year too as you make sustained progress. This is the perfect time to launch yourself; what a wonderful phase to end and start a year, says Ganesha!

SAGITTARIUS

THE MONTHS AT A GLANCE

January

There will be tricky domestic problems to handle. But this apart, in general, the circumstances of your life and your inner energies are working quite well together.

February

You are moving ahead fast and in a very flamboyant manner. Do get succumb to ego drives and excessive pride. Take care not to act in an overbearing manner as there will be opposition to your plans and you will gather more enemies than you need to.

March

You are in a period of incorporation and assimilation; the universe throws many things at you and you accept whatever can nourish and support you.

April

There is recognition for your achievements. Employers and your peer group will be impressed with your diligence. You have many new offers coming your way and it is a good time to go flat out which you do.

May

This period is very intense and you will need to be very flexible now. Towards mid-month, with the influence of Aquarius, you are filled with new thoughts and make many changes to your life.

June

This is also a period of new beginnings. You are networking

well and are super-charged. You will widen both your personal horizons and the scope of your activities.

July
This is a very ambitious period when you push ahead on all cylinders. This is a phase of hard, sustained work. At times, you will not have time for yourself.

August
You are a mix of several influences now: you are exceptionally creative, and also willing to help the needy and the downtrodden. You will be far more composed, caring and calm.

September
There is tremendous movement in all directions. You are obsessed with reaching out to people who matter to you. You also win applause at work and find recognition.

October
Valuable time is spent with domestic issues that hog your time and attention. The health of elders may need attention. While you work hard, you also pay close attention to your inner voice for guidance. Mercury, the mighty planet, is all-powerful now. You will be zooming ahead like a spacecraft, says Ganesha.

November
The influence of Mercury continues for a while and you will be in the throes of communication and expansion. You display a tremendous ability to make friends, socialize, give and receive love. Success is yours!

December
As the year ends, Mercury is powerful again. Its influence will spill into the New Year too as you make sustained progress. This is the perfect time to launch yourself; what a wonderful phase to end and start a year. Ganesha blesses you.

SAGITTARIUS

WEEKLY REVIEW

(By the Phases of the Moon)

January 1 - Moon's first quarter in Aries

The pace with which you get work done is nothing short of amazing. You are firing on all cylinders and blazing the turf. Your speed is demonic; you are a person in a hurry and will brook no opposition. You tend to get too aggressive and this is something you have to guard against. Don't shoot your mouth off even when provoked. Keep a tight lid on yourself. This can be a time of balance and order in your life. Your professional life is well organized and you reap the benefits of years of hard work. You see clearly how various parts of your life are working. Your attitude is pragmatic and practical and you look at all sides of the coin. You are willing to work at improving a bad situation. Please remember that the choices you make now will significantly impact your future. Colleagues, peers and bosses also see your side of the story and there is substantial give-and-take. You are a team man (or woman) who leads from the front. Take Ganesha's blessings and sally forth.

January 9 - Full Moon in Cancer

You handle the emotional situations that crop up well. There will be tricky domestic problems to handle. There may be issues with the spouse and in-laws. So you will have to manoeuvre this path with dexterity. But this apart, in general, the circumstances of your life and your inner energies are working quite well together. Your life seems to run smoothly, and all your dealings will come out well. Without stretching yourself you are able to make significant progress. So you manage to accomplish much more than you normally would. Accept all opportunities that come your way with open arms as you will be able to build a bulwark against possible adversity later on. There will be expenses and illness in the family and you will have to cope. Children, in particular, can be a source of worry. Trust in Ganesha to take you over the coals.

January 16 - Moon's last quarter in Libra

There is love in your life and you will be on cloud nine. You may also be in the throes of an extra-marital affair if you don't watch out. You will be faced with many critical developments as you will be challenged by a slew of factors. You love your freedom and hate being tied down but now you will have to make compromises and adjustments. Your vitality may be at low ebb and your morale too. Go with the flow; better times will follow. Patience and perseverance will carry you through. Ganesha ensures that. Authority figures may be difficult to deal with. Your plans, ideas and suggestions may be resisted initially. Work around the obstacles like water around a boulder and you will find light at the end of the tunnel. But, despite it all, you are still a hit on the party circuit. You also made substantial headway at work. Expenses multiply but you will recover as the year gets going.

January 23 - New Moon in Aquarius

New thoughts and processes occupy you. There is a tinge of sadness and regret as melancholy and regret overtake you. Many of the difficulties you encounter now seem totally unexpected. They have emerged from out of the blue. This is a period of trial and anything that is invalid is likely to fall by the wayside. Your burning ambitions may be thwarted temporarily but hang on. Despite the tough road, you can still accomplish a great deal by transferring your energies to more productive areas. The energies that are flowing now are very powerful and formidable. You are generally a positive and fun loving person who rarely takes life seriously. But this time the knives are out and you will go through fire. Ganesha is with you and you will come out clean!

January 31 - Moon's first quarter in Taurus

You get down to solid work. A lot of valuable time has been lost and you try to turn the clock back. This can be an excellent time to make headway. Watch out for the usual pitfalls and keep restrained. Do not go overboard at the slightest pretext. Do not squander valuable resources. You are a spendthrift and have been lucky so far. But luck can also run out. If you are careful and manage to fine tune your work, there is scope for real growth and expanded opportunities. It is a matter of how much control you have over yourself. You have to know precisely where you are and what your real needs are to make the most of this time. Do not over stretch; know your limits. You expand your work area and make money. There may also be a short holiday with the family. You also manage to make intelligent realty purchases. There are meetings and collaborations as you slowly make your way into the elite circles. Take Ganesha's blessings.

February 7 - Full Moon in Leo

With the full moon in Leo, you are moving ahead fast and in a very flamboyant manner. Do not succumb to ego drives and excessive pride. Take care not to act in an overbearing manner as there will be opposition to your plans and you will gather more enemies than you need to. Avoid conflicts with the law, the police or with authority. Do not harp on issues like outraged honour and dignity. Instead, find a middle path and arrive at a mutually satisfactory solution. Various aspects of your life may be transformed. There will be new persons, circumstances or even possessions and you will have to move like water to accommodate all the changes that are happening so rapidly in your life. You will realize, much later, that all these changes were for your betterment. They will lay the foundations for sustained growth later on. Believe in Ganesha whatever happens.

February 14 - Moon's last quarter in Scorpio

This is a period of love, joy, eros and merriment. You will be surrounded with love and, I dare say, what a way to be! You could be in the throes of unmitigated passion. You may seek the romance of the hills, the mountains or the beaches with your partner. The period will be sizzling. You will lose all sense of propriety as you delve without restraint or thought into the arms of passion. This is an extremely positive time. You feel emotionally secure and in touch with your feelings. You express yourself clearly and honestly. You are also generous to a fault and may make many expensive purchases for your beloved. You feel like nurturing, protecting and supporting. Most importantly, you feel love. And, as we all know so well by now, it is love that makes the world go around. There is work calling, and many responsibilities at home. But right now you are in the arms of Amora! Ganesha blesses you.

February 21 - New Moon in Pisces

Your home and personal life are very important to you suddenly and you decide to make this area as positive as possible. You may simply make your home more comfortable and elegant, or on a more psychological level you may bring friends and neighbours to your home in order to make them feel good; this way you also pamper yourself. You remember the past with fondness and want to be surrounded by things that remind you of times gone by. This is a good time to go home and meet old friends and loved ones. If you haven't met your parents for a while, spend time with them. It will be well worth it. Who knows what the future has in store for all of us? Even I say that sometimes! Take time off your busy schedule and make more room for nostalgia. You are in that sort of mood. So indulge it, says Ganesha.

March 1 - Moon's first quarter in Gemini

You are thinking out of the box. Your mind is in a flurry. There is a lot to do and very little time to waste. New people will enter your life and there may be a woman – regardless of your gender - who suddenly comes into your life to help you out. This will be a windfall; so accept it happily. There will be many experiences now that will be difficult to fathom. Do not linger on them too much. Just believe that it is all Ganesha's blessings and go about your tasks with a clean conscience. You are in a period of incorporation and assimilation; the universe throws many things at you and you accept whatever can nourish and support you. You are not one to show your emotions often, but this is a time when you might just do that. The universe is showering its largesse on you and you are overwhelmed and filled with gratitude.

March 8 - Full Moon in Virgo

There is a semblance of stability in your affairs and you forge ahead. You feel quite good about yourself with enough confidence to handle just about anything. You feel happy and optimistic and manage to achieve a lot. The mood is also contagious and colleagues rally around you. You have put your fingers in several pies and now are caught in the rut of work and more work. But do not worry, says Ganesha. The payments will also come in due course. Hard work and perseverance have never let anyone down. Genius has always been about perspiration, and this could be the time to show the world your genius. Keep at it without thinking about the rewards and in time the lords will shower their bounty on you.

March 15 - Moon's last quarter in Sagittarius

The last quarter is in your sign. You are on the go and achieving a lot. This is a splendid period, so, make the most of it. Ganesha's blessings are with you. You seek to grow in various ways through your closest contacts. You try to create relationships that will enrich your life. You meet people and there will be mutual growth. There will be new and fruitful partnerships, new ventures and a lot of money to be made. There will be new, profitable personal associations too. There could also be a new romance in the air. Right now, your world is pregnant with possibilities.

March 22 - New Moon in Aries

You forge ahead; nothing can stop you. The world is your oyster. You clear debts/loans and come out on top in any business litigation. This is also a great time for an intimate relationship. You and your partner are in perfect sync and work at helping each other grow. There will be freedom and open expression in the relationship. There will be happy times; do not force the pace – let the relationship run its course and find its level. Additionally, you make money, expand your business ventures and spend happy times at work and play. There is money and honey, says Ganesha. Is there any need to complain?

March 30 - Moon's first quarter in Cancer

The mood becomes mellow and soft. This is a time of preparation for the events that will possibly follow. Do not worry; I am not saying they are bad or unfortunate events at all. Use this period well to make your world strong and secure. If you can, try also to build your physical strength. You may take up a gym membership or take to alternate therapy and massages which can have a rejuvenating effect on you. You need the health and energy for the challenges of the future. Family life is good but there are expenses on the domestic front in the form of medical bills. But nothing too serious, assures Ganesha. Many people assist you and you come through in one piece. Spend time with the family. They may need you now and may not really express that need.

April 6 - Full Moon in Libra

It is the time for the good life. You buy and spend without a thought. There is recognition for your achievements. Employers and your peer group will be impressed with your diligence. You have many new offers coming your way and it is a good time to go flat out. You feel optimistic and generous. You are in love with yourself and with the world at large. You will attract favourable circumstances and resources with little effort. This is a very soft, kind and pleasan0t time, says Ganesha. You keep meeting people and making associations that benefit you professionally. You will also be in a stable, balanced frame of mind.

April 13 - Moon's last quarter in Capricorn

Without a doubt, there is a lot of progress. You are moving ahead at breakneck speed. Along with the hard work, new gains and the money you make, you may also be excited by a new interest in religious and spiritual thought. You delve into spiritual matters much more than religious rituals and feel at peace and satisfaction with yourself. Ganesha is happy for you. But you still manage to work hard and spend money on the good life. There are happy moments too with the spouse, children and the extended family. Your joy spreads everywhere like the fragrance of wild flowers. Let the earth share your happiness.

April 21 - New Moon in Taurus

This is a period when stability reigns. You progress a lot too. There is balance and equilibrium in your life. The ball is rolling and your affairs seem to run smoothly and without much effort. You are content with the fact that your life is working well. There is growth at many levels - in consciousness, in your profession, in your social life, and in all personal matters. Ganesha has given you stability in this period and you enjoy the moment with open arms. Family life is congenial and you manage to hum a happy tune to bed.

April 29 - Moon's first quarter in Leo

While everything is going well for you, this is not the time to get lax or lethargic. You can use the good energies to examine your life and leverage the moment for greater impact. You can look at yourself, your work, your family and the world with reasonable calm and detachment. Your perspective is mature and reasonable and you can see through the labyrinths of life with crystal-clear vision. This is also a good time for higher knowledge, education, either formal or informal, self-awareness, occult studies, and travel. Grab the moment, says Ganesha. If you use this period of stability and peace wisely, you will reap the whirlwind in times to come.

May 6 - Full Moon in Scorpio

The period becomes very intense now. There are new and

profitable business transactions or negotiations. You expand your work arena and make huge gains. All your affairs continue to run smoothly. But please remember that with every expansion there is an investment of time and money. You will also need to be very flexible now. It will be a good idea not to hold on to circumstances, possessions and relationships that have outlived their utility. You have to move ahead all the time and so do not live in the past. Make new discoveries and challenge the boundaries that you have set for yourself. Ganesha is with you. Friends and loved ones also understand you well now. There is support from all quarters as you take more control of your life and your subconscious drives.

May 12 - Moon's last quarter in Aquarius

You are filled with new thoughts and make many changes to your life. You may also get a bit morbid or melancholic but it is a passing phase and will not bog you down. There will be many surprises in store. Just go with the flow and trust in Ganesha. He will not let you down. If anything, the new processes can be quite exciting and will certainly inject an element of surprise and freshness into your life. You will also have the wisdom to understand it all as you have gone through the processes earlier. You make waves as you become a well rounded person and the world sees it with grudging admiration.

May 20 - New Moon in Gemini

You will break free from the restrictions and obligations of the past. This need for newness in your life will be a powerful force and could change you from the inside out. In the end, you will enjoy all the processes that are taking place in your life. There is new freedom and you have to use it wisely. But, despite it all, you make the correct decisions. There is travel thrown in and you make contact with people in a big way. Your progress is unhindered as you move ahead on the fast track, with Ganesha's blessings. You love communicating with all types and earn brownie points on the popularity charts.

May 28 - Moon's first quarter in Virgo

Your relationships are especially affected by this influence as a partnership, either marital or business, may be quite difficult to maintain. It may be necessary to give your partner all the freedom he or she needs. Follow the same principle in business; if it is not working well for you, let it slip away. Do not hold on to things that don't work anymore. That is the message of the moment, says Ganesha. There will also be other forces at work in this period. You keep meeting people who play some role or the other in your life, each as valuable as the other. All these influences, though disruptive, can be very valuable to your growth as a person and as a professional. Your life also gets injected with new energy that keeps you alive. All is ostensibly well on the domestic front but you have little time for it. You are occupied with many higher thoughts. You open the higher charkas and wear the mantle of nobility with ease and pride.

June 4 - Full Moon in Sagittarius

You will be on a quest to acquire true knowledge and wisdom. You will be motivated by new learning and will seek knowledge not merely for gain but out of sheer love for it. A frantic week lies ahead with a lot of socializing. There will be parties and meetings. You are filled with confidence in your own abilities and are charged with vision, optimism and faith. There is also room for passionate bondings, love and romance. But your main thrust will be a desire for true knowledge that can uplift you and make the world a better place to live in. There are also romantic liaisons and behind-the-scene activities. There is more happiness and contentment and joy in your interactions. You look at life from a different prism and perspective. Ganesha blesses you as you forge ahead with the full moon in your sign. Make the most of this period.

June 11 - Moon's last quarter in Pisces

This is a period of new beginnings or a new way of handling life. The key words will be bonds/connections/relationships. This will be the keynote for this period. You will try your best to improve communications at all levels. Do not display negativity and be on a solo run; work in a team with others. It is with the support of people who matter that you will realize your dreams. There are strong indications of travel as you make many new and supportive connections. You are networking well and are super-charged. You are agile and strong, both physically and mentally, and handle whatever is thrown at you with flair and élan. There are maudlin moments too, says Ganesha. But this makes for a well-rounded personality. All the trends at play now will be good for you in the long run.

June 19 - New Moon in Gemini

There is a lot of mental and physical movement now. You will widen both your personal horizons and the scope of your activities. You reach out and extend the scope of your interactions and relationships, fanning out to people and places. You get along well with others and make rapid progress. There will be many gains from your changed attitude and thinking. There will be fresh acquaintances and contacts. Ties and bonds of a totally different nature - those that last a lifetime - are also very strongly in focus. You could be forging new bonds that are intense and deep. Your search for new experiences and knowledge takes you farther afield and you are determined to give a fine account of yourself. You are a people's person without a doubt but you also need to be less subjective and more objective about issues that matter. You want to do too many things at the same time and that could be a problem. Believe in Ganesha and all will be well.

June 27 - Moon's first quarter in Libra

There is a lot of buying and selling now. If you are with the stock market, there is a lot to gain. You enjoy the challenge of work. You tend to work cheerfully and uncomplainingly, enjoying the task itself without caring for the results which is really the best way to be. There are many happy outcomes now and they could manifest in several pleasing ways. The possibilities are endless. Ganesha says there could be recognition of your worth, public acclaim, letters of appreciation, good write-ups about you if you're in the public eye, promotions, perks, a jump up the corporate ladder. You will truly get what you deserve. The home front will be peaceful with a lot of bonding and intimate moments. This is a good period of joy, happiness and peace and you revel in it.

July 3 - Full Moon in Capricorn

This is a very ambitious period when you push ahead on all cylinders. This is a phase of hard, sustained work. You are spurred to work and there are expected rewards. The full moon in Capricorn makes you want to climb to the top rung in the ladder. If you have been somewhat stressed out or run-down or just out of sorts that will now come to an end. There is greater energy now and your plate is filled with new, exciting possibilities. There is great rapport and bonding with loved ones and much more warmth and tenderness in all your relationships. You make serious connections with extended family, colleagues, subordinates, peers, superiors. You feel much more relaxed, happy and truly at ease. Ganesha blesses you as you move from one frontier of achievement to another.

July 11 - Moon's first quarter in Aries

You keep at it like a man possessed. You break down all opposition in your quest for money, power and security. Your efforts and endeavours of the recent past give you great success and confidence. Your self-belief is at an all-time high. Your rapport with spouse, children and other family members gets better. Your positive and happy approach to life helps you handle the most difficult situations. You sail through with aplomb. You are also creative and revive old hobbies and leisure pastimes and/or a sport that interests you, or even take up something new. Ganesha ensures that you love, enjoy and appreciate all the good things of life. Indeed, life is a celebration! Money is there for the asking along with the fun times too!!

July 19 - New Moon in Cancer

Many domestic issues take over your space. There is, ironically, a relaxed attitude and also great mental activity and agility. You are full of progressive, even daring ideas, for career advancement and financial success. You may even think of freelancing and/or moonlighting to augment your earnings. You are in great demand and have struck a purple patch. What also inspires you to such great and sustained effort is a) your love for your family and b) a desire to achieve your true potential. You are committed to caring for your loved ones. It is this theme that makes you love, provide for and nurture your family, children, and older relatives. There is a philanthropic streak in you and you want to help people. Ganesha is with you on this noble quest. The world needs more people like you.

July 26 - Moon's last quarter in Scorpio

The intensity of the phase takes you by surprise. It is the influence of Scorpio. You adopt new methods to study ways and means of improving your personal and family life. You know that people and your interactions with them will be central to all your plans. There is also luck at lotteries, games of chance, winning at the races. The money angle is well covered. It is steady, secure, if not spectacular. Ganesha says that you will be honing, improving and perfecting your people-skills and putting them to good use. Consequently, you perform brilliantly at meets and conferences and are equally successful at partnerships and human relationships. Relations with superiors, co-workers and dependents are important this week and you make sure you are exceptional in your role as a team player. Family life is just bliss. What more can you ask for?

August 2 - Full Moon in Aquarius

New thoughts and new activities push you. You may also plough deeply into spiritual pursuits. You are a mix of several influences now: you are exceptionally creative, and also willing to help the needy and the downtrodden. You will be far more composed, caring and calm. Your caring and loving attitude takes you away from purely individualistic concerns. You attention is drawn to the family, and domestic matters. The focus is finances. Property and legal matters may get favourably resolved. There will be maudlin moments too but all this is a part of the package of life and individual biorhythms. You can't escape it. So why not revel in it, says Ganesha. The world has to go through with moods day in and day out and you cannot be an exception.

August 9 - Moon's last quarter in Taurus

There is more stability as your inner pursuits now become more concrete in this earth sign phase. You are still concerned with personal progress, but you are also distracted by domestic expenses. Family funds, acquiring possessions, extending or renovating your home and your wardrobe, and several other pending issues take up your time. You manage to invest wisely and find yourself entertaining lavishly. You have done well, most of your material dreams have been met, and now you just let go. A good idea too, agrees Ganesha.

August 17 - New Moon in Leo

There will be personal and/or emotional gains. There will be new bonds, a touch of romance, of glorious passion and sex. There is a lot to look forward to. You personal interactions, particularly the marital bond, will have more depth, intensity, harmony. You will find that a vastly, perhaps even diametrically, different dimension to your growth takes place now. There is movement of all kinds - from shifting house to a promotion at work, more money and varied emotions. You deal with joint funds/joint finances/legacies and inheritance/loans/capital. There is personal advancement and money plays a big role. Go for it, urges Ganesha.

August 24 - Moon's first quarter in Sagittarius

This is a period of hope and promise. You will now actually see the summit. Your earlier efforts have borne fruit. You will learn to be objective, pragmatic, balanced and peaceful. You will be able to take criticism sportingly which means that you are able to a) handle the demands on you and simultaneously, b) pursue your inner growth. You will also find yourself far healthier, more productive and useful. There will be domestic distractions though: pets will need extra attention as also your children and dependents. Even in-laws and older relatives will have to be taken care of. This phase is a valuable learning experience, says Ganesha. As you can see, the early part of the year has been wonderfully rich and flamboyant and packed with activities and influences. Go with the flow, says Ganesha.

August 31 - Full Moon in Pisces

This is a slightly sensitive and emotional period for you. From time to time, the real world yanks us back. You will find that you are once again a player in the game of life. You will have to deal with finances, push through business transactions, and deal with legal matters even. It is more prudent to negotiate an out-of-court settlement rather than get embroiled in a long drawn-out wrangle. You have acquired the necessary negotiating skills and wisdom. This is the right time to put them to good use. You need peace of mind more than anything else. Avoid any kind of mental fatigue, advises Ganesha.

September 8 - Moon's first quarter in Gemini

There is tremendous movement in all directions. You are obsessed with reaching out to people who matter to you. You believe in communicating on a one-to-one basis. You feel good about yourself and are motivated to work behind the scenes in humanitarian activities. This is an ideal way to gain peace of mind for yourself which is, after all, what you want most. However, the focus in this period is definitely that of reaching out - whether to new places, or to new people and old friends, acquaintances, lovers, relatives - the works! You also win applause at work and find recognition. There could be awards for the asking. This is a good time and you have to make the most of it, says Ganesha.

September 16 - New Moon in Virgo

You make steady progress. This phase grows logically out of the previous one. Now, the new moon ushers new trends: hospitality, guests and visitors, developing social interactions. Ganesha says that you will make rapid progress as you plan and execute important projects. You make headway as you will be extremely alert, positive and creative. Do not display negative attitudes or let communications deteriorate. It's not that you are critical, but that your valid suggestions for change can be taken as criticism. Tone down your aggression and your outspoken nature. You have so much - all kinds of delights that tickle the taste-buds - the joys of family life, the security of money in the bank. This is a good period and all you have to do is to consolidate it.

September 22 - Moon's first quarter in Capricorn

The progress you make is steady and visible. Your gains are palpable. You provide for those you love and care for. You find yourself giving money matters extra time and grab all financial opportunities that come your way. You are in a giving mood and sometimes feel exploited which you have to guard against. Such feelings could unnecessarily lead to hurt and disappointment. House, home, property are the main focus even if it's just renovation, refurbishing or redecoration. Your relationships will also be on an even keel. As I have mentioned many times, a lot depends on the individual horoscope and this holds true for all signs. These are, at best, generalizations but Ganesha believes that you are on the fast track to success. Need I say more?

September 30 - Full Moon in Aries

The year is working out well for you and you bask in the limelight. It is indeed a blessed period. Away from the work scene, a huge shift, almost a sea-change, takes over your interests and orientation. The new, the unique, and the mysterious, will attract you. It will also lead you to great new ideas and ingenuity at work. It will add a new twist and dimension to your life. You are much more secure and confident than you were at the beginning of the year. You are able to relax and involve yourself with hobbies and sports, love and warmth. You realize all this and thank Ganesha profusely.

October 8 - Moon's last quarter in Cancer

Valuable time is spent with domestic issues that hog your time and attention. You nurture family members who may not be well. The health of elders may need attention. While you work hard, you also pay close attention to your inner voice for guidance on what you need to do, and how to do it, in order to excel at and achieve what you want. Your goals may now be prestige, social status, promotions, awards and rewards. You enjoy your work which is a blessing in these times and don't want to bank too much on luck and favourable circumstances; you prefer to rely on your own efforts. You deserve your success, says Ganesha. There may also be travel, new friends and new contracts/contacts. Make the most of it.

October 15 - New Moon in Libra

There is love in the air and you are lost in its arms. You love to flirt but this time it could be more serious. Go with the flow and see where it leads you. It is fine if you are single. But there could be many consequences if you are married and you will have to take all this into account. At the workplace, you add to your knowledge, skills and expertise. New work-related avenues open up. You know that you can carry through demanding schemes, schedules. You have the know-how to make even seemingly far-fetched schemes turn out well. And they do! You experience the satisfaction and joy of living up to your true potential. As you can see so clearly, Ganesha is with you!

October 22 - Moon's first quarter in Capricorn

There is rapid progress. Your self-confidence grows in leaps and bounds. You spend more time in entertainment, recreation and socializing. You are in a celebratory mood. Many serious pursuits take over your mind and heart. It is the unknown, the uncharted seas of the mind, tantra and mantra that draw you powerfully. You delve into discoveries, inventions, research. Astrology, New Age living, metaphysics, space travel, scientology or just computers and technology – they all fascinate you. You are energized and gung ho about life. You look for gurus and higher spiritual knowledge. Ganesha guides you gently along the path of new discoveries.

October 29 - Full Moon in Taurus

There is great stability now and your progress is impressive. There are also many expenses. You dwell a lot on finances: be it investing, or raising funds, buying/ selling, and new acquisitions like looking out for the latest clothes, a new summer wardrobe, perhaps, or you could be shopping for the home - giving it a new look, a makeover. All this comes from a genuine desire to see both your personality and your aspirations reflected around you. The money trend now becomes the primary concern. More than financial gains, it is what you can do with money that will be important for you. You know that it is just a means to an end and not the end in itself. Along with this is a very serious and important trend. Mercury, the mighty planet, is all-powerful now. It favours travels/ meetings/ conferences/ interviews/ trips/ more brain power/ contacts/ communication/correspondence/contracts. Mercury has a special connection with the circuits of the brain. Chess, crossword and other such games belong to Mercury. Also, short distance runners and spin bowlers are controlled by Mercury. Mercury, in short, is the ambassador and salesman of the zodiac. It is very important and occupies a prominent position. You will be zooming ahead like a spacecraft, says Ganesha.

November 7 - Last quarter in Leo

The influence of Mercury continues for a while and you will be in the throes of communication and expansion. You display a tremendous ability to make friends, socialize, give and receive love. But you must guard against disregarding the welfare of others, or going to emotional extremes in order to soothe feelings. You have a lot going for you. Just let it work its own magic. Your sphere of interests expands, letting your personality shine through. Ganesha says, all this will reflect on and impact your personal life as well. You will become more independent and also more focused with friends and colleagues at work and with money. So, there is far more understanding and warmth in all your dealings. Your growth is multi-dimensional and profound.

November 13 - New Moon in Scorpio

A very intense phase kickstarts now. Success comes to you both at work and in your personal life. Your renewed confidence in your capacity for a) hard work and b) the genuine ability to take on the most onerous of duties, the hardest of tasks and perform them brilliantly, reaps dividends. You will focus with all your might on what needs to be done. As you see it, it will be a) generating a good income and b) spending it to get the maximum value from it. I am not talking only of market value/worth but also social approval, and your own satisfaction. It represents true recognition of your worth. Apart from work, it will also be a fun-filled period with many friends dropping in. Home/house/property affairs come into sharp focus. There is a lot of social intercourse and you enjoy it fully, adds Ganesha. The influence of Mercury is still evident and you make rapid progress. Those in the print and electronic media have a very successfully period.

November 20 - Moon's first quarter in Aquarius

Different thoughts occupy your mind. Try not to get too dark or morbid. There is progress but you get a bit soft in the head and heart and spend time in the woods gardening, landscaping or just enjoying the simple pleasure of the lush green that surrounds you. There is progress in several spheres of your life and you are just taking a break from it all. Pending matters are resolved, and solid foundations are laid for new projects. Stay away from forcing issues to a conclusion that may stir up trouble for you. Wait and watch. Do not get too pushy and aggressive. You will get what you are trying to achieve sooner rather than later. That much is certain. All your efforts and endeavours, your energized and creative approaches, will finally bear fruit. All the P's that matter - power, promotion, perks, position, pelf, even pets, show a steady upward climb. You make the greatest P – progress with a capital P, says Ganesha.

November 28 - Full Moon in Gemini

You look at many new avenues for professional and personal growth. In this phase you will not only strive for greater balance and poise but also try sincerely to favour softer options, and keep the atmosphere pleasant. You could start new collaborations/ ventures or secure a grant/loan of some kind. There is a whole new meaning to the concept of progress. You undertake further study. Higher education, research, religious impulses, new discoveries will all absorb you and lead to a greatly improved, more balanced and pleasing mindset. You will concentrate on being gentler, more approachable, so that your interactions with those whom you love will be warm and cordial. You will experience and share warmth and joy with parents and family and especially children. There is well-rounded progress, says Ganesha.

December 6 - Moon's last quarter in Virgo

The focus is on loans and investments. You continue making progress but at a steady pace, not a showy one. You realize that your greatest gains are knowledge, skills and wisdom. Your positive approach and energy will be sustained and further enhanced, leading to happiness in relationships and better focus on your work and profession. A lot of time will be spent dealing with matters pertaining to money and finance - funds, grants, loans, joint finances, and raising of capital. You are also busy spending that money, but on professional rather than personal needs. You are prudent enough to make sensible investments and ensure a nest's egg for you and your family.

December 13 - New Moon in Sagittarius

The new moon is in your birth sign and there is a lot to do. There will be a flurry of activity. There is all-round growth, advancement and betterment of your life and prospects in every sphere of activity. You are in fine fettle. This week will see you being the life of the party circuit enjoying yourself without a care in the world. You will interact happily with all types of people from all strata of society. You will live intensely, affirms Ganesha. There is a hint at over-indulgence too but you are in a celebratory mood. Tomorrow is another day, and who knows what it holds in its bosom? So you decide to live to the hilt and seize the moment as though it were a lost butterfly!

December 20 - Moon's first quarter in Pisces

You will gain appreciation, perhaps even applause. Your efforts are well rewarded and you bask in the glow of well-earned plaudits. There is a wondrously pleasing influx of money. There may be an addition to the family too (another form of wealth, I dare say). It may add in some ways to the demands on you, but you take it in your stride. You have acquired great mental strength that sustains your actions. You revel in the glow of genuine popularity. You are the toast of the town in the circles that matter to you. The year is slowly ending and the mood is good. You have had a successful year by any yardstick, says Ganesha.

December 28 - Full Moon in Cancer

As the year ends, Mercury is powerful again. It favours travels/ meetings/conferences/ interviews/ trips/ more brain power/ contacts/ communication/correspondence/contracts. As I have said earlier, Mercury is the ambassador and salesman of the zodiac. It will spill into the New Year too as you make sustained progress. This is the perfect time to launch yourself; what a wonderful phase to end and start a year, says Ganesha! There is a widening of the vistas of your life. You undertake travel and journeys, partnerships and new beginnings. A new venture (perhaps even long-delayed) maybe set up or a new project may take off to an exciting start. Your interactions will be filled with intensity and excitement. Love will play a heart-warming part. You meet work challenges head on. In this phase every activity is more meaningful and joyous. You are involved with socializing, networking, firming up relationships with friends, enhancing your social status. You will also work hard at your personal bonds and emotional attachments. You will refresh your marital and emotional interactions, reiterate your love, caring, concern. Wow, what a way to be!

SAGITTARIUS

KEY DATES

January

1*, 4-5, 9-10, 14*-15, 19-20, 23*-24, 27*-28.

Loans and investments of all kinds are important. Therefore, all financial activities keep you busy.

February

1*-2, 5-7, 10*-12, 15*-16, 20-21, 23-25, 26.

Inspiration, publicity, ceremony. It's time to see great achievements, both personal and professional.

March

1-6, 10*-11, 14-16, 19-20, 23*-24, 27-28.

Power, position, promotion, in short Ganesha's plenty comes to you know.

April

1-2, 6*-7, 11*-12, 15*-16, 19*-20, 23-25, 28-30.

Excellent, all-round performance sum up this month for you. A fine phase, comments Ganesha.

May

1-5, 8-9, 12-14, 16-18, 22-23, 25-27, 30*-31.

Both the good and the not-so-good are highlighted; you seek to create harmony. Expenses have to be dealt with, too.

June

1*, 4*-6, 9-10, 13*-14, 17*-18, 22*-23, 27*-29.

Reaching out to people and places as never before; you seek to reconcile different trends in both personal life and work/ profession.

July

1*-3, 6-7, 10*-11, 14-16, 19-20, 24*-27, 29*-30.

Finances are highlighted this month and therefore, obviously work. No easy money, but the money's there.

August

2-3, 7-8, 11*-12, 15-17, 20-21, 25*-26, 30*-31.

All the possible means of communication and trips will be in focus as you seek to reach out, make waves, make friends.

September

1-2, 3*-4, 7-8, 12-13, 17*-18, 22-23, 26-27, 30*.

House, home, office, and shop will be top priority says Ganesha. The key word is enhancement of property.

October

1*, 4_6, 9*-10, 14*-15, 19*-22, 23*-24, 27*-28.

Plans/projects will now be put into practice, so expect both great activity and great progress.

November

1*-2, 5-7, 10*-12, 15-17, 20-21, 23*-25, 28-29.

Work, health and money will be the main issues you address. All are important for progress and gain.

December

1, 2*-4, 7*-9, 12*-14, 17*-18, 21*-22, 25-26, 30-31.

Money and your mate/spouse/partner are the twin themes. Also, the 3rd M of marriage.

Capricorn

December 22 - January 19

CAPRICORN

(December 22 - January 19)

ELEMENT AND RULING PLANET: Earth and Saturn.

STRENGTHS: Sure footed, reserved, seek security, acquisitive, cautious discipline and determine.

WEAKNESS: Pessimistic, gets pulled into depression, undue materialism, conservative.

SYMBOL: The Goat- The goat is sure footed as it finds its way through obstructions and climbs up hill of success.

MATCHING SIGN: Cancer.

MAGICAL BIRTHSTONE: Garnet – attracts popularity high esteem and true love.

CAPRICORN

YEARLY FORECAST

Main Trend

Ganesha says the desire for a make-over that first came to you two months ago now takes on a definite shape and plan. You may a) Change your job, or even your career/ profession, searching for new pastures; b) Embark on a mission of self-improvement. This will include, with your attention-to-minute details, diet, grooming, healthcare, wardrobe (c) See scope for improvement in all your relationships, from professional colleagues to loved ones and dependents. In all, you are willing to put in extra effort. But here too, I detect a tendency to go overboard in the other direction. You can get too involved, too concerned with other people's problems and hang-ups. It may lead to stress on you, if not conflict with others. Here, too, Ganesha advises moderation. It's the best way - the middle path (as they say in Buddhism). Don't overdo things, either way. One word sums up the various activities you engage yourself in. You seek CHANGE -- for the better, of course. Even fools don't want things to get worse. But you'll elevate to a fine art, in terms of the detailed attention and time you devote to it. Ganesha says in conclusion: It is a time when less is more, so don't think of sweeping or drastic changes.

"Maybe, by raising my voice, I can help the greatest of all causes: goodwill among men and peace on earth"

– Albert Einstein.

This quote from Einstein is very apt for you, Capricornians. Believe it or not, I feel the future of the world will depend partly upon you. So intense will be your responsibility and role in helping the cause of human justice and joy that I laugh and cry for you. It is as if some forces, maybe the Furies, are driving me to extol your virtues and your greatness. I am not a Capricornian; therefore I can be completely objective in what I predict about you.

You will be helped greatly by Jupiter. Jupiter will be in your sixth angle.

a) Work is an antidote to boredom;
b) Work is the master key to good health.
c) Work is worship; it brings about a golden harvest, a reward from heaven as well as the satisfaction of a job well done.

Ganesha says, loans, funds, taxes, colleagues, servants, and promotion, perks are predicted. In short, Jupiter in your 6th angle will pep you up. It will give you both push and go.

'No fine work can be done without concentration and self-sacrifice and toil and doubt'.

-Max Beerbohm.

'All work is empty save when there is love'

-Khalil Gibran.

I am sure, dear readers, you will now understand what work is all about.

We are rolling baby! Show time! Jupiter, the planet of God's plenty, will be in your 6th angle. Ganesha says, the smoking gun, the *raison d'être* as the French say, the main reason for your success, dear Capricornians will be the joint formation of Jupiter (money), Saturn (limitations), and the electric planet of sudden events, namely Uranus (spirituality). Simply put, this trio leads you to fame and glory. How?

Let us first call Jupiter on our astro-radar. Jupiter will be in your 6th angle. You will be interested in Cosmo-biology, the study of the living universe. This will make you a caring and a daring person.

'Work is not a curse; it is the prerogative of intelligence, the only means of manhood, and the measure of civilisation. Savages do not work'.

Work, work, and work - you will be great at it, especially handling public relations with both flair and sincerity; and it pays great dividends. Dealings with bosses/ employers/ superiors are as good as your vibes with colleagues, subordinates, employees, even children, pets, dependents. There could be some tension and also health hazards to reckon with, too, around this time. Play down the self and ego angle in conflicts and confrontations, and you should be able to come out on top. Try and put your personal interests temporarily on the back burner. There is an astro-reason. Jupiter is in your sixth house of income, profession, service and livelihood, honours and rewards from higher up. You have a lot to gain, and a lot to lose if you don't handle it well.

Future gains and added prosperity could sum up the financial angle. You can well afford to take a short trip/ holiday. Or have a weekend getaway and come back with your batteries recharged and equilibrium restored. Domestic bliss, much more harmony in the home and family, romance, love and marriages are the added benefits. Friends are both numerous and sincere and add greatly to the quality of life.

Here are a few extras: loans and funds, health and hygiene, exercise and workouts, the recovery of important goods and items. Please also add relationships with servants, employees and colleagues, recovery from diseases, injuries and illness. You will be in fine fettle, and above all, have the ability to communicate. Wow! What a list.

Ganesha says, loans, funds, taxes, colleagues, servants, promotion, perks have all been mentioned. I deduce, therefore, that as a result of your creative energy, you will get a promotion, or if unemployed, you will get a job, and if you have been down in health and energy, both will definitely improve. Jupiter in your 6th angle will act as an energy-booster. It will give you the push and go to be a winner.

Let me update you with more information about Jupiter. Jupiter will lubricate your intellect, pep it up with all sorts of pills and goodies, so to say, and thus your brain will send messages which will galvanise you into great action. True, I might have mixed my metaphors. True also, I might have gone medicinal in my approach. But there is no doubt about my meaning. You will sizzle with ideas. And you will carry these ideas out, the latter being as important as the former.

Goodies of Jupiter:

a) Health, pets, relationships with colleagues and subordinates; if you are the boss, hiring and firing of staff;
b) Focus on the services you and your company give to the customer; in this I also include after sales services;
c) Different systems and techniques of working;
d) Top notch performance; results will be targeted and handsomely achieved;
e) Lost valuables may be recovered;
f) Loans can be taken, if necessary;
g) The maternal side of the family will have much to do with you.
h) You will be extremely conscious of your diet, exercise, food, flavours, aroma, and the right way to prepare and also serve food.
i) Fast recovery from injuries (and there may be hospitalisation or a medical check-up).

It is said that there is a time and a place for everything. Jupiter will be in your 6th angle of health. I am listing some new gadgets and gizmos for your well-being:

1. Handheld scanner
2. Anti-Gravity Treadmill
3. Implantable solar cells

4. Black Box Cleanser
5. Glove for stroke victims
6. ThinQ Pedometer
7. Artificial foot
8. Pregnancy sound system
9. Tennis elbow cure
10. Wireless toothbrush cam

Neptune:

Neptune is in your 2nd and 3rd house of communication, finance and family. It means, in simple language, fame and fortune are all-inclusive. It will hone your ambition, and you Capricornians are perhaps the most ambitious of all. Buying and selling, sales, and service, commission and brokerage, lending and borrowing, stocks and shares should be what swing the deal for you.

Mercury:

Mercury is in charge of your sectors of publicity, alliance, marriage, and journey from 1st to 27th January. Mercury performs marvels, resulting in the achievement of goals and victories. You will balance work and pleasure in almost ideal proportions. There is also a chance of wedlock, an engagement, a business deal, or major contract or even a hugely successful publicity campaign coming through. You will gatecrash headlong into the corridors of fame. Travel and collaborations are likely. Yes, you can start a project. This is a time when you will have renewed vigour and verve, and feel at your optimistic, ebullient best. 'Attitude spells attainment,' which is an original quote of mine, is what you will personify now.

Venus:

Venus will be lucky from 24th June to 1st August. You will have a chance to marry, love well, if not entirely wisely (there can never be both), an opportunity for warm emotional bonds and relationships to develop. We achieve true comfort and solace in love. Relationships of all kinds will be in strong focus. Collaborations and ties, journeys and publicity, rivalry and competitions, legal cases and confrontations, ventures and adventures, are the other salient features. You sporty Capricornians usually like to take chances in life.

Mars:

Mars moves in your sign only from 18th November to 16th December. And this planet helps you in different ways. If married, your spouse could have a minor or major wish coming true, your children and you might be involved in a major shift. Professionally, there could be important changes in your work area and you will have to work that much harder and possibly longer.

Saturn:

I have said again and again that Saturn will be in your 10th angle of power, prestige, pelf, till 5th October 2012. Let me explain this differently. In the World Cup series of April 2011, the pressure was on India, Pakistan, Srilanka and Australia, and the last four cricket teams were simply awesome. For you Capricornians, pressures will continue till 5th October 2012. This is the key and the secret. If you push too hard, you will fall.

Try to remember that if you bulldoze people, people will finally get together and throw you out. I know and recognise your tremendous ability to organise, plan, manage and execute wonderfully well the greatest of projects and campaigns. But sometimes you are uncaring, brutal and absolutely ruthless. That is not the way to win hearts. Finally, it will result in your own downfall. From 6th October, Saturn changes signs by western astrology. Pressures will ease. You will be softer and easier with people, and your bosses. The going will be sweeter. Your main strength will be in team work, group activities, and sweet leadership. So, there is a good chance of a dream coming true, a wish fulfilment, or the attainment of objectives. But remember, patient, solid, methodical Capricornians, the results will be spread out over the next two and a half years. The bottom-line is you will hit the target and shoot a magnificent goal.

CAPRICORN

MONTH-BY-MONTH

JANUARY

It is around your birth month that energies can be very powerful. Start the year by asking Ganesha for his blessings. You can't go wrong here. This month brings warmth and an added dimension to your personal life. You have the power, the charisma to handle everything. Remember, of course, that this is your birth-month phase. Financial matters too will be of great importance so you will really have your hands full. Journeys and travel plans also conspire to keep you occupied, especially around or after the middle of January. All in all, both money and honey, and reaching out, will be what you're involved and busy with. You are in for a power-packed start to the year. You are zooming ahead and expanding in every sphere. You move off the blocks like a Formula 1 race car. You reach out to people and places, sign huge deals and truly believe that this is the best period for you. You are stacked with energy and stamina and will even sprint the marathon. This is your month for sure. Nothing can stop you.

You are aided by Mercury, the mighty planet, which is all-powerful now. Mercury, in short, is the ambassador and salesman of the zodiac. You have scorched the track for sure in the early part of 2012. Your strengthened will power and mindset prepares you to take all kinds of chances. Financial dealings and money matters will be handled with flair, intelligence and great savvy. In the last phase of the month, there are burdens and responsibilities and the hard slog. There is little time for fun and frolic as expenses skyrocket. There could also be health issues to deal with. You will now truly embrace the joys, comfort and support of family life and draw further strength. The support systems are in place and nothing will hold you back.

FEBRUARY

There is a lot going for you and Ganesha stresses that luck is on your side. Your money angle was tremendously activated and energized in January itself, but now money/finances become the main focus. Your job, emoluments, perks will be mighty important. Some good investments can be made around this time, but once again a touch of caution and restraint will also need to be exercised, along with careful planning. All your activities will get supercharged and powered by Jupiter from the first week of February onwards. Remember, your symbol of the goat climbs sure-footedly over difficult paths strewn with rocks and obstacles. There are new expenses and the expansion plans continue. Your efforts of the past weeks will yield results. There is room for romance, fun and games, pleasure and publicity, ceremonies, functions perhaps even a wedding or marriage. This is a period of both recognition and genuine contentment. You will earn the respect of peers and will be conferred awards/rewards, promotions, perks. There will be great stability in most of your financial matters. Towards the month-end, the softer aspects of your personality come to the fore.

MARCH

Ganesha tells you right at the start of the month that there will be many kinds of pressures this month. Your people skills could really make or break you now. A good time to learn to curb your temper and irritability, learn not to be too touchy. Be more forgiving, tolerant and easygoing. It is not the usual Capricorn temperament, but you can always cultivate good qualities, a better attitude, counsels Ganesha, especially when you know how much is at stake. The tempo and pace of life will speed up even more. You have much socializing in store – functions, ceremonies, festive occasions, even travel, visits to shrines and holy places, or pilgrimages. Your earlier successes will inspire you to try to scale new heights. At work, your performance will be spectacular as all ventures, plans, projects, even new and existing businesses and other enterprises are crowned with success. As the month progresses, there is a steadying of your affairs and a definite shift in focus which makes you much more keen on achieving peace of mind, harmony, balance with your own self, your life, work, and immediate and extended environment and family. The focus will also be on the home front. The main trend for this phase is a somewhat nebulous one with several influences and pulls.

APRIL

Success is knocking at your doorstep. All you have to do is to open the door and welcome success in. Publicity, travel, and the print and electronic media keep you on your toes. The net results will be more than satisfactory – profits and rewards galore. Egoistic and carping tendencies need to be curbed, says Ganesha. There are good times to be had but many expenses too. There could be medical emergencies for yourself and for the extended family. With work and money issues at the forefront, you will also focus on personal, social and professional relationships. The moon's last quarter is in your sign towards mid-month. While there is expansion and several profitable opportunities coming your way, relationships will continue to dominate your thinking, and perhaps even dictate your actions. There are actually three main considerations to be precise – domestic pursuits, children and your own creativity and talents! This could be a very happy and fulfilling period as dreams and hopes come through to glorious realization. You feel pleased with life! It will impact both your relationships and your own mindset very favourably. There are strong indications of a wish-fulfilment on the professional or personal spheres.

MAY

This is an interesting month and you will be doing so many different things and all at once too. You will have to focus and concentrate hard. Ganesha also blesses you with large dollops of luck. There is goodwill, high approbation and love to be experienced and basked in, during this lovely month. Your angle of love and relationships will be sweetly rewarding and fulfilling, giving you much joy. A month of gains all-round in which the confusion of the past weeks will decrease. Your confidence will increase, and dealings with people as such will be on an even keel. Comfort and care – the two are different – are found in abundance this month. There will be gaiety and laughter, a very pleasing wish-fulfilment. The intensity of the period may take you by surprise. The gentle, caring side of you emerges as you help the needy and the less privileged. There is hard work in store with several factors taking your time and resources. You won't have a moment to spare; pets, family, projects, loans, funds and finances will take your time but you handle all the challenges with care as well as flair. The trend for the month widens to include rituals, rites and ceremonies. There could be profitable travel and many new beginnings. In this phase, it is a toss-up between your creative talents and your family, to see what inspires you and pleases you more.

JUNE

You will be making fresh evaluations and assessments, especially of goals and orientations. Ganesha insists that this is a time for thought, for planning rather than rushing into action. You have to make time for plans and ensure that you carry them through to the minutest detail. Your energy levels and self-confidence are sky high. You look firmly ahead at what the future has in store for you. You have the confidence and self-belief to plan both ambitiously and systematically. You will initiate new projects, business plans, exciting and novel ventures. There are many emotional moments too. Your mind will be in a whirl with many maudlin thoughts jostling for space. Whatever said and done, financial security is usually important for you and makes you emotionally secure. Property matters, loans, funds, domestic issues, home affairs and improvement conspire to keep you occupied. Use your head, says Ganesha.

JULY

There is luck going your way till the middle of the month as both Mars and Venus help out. If the planets favour you, what more could you ask for? You will have more than enough money to cope with the many demands on your pocket. Your family will both merit and demand your attention. Give it ungrudgingly and see huge gains in terms of love, affection and popularity. Ganesha says – this is the time for action. You are competing with yourself, and pushing yourself to the limits of excellence. The full moon is in your sign and there will be sustained progress. There will be new visions and the higher self will occupy your mind. There may also be a change in career/job/business. In the long run, it will work to your advantage. Accept whatever comes your way. You are on the fast track to success. This is a good phase for media folk as you make inspiring interactions. You overhaul your career and finances and renew old contacts. The intensity of the last quarter takes you by surprise. You have made some good decisions over the past weeks and it's payback time. There are many gains in personal esteem, belief and credibility.

AUGUST

Ganesha implores you that caution and restraint will need to be exercised. Do not try to be all-knowing, all wise, the supremo of all that you see and do. In short, try not to stir up a storm of controversy and conflict. It won't help anybody; believe me on this, if nothing else! Don't try for too much, too soon or too fast. The money continues to be good, steady rather than spectacular – and that's fine with you! The family scene is heavily emphasized, even in this context. It is a good time for creating or investing true meaning in your interactions. If you tweak it right, this could be a marvellous phase of fulfilment that both enlightens and illumines your life. Keep a check on your anger and impatience. Your focus shifts to the quality of life you envisage for family, loved ones and, of course, yourself. Towards the middle of the month, you make time for love, romance, parties, hobbies, children, partner/ spouse and the other sundry little things that make life charming. The chances of travel are high and you make many new contacts. Towards the month-end, new vistas open up and you are tested. Nothing great comes easily in life and you have to come through fire. Expenses will skyrocket, so also will health problems.

SEPTEMBER

There is an upward swing in all your affairs. This is a good time and you will do well to maximize your potential. Your personal as well as public image gets an almighty boost. And the astro-reason is a blessing from Ganesha. You positively shine at inter-personal relationships and interactions this month. Contracts, deals, assignments and projects almost fall into your lap. Along with the camaraderie and companionship you enjoy with friends and colleagues, there are 3 other C's – co-operation, correspondence and communication – in store for you. Your public persona has perhaps never been as scintillating as it is this month. You open new windows of your life and move from aesthetic appreciation to intellectual gains. Further study, research, or further professional training will interest you greatly. I must add here that a lot depends on the exertion of your free will. Astrology does not compel, it only impels. You look at the larger issues of love, spirituality, New Age living and alternative lifestyles. There is sharing, laughter, joy and group activities. Later in the month, the moon's first quarter is in your sign and this could be a very significant period. You indulge the more material side of your nature.

OCTOBER

The domestic scene will take a lot of your time. You will make progress but you will have to sort out the issues that confront you, says Ganesha. You will have to work things out delicately. Work, career and business on one hand, and house and family on the other, demand your special attention this busy month of October. Home will be what you build on and home-based activities are so important that you may even make it your base of operation, or your actual work-place. Your status and respect in the immediate or extended family, the vicinity or the community, or even society at large will be enhanced due to your own efforts. The truly interactive, sociable side of you will be at the forefront. There will be gatherings, reunions, ceremonies and get-togethers, all kinds of functions, celebrations, outings with near and dear ones, and also meetings with close relatives and kin. Towards the month-end, you feel happy and fulfilled. You have become totally convinced of the fact that interactions with people bring you joy. You strive for a grand reaching out to both, people and places.

NOVEMBER

The theme of the month can change dramatically. There will be many changes in store for you, says Ganesha. There will be a sudden slowdown in which nothing will seem to make progress. There are bound to be glitches in your plans and you will be terrified by the prospects of failure. You will have to distinguish friends from rivals and fact from fiction. The main focus though will be the 3 P's – projects, productivity and pets. Plans and long-delayed projects will move ahead now. Ganesha asks you to be wary as you will be prey to anxiety, overstrain, perhaps even health hazards. But as the month wears on, you enter a spell of unusual activity. You will experience achievement and enjoyment. There will be laughter, love, recreation, functions, parties, wining and dining, even a new relationship. You will also do well financially. You will inspire many emotions and reactions – from love to hatred even. As the month ends, a million thoughts bounce off your mind. You are filled with plans and ideas and don't know where and how to start or stop. You are riding high and feel that the world is your oyster.

DECEMBER

The year ends and Ganesha blesses you. The mountain goat has been able to achieve the impossible in most areas of life and you will be filled with a deep sense of satisfaction. December is a time for reaping rewards, meeting the opposition head-on, improving your long-distance performance, collaborations, communication, contacts and publicity. You have the need to reach out to people on a global scale. Ganesha wants you to plan ahead and opt for a less argumentative approach in your dealings. You'll win more people over to your way of thinking that way. It is in your interests to be positive and optimistic of all outcomes as negativity only breeds negativity. Keep your ego in check. You end the year on a high note, reaching out in all possible ways, says Ganesha. This is a period when you gain much, get things done, meet deadlines, wind up pending matters and, of course, look ahead. There are negotiations, meetings, collaborations and settlements. Destiny deals you the winning hand and so all money-making activities will be pleasingly fruitful. As the year ends, property and land-related matters will also take up a lot of your time. But you plunge into everything with eagerness. Those in the media will do exceptionally well.

CAPRICORN

THE MONTHS AT A GLANCE

January

You have scorched the track for sure in the early part of 2012. Your strengthened will power and mindset prepares you to take all kinds of chances. Financial dealings and money matters will be handled with flair, intelligence and great savvy.

February

There is room for romance, fun and games, pleasure and publicity, ceremonies, functions perhaps even a wedding or marriage. This is a period of both recognition and genuine contentment.

March

As the month progresses, there is a steadying of your affairs and a definite shift in focus which makes you much more keen on achieving peace of mind, harmony, balance with your own self, your life, work, and immediate and extended environment and family.

April

While there is expansion and several profitable opportunities coming your way, relationships will continue to dominate your thinking, and perhaps even dictate your actions. There are actually three main considerations to be precise – domestic pursuits, children and your own creativity and talents!

May

The trend for the month widens to include rituals, rites and ceremonies. There could be profitable travel and many new beginnings.

June
Property matters, loans, funds, domestic issues, home affairs and improvement, conspire to keep you occupied. Use your head, says Ganesha.

July
You are on the fast track to success. This is a good phase for media folk as you make inspiring interactions. You overhaul your career and finances and renew old contacts.

August
Your focus shifts to the quality of life you envisage for family, loved ones and, of course, yourself. Towards the middle of the month, you make time for love, romance, parties, hobbies, children, partner/spouse and the other sundry little things that make life charming.

September
You open new windows of your life and move from aesthetic appreciation to intellectual gains. Further study, research, or professional training will interest you greatly. You look at the larger issues of love, spirituality, New Age living and alternative lifestyles.

October
The truly interactive, sociable side of you will be at the forefront. There will be gatherings, reunions, ceremonies and get-togethers, all kinds of functions, celebrations, outings, with near and dear ones, and also meetings with close relatives and kin.

November
There will be laughter, love, recreation, functions, parties, wining and dining, even a new relationship. You will also do well financially.

December
There are negotiations, meetings, collaborations and settlements. Destiny deals you the winning hand and so all money-making activities will be pleasingly fruitful.

CAPRICORN

WEEKLY REVIEW

(By the Phases of the Moon)

January 1 - Moon's first quarter in Aries

You are in for a power packed start to the year. You are zooming ahead and expanding in every sphere. You have set your targets high and want to achieve all that you have set out to do. At the pace at which you have begun the New Year, there is very good chance that you will accomplish everything. Capricorn is one of the most practical and ambitious signs and they can often be ruthless too to get what they want. There is expansion at work and accolades and applause. You move off the blocks like a Formula 1 racing car. You reach out to people and places, sign huge deals and truly believe that this is the best period for you. You are stacked with energy and stamina and will even sprint the marathon. Ganesha is with you in this bright, beautiful and bountiful period of your life.

January 9 - Full Moon in Cancer

This is your month for sure. Nothing can stop you. You are the fastest, strongest and fittest by far. You could win the Olympics. Luck favours you too. The planets are your great allies as you make short work of all opposition and zoom away to glory. What a start! Even Ganesha is amazed. You are aided by Mercury, the mighty planet, which is all-powerful now. It favours travels/ meetings/ conferences/ interviews/trips/ more brain power/ contacts/ communication/correspondence/contracts. Mercury has a special connection with the circuits of the brain. Chess, crossword and other such games belong to Mercury. Also, short distance runners and spin bowlers are controlled by Mercury. Mercury, in short, is the ambassador and salesman of the zodiac. It is very important and occupies a prominent position in your chart now. It is time to reap the whirlwind. Of course, I must add here that these are generalizations and I haven't seen your personal chart. In this phase, you understand material comfort and go all out to get what you want. You are also at your creative best and this could be a great time for those in advertising and journalism. You think of new ideas and are the toast of the office. You have scorched the track for sure in the early part of 2012.

January 16 - Moon's last quarter in Libra

The expansion phase is still in progress. You are the soul of the party and make substantial purchases. Most of them, let me add, are wise investment decisions. In the mode you are in now, there is very little that you can do wrong. Your strengthened will power and mindset prepares you to take all kinds of chances. Financial dealings and money matters will be handled with flair, intelligence and great savvy. But you also need to be sensible and take adequate precautions and guard against all eventualities. Taxes, funds, buying and selling, deals of every kind, are definitely going to be the trend for the month. Please read all documents carefully, examining the hidden agendas, if any. Pore over the fine print and built–in clauses. You are on a high at this moment and could turn careless. It is better to warn you to keep your feet on the ground. Ganesha blesses you. These aspects I mention are particularly important if it is a family business or if you are an entrepreneur doing a solo show. If you are in a job, the growth processes are different with promotions and added perks.

January 23 - New Moon in Aquarius

There are burdens and responsibilities and the hard slog on the cards. There is little time for fun and frolic as expenses skyrocket. You are smart enough to know that if you don't put a lid on it urgently, the financial implications could get worrisome. There could also be health issues to deal with and you may need to be hospitalized or be admitted for a check-up. You have been burning the candle at both ends and it can take its toll. You will seek out solutions in prayer, contemplation or even just introspection – whatever works best for you. Ganesha is with you. Despite the challenges, you manage to zoom ahead. The force is with you.

January 31 - Moon's first quarter in Taurus

You are back to expansion mode after the blip on the radar. You will now truly embrace the joys, comfort and support of family life and draw further strength. Your siblings, spouse/partner, parents and extended family are a source of great strength. It is stock-taking time for you, and tradition, family, shared bonds assume both, significance and value. You look for new ideas and inspiration as you launch into attack mode like Shahid Afridi or Yusuf Pathan or Virendra Sehwag. You are in a mood that literally wants to blaze the track. The support systems are in place and nothing will hold you back. Go for it, says Ganesha.

February 7 - Full Moon in Leo

There are new expenses and the expansion plans continue. Your efforts of the past weeks will yield results. Finances and work pressures will ease. Family support and the encouragement and input of well-wishers and friends have given you more confidence and you slowly taste the rewards of unstinted, hard work. There is room for romance, fun and games, pleasure and publicity, ceremonies, functions perhaps even a wedding or marriage. You are in a happy phase. Ganesha is pleased. This is a period of both consolidation and expansion. There will be valuable travel and many new contacts.

February 14 - Moon's last quarter in Scorpio

This is a period of both recognition and genuine contentment. You will earn the respect of peers and will be conferred awards/ rewards, promotions, perks. There will be great stability in most of your financial matters. There will be profitable interactions and relationships which will also include not just family but someone special who finds a place in your heart. There is love in the air and many beautiful, soft and mushy moments. You will also be in an indulgent and generous mood and shower your loved ones with many gifts. Way to go, assures Ganesha. Incidentally, it is also Valentine's week!

February 21 - New Moon in Pisces

You are now inspired to great heights of achievements. You also find time to help out the less fortunate, the needy, the poor and the destitute. You embark on a self-improvement drive, which will be genuine and sincere, based on the courage of your convictions, high ideals, and lofty sentiments. All this will generate much warmth, care and loyalty in others towards you. Even acquaintances, colleagues, superiors, your own children rally around you, and their support and encouragement will inspire you to new heights. This is time well spent as there are many gains. Ganesha is happy with this facet of yours. While you are blazing the track, the softer aspects of your personality also come to the fore. You show the world that you are also capable of kindness, sympathy and empathy.

March 1 - Moon's first quarter in Gemini

You are swimming in new ideas and approaches to life and work. Your earlier successes will inspire you to try to scale new heights. At work, your performance will be spectacular as all ventures, plans, projects, even new and existing businesses and other enterprises are crowned with success. Friends, family, well-wishers and loved ones join in the celebrations. You are creative at work and also find happiness at home. You know that you have got what it takes and are keen to do justice to your skills, talents, potential. This is a great time for people in advertising and journalism as you blaze new trails. Ganesha is with you all the way and wishes you well.

March 8 - Full Moon in Virgo

This is a good trend and Ganesha is more than pleased. There is a steadying of your affairs and a definite shift in focus which makes you keener on achieving peace of mind, harmony and balance with your own self, your life, work, and immediate and extended environment and family. You will realize how much you value people, both in your personal life and at work. You will now try to make them aware of it, too. Attachments, ties, and bonds will be of paramount importance and the pleasing fall–out will definitely be your gains in the areas of love, romance and marriage. It is here that you will find fresh strength, excitement, joy. You are able to prioritize your life and make steady progress.

March 15 - Moon's last quarter in Sagittarius

You are moving ahead with dynamism and élan at work. The focus will also be on the home front. Associated issues like land, property, building and construction will receive attention. Deeds, documents, legal issues pertaining to home and property, will be important and must be handled carefully. You will put your house in order and attend to renovation, refurbishing, improvements, add-ons of all kinds. There will also be new financial dealings as your confidence skyrockets and you feel ready to take on all–comers in a splendid show of strength and valour. There is the danger of getting too ruthless and brutal too and you will have to watch your step. There is no use in ruffling feathers. Ganesha says it is better to go slow and be more tolerant of people than mow them down to meet your ends. You will get your due in life. Do not worry.

March 22 - New Moon in Aries

The push ahead continues unabated. It is difficult to stop you once you are on the go. Take adequate precautions though as there could be a really confusing, paradoxical week ahead. The main trend for this phase is a somewhat nebulous one with several influences and pulls. Passions, a riot of emotions and feelings, high finances, borrowing and lending, even some financial wheeling, dealing, creativity, sex and religion as well as ceremonies and prayers for the living and dead; the entire package falls on your lap. There is a lot happening and in the blitzkrieg of events, there is a chance of illness, accidents, trauma and loss. There is romance and expenses and you seek out money, power, recognition and security. There could be domestic worries, maybe a divorce and unnecessary litigation. Hang in there, suggests Ganesha.

March 30 - Moon's first quarter in Cancer
The mood turns mellow. Your eyes open to new possibilities. You look to somehow impart joy, security, harmony to those you love. You have neglected the family and paid the price for it. You haven't even met your siblings and extended family for a long time. You have realized your mistake and it is time for some deep bonding. You also work hard and sincerely as work defines who you are. You and your work and there is no way you want to be disassociated from it even for a moment. This is, of course, stretching it but I am sure that you get my drift. There is more to life than climbing the ladder and making money. If you don't see it, life will open your eyes to it. Ganesha blesses you.

April 6 - Full Moon in Libra
There are good times to be had but many expenses too. There could be medical emergencies both for yourself and for the extended family. With work and money issues at the forefront, you will also focus on personal, social and professional relationships. There are mandatory domestic obligations to attend to as well as business deals. You may be sticking your neck out, and getting saddled with tremendous responsibilities and liabilities. But your luck pulls through. There is time for love, new purchases and some real fun times. The good and the bad are thrown your way this week. Make your choice. Ganesha is with you any which way.

April 13 - Moon's last quarter in Capricorn
The moon's last quarter is in your sign. While there is expansion and several profitable opportunities coming your way, relationships will continue to dominate your thinking, and perhaps even dictate your actions this week. But there will be other strong predilections that will both enthuse and drive you. There are actually three main considerations to be precise – domestic pursuits, children and your own creativity and talents! You will centre your work and activities

around people; personal relationships will be heightened. Your feelings and emotions, your bonds and sharing, will all be at fever pitch. There may also be a great love affair or a great business move. One way or the other, you go for gold! Trust in Ganesha.

April 21 - New Moon in Taurus

This could be a very happy and fulfilling period as dreams and hopes come through to glorious realization. You feel pleased with life! It will impact both your relationships and your own mindset very favourably. There are strong indications of a wish-fulfilment on the professional or personal spheres. There are family reunions and the possibility of an addition to the family. For the singles, there is romance in the air which could lead to the next level depending, of course, on several factors including the personal horoscope. But this is a time of stability and sustained progress. Ganesha is with you.

April 29 - Moon's first quarter in Leo

This is a dream run for you. People rally around you as friends, lovers, mate/spouse, sweethearts and several acquaintances from the past emerge from the woodwork. You are kept busy walking the tightrope. Work is also in an expansionist mode. There is money to be made and also new expenses. Home and home-based activities come strongly into focus. You will be doing a fair amount of re-organizing, shifting around, chopping and changing at home. In your personal space too there will be a re-allocation of priorities as you try to make life easier and comfortable. This could be a truly busy week as you try to fit in partnerships, collaborations, family commitments, bonds and ties with loved ones and your profession. But take heart as Ganesha believes you will do rather well. You will emerge from it all unscathed.

May 6 - Full Moon in Scorpio

The intensity of the period may take you by surprise. You know that you can give a really impressive account of yourself but there will be roadblocks to progress as practical matters, money concerns, work and family come into sharp focus. Your hands will be full as you handle investments, domestic funds and other matters. The gentle, caring side of you emerges as you help out with the needy and the less privileged. There is hard work in store with several factors taking up your time and resources. You won't have a moment to spare; pets, family, projects, loans, funds and finances will take your time but you handle all the challenges with care as well as flair. Ganesha blesses you. There could also be several new love interests. Take care not to go overboard.

May 12 - Moon's last quarter in Aquarius

This is a relaxed period. You will be far more easygoing and fun-loving this week. You have braved and weathered the storms of life and, like a grand reward, this is the time for love and laughter, warmth, friendly interactions, companionship and shared joy. The trend for the month widens to include rituals, rites and ceremonies. You find yourself looking into the future and have flashes of inspiration that will help you align your priorities. There could be profitable travel and many new beginnings. There is success awaiting you. Are you ready to accept it? You are in an introspective mood which is not a bad thing at all. Ganesha is with you.

May 20 - New Moon in Gemini

Brilliant ideas catch your fancy and you don't know where to stop. You continue to be busy and gainfully employed in several activities, all at once. It is a toss-up in this phase between your creative talents and your family, to see what inspires you and pleases you more. There could be expenses galore and also a certain experience of loneliness, a kind of angst, if not grief. You can't put your finger on this mood and you can't pin it down to any particular reason. But it is there as large as life, and you will first have to sort it out before it blows in your face. Travel could help elevate your mood. There is tremendous joy from children, and the love and support from your mate and family will really help. It will also do wonders for your morale. You realize that none of your feelings of neglect are realistic; it is just the imaginings of your fantasy world and will pass by in due time like monsoon clouds. Ganesha wants you to be calm until the moment passes over. There are these periods in everybody's life and they come and go. It is important to remain calm right through.

May 28 - Moon's first quarter in Virgo

There is a semblance of stability but it can also be a mirage. You will have to differentiate between fantasy and reality. Romance blooms in your life and people around you are more than friendly. Social and business gatherings, dinners, conferences and get-togethers find you in your element. You will also be successful at interviews, examinations, and even the tests that life challenges us with. There will be great joy, satisfaction and pride to be derived from children. Ganesha insists that it is a good week. You have quality bonding with the people you love. The work front is also all agog with new areas to be exploited. With the right dose of luck, you will be going places!

June 4 - Full Moon in Sagittarius

There are many new influences in your life. You have never lacked in insight and understanding but now you will be aware that you have a lot to be happy about. You will continue to go places in life! Your energy levels and self-confidence are sky high. You look firmly ahead at what the future has in store for you. You have the confidence and self-belief to plan both ambitiously and systematically. You will initiate new projects, business plans, exciting and novel ventures. Ganesha urges you to go with the flow. There is travel on the cards and several profitable meetings. You will also be on a spending spree but it is all worth it.

June 11 - Moon's last quarter in Pisces

There are many emotional moments. You will go through the grind and feel ultra sensitive. Your mind will be in a whirl with many maudlin thoughts jostling for space. You will wrestle with it bravely and come out a better person. There is success at work too which is hard-earned and richly deserved. It also generates a more than satisfactory income, and money, whether we like it or not, is still the ultimate yardstick or benchmark of success as we know it in the real world. All your efforts reap rewards as a tremendous sense of well-being is generated in you. On the flip side, there are religious and spiritual inclinations and maybe even a new relationship which threatens to sweep you off your feet. You are normally a person with your feet firmly on the ground but, as we all know so well by now, nothing can be predicted about matters of the heart. Ganesha is with you.

June 19 - New Moon in Gemini

The trends continue. You are meeting new people and taking it easy in a way. You are removed from the hard slog and looking for moments to enjoy yourself. But you are not one to let go of an idea, a belief, or a course of action. You could also be switching jobs. There could be a promotion or even a more lucrative line of business. There will also be greater bonding at the domestic level. Whatever said and done, financial security is usually important for you and makes you emotionally secure. Property matters, loans, funds, domestic issues, home affairs and improvement, conspire to keep you occupied. But your emotional life could be chaotic with many love interests sharing space. There could be an extra-marital affair or even a divorce. It all depends on the personal horoscope as these are mere generalizations. Use your head, says Ganesha, before you plunge headlong into the arms of passion.

June 27 - Moon's first quarter in Libra

The fun times continue. You realize that you derive great strength from the people in your life and so you need good people skills. There may be ties of love, partnerships and collaboration. You may feel duty bound to honour some commitments, especially to near and extended family. Along with the huge demands of work, there are several domestic commitments too. There may also be journeys, lawsuits, legacies and trusts, and other fiscal instruments occupying your time and space. Expenses continue to soar and this could get you perturbed. Ganesha is with you.

July 3 - Full Moon in Capricorn
The full moon is in your sign and there will be sustained progress. There will be new visions and the higher self will occupy your mind. Charitable activities and welfare interests will be the focus this week. Of course, practical and financial matters will have to be dealt with. Budgeting your finances may be necessary both at home and in the office. There may also be a change in career/job/ business. In the long run, it will work to your advantage. There may be an addition to the family; it is also a good time to adopt if you are thinking about it. You are also on the lookout for exotica, maybe even an unusual pet like an iguana. Accept whatever comes your way, says Ganesha.

July 11 - Moon's first quarter in Aries
You are on the fast track to success. Your worries ebb and you are able to take a breather. All kinds of papers, documents, legalities have to be dealt with. There are also new contracts, partnerships, collaborations and deals. All this will extend over a period of time and so a promising phase sets in. The good times start to roll as you are inundated with the 3F's - food, fashion and finance. There are expenses too but you find new ways of earning and more than balance the budget. Ganesha sees to it that all is well.

July 19 - New Moon in Cancer
There are emotional moments with the family and some great bonding too. Your focus shifts to domestic issues and the fine arts like music and theatre which will enthrall and excite you, and even open up new avenues for gainful work. This is a good phase for media folk as you make inspiring interactions. You overhaul your career and finances and renew old contacts. This could also be the right time for a family holiday or to acquire a home away from home. You are looking at new investment options and may pick on realty as a good bet. Life is good and it all depends on your perception and attitude. Ganesha blesses you.

July 26 - Moon's last quarter in Scorpio

The intensity of the period takes you by surprise. You have made some good decisions over the past weeks and it is payback time. There are many gains in personal esteem, belief and credibility. There is also greater authority and popularity, more perks and prestige. You may also see the need to resolve some past issues that keep resurfacing; they are nestled deep in your subconscious and you will have to deal with them as soon as you can. You will need to learn tact, diplomacy, even kindness, and will need to be more pliable in problem solving. There is also the distinct possibility of a new love. It could take hold of you like a storm surrounding a daffodil and tear you to smithereens. Take care, says Ganesha.

August 2 - Full Moon in Aquarius

Your mind wanders in many directions and you lose your famed stability and poise. There are also morbid thoughts that occupy your mind. You make great effort to find peace and get back your relaxed persona that is now struggling with anger, bitterness and many demons. You manage to overcome the nightmares and are successful at work and get on wonderfully well with those around you. There is popularity and a shining new image on offer. You now get focused, action-oriented and positive in all that you do. If you tweak it right, this could be a marvellous phase of fulfilment that both enlightens and illumines your life. There is conviction to your beliefs and gentleness to your dealings as you develop much more tolerance and a truly caring attitude. You will now live life to the hilt with courage, joy and energy. Of course, before all this happens, you have to eradicate the demons that chain you so relentlessly. Keep a check on your anger and impatience. Ganesha is with you.

August 9 - Moon's last quarter in Taurus

There is more stability now. Your focus shifts to the quality of life you envisage for family, loved ones and, of course, yourself. Family affairs, possessions and assets, investments and even, perhaps, the unloading of shares in the stock market will be important. Your prime goal now is to secure your family. You are determined to achieve your targets and are resolved to do well, come what may. You are in the mood to obliterate all opposition. As a result, there is enhanced income and prestige. You feel more secure now and that makes you happy. You also feel that it is time to go flat out and secure all your aspirations. The sun is shining and you have to strike now. Ganesha nods in agreement.

August 17 - New Moon in Leo

There is love that once again creeps in on you and catches you off guard. You feel that work, money, dealing with practicalities, is not all there is to life; you want much more out of life. You make time for love, romance, parties, hobbies, children, partner/spouse and the other sundry little things that make life charming. The work front is functioning smoothly and efficiently. You have put in long hours to achieve this and now you see it all coming together rather beautifully and pleasingly. The aggressive work stance that you had adopted from the beginning of the year softens and the other side of your nature - your aesthetic self, appreciating all that is beautiful, artistic in life, art and nature - will now help you perceive and impart a sense of beauty and wonder to even the most utilitarian and mundane of tasks. Ganesha is happy with you.

August 24 - Moon's first quarter in Sagittarius

The chances of travel are high and you make many new contacts. There could also be profitable overseas associations, both professional and personal. You may get romantically involved with a person culturally opposite to you. The sparks will fly and this could even work out to be a meaningful and beautiful association. Your desire for improving the quality of your life will centre on the fact that the change has to be from within. You set new standards for yourself and turn your attention to the higher plane. Spiritual pursuits, tantra, mantra, issues of social balance, justice, law and order may attract you. You look at larger issues, cosmic concerns, higher pursuits and will experience a strong desire to study and understand them. You may take to yoga, meditation and time off in a health resort far from the madding crowd. You have a new vision and charisma and look at the future with immense possibilities in mind. You are riding the crest of a wave and feel that the world is yours to conquer. Your planning has been meticulous and your sustained efforts are finally paying off. You are on the verge of a giant makeover, says Ganesha, and he wishes you well.

August 31 - Full Moon in Pisces

New vistas open up and you are tested. Nothing great comes easily in life and you have to come through fire. Expenses will skyrocket, so also will health problems. Family issues will also rear their heads. Your spouse, children, in-laws, parents, extended family will all come into the picture and demand a lot out of you. There may be a divorce, litigation, child custody, payments and several other tough issues to handle. The law may also knock at your door. You will make personal progress but you will need to curb your temper and your ego when situations are fraught with conflict. Strive for emotional balance and restraint. You will now require all the mental reserves that you have built up. This phase will also pass, says Ganesha, and there will be happier times. But just hang in there!

September 8 - Moon's first quarter in Gemini

Your first impulse is to fly off the handle. But you have learnt to calm down. Life is a great teacher and it has taught you many lessons. You open new windows of your life and move from aesthetic appreciation to intellectual gains. Further study, research, or further professional training will interest you greatly. This will be both to get ahead financially/professionally and also for a genuine desire to enhance your knowledge and skills. You will interact with friends, in-laws, superiors, co-workers and subordinates and this interaction is likely to be warm, supportive and mutually beneficial. I must add here that every week (valid for every sign) there are new influences and a lot depends on the exertion of your free will. Astrology does not compel, it only impels. Personal decisions, circumstances and a number of factors influence one's life. Just believe in Ganesha and go according to your conscience.

September 16 - New Moon in Virgo

There is a semblance of stability. You decide to just let the world and its worries take care of itself for some time. You have a fun-loving streak and so decide to just let go. You are determined to live for the moment and instead of focusing on nitty gritty and the micro picture, you look at the larger issues of love, spirituality, New Age living and alternative lifestyles. There is sharing, laughter, joy and group activities. Despite the shift in emphasis and focus, you will always have an eye on practicalities. But you let your hair down and love the moment. There are many distractions too and several business and personal associations with potential. Use the moment well, instructs Ganesha.

September 22 - Moon's first quarter in Capricorn

The moon's first quarter is in your sign and this could be a very significant period. You indulge the more material side of your nature and realize that to even maintain the status quo you need financial security. Money is honey and it does buy you happiness. It certainly oils the wheels of life. It is a rare and pleasing time in which your past efforts bear fruit. You work hard, earn well and earn the respect of peers. There could be rewards and awards, applause and plaudits. Ganesha is with you.

September 30 - Full Moon in Aries

You move fast and make rapid progress. You realize that you will have to generate the income for your needs and assets yourself, no one really helps when the chips are down – and you go about it with dogged determination. You focus on land, property development, deeds, bonds, insurance and other instruments of investment. Adequate rest and sleep and health safeguards are necessary if you want to see the desired results. There is little point in falling sick and so taking a little time off to meditate will help you stay both relaxed and focused. The full moon phase is a good time to move fast. Ganesha wishes you well.

October 8 - Moon's last quarter in Cancer

You spend time bonding with the family and there will be many happy, joyous and intimate moments. The truly interactive, sociable side of you will be at the forefront. There will be gatherings, reunions, ceremonies and get-togethers, all kinds of functions, celebrations, outings, with near and dear ones, and also meetings with close relatives and kin. You are at the helm of family affairs, and you quite enjoy it! There will also be alumni meets and you will be meeting school and college buddies and having a great time. You are in the right frame of mind to hit the party circuit and make merry. But that's not all that interests and draws you. There is, also, an equally deep involvement with home, family, the joys and cares of parenting. There is growth in all areas of your life and you become a truly multi-dimensional personality. Ganesha is happy for you.

October 15 - New Moon in Libra

You make money, spend money and feel good with yourself. You buy expensive and tasteful accessories and artefacts. You are now comfortable monetarily and socially. You feel that you can afford to be more easy-going and laidback. The frantic pursuits that have kept you busy for the last two weeks ease off now and there is time for leisure and pleasure. You feel that you have managed to get a lot done, put your house in order, so to speak, and can now justifiably afford to relax – in the work place and in the family circle. You are in an indulgent mood and you have earned every bit of it. There is harmony and balance in life and Ganesha is pleased.

October 22 - Moon's first quarter in Capricorn

You are happy and fulfilled. You have become totally convinced of the fact that interactions with people bring you joy. You strive for a grand reaching out to both people and places. You will do well at public relations, managing events and interacting with people at all levels. But there are also pinpricks as you could be burdened with nameless discontent, restlessness, even inertia. You focus on finance, property, gains, friendship and fraternity. But, like always,

I add here that a lot depends on the individual horoscope. I have seen several times in my vast career that generalizations can lead a person into a false sense of complacency. Please remember that these are all mere pointers and you do not have to be condemned or liberated from them. You have to use them as guideposts or signposts. Ganesha nods in agreement.

October 29 - Full Moon in Taurus

There is a lot to be done and your plate is overflowing. You may well feel that there is so much to be done and so little time left. The home front requires a lot of your time and attention. There could be repairs, renovations, and improvements to property, even some kind of construction or just buying things for the home. Additionally, there will also be elders, dependents and pets to be cared for. But you will cope. You turn to practical and down-to-earth considerations and deal with all challenges efficiently and strongly. If you are an electronics buff, you spend on new gadgetry. Computers, iPods, mobiles, cameras, music systems and the like hold a deep fascination. Have fun. Ganesha blesses you.

November 7 - Last quarter in Leo

Your mood is once again buoyant and positive. The good times roll and you are filled with joy and fulfilment. You will excel at work and at personal relationships. However, pay close attention to money matters as you may have to deal with loans, funds, even leases and rentals. There are many expenses along with several opportunities to make money. You also look at new lines of business and investments. There are new business associates and a lot of travel, wining and dining. You are determined and fixed and are known for your persistence. Once you decide on a course of action, you generally pursue it wholeheartedly. You put in your best and sincere efforts at the workplace and there will be enhanced power, prestige, status and pelf. Your energy levels and self-confidence are high. There is balance and stability in your life. Ganesha is with you.

November 13 – New Moon in Scorpio

You are re-energized and now enter a spell of unusual activity. You will experience achievement and enjoyment. There will be laughter, love, recreation, functions, parties, wining and dining, even a new relationship. You will also do well financially. There will be expenses to deal with and some extra time and thought will have to be devoted to managing your cash flow. You will also be introspective and juggle the challenges of many worlds. This could be a demanding phase in which you will have to call up reserves of energy and stamina to cope with it all. The big danger, if I can call it that, will be with regard to someone stealing your heart. You could lose all sense of propriety and may even leave a stable home behind for the lure of new, mysterious charms. Watch your step, cautions Ganesha.

November 20 - Moon's first quarter in Aquarius

There is a lot to cope with. Financial matters, spiritual concerns, family commitments and a hectic social life all come together, with their demands and, of course, expenses. Money matters will have to be dealt with along with other commitments. You will inspire many emotions and reactions – from love to even hatred. Money is normally the root cause of all evil. Position and status are other ego issues that cause animosity. Do not do anything that exacerbates friction in the family. If you live in a joint family, there could be many pulls and pressures. This is a strange period of many extremes. There is strife and tussle and also great moments of joy and satisfaction. You may also indulge in social work, gardening and take time out in the zoo or in the woods. It will be good to get away from the scene of action for a while and recharge your batteries. Ganesha blesses you.

November 28 - Full Moon in Gemini

A million thoughts bounce off your mind. You are filled with plans and ideas and don't know where and how to start or stop. You are riding high and feel that the world is your oyster. There are happy times and enhanced power and prestige as a result of your own efforts and hard work. You also pay attention to grooming, social skills and manners. You complete pending work and clean the table of old files. The year is ending and you want a clean slate. You want to forget all acrimony and embrace humanity. You are filled with gratitude and may even plan an exotic holiday with the family or a special partner. Way to go, says Ganesha.

December 6 - Moon's last quarter in Virgo

Hectic times are here again. You will deal with marital funds, shared resources, inheritance, wills and family accounts. There are many domestic demands on your time and energy. However, by and large, it is also a lucky period and you can get away with some cheeky risk taking. You will also attempt to review your own achievements, your goals and your stance in life. Ganesha feels that this is a period when you gain much, get things done, meet deadlines, wind up pending matters and, of course, look ahead. There are negotiations, meetings, collaborations and settlements but you wish to put your feet up and relax a bit. It is not that you are tired. But you just want a break. Ganesha wishes you well.

December 13 - New Moon in Sagittarius

You are materially successful as luck is still very much on your side. Destiny deals you the winning hand and so all money-making activities will be pleasingly fruitful. There are also happy times spent with family and friends and you find great joy in the company of like-minded people. There could also be a windfall coming your way as a family settlement or an inheritance will come through depending, of course, on your personal horoscope. This is a great way to end a year and start another. You overcome all obstacles and feel pleased with yourself. And why not? Ganesha is happy for you.

December 20 - Moon's first quarter in Pisces

You focus on the welfare of the family and the neighbourhood. You also come to the aid of relatives, friends, acquaintances, even subordinates and score several brownie points. You rise in popularity and also realize your potential of being able to give ceaselessly which is indeed a great trait. Life has no free meal and you are capable of generosity without calculating the pennies. I don't have to say this but everyone loves you in this mood. You will have many hangers-on as others discover the hidden depths of your character and the infinite capacity for good that you are capable of. This will be a period of give and take, caring and sharing, loving and being loved. This is also the period of your birth and you are truly on a high.

December 28 - Full Moon in Cancer

You take your family responsibilities seriously. Property and land related matters will also take up a lot of your time. But you plunge into everything with eagerness. The creative pursuits, hobbies, interest in the arts, theatres, TV, cinema will be activated. Those in the media will do exceptionally well. There is also a fair amount of partying and socializing and the mood is happy. A touch of class, of style, in all your dealings helps you dish out an outstanding performance. Ganesha wishes you a great year ahead.

CAPRICORN

KEY DATES

January

2*-3, 6*-8, 11*-13, 16*-18, 21*-22, 25*-26 29*-31.

January to March form a bridge for you in every possible way – for example, business, marriage, foreign connections, trading, expansion, children.

February

3-4, 8-9, 13*-14, 17-18, 21*-22, 26-27.

Important for finance; pending work will be done. Partnership, joint-finance, house and office shift, work with the government, multinationals, loans and funds.

March

2*-4, 7*-9, 12*-13, 17*-18, 21*-24, 25-26, 29-31.

Launch pad to success, just as GSLV's success puts the country in the reckoning for a share of the $10 billion global space business.

April

1-5, 8*-11, 13-14, 17-18, 20-22, 26-28.

Power, promotion, perks, pelf, position, all the P's summarize this month.

May

1*-2, 6*-7, 10*-11, 15*, 19*-20, 23*-24, 28*-29.

You will be straining every sinew and muscle to push your way to the top. Yes, you will get there. Funds will be available for home and new projects.

June

1*-3, 7-8, 10-11, 14-16, 18-20, 23-25, 29-30.

June will blow hot and cold for you. Expenses will be heavy but the work will be done. Journey and secret dealings/ affairs will be highlighted. The last 10 days will be the best, announces Ganesha. *June through September* will decide your future.

July

1-2, 4-5, 12-13, 17-18, 22-23, 26-31.

Away to a head-start. Work will be done. People will respect you. Success in new projects and a mighty romance, says Ganesha!

August

4-6, 9-10, 13-16, 18-19, 23*-29.

Honey and money; a turning point, says Ganesha! Income increases, expenses multiply, you'll buy and sell. It's also party-time.

September

1*-2, 5*-6, 9*-10, 14*-16, 19*-21, 24*-25, 27*-28.

Travel, news, computers, exciting news, contacts, contracts, trips, ties, victory.

October

2-3, 7-8, 9-13, 16-18, 21-24, 26-27, 29-31.

The focus is on home, house, office, shop, godown, i.e. property. You will be working very hard. Do rest from time to time.

November

1-4, 8-9, 13*-14, 18*-19, 22*-23, 26*-27, 29*-30.

Romance and drama, contacts, companions, attachments. A lovely month for marriage, companionship, partnerships, journeys, collaborations, children, sports, arts and crafts, scholarships.

December

1, 5*-6, 10*-11, 15*-16, 19*-20, 23*-24, 27-29.

Important for work and partnership. December means a job switch/ promotion, income from different income sources, exceptional hard work, good rewards.

Aquarius

January 20 - February 18

AQUARIUS

(January 20 - February 18)

ELEMENT AND RULING PLANET: Air and Uranus.

STRENGTHS: Assertive, independent, aggressive analytical original and inventive has strong dislikes and firm opinions.

WEAKNESS: Fixed ideas, rebellious for once own sake, coldness. Can also be eccentric at times and so, may attract by narrow by narrow minded people.

SYMBOL: the Water Bearer- dispending that flows freely and equally to all, representing creation and the giving of life.

MATCHING SIGN: Leo.

MAGICAL BIRTHSTONE: Amethysts – bring faithfulness in love and bestows the gifts prescience.

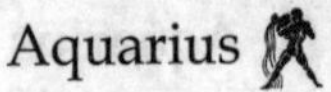

AQUARIUS

YEARLY FORECAST

Ganesha says the meltdown and the leaking of the Japanese Fukushima took the world by great sorrowful surprise in 2011. But you, Aquarians, will spread sunshine and radiate cheer, joy, happiness. Three cheers!

Thanks to Jupiter and Saturn, You will experience the timeless rhythms that celebrate the renewal of life.

Main Trend

Ganesha says that from the word 'go', almost all spheres of activity are abuzz this year. Communication and contacts with both the masses and classes will start from this month itself and last throughout the year. Love will definitely take a front seat and so indeed will finances and money matters. In fact, they will all be jostling for space in your life, your mind, and your pursuits. In terms of the main trend, though, staying close, total connectivity and bonding are the main thrust – and will continue to be for some time. Journeys or plans to travel are probable. You might also suffer from the new social disease, 'information obesity' because people will be bombarding you with faxes, e-mails, phone calls and voice mail, you name it. You utilise technology fairly extensively, both for pleasure and for profit. Partnerships, new deals, positive tie-ups are emphasised, so also are collaborations, local and foreign. There could be marriage, legal affairs, open and hidden rivalry or perhaps only examinations/ tests/ interviews or group discussions – in fact, the entire gamut of interpersonal relationships. The result?

A full plate of events. You will be kept busy at home, at work, and at the extended family level, and could be running around helter-skelter trying to fulfill several commitments simultaneously. Try to take a breather and fix priorities.
"Let's drink and dance and laugh and lie; love, the reeling midnight through, for tomorrow we may all die!"

Beginning Anew
Another fresh New Year is here.....
Another year alive!
To banish worry, doubt, and fear;
To love and laugh and give!
This bright New Year is given me
To live each day with zest....
To daily grow and try to be
My highest and my best!
I have the opportunity
Once more to right some wrongs,
To pray for peace, to plant a tree,
And sing more joyful songs!

- Willam Ward.

If you put all this together, you will get, both, the significance and the ambience of love, life and laughter brought about by a jovial Jupiter whirling in your 5th angle.

I will illustrate it by citing the example of that leviathan of the sea, Ronald Reagan No. 76, an aircraft carrier, which has been nuclear fuelled for the next 50 years! This information was gleaned from a special feature on it on National Geographic Channel, on April 13, 2006, 8 pm. The ship or carrier was so huge that men were attired in different colours, blue, white, green, red and yellow, to help them categorise the different duties they were carrying out. Dummy bombs, landing or launching of navy aircraft in rapid revolving fashion, and the sheer regularised, smooth, computerised management of this juggernaut is typical of your sign Aquarius at its best! Ganesha says, therefore, take heart. It is the Aquarian Age. It is your Age, Aquarians. Incidentally, President Reagan was also an Aquarian. The number of the aircraft carrier is 76. 7+6=13. 1+3=4. Number 4 is the numerological equivalent of your sign, Aquarius! Exciting, eh?

Here are the facets of Jupiter in your 5th angle:

a) Wish-fulfilment and hope, and we do know, it is hope that keeps the world going, just as, in all fairness, love keeps it passionately alive;
b) Old acquaintances, new friends, sweethearts and loved ones, mate and companions, all form a full circle of happiness for you - well, for the most part, at least;
c) Your income could come from more than one source, and here, one of the secrets would be socialising and fraternising;
d) You must learn not to offend those who love and support you. Not ego, but love, will get you where you aspire to be;
e) Jupiter could also make you spend too lavishly for your own good, or over-reach in business deals and investments, because Jupiter means expansion at all levels, and that applies to your wallet/purse too;
f) Possessions, fusing substance with style, say in clothes, work, home, renovation/decoration of either new or ancestral property is foretold;
g) Good news about children and romance, hobbies and sports;
h) Pious deeds, charitable acts, the elder brother, paternal uncle, the longevity of your mother, finding lost/stolen goods/ valuables, treasures, lotteries and windfalls, recovery from illness and, therefore, returning from hospital, medical centres, are the other salient points or the attributes and power of this placing.

Jupiter is the panacea, the cure-all, the magic wand for the ills of the world. It is Jupiter which helps you attain the pinnacle of success and the highest position in life. The notorious gangster Bernardo

Provenzano, arrested on April 13, 2006, was called the 'Capo Dei Capi', namely boss of bosses! Yes, Jupiter is the Big Boss, the Capo Dei Capi of the planets!

Like the three musketeers created by Dumas, let us call into action Neptune, Pluto and Uranus.

Neptune:

Anger lives like a lightning flash. Friendship endures like a line inscribed on a rock. Now, the choice is yours...
Neptune on the positive side will give you inspiration, imagination, intuition, ESP. Therefore, Neptune works for those of you who are artists, especially musicians and poets, film stars and those into therapy and healing. By modern astrology, Neptune is one of the main planets for films. On the negative side, Neptune represents drugs, illusions of grandeur, and deceit as well as double-dealing. Therefore, see to it that you are not cheated and conned. Misunderstandings and separations are possible. They are part of life.

Pluto:

Pluto whirls in your 12th angle, you can pray, **"O Thou, soul Reality, Light of our light and Life of our life, Love supreme, Saviour of the World, grant that more and more I may be perfectly awakened to the awareness of Thy constant presence".** Pluto refers to expenses, secret and open love affairs, matters concerning power and relationships, spiritual practice and religious rituals, life, death, rebirth, salvation. Naturally this is a mighty interesting and exciting menu. You will not be able to taste all the dishes. But whatever you have should be tempting.

Uranus:

By modern astrology, you are under the influence and sway of Uranus, also called 'The Great Light.' Uranus is the indicator of the New Age. Uranus will be in your angle of wealth, speech, physical enjoyment, trading in ornaments, pearls and diamonds, buying and selling in general, accumulation of wealth, earning through self-effort, acquisitions from the father, truthfulness and falsehood, inclinations, food, taste, clothes, eloquence, humility, steadiness of the mind, learning, education, letters, anger, deceitfulness, family members, friends, enemies, servants, close followers, self-control, and death.

I have given you this exhaustive list from Vedic astrology so that you get an idea of the power and effect of Uranus; EVERYTHING stated will obviously not happen. Only a few events will occur.

SPECIAL MONTHS

Ganesha says, Jupiter in your 5th angle leads to gains, gaiety, a touch of class and genius in all that you say and do. Yes, a minor or major wish-fulfilment will be the gift of Pluto.

Mercury:

Mercury speeds away in your own sign from 28th January to 14th February, as did Malinga, one of the world's fastest bowlers. Ganesha claims that Mercury has jurisdiction over creativity, children, sports, entertainment, pleasure, freedom, funds, loans and joint-finances, buying/selling/investing. These areas will be wonderfully activated. Go all out with guns blazing and grab what you want! It's a good and lucky period for you.

Venus:

Venus glides into your sign from 1st January to 14th January. Venus represents house, home, parents, comforts of the home and a happy retirement. I have seen even poor Aquarians having a reasonably comfortable old age, though I know that comparisons will be made with other signs. Usually, Aquarians have a few really good possessions, use them well, and are happy or, at least, content. Venus also stands for journey, connections, computers, and communication, and here you Aquarians come out right on top. Aviation and science also come within this ambit.

Mars:

Mars, the muscular planet, energises you from 27th December to 2nd February, giving you enthusiasm and ebullience. At work, you will go through all impediments and still register progress. Honour and status, you will have as your rightful due. Friends, supporters, the boss, and the general public will be on your side and that should encourage you to give work your best shot. Yes, awards and rewards are foretold. New vitality surges within you. You respond like a powerful steed, spurred to gallant galloping. Profit and pleasure fuse grandly. It's time to show the world your paces.

Saturn:

Ganesha says, the Star Trek slogan: "To go where no man has gone before," applies to you perfectly.

Singer Don Stevenson sang "All I seek is the heavens above and the road before me." You Aquarians will expand your physical, mental, emotional, spiritual, psychic horizons. Saturn will be the drug to make you aware and conscious of the pulse and purpose of the world and the cosmos. Paradoxically, it will also turn the searchlight within you and thus will have rare and new insights about yourself. I have laid it on thick and fast, because you deserve it.

Saturn, the planet of knowledge, wisdom, right, thoughts, words and action will be in your 9th angle till 5th October, 2012. It is a time of intuition, imagination, and inspiration. Your dreams will come true. Your words will have power. Your actions will shake the world. You could well be a prophet, says Ganesha.

"The most beautiful experience we can have is the mysterious. It is the fundamental emotion, which stands at the cradle of true art and true science."

-Albert Einstein.

"Research is to see what everybody else has seen, and to think what nobody else has thought."

- Albert Szent-Gyvrgi, American biochemist

Ganesha affirms that these two quotations best elucidate 2012 for you impulsive, energetic, go-ahead, Aquarians Remember, dear readers; both these quotes are from scientists. Yet, both talk of the vision and mystery needed for true research. Einstein talks of the "mysterious." It could also mean genuine spirituality and intuition. The reason I have emphasised these aspects is that Jupiter, the planet of wisdom (different from intelligence and cleverness) will be in your 9th angle of evolution. This is the crucible, the melting pot, the turning point, for you. Science will be wedding religion! The beginning of a NEW ERA! Happiness will be trickling in!

Just as modern 'smart bombs' seek out targets before release - here, I must hand it to technology and weaponry - so also will Jupiter seek out your material comforts. Ganesha willing, my words will prove prophetic. Jupiter will help you in marriage, journey, collaborations, ceremony, social and financial advancement, property and land value, and anything with a foreign slant to it, says studies, business, immigration, crash courses, and visits, holidaying or having a home-away-from-home. Astro-advice? Even if you are called a 'quark' which is now used to mean eccentric, it would pay to follow your ideas and intuition. As said at the outset, God is with you this year! This is also an absolutely top-drawer time for the T's - travel, ties, telecommunication and transport. A few of you could have glimpses of God, a feeling that He is by your side, or He could appear in your dreams and manifest Himself to you. I understand that people can also have delusions in this matter and mistake them for the real thing. This is also one of the possibilities suggested by this placing of Jupiter.

Poets, writers, researchers, teachers, doctors, healers, psychiatrists and health buffs, scientists and statisticians, cost accountants and librarians, philosophers and policemen, will all be truly inspired. It will be as if they are carried forward on a huge tidal wave of progress and action.

Saturn in your 9th angle will help you to prepare a blueprint of all that you want to achieve. It should also make you positive and hopeful. Also remember that people from distant places will play a vital, even pivotal role in your affairs. Your in-laws will see more of you.

Final word on Saturn:
Listen Aquarians, Saturn will shift gears in your 10th angle from October 6th, 2012. It means two different things:

a) You will be at peak power and performance;
b) But if you push too hard and become a dictator, you will be thrown out.

In other words, you will fall from power. Therefore the advice of Ganesha is: Be ambitious, earn good money, but respect the feelings, ideas, and opinions of others also. Be reasonable; if you do this all will be well.

We will talk more, much more about Saturn in your 10th angle in the next two years.

AQUARIUS

MONTH-BY-MONTH

JANUARY

There is a lot on your plate and you start the year with a bang. This is not the time to be morose or morbid. You will have to learn to take others in the team along with you. This is not the time for an ego-oriented, individual effort. Your gentle approach will bear pleasant fruit as your birth month comes closer. Jupiter is in a favourable placing till 4th February. So, expect better family ties, dinners and parties, important social events, appointments and power lunches. From the beginning of the year, Ganesha creates an unusual combination – both love and money. You capitalize on your bondings and contacts. Ganesha advises you to go all out with work. You will find the rewards soon enough. And when work is both lucrative and satisfying, your entire attitude/approach to life is much more relaxed.

This year may open up new frontiers at work. You carry through demanding schemes/schedules. You have the knowledge and expertise to make even seemingly far-fetched schemes come good. You grow in self-confidence. You focus on finances; nothing wrong with that, assures Ganesha. You display a tremendous ability to make friends, socialize, give and receive love. There is a lot going for you and the focus is now on human relationships. There is high adventure, torrid romance spirituality, tantra and mantra, all thrown into the cauldron. You will be busy moving ahead in all directions. Your focus shifts to inner growth. You have the freedom now to devote time, attention, effort to your inner advancement. You show spectacular results in whatever you undertake. A fine, lively, even cracking pace will be set as you delve into new avenues of thought and discoveries. You participate in life fully.

The end of the month is a powerful period and you have to make the most of it. You are an ideas person and this period will suit you perfectly. Mercury, the mighty planet, is all-powerful now. Mercury, the ambassador and salesman of the zodiac, occupies a prominent position now. This is evidently a significant period with many far-reaching consequences. You make waves and there will be prestige, social status, promotion, triumphs, awards and rewards. Ganesha's blessings are in abundance.

FEBRUARY

You will be meeting a lot of people from a variety of persuasions. Ganesha assures you of success in all your new collaborative ventures. You will be spreading your wings far and wide. The focus in the second month of the year is on contacts and communication. You will be lucky in business partnerships, joint endeavours and ventures. You can also indulge the nurturing and caring side of your temperament, along with being a good provider. Ganesha sharpens the loan and funds angle which will prevail throughout the year. But so also will legal matters, lawsuits or disputes. In fact, Ganesha goes a large step further. You concentrate on money in several manifestations now. It is more on the larger scale than on personal or domestic income; mega-finances will be arranged. It will ensure greater progress for you. Individual freedom and pleasure, creative pursuits will all be sources of immense satisfaction. There could be health issues if you stretch yourself beyond manageable limits. Towards mid-month, there could be an intense and romantic phase in which you may have a string of affairs. Do not break the bounds of propriety. I underscore the fact that all trends are subject to individual horoscopes but these are reasonable generalizations.

Towards the end of the month, many sensitivities and insecurities pile up. But there will still be a boost in will power, optimism, vision. You enjoy exploring new avenues, and several vistas are opened. There is a financial focus too now as budgeting and personal cutbacks may be necessary. The emphasis is on loans and funds, and employment, projects. A career/ business/ vocational change may also be contemplated. Ganesha blesses you as you take the necessary steps for personal advancement.

MARCH

The trend is about making some money now. You make swift decisions and capitalize on them. There is money and honey in the kitty, says Ganesha. Now, your reach is wider, your vision larger and the scale of operation bigger. Ganesha will support you, Aquarians. He decides to extend help vis-à-vis taxes, funds, insurance, joint finance and loans. Your income will be enhanced and possibly accrue from several sources. The fine influences still continue to dominate both your purse and heartstrings; love is also greatly energized. In fact, you will definitely be seeking greater depth, vitality, vibrancy in your emotional attachments and involvements. While a true love affair may blossom, there may also be strange encounters. You will have to bank heavily on your innate caution, as well as a strong sense of commitment to family, society, loved ones - but you do come out a winner. Commitment and caring is what you are good at.

In the beginning of the month, you make progress at a steady pace. You are filled with positivity and new energy. The main thrust of this period pertains to money and finance - funds/ grants/ loans/ joint-finances/ raising of capital. There will be a resolution of several problematic issues and you display great mental strength, stamina and wisdom to deal with all that is thrown at you. You are full of positive energy, but health has to be guarded. Ganesha advises you to go slow. There are many distractions as people come to you with their problems and you solve them. Towards mid-month, you strive for greater balance and poise. You could start new collaborations/ventures or secure a grant/loan of some kind. Higher education, research, religious impulses and new discoveries will take your time and grab your eyeballs. Ganesha is with you. There will be family outings, possibly a holiday together. But you are not at peace; something under the surface is frothing and it is disturbing you enormously. Try to get away to a quiet corner and understand the feeling better. As the month ends, you will be spending more time with the family. People from all over the world will drop in and there will be many happy moments. There is success at work too but it is not the thrust of this period. Home/house/property affairs come into sharp focus and socially it turns out to be a lively and exciting time.

APRIL

There is a chance that you don't fit in with the masses as you believe in following a different drumbeat. You may be difficult to figure out for most people. But things change for a while now. You possess a quality that is rare – people skills – and it will give you a global reach. You are much more tolerant and gentle with people whose lifestyle, values, even behaviour are different from your own. You are eager and willing to help relatives, parents, and in-laws and/or to travel. Ganesha says that this is a month of huge, invisible gains. There is a side of you that truly thrives on being there for others. You love doing it and apply it to the family level and the material plane too. Personally, however, you now turn to study, learn new skills and strategies, improve your mind, and be open to suggestions, ideas and opinions quite different from yours. Your willingness and desire to grow is great indeed. In the cognitive processes, thinking, meditation, contemplation are both positively reinforced and improved. True spirituality will therefore be a major gain. There is also love in the air. You are off on holiday with loved ones and have wonderful times. There are relationships, associations, marriages, engagements, concerts, get-togethers. Your empathy and philanthropy earn acclaim as people seek you out. This is truly a wonderful period, says Ganesha.

Towards mid-month, there is time for celebrations. There are happy moments in the family. This phase has you turning to the home, hearth, home-away-from-home, domestic and filial duties. You will seek to strengthen, reinforce bonds and ties and turn to family matters. There is enhanced confidence, sharing, love and self-belief. As a result, your efforts will peak and you will take on life with renewed zest, zeal and enthusiasm. As the month ends, you will also be fascinated by tantra, mantra, spiritual questioning and the inner life of the soul. This is an interesting mix along with the passions and emotions of the physical plane. You desire a certain depth and intensity in your life, and you will have it for sure. This is also a lucky phase with money.

MAY

You strike a purple patch. The going is good and you do exceedingly well. Your upward trajectory has no roadblocks. The very favourable Sun-Jupiter combination dominates your sign, empowering and inspiring you greatly and enabling you to win laurels and outshine all other contenders. The emphasis on loans and funds remains as strong as ever this month, too. There is also genuine love and romance, parties and fun, the warmth of friendship and social gatherings. There are celebrations at home and at work. There is better rapport with colleagues, associates, peers and family. There is greater harmony, peace and contentment in your life. This is a time for bonding, a sense of being truly comfortable in your own skin.

As the month moves ahead, you spend a lot of time on renovation, construction and house-warmings. The theme in this phase is the enhancement of property, assets and other such acquisitions. Ganesha blesses you as you brook no opposition to your plans. As May ends, emotions are intensely experienced. There could be travel and several new connections. You also spend time with family finances and your personal wealth/ income/ assets/ investment portfolio. There could also be many expenses and the risk of ill-health.

JUNE

You push ahead on all cylinders. There is no letting go of the pedal. Saturn retrogrades in your angle of work; this is an apparently reverse movement, but it draws your mind towards work with renewed energy after the 10th. It's common knowledge that the movement of Saturn is always slow. But there is good news. The quality of work you put in will not only be admired and appreciated but will lead to gains and progress that are visible, concrete, exciting. The sheer necessity of routine work will be converted into inspired - and inspiring - activity. But it's not all work for you. You also relax, let your hair down, enjoy yourself - and that you do with much socializing, happy times with friends and loved ones. The strong trend is that you will be relating better to people, especially those closest to you. You define yourself through your work and make several amendments to your working style. Whatever changes you make now will be an extension of the greater confidence and energy that you possess and this will underline the changes that you make on the home and work fronts as well. Health is also good. What more can one ask for, says Ganesha.

Towards mid-month, with the new moon in Gemini, you are flying off in many directions. Your creative juices are flowing and those in the media do exceedingly well. You have a much larger vision of the world now. Your interests expand to research, higher study, or just enhancing your knowledge and skills. There is also time for love and laughter. Your will power, optimism, vision and aspirations favour you to breach all boundaries. As the month ends, you focus on relationships and ties, bonds and commitments. You focus on the people you value, and are more involved and caring with loved ones. The extended family of children, siblings, in-laws and other relatives will crave your time and attention. You are the soul of the family and Ganesha is happy.

JULY

You have to be wary this month as there are many contrasting and contradictory pulls and pressures. You will have to seriously examine the middle path and find a neutral way out. There will be conflicting pulls this month. But, thankfully, your mate/partner is supportive and understanding. There may also be health problems/medical expenses for family members, perhaps an older person. It is a challenge for you to balance your personal life, commitments, work requirements, but you do it. Ganesha cautions against signing contracts or enter profit sharing or other financial agreements hastily. There may also be some dangers in travel and so it will be a good idea to take the precautions necessary. This can be an intense, demanding but greatly fulfilling period. The big trend for this month is definitely relationships. There will be warmth, closeness and happiness in your life. As July moves on, many emotions come to the surface but you are on stable ground and make huge gains. There may be some misunderstandings that need to be urgently sorted out before they manage to take on gigantic proportions. You will rise to the challenges and your performance will be awesome, impressive and inspirational. There is also a hint at overindulgence in this period. But you are destined for good times, as Ganesha is with you.

AUGUST

There is a lot of movement in your life and you will be in the thick of innovation and strategizing. There will be new winds pushing your sails. You will be blessed with a feeling of relief this month. The odds favour you. All you need to do is go out and win! You will instinctively know the good moves, the right things to say/do – and the results will show. You seem to be spinning around, moving fast in all directions. You start the month with the full moon in your sign and this can be significant. You will look at ensuring success in all your ventures and projects. This is a really favourable phase, which brings about better results at work, respite from stress, somewhat better health and better family ties. You will be completely absorbed in activities that will enhance your vision and intellectual powers. Please remember that this phase is full of hope and promise with infinite possibilities. Also remember that these are generalizations and a more accurate pronouncement will depend on your individual horoscope. It goes without saying though that Ganesha wishes you well.

There is a strengthening and widening of the relationships theme as the month moves on. There are new ties of love and affection and also partnerships, collaborations, and tie-ups at work. Health may need extra attention as you have been burning the candle at both ends. It is also a good time for writing, academics, even delivering guest lectures and attending symposia. As the month ends, there is a lot of movement and possibly overseas travel. You make many new connections and expand rapidly at work. But please remember that life is not all champagne and strawberries. There could be legal issues and domestic strife. This is not a good time to take risks. Keep away from gambling/speculation. This could be a very sensitive period when old wounds show up. But please do not be too soft in your decision-making. Be more dispassionate and objective. You are in a very abstract and subjective mood now and could make decisions from the heart.

SEPTEMBER

There is a lot going for you as the year turns the corner. Ganesha says, perks, promotions, plaudits, plans, projects – all the P's will be there. New projects and assignments are bound to materialize; this is also a good month in terms of both the F's – family and finances. My advice is - eat, drink and be merry, and give thanks to Ganesha! The presence of Mars in your sign energizes you, imbuing you with renewed zest and enthusiasm. All this makes for great power and the determination to overcome all obstacles. Close bonding, warmth, tenderness are also your gains in this month. People, in general, will expect a lot from you in this phase. Ganesha advises you to deal with your duties and chores with commitment, and simultaneously find the time to unwind. Towards mid-month, many new forces will be at work in your life. You need to be unemotional, objective and dispassionate. You also need to re-evaluate and reassess strategies, objectives and, above all, your attitude. There will be times when you will be severely tested. All this, let me add here, will only make you a better person. When the month ends, there will be a lot on your plate. Your income and finances will be on the upswing. There is a possibility of forging a strong partnership based on loyalty, trust and bonding.

OCTOBER

There will be many domestic issues that take up your time. There will also be time spent with old friends and distant relatives. The focus returns to hearth and home this month. In fact, it is as if the world itself is your family. This will include partnerships, tie-ups, and collaborations. You have tremendously exciting chances to make a quick turnaround, a fast buck, a killing in the stock market. In addition, the strong emphasis this month will be on cyber communication, contacts and contracts. The good times continue – in fact, they get even better. This could be a very busy month with love and romance along with legal and financial matters. There is money and honey. You make many plans for the future and also immerse yourself in local affairs. You are on firmer ground as the month ends. Ganesha ensures that there is recognition as well as a feeling of self-worth that enhances both your confidence and your performance in the professional sphere. The full moon is in Taurus as the month ends and there is stability and progress. Your quest for new ideas and concepts, the constant desire for achievements, will be further stimulated. You are cherished, loved and popular.

NOVEMBER

Ganesha cautions you that this month has many ups and downs. The year ends in a flurry of activity and you will be running in many directions. There will be a lot on your plate and you may be chewing more than you can digest, metaphorically speaking. Ganesha advises you to concentrate on loved ones and family, and the joys of domesticity. This could also reduce your stress levels. Equally important will be the paradox that, despite pressure-cooker activities, you will be in an introspective, assessing mood, thus giving an extra dimension, more or less, to your personality, persona, intellect. It is the qualities of the mind that you will value cherish and seek to enhance. There are many expenses, and travel too. You make many new associations and contacts as you sally forth in the world of business. Your new ideas and ingenuity will lead to progress. There is also spiritual and emotional growth. There is a new purpose to your life now. You are brimming with ideas. Your performance is scintillating. As the month progresses, the intensity increases with the moon's first quarter in your sign. You manage to find the time to do justice to whatever is thrown on your plate and, believe me, there is a lot. Life is frantic and frenetic. It may be time now to go slow on the pedal and take time off to explore your motives and inner impulses. True soul-searching and self-examination will be of great help. Ganesha encourages you.

DECEMBER

Another year ends and it is all finally well worth it. This can be a great time to be. You are burning the candle at both ends for sure. The year ends with a flurry of activity. Ganesha warns you of burnout because you will be spreading yourself too thin. But, once again, it is your own people skills and your presence of mind that will stand you in good stead. You will certainly reach out to people and places, sign contracts, your prestige will soar, and that is always good. In addition, it brings with it perks, pleasures, profits and plenty. December is definitely a power-packed month, which finds you going great guns, both financially and socially. It endows a fresh sparkle, a touch of glamour and style, to your creative endeavours. Artists born under this sign will give off their best now. It is holiday time as well, but avoid indulging in a spending spree as there may be a sudden financial squeeze. However, good times are just round the corner in January guaranteeing you energy, enthusiasm, and ebullience. You feel loved and cherished, along with being appreciated and understood as an individual. You have self-belief and confidence and a strong will to grow in your job. As the month moves on, you are on the fast track to success. Your determination to succeed is unmatched. There will be good money, good prospects, good moves at work and good times at home, says Ganesha. As the year ends, you have inner peace and a sense of balance. You move into the New Year with greater confidence.

AQUARIUS

THE MONTHS AT A GLANCE

January

Mercury, the mighty planet, is all-powerful now. Mercury, the ambassador and salesman of the zodiac, occupies a prominent position now. This is evidently a very significant period with many far-reaching consequences. You make waves and there will be prestige, social status, promotion, triumphs, awards and rewards.

February

The emphasis is on loans and funds, employment, projects. A career/business/vocational change may also be contemplated.

March

There will be a resolution of several problematic issues and you display great mental strength, stamina and wisdom to deal with all that is thrown at you. You are full of positive energy, but health has to be guarded.

April

You desire a certain depth and intensity in your life, and you will have it for sure. This is also a lucky phase with money. You may spend a lot of time too helping and counselling others.

May

The theme in this phase is the enhancement of property, assets and other such acquisitions. Ganesha blesses you as you brook no opposition to your plans.

June

Your creative juices are flowing and those in the media will do exceedingly well. You have a much larger vision of the world now.

Your interests expand to research, higher study, or just enhancing your knowledge and skills.

July

The big trend for this month is definitely relationships. There will be warmth, closeness and happiness in your life.

August

This is a really favourable phase which brings about better results at work, respite from stress, somewhat better health and better family ties. You will be completely absorbed in activities that will enhance your vision and intellectual powers.

September

When the month ends, there will be a lot on your plate. Your income and finances will be on the upswing. There is a possibility of forging a strong partnership based on loyalty, trust and bonding.

October

This could be a very busy month with love and romance along with legal and financial matters. There is money and honey. You make many plans for the future.

November

There is also spiritual and emotional growth. There is a new purpose to your life now. You are brimming with ideas. Your performance is scintillating.

December

A power-packed month which finds you going great guns, both financially and socially. It endows a fresh sparkle, a touch of glamour and style to your creative endeavours. Artists born under this sign will give off their best now.

AQUARIUS

WEEKLY REVIEW

(By the Phases of the Moon)

January 1 - Moon's first quarter in Aries

You move fast and furious as the year unfolds. You have great ideas and are often misunderstood as you work from an entirely different perspective. You are normally far ahead of your times. This year you work hard and qualitatively too. You may open up new frontiers at work. You know that you can carry through demanding schemes/schedules. You have the knowledge and expertise to make even seemingly far-fetched schemes come out good. You experience the joy of exploiting your true potential. You grow in self-confidence. You focus on finances: be it investing, or raising funds, buying/selling, getting yourself new acquisitions. Money matters become a primary concern. Nothing wrong with that, assures Ganesha. Unless your home is well-stocked, there is no point in solving the problems of the world. Every spiritual master tells you to listen to him or her on a full stomach to get the true import of what is being said! The year will have many colours like a huge Holi party and you will revel in it.

January 9 - Full Moon in Cancer

You have many moods and not all of them are usually pleasant. But there is no harm in showing the world the sunny side always. You display a tremendous ability to make friends, socialize, give and receive love. There is a lot going for you and the focus is now on human relationships. Your sphere of interests expands. Your personality shines as you become more independent and focused. You look for a global vision and are interested in news, messages, journeys, study courses, a penchant for knowledge and information, a bonding with relatives and friends. There is high adventure, torrid romance, spirituality, tantra and mantra, all thrown into the cauldron. There is great spiritual progress, says Ganesha. You will be busy moving ahead in all directions. Many new attractions and distractions will be thrown your way and you will have to choose intelligently.

January 16 - Moon's last quarter in Libra

You materially prosper and make substantial spiritual progress too. Your focus now shifts to inner growth. Relationships are important too. You may find yourself losing the affection of someone you cherish, or hold dear. It would be best to keep all associations at arm's length lest they blow up on your face. Keep all your dealings cool, unemotional and objective. Ganesha is with you. You have the freedom now to devote time, attention and effort to your inner advancement. There are sundry expenses too.

January 23 - New Moon in Aquarius

You are energized, excited and enthused by life. You show spectacular results in whatever you undertake. A fine, lively, even cracking pace will be set as you delve into new avenues of thought and discoveries. Your mind is razor sharp as you tackle new challenges with dexterity. You participate in life fully. There is entertainment, romance and sheer joie de vivre. You are able to juggle several aspects of your life beautifully. Ganesha blesses you all the way. You embark on a new phase of achievement and hard work.

January 31 - Moon's first quarter in Taurus

This is a powerful period and you have to make the most of it. You are an ideas person and this period will suit you perfectly. Mercury, the mighty planet, is all-powerful now. It favours travels/ meetings/conferences/ interviews/ trips/ more brain power/contacts/ communication/correspondence/contracts.

Mercury has a special connection with the circuits of the brain. Chess, crossword and other such games belong to Mercury. Also, short distance runners and spin bowlers are controlled by Mercury. Mercury, in short, is the ambassador and salesman of the zodiac. This is a very significant period with many far-reaching consequences. You make waves and there will be prestige, social status, promotion, triumphs, awards and rewards. Way to go, says Ganesha. Your ideas receive acclaim. For those in print, radio and broadcasting this is a particularly good period.

February 7 - Full Moon in Leo

There is palpable power and direction in whatever you do. Your new perspective gives you many gains. Individual freedom and pleasure, creative pursuits will all be sources of immense satisfaction. There could be health issues if you stretch yourself beyond manageable limits. You need to maintain a sense of proportion, and balance work and recreation, both of which Ganesha gives you in ample measure this week. You make the necessary adjustments in your values, lifestyle and orientation. You finally find balance, peace and equanimity. Ganesha is happy for you. You consolidate your gains and make great strides at work and play.

February 14 - Moon's last quarter in Scorpio

This could be an intense and romantic phase in which you may have a string of affairs. You will fly off the handle for sure. Ganesha urges you to have some restraint. Do not break the bounds of propriety. I underscore the fact that all trends are subject to individual horoscopes but these are reasonable generalizations. You are riding a tiger. There is romance that catches you off guard and you may, in all probability, lose your senses to the aroma and excitement of a roll in the haystack. There will certainly be no holes in your pocket and no financial worries. But there is still a need to conserve both your vitality and your funds. You seek a wider perspective and sharpen your communication skills. You will be reaching out to people and places. There is very little to halt you in your tracks. You are blazing it, or rather torching it!

February 21 - New Moon in Pisces

This is a mixed period with many sensitivities and insecurities piling up. Sometimes your plans and actions may not pan out as anticipated but there will still be a boost in will power, optimism, vision. You enjoy exploring new avenues, and several vistas are opened. In addition to your normal pursuits, you will dabble in metaphysics, astrology and other related sciences. There is a financial focus too now as budgeting and personal cutbacks may be necessary. The emphasis is on loans and funds, employment, projects. A career/business/vocational change may also be contemplated. Ganesha blesses you as you take the necessary steps for personal advancement. Finances will be the dominant trend, be it buying/selling/loans/stocks/realty. You earn, spend, speculate, gamble and understand the ground realities of finance better.

March 1 - Moon's first quarter in Gemini

You make progress at a steady pace. You realize that your greatest gains are your added knowledge, skills and wisdom. You are filled with positivity and new energy. There is zest in whatever you undertake. There is happiness in relationships too. The main thrust of this period pertains to money and finance --- funds/ grants/loans/joint-finances/ raising of capital. There are many expenses too on both the professional and personal fronts. You also look at tantra and mantra and spend time in esoteric and spiritual pursuits. Your core wants complete, all-round growth. It will happen, assures Ganesha. There are domestic issues too which will take your time.

March 8 - Full Moon in Virgo

There will be a resolution of several problematic issues in this period. You have great mental strength, stamina and wisdom to deal with all that is thrown at you. You will be addressing conflicts and problems at work, sharing with your boss, co-workers, subordinates, children, dependents, even extended family, in-laws, friends, and the community at large. There will be some underlying turmoil and tussle, but you manage to cope. You are full of positive energy, but health has to be guarded. Ganesha advises you to go slow. There are many distractions as people come to you with their problems and you solve them. You will have to be clear about your priorities. It is futile to spread yourself too thin and be taken advantage of.

March 15 - Moon's last quarter in Sagittarius

There is a lot of movement. You strive for greater balance and poise. You could start new collaborations/ventures or secure a grant/loan of some kind. Higher education, research, religious impulses and new discoveries will take your time. Your interactions with those you love will be warm and cordial. There will be great happiness at home as children will be a source of joy. There is hard work too and you solve pending issues and lay the foundations for expansion. Ganesha backs you right through.

March 22 - New Moon in Aries

Expenses pile high. You are on overdraft mode. You need to sort this out before it gets the upper hand. Money is never your reason to live but it should also not bog you down. You display a tremendous ability to make friends, socialize, give and receive love. There will be family outings, possibly a holiday together. But you are not at peace; something under the surface is frothing and it is disturbing you enormously. Try to get away to a quiet corner and understand the feeling better. It will be well worth it, says Ganesha.

March 30 - Moon's first quarter in Cancer

You will be spending more time with the family. People from all over the world will drop in and there will be many happy moments. There is success at work too but this is not the thrust of this period. Home/house/property affairs come into sharp focus, and socially it turns out to be a lively and exciting time. At many levels, it is a frantic period as you move about getting your house in order. It may be a good time for introspection. Get into your corner and try to disconnect, says Ganesha. You have nothing to lose and a lot to gain. Silence is always the best teacher. The madding crowd can have dissipating energies and you are beginning to feel it. It may be worth your while to take a break and visit a sanctuary or monastery for some peace and quiet.

April 6 - Full Moon in Libra

Once again, there is love in the air. You are off on holiday with loved ones and have wonderful times. You resolve pending matters and lay solid foundations for new projects. All your efforts and endeavours are energised leading to power, promotion, perks, position and pelf. There are relationships, associations, marriages, engagements, concerts, get-togethers. Your empathy and philanthropy earn acclaim as people seek you out. You bask in the admiration of friends and loved ones. Even your foes are silenced. This is truly a wonderful period, says Ganesha.

April 13 - Moon's last quarter in Capricorn

You are focused at getting your life, financial affairs and commitments in proper order. Home and family are top in the order of priority. You also work on finances to ensure a steady source of income. You may look at moonlighting or take up an extra job to garner your resources. You will be keen to make a quick buck so that you have liquid cash at hand for possible emergencies and, of course, the little luxuries and extras that add to the quality of life. There could also be a swift affair in this period. You widen your horizons and reach out to people and places. There is sustained progress as you dig your feet in and slog away. You grab every opportunity that comes your way. Ganesha wishes you great luck in all that you undertake.

April 21 - New Moon in Taurus

This is the time for celebrations. There are happy moments in the family. This phase has you turning to the home, hearth, home-away-from-home, domestic and filial duties. There is a sense of satisfaction when you fulfill the hopes and expectations of those you love. You will seek to strengthen, reinforce bonds and ties and turn to family matters. You will also try to improve parent–child relationships. There is enhanced confidence, sharing, love and self–belief. As a result, your efforts will peak and you'll take on life itself with renewed zest and enthusiasm. There is no time now for mood swings and a fickle temperament. This is a period to enjoy yourself without a harness, says Ganesha. There could be an addition to the family and many happy moments.

April 29 - Moon's first quarter in Leo

A lot is happening in your life now. You have managed to reinforce, enhance and strengthen family bonds. There is love and passion in this period and you may even take the new person in your life to the altar. You will also be fascinated by tantra, mantra, spiritual questioning and the inner life of the soul. This is an interesting mix along with the passions and emotions of the physical plane. You desire a certain depth and intensity in your life, and you will have it for sure. This is also a lucky phase with money to be made in gambling, speculation or at the stock market. Life is interesting, to say the least. Ganesha is happy for you. This is a lucky streak and you can cash in on it.

May 6 - Full Moon in Scorpio

You have made rapid progress on all fronts. You now feel that you can afford to relax a bit. There is genuine love and romance, parties and fun, the warmth of friendship and social gatherings. You pay more attention to your own creature comforts, your pleasures, leisure pursuits and above all, to your personal, intimate bonding and involvement with your partner/mate/spouse/lover. There are celebrations at home and at work. There is better rapport with colleagues, associates, peers and family. You wonder how strange life is -- barren at times with nothing happening, and then, suddenly, without warning, an avalanche of activities. Ganesha, who knows it all, chuckles. The force of events that engulf you, takes you by surprise.

May 12 - Moon's last quarter in Aquarius

People continue to be important this week. Local and domestic affairs need to be handled first as also some long-pending issues. There is greater harmony, peace and contentment in your life. This is a time for bonding, a sense of being truly comfortable in your own skin. Your personal space and life will continue to be your main focus. You may seem off tangent but you are still full of progressive ideas. The mood is good and you are at your creative best. You win applause. Ganesha is happy for you.

May 20 - New Moon in Gemini

You spend a lot of time on renovation, construction and house-warmings, maybe even dealing with a 'Vaastu' problem in the house - the theme in this phase is the enhancement of property, assets and such acquisitions. You have a genuine desire to address all your domestic requirements. Your agenda is very clear and the family is happy that, for once, you are on a truly practical mode. You spend all your time poring over financial instruments and downloading to the bin what you don't need. It is important to de-clutter and you are doing just that. You are emptying the vessel for new water to be poured in. There is need for cash in hand. Ganesha blesses you. You brook no opposition to your plans. Money has been well earned and now well spent too.

May 28 - Moon's first quarter in Virgo

This could be a complicated and intense week as emotions are intensely experienced. There could be travel on the cards and several new connections. You are on the fast track this week. In fact, you are ready to pull out all the stops, work super-fast and extra long in your hurry to achieve, to get things moving to your satisfaction. Ganesha tells you not to be rash and hasty in your decision-making as that could boomerang on you. You spend time with family finances and your personal wealth/income/assets/ investment portfolio. There could also be many expenses and the risk of ill-health. You may lose your cool and have unnecessary altercations. Avoid all this, advises Ganesha. Learn to keep your cool as anger is a sign of weakness and not strength. Anger is detrimental to health and the wellbeing of everyone present. It kills slowly; try to find ways to handle it. If you act in anger, the results are almost always detrimental.

June 4 - Full Moon in Sagittarius

The strong trend now is that you will be relating better to people, especially those closest to you. You will also expand at work/ business. You define yourself through your work and make several amendments to your working style. Whatever changes you make now will be an extension of the greater confidence and energy that you possess and this will underline the changes that you make on the home and work fronts. The new initiatives will not be easy and your task is somewhat burdensome. But Ganesha blesses you and you come out trumps despite the many challenges thrown at you. New opportunities come your way and the future is dependent on how you are able to utilize them.

June 11 - Moon's last quarter in Pisces

Emotional issues are at play now. Life is relatively comfortable as your finances are in order and you feel that you can afford to take it easy. You will find time to be with loved ones and friends. There will definitely be better bonding and closer interaction with your children/parents. This is a pleasant time as you are mentally and emotionally much more relaxed and at ease. Health is also good. What more can one ask for, says Ganesha. There can be no visible worry if work and health are good and loved ones well taken care of. This is, without a doubt, a great time to be. You revel in the bounties of the moment.

June 19 - New Moon in Gemini

You are flying off in many directions. Your creative juices are flowing and those in the media do exceedingly well. You have a much larger vision of the world now. Your interests expand to research, higher study, or just enhancing your knowledge and skills. A good time to travel or make travel plans which is all a part of the overall theme of wider communication and mental growth. There is also time for love and laughter. The warmth of human relationships is pleasing. There is joy in bonding and you experience the richness of human contact. You have blissful times. Your will power, optimism, vision and aspirations favour you to breach all boundaries as you expand and excel in whatever you undertake. Ganesha blesses you. It is a time to experience the richness of true bonding.

June 27 - Moon's first quarter in Libra

Your mood is stable now. If anything, you could be deliriously happy. The focus is on relationships and ties, bonds and commitments. All these may either be personal or professional. You focus on the people you value and are more involved and caring with loved ones. You may even accidentally meet someone you find especially compatible. It could be the beginning of a lifetime bond. The extended family of children, siblings, in-laws and other relatives will crave your time and attention. You are generous with them and take them out for sumptuous treats. You are the soul of the family. What a great way to be, says Ganesha.

July 3 - Full Moon in Capricorn

There is a lot of buying and selling. There are also solid expansion plans in the offing. You will now acquire a changed perspective and a totally different slant on contacts and communications. You are filled with new ideas along with the energy to carry them through. You display outstanding mental capacity but must think carefully and long before forming opinions or taking vital decisions. It might be a good idea to postpone important decisions for later, as haste may bring waste. Slow down. You seem to be in a tearing hurry. Ganesha cautions you against signing contracts or entering profit-sharing or other financial agreements hastily. There may also be some dangers in travel and so it will be a good idea to take necessary precautions. Avoid drunk driving and the fast lane. There is free will too to fashion your karma. This is an intense, demanding but greatly fulfilling period. There are also new expenses but you are sensible enough to make the right investments. Nothing ventured, nothing gained, and unless you throw some money around you will not earn anything. Reap the whirlwind now. It is your time in the sun.

July 11 - Moon's first quarter in Aries

You are zooming ahead. The foundations have been well laid and this is the right time for sustained progress. You handle life positively, full of vision, optimism and faith. It makes for a very warm atmosphere at home and at the workplace. If you are self-employed, there could be many renovations to the office. The employed may see a rise in perks and a promotion. There could also be an addition to the family; something good is bound to happen. You gain the support, companionship and camaraderie of friends, admirers, acquaintances and lovers. The big trend for this month is definitely relationships. There will be warmth, closeness and happiness in your life. You achieve a lot and the results are spectacular. Your dark moods are a thing of the past. You realize that nature has been very kind to you. Ganesha is with you, for sure.

July 19 - New Moon in Cancer

Many emotions come to the surface but you are on stable ground and make huge gains. All this will happen thanks to the changed mental ethos that you have created within you, caring for those around you without making demands, being tolerant and less critical. This softer persona makes for much more happiness and contentment in your family. It also helps garner the true co-operation of those around you, especially of your colleagues/co-workers, bosses/sub-ordinates/employees. Your voice is heard and your words accepted for their import and impact. Domestic issues will grab your attention and there could be minor expenses. Believe in Ganesha to carry you over the coal.

July 26 – Moon's last quarter in Scorpio

There may be some misunderstandings that need to be urgently sorted out before they take on gigantic proportions. Out of court settlements are suggested. Please stay calm and remain receptive to bright and new ideas. You will rise to the challenge and your performance will be awesome, impressive and inspirational. You will plan/undertake new ventures that will bring out the best in you in terms of both ingenuity and creativity. You will also revel in relationships that, Ganesha willing, may ripen into something more intense, more joyous and fulfilling. There is a hint at overindulgence in this period. But what the hell; life is for fun and merriment and not for watching your back or your wallet all the time. Live in the present and try not to be suspicious of people and events. You are destined for good times.

August 2 - Full Moon in Aquarius

The full moon is in your sign and this can be very significant. You will look at ensuring success in all your ventures and projects. This, of course, may require a hard slog. Do not get carried away by the moment and make decisions in haste. Do not, also, get too judgmental. This is a really favourable phase which brings about better results at work, respite from stress, somewhat better health and better family ties. You have realized that all work and no play make Jack a dull boy. You are also convinced that you need holistic growth for true happiness. These are vital realizations, says Ganesha. It will be a great step forward if you can manage this new-found lifestyle for keeps. Life is a long process of teachings, and as you move up the ladder of success and fame you also grow as a person. But money and fame have never spurred you to great heights. You have always looked for more intrinsic and substantial growth. In your heart, you know that money can only buy you worldly goods and nothing more.

August 9 - Moon's last quarter in Taurus

There is more stability and progress. There are also many expenses and a touch of love. So, this week, you have a plate that is filled with many aromas. You are determined to sustain the growth that you have achieved and also add to it. You will be completely absorbed in activities that will enhance your vision and intellectual powers. You are keen to grow as a person of consequence. Family ties could exert a strong pull; you will also be more tolerant of those close to you. In this phase, you have the moral strength and dedication to sustain huge efforts at work and play. Avoid harshness in your dealings and do not speak disparagingly of those around you, even though it may be justified. Please remember that this phase is full of hope and promise with infinite possibilities. Please also remember that these are generalizations and a more accurate pronouncement will depend on your individual horoscope. It goes without saying though that Ganesha wishes you well.

August 17 - New Moon in Leo

Expenses mount and you have to be careful with your purse strings. You may overextend yourself. You have to be shrewd and discreet and make the correct decisions and the right moves since you have a lot going for you that will be positive and pleasing. There is a strengthening and widening of relationships. There are new ties of love and affection and also partnerships, collaborations, and tie-ups at work. Good social interactions will step up your entertaining time. There is a note of warning though: watch your step, as accidents and traumas as well as let-downs are possible. Be vigilant, suggests Ganesha. You do not need a breakdown at this stage of your life. Health may need extra attention as you have been burning the candle at both ends. It is also a good time for writing, academics, even delivering guest lectures and attending symposia. You will make your presence felt despite the odds stacked against you. There is some rough weather but Ganesha is in the cockpit and he will steer you to safety.

August 24 - Moon's first quarter in Sagittarius

There is a lot of movement and possibly overseas travel. You make many new connections and expand rapidly at work. If employed, there could be perks and promotions in the offing. But there are other forces at play too, some of which are somewhat disconcerting. You will find yourself almost yanked back to what is nowadays frequently referred to as the 'real' world. There could be rude shocks or a reality check. Life is not all champagnes and strawberries. There could be legal issues and domestic strife leading to arguments and face-offs. This is not a good time to take risks. Keep away from gambling/speculation. This is a period when you have to roll up your sleeves and dirty your hands. There are several pressing domestic and professional demands on you. But you are blessed by Ganesha and he will clear the obstacles from your path. Just keep the faith.

August 31 - Full Moon in Pisces

This could be a very sensitive period when old wounds show up. The focus is on love and the home. You and your partner could take love to another level and there could be powerful bonding. There will be several domestic issues to deal with, like children's health and schooling and the welfare of elders. But this can also be a time of joy, happiness and contentment. You are cheerful and warm and more accepting of people. But please do not be too soft in your decision-making. Be more dispassionate and objective. You are in a very abstract and subjective mood now and could make decisions from the heart. You are insightful, sensitive and caring. Ganesha blesses you. You may bring home a new pet, probably an exotic one. Or you may indulge in gardening and landscaping, depending on the size of the area you are working on. If it is tiny, you could be just pottering around with plants on the terrace.

September 8 - Moon's first quarter in Gemini

You continue to spend time with family. There could be weddings, anniversaries, birthdays and several family outings. People, in general, will expect a lot from you in this phase. Ganesha advises you to deal with your duties and chores with commitment, and find time to unwind simultaneously. Both your health/vitality and personal interactions could suffer and you certainly do not want that. As I said last week, objectivity will be your best bet. You will be loving yet unbiased when dealing with matters concerning dependents - your children, loved ones, old people, or even pets. Don't neglect your health or be careless about food and nutrition. This is also a period when you are infused with powerful creative energy. Those in the media could be in great demand.

September 16 - New Moon in Virgo

Many new forces are at work in your life now. You need to be unemotional, objective and dispassionate. You also need to re-evaluate and reassess strategies, objectives and, above all, your attitude. New ventures will work out well if you avoid mistakes and over-confidence. Be fair in profit-sharing. This will apply more to work, of course, but also partly to the extended family. There could also be a danger of procrastination and letting matters slide. Do not allow communications to deteriorate in depth and meaning. Associates and colleagues may not read hidden signals, and will need to have things spelt out. They may not understand you and may misread your intentions. But Ganesha is with you all the way. The year, as you have seen, has had many trends and will continue this way. You will have to work hard for stability. There will be times when you will be severely tested. All this, let me add here, will only make you a better person. Do not get depressed or worried or suicidal. The storm clouds will pass and the sun will shine again. It is the way of all life --- no man or animal life is exempt from it.

September 22 - Moon's first quarter in Capricorn

There is a lot on your plate and you are munching away in glee. You have a lot to do, and several concerns to keep you not just occupied but heavily involved. Your income and finances will be on the upswing - increased funds, employment benefits, gifts, or an inheritance may be coming your way. You will spend time working on the right investments to be made; after all, the family needs to be secured. There is also the urgent need to work towards building greater accord and harmony in the home or with family members. There will be several profitable discussions with friends/ co-workers/partners or like-minded people. You may also check out the occult sciences or astrology. You realize that you may benefit from a fuller life and move ahead in that direction with some purpose. All this is not easy and you may feel like throwing in the towel, but remember that nothing lasts forever and there is no point in either depression or elation. Many emotions are just wasted. Life is all about perseverance and the right attitude. Ganesha is with you; be rest assured of that.

September 30 - Full Moon in Aries

There is a lot of movement now and you are back to solid work. Your new ventures/projects could already have started showing pleasing results, but you need to make further efforts to ensure that this progress is not only maintained but also speeded up. But there will be hindrances of different kinds, disappointments, family conflicts, many disagreements and misunderstandings and you will have to steer the boat with dexterity. This will be the case particularly if family assets are being divided, apportioned and shared. You need to stay calm and focused to ride the storm. There is a possibility of forging a strong partnership based on loyalty, trust and bonding that helps you build for the present as well as the future. Meticulous planning will be required with the handling of funds to actualize and implement all the great ideas, plans and projects that are now seeking a way out of your grey cells. If you plan carefully, there is recognition and applause coming your way. Your plans are creative and could lead to many new money making opportunities too. Ganesha is happy for you.

October 8 - Moon's last quarter in Cancer

Emotions play a vital role now. There could be problems with teenage children. If you don't nip their activities now while there is still time, it could blow up. But you will also be energized and humming a happy tune. This could be a very busy period; love and romance vie for your attention along with legal and financial matters. You also keep an eagle eye on investments with long-term gains. You could be handling the family finances and also reorganizing your existing resources. Money matters, at every level, will therefore be vital. Tact, diplomacy and gentleness will help you a great deal. This is a period for discretion. You must safeguard your secrets and not disclose your assets. Away from the money angle, there will be harmony at home with family, your loved ones and above all your mate/partner. You are a picture of domestic bliss. Ganesha nods in approval. As I have pointed out several times over the years, the tide changes rapidly.

October 15 - New Moon in Libra

There is money and honey as you spend on goodies. The ambience is pleasant. The spell of peace, amicable interaction and genuine harmony that you have been able to create will extend to all your relationships. Practical day-to-day matters will become much easier to handle as you feel more comfortable in your own skin. A legal issue may be successfully resolved and you manage to keep your commitments to friends and organizations. You make many plans for the future and also immerse yourself in local affairs. You may get involved in social work and may join some organization to clean up the neighbourhood. You are involved in many activities and this is also a pleasant distraction from the cares of the world which you so happily carry on your overburdened shoulders. Sometimes, you may feel that you are on the cross and even think that it is your duty to the world. Do not be so self-sacrificing.

October 22 - Moon's first quarter in Capricorn

You are more settled now and on firmer ground. It is important to get out of the maudlin mood that you often find yourself in. Do not develop a persecution complex as it won't do you any good. Ganesha ensures that there is recognition as well as a feeling of self-worth that enhances both, your confidence and your performance in the professional sphere. You work hard and well but the truly sparkling display will be if you are involved in, or now start up, a venture involving overseas business or trade. Loans/funds/capital/seed money/mutual funds/mortgages work out easily and there is harmony in domestic affairs. You are warm, affectionate and caring, and generate warmth and care in return. But you have this tendency to warm up to losers in life who take away a lot of your valuable time. You feel that you are helping them but, in actuality, you are not. You are, in fact, only harming yourself in the process. And, may I add, harming them too. Just show the path and move on.

October 29 - Full Moon in Taurus

There is stability and progress in this phase. You have a balanced mind and new ideas and thoughts come flooding in. Your quest for new ideas and concepts, the constant desire for achievements, will be further stimulated by social activity, entertainment, creative interference and pursuits, and relationships with children/friends/loved ones. At the same time, you are also content to work quietly behind the scenes rather than project a high-profile image. You are pretty sure of yourself and don't need to win the approval of others. Your self-esteem, which often takes a beating, is at a high now. Go for it, says Ganesha. You are cherished, loved and popular. There is no need or reason to feel that you are the cause for everything bad or ugly that happens in the world. You have every reason to stand up proud with your chest held high. Please remember that you have done your bit.

November 7 - Last quarter in Leo

There are many expenses, not all of which are pleasant, and travel too. You make many new associations and contacts as you sally forth in the world of business. Your new ideas and ingenuity will lead to progress. Changes and commitments that you make, especially on the work front, are likely to be long-term. There is also spiritual and emotional growth. You will move ahead in creative pursuits. On the domestic front, you will find lasting solutions for happiness and contentment with your mate/spouse and children. There is new study, learning, mental growth, and philosophical insights as you grow in every sphere. Personal relationships will be cordial. You work constantly on improving yourself and your relationships. There is the possibility of a child leaving for overseas studies and you will be moist eyed about it. There may also be a bereavement of some kind. Many facets of life will be revealed to you now. This is a valuable phase, says Ganesha, and you have to make the most of what is thrown at you. Life teaches you many lessons.

November 13 - New Moon in Scorpio

There is a new purpose to your life now. You are brimming with ideas. You take on a lot at work and fulfil all your commitments. You work hard at fulfilling the many demands on your time and purse. You are now pursuing high-end goals, and tact and diplomacy will stand you in very good stead. Your performance is scintillating and this helps your relationship with your superiors, peers and those in authority. On the domestic front too, there is joy. There are growing demands on your time and you will fulfil all your obligations willingly and happily. A good way to grow, says Ganesha, as all your interactions will be stronger and more meaningful. The year seems to ending well for you.

November 20 - Moon's first quarter in Aquarius

The intensity increases with the moon's first quarter in your sign, and the pace could be scorching. There are many commitments and you don't shirk them. You work hard at fulfilling the many demands on your time and your pocket. You are now pursuing high objectives and will do a fine balancing act with family time, personal interactions and work needs. Activities involving your superiors are important but so are parental ties and duties. You manage to find the time to do justice to whatever is thrown on your plate and, believe me, there is a lot. Your approach is gentler and more balanced, laced with tact and diplomacy. You are sincere and humble and this phase is therefore, truly, a learning experience. You have learnt to give work your best shot, and to also value and improve your own relationships. You realize that both aspects of your life are equally valuable, valid and important. Ganesha is a fellow traveller, always guarding you.

November 28 - Full Moon in Gemini

Life is frantic and frenetic as you bust forth on multiple cylinders like Asafa Powell, the great hundred meters champion. The home front has many challenges and the work station also draws on your time, energy and resources. You rise in the office hierarchy as your sustained efforts have been noticed by the bosses. There is growing popularity too. It may be time now to go slow on the pedal and take time off to explore your motives and inner impulses. True soul-searching and self-examination will be of great help. You want to get in touch with yourself and this is the best way. You also want others to be aware of what makes you tick, of your true self, and to love you the way you are - warts and all. Ganesha encourages you and hopes you give this journey of self-discovery the best shot. You need to get away from the madding crowd and this could well be the time for it.

December 6 - Moon's last quarter in Virgo

There is recognition at work but personal joy, satisfaction and true pleasure are what Ganesha has now decided to give you. Popularity and warm relationships will add not only to the 'feel-good' factor but to the inner security that being loved and valued gives you. You feel loved and cherished, along with being appreciated and understood as an individual. There are concrete gains and rewards/power/prestige/ pelf/prosperity. Your new priorities will centre around the people you love, and will be infinitely more satisfying and rewarding. Despite some conflicts and confrontations, you are able to pursue your goals and realize them too. There are challenges but you face them with great strength of character. Ganesha blesses you.

December 13 - New Moon in Sagittarius

You have new self-belief and confidence and a strong will to grow in your job. You may, however, need to handle some matters from the past in order to make substantial progress. There may be old wounds or old patterns of thought and action that need addressing. You realize that you need to change your attitude and shift your stance to one of true flexibility and adaptability. This needs to be done both at home and at work. This is what will work best, and be less stressful too. Friends, family and loved ones are solidly behind you. You are enveloped by warmth and caring. You are filled with gratitude as you couldn't have expected more. You are aware of Ganesha's benevolence.

December 20 – Moon's first quarter in Pisces

You are on the fast track to success. Your determination to succeed is unmatched. Now the results will start showing and they will be glorious. There will be good money, good prospects, good moves at work and good times at home, says Ganesha. Loved ones spouse/partner and friends draw closer to you. What adds to your 'feel-good' mood is the fact that there are huge opportunities for advancement in your chosen vocation, job or specialization. You have given a lot of yourself to the people around you and there have been moments of loss and despair. You have felt like throwing in the towel many times and have clung to life precariously. On many occasions, life was like a choppy sea and you held on desperately to the lifeboat thrown at you till your knuckles turned white. But, with Ganesha's help, you managed to come out in one piece, and a wonderfully well fashioned piece at that!

December 28 - Full Moon in Cancer

As the year ends, you have inner peace and a sense of balance, too - the good and the bad in perfect equipoise - which is necessary for true advancement. You will grow in another way, too – learn more about negotiation, management, and some job-related skills. You move into the New Year with greater confidence. This is party time and there will be great socializing, fun times even love and romance. Do not be a dispassionate, objective bystander, internalizing, rationalizing and assessing experiences and objectives. Throw caution to the winds and have fun. Ganesha wants to take you to the next year in a happy mood!

AQUARIUS

KEY DATES

January

1, 4*-5, 9-10, 14-15, 19*-20, 23-24, 27-28.

Work, home, love, journey, the satisfaction of achievement, possible change of a job or a promotion. Stress and strain, though unavoidable, are not good for your health; rest and care is essential.

February

1*-2, 5*-7, 10*-12, 15*-16 (important), 19-20, 23*-25 (important).

Marriage, partnerships at all planes, journeys, stopovers, ceremonies, collaborations. Quite an armful! At the crossroads, says Ganesha!

March

1*, 5-7, 10-11, 14*-16, 19-20, 23-24, 27*-28.

A pivotal week. Hard work, loans, funds, investment, joint-finance for working full speed ahead. Gratuity and pension for retired Aquarians.

April

1*-2, 6-7, 11*-12, 15*-16, 19*-20, 23*-25, 28-30.

You climb the ladder of success and also achieve real happiness. What is left to say?

May

1-2, 8*-9, 12-14, 16-18, 21*-22, 25-28, 31.

Tremendous hard work, mighty success; it will be a carryover from April. Friends, supporters will be with you. Guard your health.

June

1, 4*-6, 9-10, 13-14, 17-18, 22-23, 27-28.

A month of happy results, fulfillment, the realization of hopes, dreams and ambition, predicts Ganesha! You will love and be loved.

July

1*-3, 6-7, 10-11, 14*-17, 23*-25, 28*-30.

Expenses mount, but from the 14th onwards, there is improvement. Health-care is essential; learn to be well-organized, says Ganesha!

August

2-3, 7*-8, 11*-12, 15*-16, 20*-22, 25*-26, 30-31.

Life really begins now. You will pick up strength, energy and, therefore, be successful. Love and gains make you happy. New ventures can be launched.

September

2*-4, 7*-8, 11-13, 16-18, 24-25 (important), 29-30.

Hard work and good reward. Foreign lands beckon. Buying, selling, leasing, funding, investing will be important. Money comes and goes.

October

1, 4*-6, 9*-10, 14-15, 19*-24 (important), 27-28.

October to February will make one unit. The salient features will be employment, property, news and views, inventive genius, ability and the courage to take chances, says Ganesha!

November

1*-2, 5-7, 10-12, 15*-17, 20*-24 (important), 28-29.

November and December also run into one unit. House and home, journey and contacts sum it up.

December

2-4, 7-9, 12*-14, 17-18, 21*-22, 25*-26, 30*-31.

Thrills, spills, mental brilliance, speculation, courtship, wedding nights. They all last long because you have much to share in every way. In short, happiness and satisfaction.

Pisces

February 19 - March 20

PISCES

(February 19 - March 20)

ELEMENT AND RULING PLANET: Water and Neptune.

STRENGTHS: Pieces is receptive intuitive and emotional imaginative romantic impressionable and mystical adaptable and very changeable.

WEAKNESS: Often always in doubt, not serious in life lackadaisical complicated, impracticable and imbalance.

SYMBOL: Two fishes tied to one another swimming in opposite direction-signify hidden depths, shifting emotional currents, conflicts desires and extremes of temperament.

MATCHING SIGN: Virgo.

MAGICAL BIRTHSTONE: Cats eye and Aquamarine – magnifies occult power and brigs serenity of mind. It also protects its wearer while travelling on sea.

PISCES

YEARLY FORECAST

*** "Mi Casa Su Casa." My house is your house.**

*** "A man's home is his wife's castle" A. Chase**

Main Trend

Your days of planning and strategising will be over. It will be totally action time. 2012 brings you a large agenda of things to be done, at least in terms of what's expected of you - personally, professionally and family-wise. It will lead to several new avenues, beginnings, and start-ups. For all of this, a more objective, pragmatic approach will prove to be a good bet. You will thus be able to prioritise what needs to be done, and also decide how best to cope, especially in finances and expenses, but also with your time and effort. Where there was just a general stepping up of activity in June, there is now a clearly defined trend. This July the focus is sharp and clear in home, house, property, the domestic scene, with intermittent spotlights on the outside world.

A family gathering is also quite likely and so, paradoxically, is a home-away-from-home. It could be a holiday cottage, weekend pad or even a second establishment, which you find necessary for work or your professional consultations. Around March and onwards you may expect a bit of peace and domesticity, too. Renovation and decoration, buying and selling, refurbishing and designing will all keep you on your toes. July centres and focuses you, gives you grounding, a base, especially on and after the 9th. Community affairs, pending work and in a few cases retirement may be likely.

But there are equally likely to be hassles, conflicts, differences here, too. Learn to be diplomatic and tactful in your dealings. You'll achieve desired results with far less stress on yourself and less expense, too. The rewards are promised by Ganesha, who also claims in conclusion that June is a slightly difficult customer to handle in the sense that too much is expected --- lots to do, lots to handle. **But challenges are what make us humans grow and also realise our own true potential.**

Jupiter:

Ganesha says, the focus is very strong and sharp on the home; a home which will be a haven as well as a 'tavern' and a meeting place for friends, a harbour for your mate, and everything nice for yourself.

Yes, the home could also be the base of operations, the fulcrum around which your life rotates. Buying/ selling/ leasing/ renting of house and or shop and office are also more than possible. You will say, with Edward Coke, "A man's home is his wife's castle", and you will repeat with Pliny, "Home, is where the heart is." I know you have begun to ask yourself about the heavy concentration on the home front! The reason is, you will say, "Mi Casa es tu casa"- my house is your house. To Adam, paradise was home. To you, home will be paradise.

The astrological reason is the placing of Jupiter in your 4th angle of house, home, property as such, including land, agricultural holding and so on; the spotlight is also on parents, in-laws, the elders, boss, relatives; the later part of life and the happiness/ comforts to be had from it. This could also deal with retirement; a home-away-from-home comes under this particular Jupiterean ambit. Renovation and decoration, buying/ selling, alteration and installation of gadgetry, even refurbishing are also within the same ambit.

Ganesha points out that the world's most expensive dress worth $2,000,000, embellished with 2000 carats of emeralds and 400 carats of diamonds – was shown off by a model at a fashion show held recently at the national history museum. In addition, the Kohinoor diamond, the cash value of which can financially support and sustain the entire world for two and a half days, could well come your way, for right now Pisceans, beauty and glamour is your birthright.

Ganesha says, it is your destiny to deck yourself in style, enjoy the goodies of life, entertain and be amused, and possibly continue with renovation/ decoration/ investing/ buying/ selling/ mortgaging of land, property, building, shop, office, godown, warehouse and farmhouse.

Jupiter will swish away in your 4th angle, emphasising:

a) Buying/ selling of house/ office/ shop/ godown/ warehouse;
b) Renovation/ decorating/ altering; adding a room or so;
c) Better health and more cheerful ambience/ surroundings;
d) Improving your entire base of operations and that, says Ganesha, is both extremely important and absolutely necessary;
e) Taking an active interest in all your surroundings, as we Indians say, but that does not mean that you have to be nosy and interfere in the affairs of others, though most of us do it in India!

The 4th angle is also normally associated with the later part of life, old age, retirement, and paradoxically, with a few new activities, which do not require sinews and muscles or sheer physical strength. Major streamlining of the home and house, office and shop, also come under Jupiter in the 4th angle, almost as a natural corollary. You will want to make your working conditions easier, pleasanter, more comfortable, perhaps more plush.

You will demonstrate considerable managerial skills and artistic excellence in anything to do with property. Property is a broad, all-inclusive term for your assets. Land and farming are included in property. Finally, Ganesha points out that all matters which have not been resolved will be solved, at least to some extent. Ultimately it depends upon your individual horoscope.

Saturn:

We now turn to Saturn for further guidance. Saturn will be in your 8th angle from 13th October 2009 to 5th October 2012. This is a halfway indicator for Saturn.

I must make it absolutely clear that from time to time, your health will be down, as we say in Indian-English! There is also a slight danger of accidents and/ or operations; Ganesha says don't take risks on the health front. For example, do not eat too much stale food/ junk food and, if at the wheel of a car or scooter or motorbike, drive carefully. Have it serviced with regularity. Do this and have faith in Ganesha and Allah. Believe me, this is good advice from your astrologer.

Finances, family, property matters also come under the influence of Saturn in your 8th angle. Therefore you have to be careful of investments, joint-finance, buying and selling, wills, inheritance, and actually all transactions of money. Separations and perhaps death are possible in this placing. Astrology is not completely accurate and perfect. Sometimes the events and incidents may not happen right then, or at all. God alone is the perfect astrologer. Pray to god and seek the help of Allah/ Christ/ Ganesha, and do your duty. That is the real lesson of Saturn in your 8th angle.

Ganesha says you folks do understand that nothing in life is perfect. You are right. With Saturn in your 8th angle, the other main features will be:

a) A sharp and clear focus on joint finance, loans, public trusts and charity institution;
b) Your health and that of near and dear ones, could pose some problems for you;
c) A home- away- from- home;
d) Problems of legacy, dowry, hidden treasures, wills, codicils, legal documents pertaining to marriage, alimony, company laws, contracts regarding corporations, bonds, funds may occur.
e) Tax matters related to land, building, shop, office, godown, warehouse and so on will need to be handled;
f) The danger of low vitality, poor health, accidents, operations, wounds, injuries; once again, I must stress health concerns;
g) Lawsuits and court proceedings will have to be dealt with;
h) Also, perhaps blackmail and deceit.

Yes, I know and understand that this sounds like a terrible list of immense misery and suffering. Obviously, all of it will not happen. The main mishap or unfortunate events may have to do with finance, health, separation from loved ones, depending on your individual circumstances and/ or your personal horoscope.

Saturn in the 8th angle also implies the supreme yogi, the occult master, and the real servant of God. Taken in this light, you will be supremely spiritual. The hand of God will be on your head in benediction. The game of life will be yours. Just wait and watch, and have faith.

Ganesha says we have an extremely unique and unusual situation for you. Expect the unexpected, because Jupiter will be in the first angle and Saturn in the 8th. Prophetic vision and even liberation from worldly ties are possible. So also are lotteries, windfalls, legacies and other forms and unexpected sources of money. It may come in suddenly and surprisingly. The strange, mysterious and the bizarre or even eccentric will be likely to happen.

Saturn in your 8th angle also refers to alcohol and poison, e.g. cyanide, hydrocyanic poisoning. 0.1 percent alcohol is normal for a man by ordinary observation. At 0.2 percent he has become intoxicated. He has emotional instability. His inhibitions are greatly diminished. At 0.3 percent there is a very definite confusion, staggering gait, blurred speech. At 0.4 percent there is stupor, a marked decrease in response to external stimuli and approaching analysis. From 0.5 percent to 0.6 percent there is complete coma and impairment of circulation. There is danger of death that is virtually inevitable after 0.6 percent of alcohol in the blood.

Neptune:

Listen Piscean, Neptune is your main planet. Neptune means illusion, big dreams, great ambitions and **a heightened awareness of life.** Top notch creativity goes naturally with your sign. As an artist, you will outshine all the others. Alas, you might also outshine others as a con man. Drugs, drinks, deceit - the 3Ds - also come under your sun sign. Neptune begins his journey in your sun sign from 4th February 2012 to 30th March 2025. It is obviously a long period; it can make or break you. It depends upon your karma and efforts and willpower and determination. DO NOT TRY TO ESCAPE FROM THE HARD FACTS AND REALITY OF LIFE. But Neptune can also make you a genius.

Uranus:

Uranus does a slow run in your second angle of food, finance, family, buying and selling, friendship and hosting dinners and parties. Uranus will make you gain and lose money suddenly and dramatically. Uranus is like the tsunami which hit Japan in 2011. It lends spice and masala to life and living. You are in for a fantastic experience.

Mercury:

From 28th January to 14th February, Mercury will hit out very strongly for you just as the batsmen hit out in IPL 2009. Mercury will hone your already sharp intellect, giving editors, writers, teachers, preachers an advantage over others; it will work at a hectic pace and it will spur you into winning plaudits. Yes, you will also be interfacing with the boss, friends, parents, in-laws, relatives as never before. This, I admit, could be a slightly tall statement. Nevertheless, for the most part, it is valid. Travel and ties are confidently predicted. The more people you meet and interact with, the better for you.

Venus:

You have an ongoing hot date with Venus from 15th January to 7th February. In this period, you will flourish and do things with a mighty swish and swirl! Collaborations, long distance travel, augmentation of wealth, the securing of loans and funds and throwing parties, giving out invitations for social gatherings will keep you busy. Dazzling multi-national affairs and meets are also very probable. It is a time to show the world just how good and great you really are.

Mars:

Mars in your 9th angle moves heaven and earth for you from 18th November to 26th December. You will face intense and active competition as well as bad vibrations and accusations from your rivals, but your work will be done. Trips, ties, contacts, contracts, signing deeds and documents, floating a company, going public with shares and everything else, getting unexpected money, improving upon your finances, public trusts and funds, investing, buying and selling, and funding, borrowing and lending are the other probabilities. However, Ganesha says there is a slight danger of ill-health and accidents, operations, falls, injuries and mishaps to you and your dear ones. Do be careful.

Pluto:

Ganesha says Pluto will be in your 11th angle. Pluto means the power house of the atom bomb. The 11th angle stands for friendship, popularity, promotions, perks, gains, socialising and children. All of this will be emphasised in some way. Luckily for you, Pluto is in a fine position with Neptune and Jupiter in your sign. This will activate Uranus and Jupiter. Uranus will give you the capacity to think out of the box, i.e. to be original. The Pluto-Neptune fine formation makes you charming and exciting to others. Obviously, you will be popular with one and all.

Jupiter and Pluto also make what is called a trine till June. In other words, Jupiter and Pluto are happily placed from each other. What will be the result? Jupiter is the planet of good luck and blessings, opportunities, birth of a child, perks, bonus, pension, gratuity, loans, and funds. Therefore, you Pisceans, stand to gain in several ways. Lucky you!

Final word about Saturn

Saturn moves in your 9th angle from 5th October 2012. This is a mighty and lucky move. Saturn in your 9th angle will help you in travel, foreign affairs, preparing a master plan, publicity, advertisement, religion, ceremonies. Parents and in-laws will play a very important part in your life. But you must take great care of their health as there is a definite danger in this direction. Saturn motivates you in higher education research and creativity. Saturn will remain in your 9th angle till 23rd December 2014. THIS IS THE PERIOD WHEN YOU WILL GROW FROM STRENGTH TO STRENGTH AND FINALLY BECOME VERY POWERFUL. SATURN IN YOUR 9TH ANGLE WILL PREPARE YOU FOR GREAT ACHIEVEMENTS IN LIFE.

PISCES

MONTH-BY-MONTH

JANUARY

You start the year with a flurry of activities. There will be many sensitive and emotional moments too and you will have to wade through them all to optimize the potential of this period. Ganesha gives you a major boost, a jumpstart but you need to curb your impatience. Finish pending work or projects and get set to start a new one. A month of great progress and power. Plans, projects, ventures, launches, start-ups could all happen now and make steady progress in the months ahead. As the New Year unfolds, there is a lot on your plate. Many things have carried forward into this year from the previous year and there are several affairs that need a resolution. You will be addressing conflicts and problems at work, sharing time with your boss, co-workers, subordinates, children, dependents, even extended family, in-laws, friends and acquaintances. Both family and personal affairs will ultimately change for the better, but not without some underlying turmoil and tussles. With the full moon in Cancer, there are several emotional issues that may destabilize you. Pisceans are always an enigma but there will be many happy moments with the family, and powerful bonding will be experienced. Towards mid-month, you will seek and aspire to a wider perspective and outlook. With the new moon in Aquarius as the month ends, your thought processes are in a tizzy. Many divergent issues occupy your mind. But with the moon's first quarter in Taurus, there is stability and you make formidable progress. You are filled with new ideas and your imagination runs riot. A cracking pace will be set.

FEBRUARY

This is a very significant period. Your health will require extra safeguards and it is certainly time for a medical check-up, to prevent problems arising when you can't cope with them – either physically or financially. February will be hectic, as everything will come together, making demands on your time and attention. At work, new schemes, projects or streamlining of existing ones will be what keeps you busy. Ganesha insists that this is definitely action time! You live life king-size in this phase. You plan big and execute even bigger. You prosper materially and also achieve inner growth. Towards mid-month, the tempo increases and you are moving about frenetically. High adventure, torrid romance and yet, surprisingly, spiritual leanings, tantra and mantra occupy you. This is a very significant period for you as Mercury, the mighty planet, is all-powerful. You will be zooming ahead and achieving a great deal. Ganesha underscores the importance of this period. This is one of the best periods for a long time. Miracles happen. Your prestige rises and you are the toast of the office. Fortune is your best friend. That is the best ally to have in any situation, says Ganesha.

MARCH

The good times continue and you flourish. This is also your birth period and is even more significant. Abandon your Piscean carelessness, and exercise instead the Piscean gentleness and charm. The emphasis is now firmly on your angle of relationships. The streak of good luck is long and lovely. You make tremendous and sustained progress. The Gods seem to be smiling at every whim of yours. The main theme of this period will be money and more money. This is a very promising phase and your personal and professional growth will be phenomenal. I must add here that as the month ends the particularly lucky phase continues. Mercury, the mighty planet, comes into reckoning again. If you use this period well, you will forge ahead in all aspects of life in miraculous fashion.

APRIL

Taxes, legacy and even moving house are definite highlights, announces Ganesha. It goes without saying, therefore, that there could be some tense moments/situations ahead. Health hazards could also arise. You'll need to be very alert, indeed. You will also be hard pressed to sort out domestic issues which may rear its head all of a sudden. There could be a sharing of family assets too which you may need to look at carefully. A dynamic month definitely, and you'll have to call up tremendous reserves of energy to cope. The theme in this period will focus on relationships. Your main focus will be on love and affection, the warmth of friendship and the renewing of old acquaintances. You consolidate old ties, attachments, and the bonds of family and love. You reach out to parents/ spouse/ partner/ siblings/ extended family and revel in the bonding. This is a good period for indulgences. Additionally, there is comfort and luxury, good vibes, fresh enthusiasm and renewed energy. The moon's first quarter is in Leo towards the month-end, and your performance is nothing short of stunning. There are new expansion plans and you manage to make spectacular progress.

MAY

This could well be a period of introspection, says Ganesha. Things fall into place almost of their own accord and you enjoy all that comes your way. Your depression, or obsessive tendencies, will more or less disappear. The sunny, optimistic side of your nature will dominate. Ganesha is generous and sends you an exciting, pleasing month to cheer you up. Money pours in, entertaining and fun keep you in high spirits, the goodwill you have built up will be reflected in a million ways. Finances will be a major preoccupation. There will also be travel and a roll in the hay. This could be a period of reflection and you could develop a much wider world-view. Mid-month, you travel and also make substantial donations to homes for the underprivileged. As the month ends, you are drawn to religion, spirituality, prayer, meditation, rituals, yoga and the esoteric sciences.

JUNE

You continue to do well. Those who are on their own, those who run enterprises or are entrepreneurs, do exceedingly well. This month, too, your interactions with people hold the key. Behind-the-scene activities will be very intense. It is your mind and intellect that will dominate. There is a very mature, even a psychic, side to you, which now controls both your thoughts and your actions, and with good results. You are flying in many directions. Ganesha says that the four F's - finance, food, fun and family - are in good order and you are blessed. Mid-month can be a very explosive period with emotions and sentiments splayed all over the place. You will rework many areas of your life - physical, mental, emotional, even financial. With the influence of Libra towards the end of the month, there are many good tidings, love, warmth and deep, intimate bonding. You really have the magic touch. There will be virtually nothing you can't handle successfully in this spectacular phase.

JULY

Ganesha gives you a truly tremendous bonus of energy, confidence, and bright ideas. You will be charming, energetic, enthusiastic, productive, intuitive, and, therefore, an outright winner. This fine month will therefore be a great phase of visible success, achievements, and glory. Ganesha wants you to be assertive and grab what you want. The astro–reason is that Venus and Jupiter are well placed right now. Kudos and plaudits will automatically come your way and you will relish them. The new moon is in Cancer mid-month and the focus is entirely on family affairs. There will be fun times and many moments of celebration. There will be interesting and unusual interactions with parents, in-laws and elder relatives. You may also spend time in social work, with the old, sick, infirm and the disabled. As the month ends, Scorpio's intensity seeps through. You will be extremely ambitious, energetic and ebullient.

AUGUST

You make sustained progress. Ganesha ensures that the happy and very positive influences will mostly continue undiminished in August. Also as a rule, the influence of the planets lasts for some time after their transit in a sign. A truly pleasing and productive phase is in progress for you. There is a swell in your fortunes. You are certainly laughing all the way to the bank. The feel good factor also reflects positively on your personal life and your marital interactions. The work front is hectic as you make deals, resolve tangled domestic matters, and sort out a variety of problems. Your gentle, softer persona will serve you well now. The new moon in Leo ensures that you enter an expansive phase. As the month ends, you move in many directions. You will feel and experience true bonding and great love, perhaps more than ever before. Parents, in-laws, children all form a fine circle of care. You will truly revel in it. In the end, the full moon in your sign could be an extremely significant period for you. Dame Fortune smiles on you. In a paradoxically opposite but more elevated way, will be your interest in meditation and religion.

SEPTEMBER

There will be domestic issues to sort out. You may have to address the concerns of immediate family and sort out long pending issues. Your popularity will grow in leaps and bounds and you will be loved, feted. Ganesha decides to remain generous. The three P's - projects, productivity and pets - are all specially favoured by Ganesha. You are on a roll and the luck of the draw favours you without inhibition. There is magic in the moment and Ganesha wants you to tug at every heart string and enjoy yourself with passion. You may have to look after the elderly. Children's health may also be a concern. The influence of Capricorn mid-month could steady the boat. The mood is reasonably belligerent as the month ends and the focus will be on a variety of activities and experiences that conspire to keep you heavily involved. Social activities, time with children, dependents and pets give joy and pleasure.

OCTOBER

There could be many emotional moments with children and the immediate family. This could be a far more sober, internalized month. There may be visits to hospitals, clinics, welfare centres, places of worship and healing and health resorts, some heavy expenses, long-distance connections, secret meets and conferences. It could all be part of your growing spirituality and spirit of caring for the whole of humanity. A fine way to go, says Ganesha. There will also be journeys, ceremonies, publicity, meetings, interviews and conferences. Romance and marriage, too, for the unattached cannot be ruled out. Spiralling expenses and multifarious activities will make it a busy, demanding, even tiring phase. Take extra care of your health, funds and assets. With the moon's first quarter in Capricorn mid-month, there will be refurbishing, renovating and decorating, in short, a complete face-lift to your home. You get steady and make rapid progress as the month ends thanks to the influence of Taurus. There will be all types of romantic/ emotional/ marital bonds and a grand reaching out to people and places.

NOVEMBER

November proves vital in the sense that good things happen, particularly those of the heart, perhaps an engagement, wedding, children giving affection and joy. You can party and socialize with a vengeance, and yet be successful. Ganesha says that it will be a truly spectacular month. At the same time, nothing is totally hassle free. I want you to remember that; this is how life is for everyone. The trends of the preceding weeks culminate, come to fruition, and reach the best possible conclusion. The themes of work/ enjoyment/ pleasure will run through this really happy phase and merge into one harmonious and very fulfilling whole. You have restored your faith in yourself largely by your own efforts. Towards mid-month, with the influence of Aquarius, emotions will rule supreme. The higher self is very active in this phase and you will be drawn to religion, spiritualism, prayers, meditation, yoga, healing and the rituals of worship. As the month ends, you will be at your creative best. You have money, status and prestige as you zoom ahead.

DECEMBER

You make big plans for the next year. As the year ends, your possessions will be more precious and meaningful than ever before. Finances and family values will be paramount. Loans, funds, investments/ selling/ buying/ shopping/ leasing/ funding will play a dominant part in your affairs. Ganesha gives you a lot - travel, collaborations, future plans, making more money and having fun. The five P's of life – power, pelf, prosperity, progress and position - are yours for the asking. All aspects of your life are energized - home, career, family, entertaining, and money angles will hog your attention. Towards mid-month, there will be two prime motivators - work and finance on one hand, and love and romance on the other. A lot is on your cards, agrees Ganesha. As the year ends, you realize the need to relax, to unwind and to de-stress. There is fun to be had and a life to be lived.

PISCES

THE MONTHS AT A GLANCE

January
As the New Year unfolds, there is a lot on your plate. Many things have carried forward into this year from the previous year and there are several affairs that need a resolution. You are on your toes from the word go.

February
You live life king-size in this phase. You plan big and execute even bigger. You prosper materially and also achieve inner growth.

March
The main theme of this period will be money and more money. This is a very promising phase and your personal and professional growth will be phenomenal.

April
The focus is on relationships. There will be love and affection, the warmth of friendship and the renewing of old acquaintances. You consolidate old ties, attachments, and the bonds of family. There may even be new love.

May
Finances will be a major preoccupation. There will also be travel and a roll in the hay.

June
Ganesha says that the 4F's - finance, food, fun and family - are in good order and you are blessed.

July

Kudos and plaudits will automatically come your way and you will relish them. The new moon is in Cancer mid-month and the focus is entirely on family affairs. Health of children and elders may cause concern. There may so be a marriage or an addition to the family.

August

There is a swell in your fortunes. You are certainly laughing all the way to the bank. The feel good factor also reflects positively on your personal life and your marital interactions.

September

There is magic in the moment and Ganesha wants you to tug at every heart string and enjoy yourself with passion. You may have to look after the elderly too.

October

A fine way to go, says Ganesha. There will also be journeys, ceremonies, publicity, meetings, interviews and conferences. Romance and marriage, too, for the unattached cannot be ruled out.

November

Ganesha says that it will be a truly spectacular month. The trends of the preceding weeks culminate, come to fruition, and reach the best possible conclusion.

December

The 5 P's of life - power, pelf, prosperity, progress and position - are yours for the asking. All aspects of your life are energized – home, career, family, entertaining, and money angles will hog your attention.

PISCES

WEEKLY REVIEW

(By the Phases of the Moon)

January 1 - Moon's first quarter in Aries

As the New Year unfolds, there is a lot on your plate. Many things have carried forward into this year from the previous year and there are several affairs that need a resolution. You will be grappling with this. You may find that solutions are taking longer than you expected and are, also, perhaps much more complicated. However, you have the mental strength and wisdom to deal with them. You will be addressing conflicts and problems at work, sharing with co-workers, subordinates, children, dependents, even extended family, in-laws, friends and acquaintances. Both family and personal affairs will ultimately change for the better, but not without some underlying turmoil and tussles. You will cope well since your energy levels are re-charged and you are able to get down to some good slogging. You are full of positive energy, working hard and ready to zoom past the winning post. There is a lot that you want to do. You are ambitious and know very well too that money is honey. You work hard and grab every opportunity that comes your way. There is love and bonding in the family too and it is a good start to the New Year. Those who are keen on adopting a child may do it this year. Ganesha blesses you.

January 9 - Full Moon in Cancer

There are several emotional issues that may destabilize you. This is a mixed week with different types of tensions hidden in the bag of offerings. Your plans and actions may not pan out as anticipated but there will still be a boost in will power, optimism, vision. You enjoy exploring new avenues and there is a great desire to earn more and acquire more know-how. While you continue to work hard in your chosen field of work, you also delve into metaphysics, astrology and other allied interests. There is a desire to question yourself, delve deep into your inner psyche. The emphasis is also on budgeting, loans, funds, employment, projects. A career/business/vocational change may be contemplated. Pisceans are called the escape artists of the zodiac. They are smart, polite, diplomatic, shrewd and tactful, and their lives are normally packed with secret meetings, rendezvous, clandestine love affairs, journeys and experiences of all kinds. They spring surprises and never wear their plans on their sleeves. They are charming and seductive lovers. So Pisceans are always an enigma; one never knows what they will do next. But, still, there will be many happy moments with the family, and powerful bonding will be experienced. Children will be a source of joy and there could be an addition to the family too. For those in love, wedlock cannot be ruled out. Great going, says Ganesha.

January 16 - Moon's last quarter in Libra

You are on a spending spree. There is a lot of feel-good shopping going on in your life. You feel happy as you are riding the crest of success. You make good money and also leapfrog in the popularity charts. But there is a need to conserve your vitality and your funds; be on guard against business deceit. People may not pay you in time or avoid paying at all. Be extra careful in whatever business transaction you get into as you could be taken advantage of. You will seek and aspire to a wider perspective and outlook. You will sharpen your communication skills and will reach out to people and places. There could be travel thrown in too. You make new connections and they could all turn profitable. Ganesha is with you.

January 23 - New Moon in Aquarius

Your thought processes are in a tizzy. Many divergent issues occupy your mind. You have many invaluable new perspectives. Creative pursuits will be a source of immense satisfaction. There can be health issues if you push yourself beyond manageable limits. You need to maintain a sense of proportion and balance both at work and play. There could be visits to the doctor, and elders at home may need looking after. Children, normally a source of joy, could be a cause for concern. You strive for balance in your actions, your attitude and approach as you make the necessary adjustments in your values, lifestyle and orientation. Nothing in life comes easy. There is no free meal. You realize how true this is as you push on all cylinders and make the most of your free will. Trust in Ganesha.

January 31 - Moon's first quarter in Taurus

There is some stability now and you make formidable progress. Your feet are on the ground and you make headway. You are filled with new ideas and your imagination runs riot. You stop thinking of the dark areas of life which you sometimes indulge in. In addition to the attention needed at the work and home fronts, spiritual, religious, occult and esoteric matters occupy you. There is movement, new associations and many new realizations. You show spectacular results on the work front despite the forays into diverse areas. A fine, lively, even cracking pace will be set. It is your mind, intelligence and intellect that will dictate your desire to grow and progress. You enjoy life too and take part in entertainment, romance and sheer joie de vivre with heart and soul. You are able to juggle several areas of your life with aplomb. You are pushing ahead and doing well. This is a good trend, affirms Ganesha.

February 7 - Full Moon in Leo

You live life king-size in this phase. You plan big and execute even bigger. You play hard and party even harder. You prosper materially and also achieve inner growth. There is a shift in your areas of interest and focus to inner revisions vis-à-vis your personal foundations. There could be many new affairs of the heart and it is best not to get too involved with a colleague who stirs your affections. Keep your dealings with servants, colleagues, subordinates as cool and unemotional as possible; the buzz word is 'objective'. This will give you the freedom for inner advancement. There are many expenses on the home and work fronts. You travel and expand in all areas. You earn the respect of peers and receive plaudits. There are new challenges and you meet them all. Ganesha is with you in this powerful phase of inner growth and material advancement.

February 14 - Moon's last quarter in Scorpio

The tempo increases and you are moving about frenetically. Beware of clandestine affairs. They could ruin you and break up the family. You are blessed with a world view and a global vision. You are interested in news, messages, journeys, study courses, a penchant for knowledge and information. There is also bonding with relatives and friends. High adventure, torrid romance and yet, surprisingly, spiritual leanings, tantra and mantra occupy you. As you can see, many divergent forces are working on you. But a lot will depend on the personal horoscope as these are mere generalizations. There will be travel, possibly to foreign lands. There will be many new encounters and a possible relationship with someone from a different culture. This is a very significant period for you as Mercury, the mighty planet, is all-powerful. It favours travels/meetings/conferences/ interviews/trips/ more brain power/ contacts/communication/correspondence/ contracts. Mercury has a special connection with the circuits of the brain. Chess, crossword and other such games belong to Mercury. Also, short distance runners and spin bowlers are controlled by Mercury. Mercury, in short, is the ambassador and salesman of the zodiac. It is very important and occupies a prominent position now. You will be zooming ahead and achieving a great deal. Ganesha underscores the importance of this period and hopes that you make the most of it.

February 21 - New Moon in Pisces

This is one of the best periods for a long time. You feel the continued impact of Mercury. You can take risks and do wonders. Miracles happen. You map out your future, both the immediate and long-term, and slog away. There are many lucky breaks in this supremely fortunate period. There is travel and new work and new collaborations which are all profitable. Your prestige rises and you are the toast of the office. You may be attending conferences, gathering or conventions, giving/taking interviews and setting up appointments. You earn well and also pioneer new ideas. You are ambitious, energetic and, most important of all, lucky. Fortune is your best friend. That is the best ally to have in any situation, says Ganesha. Finally, life is all about good luck and the cards we are dealt with. Your cards are good now; exert your free will to optimize them.

March 1 - Moon's first quarter in Gemini

The streak of good luck is long and lovely. You make tremendous and sustained progress. The gods seem to be smiling at every whim of yours. Even Napoleon wanted only lucky generals; so vital is luck in one's life. You are riding the stallion of good fortune now. You will shine in academics and matters pertaining to the intellect. Your drive towards self-improvement or self-realization will push you to take up a course of study, learn a new skill or hone and sharpen an existing one. Perhaps you may even acquire a new trade as you are on a rapid expansion spree. Despite the hectic times, you will also prefer to spend time in contemplation, introspection and in evaluating yourself. This is a truly rewarding period, says Ganesha. You grow in many ways and become a well-rounded personality. Life is a great teacher.

March 8 - Full Moon in Virgo

There is a steadying of affairs. You throw anchor for a while. You are busy with the affairs of the mundane world. Once again, work is at the forefront and you will benefit from the events and gains of the previous week. Your job and its requirements will be what you concentrate on. Domestic issues will also be sorted out. The main theme of this period will be money and more money. You will expand on all fronts and may find yourself doing several things this week to earn more. You will be more than busy with buying/selling, loans, capital, funds and borrowing. This is a very promising phase and your personal and professional growth will be phenomenal. Many dreams/aspirations/hopes are realized. There may be investments in realty and stocks. You could bury yourself in small details and the fine print. Go for it, insists Ganesha. The early part of the year is a great time and you should cash in on it.

March 15 – Moon's last quarter in Sagittarius

Watch out for ill-health and hospital expenses. Also, watch your tongue as you will be shooting off and annoying or even hurting people whom you love which you certainly don't want to do. This is also a period with splendid chances and opportunities for advancement and gain. It is also a great time for earning well. In all respects, this is a really good month as you move ahead with power, lots of belief and enthusiasm, your sights firmly set on the gains of glory, achievements and recognition. You are able to identify and earmark areas of potential growth. New projects will lead to emotional, spiritual and material gains. Thus, this phase is one in which you show determination, but also gain a huge charge of energy – both mental and physical. You make carefully calculated progress. But, away from the work scene, romance rears its pretty face. You will be lost in the throes of passion. Who knows where it will lead? Ganesha wishes you well. Do not be indiscriminate in your displays of affection.

March 22 - New Moon in Aries

I must add here that this is a particularly lucky phase for you. Mercury, the mighty planet, comes into reckoning again. As I mentioned earlier, Mercury favours travels/ meetings/ conferences/ interviews/ trips/ more brain power/ contacts/ communication/correspondence/contracts. Mercury is the ambassador and salesman of the zodiac and it occupies a prominent position in your chart again. This continues for a while and you must make the most of the situation. If you use this period well, you will forge ahead in all aspects of life in a miraculous fashion. There could be rewards/ awards/ recognition/applause/plaudits and so on. Your work is well appreciated and those in the media, in particular, do exceptionally well. You gain in confidence, prestige, recognition, popularity, and are efficient and appreciated in your business or profession. You are rejuvenated, energized, alert, lively and healthy. The home front is also stable. As you can see so clearly, Ganesha is with you and goading you on to do great things.

March 30 - Moon's first quarter in Cancer

The great and profitable run continues. But there are some emotional issues that need to be tackled. Domestic issues come to the fore and you will spend a lot of time with old wounds and family tussles that need sorting out. This week, there will be travel, more work and the need for greater income-generation. You will be thinking of ways, means and fresh avenues for making more money. There will be some genuine worries for you to handle but you work hard and sincerely at resolving them. You will also involve yourself with some worthwhile cause, helping those in need, in social welfare and service, philanthropy and some secret activity. You will reach out to the less fortunate and do social work in the community. You may be visiting hospices for the destitute, old people's homes and orphanages. Keep away maudlin thoughts from occupying your time. Stay calm and focused and ride the storm, says Ganesha.

April 6 - Full Moon in Libra

The theme in this period will focus on relationships. You have become strongly aware of the value and necessity of lasting bonds and ties. Your main focus will be on love and affection, the warmth of friendship and the renewing of old acquaintances. Romance is very strongly indicated, even if you are already married. It may also be important to be responsible, caring, tactful and diplomatic in every situation. The quality and depth of your relationships will grow rapidly. There will also be expenses and a lot of buying and selling. Your work/career will also do well. Travel is also thrown in and you make many profitable contacts. Ganesha blesses you.

April 13 - Moon's last quarter in Capricorn

The focus is on people and your interactions with them. You will be a part of all kinds of group activities and interactions, of pleasant meetings and evenings of cheer. You feel wanted, cherished and loved. You also gain many new associations and will be able to judge people better and more dispassionately. You will also analyze the goals you aspire to, and also weigh up and balance your own strengths. You consolidate old ties, attachments, and the bonds of family and love. You reach out to parents/spouse/partner/siblings/ extended family and revel in the bonding. This is a good period for indulgences. You eat, drink and make merry. A wonderful time to be, agrees Ganesha. You fly and let yourself go.

April 21 - New Moon in Taurus

You are back to the slog in a big way as business and profession beckons. You become a major player in the power game, actively involved in new business enterprises and undertakings. Funds will be readily available and your interactions will take on a larger dimension, moving beyond the personal level. You charm peers and the opposition with charisma, class, optimism and the power to sustain your progress. Additionally, there is comfort and luxury, good vibes, fresh enthusiasm and renewed energy. This is a period when you make huge gains and move from strength to strength. It is an action-packed period with socializing and the hard slog thrown in and you will, most certainly, be stressed out. You need to rejuvenate. Ganesha is with you.

April 29 - Moon's first quarter in Leo

Your performance all along is nothing short of stunning. You are also more relaxed and easy going which is a great way to be. You consolidate your gains and make solid new beginnings. You spend time and money renovating, redecorating, refurnishing. Your relationships with loved ones will be great and all your interactions will be stronger, fresher, and more beautiful. There are new expansion plans and you manage to make spectacular progress. There are expenses, travel, parties, get-togethers, love affairs and the great tumble of life. You revel in it and the world loves you too. Ganesha is happy for you. Keep smiling and always remember that the world loves a lover!

May 6 - Full Moon in Scorpio

The intensity gathers and you are more focused than ever on all that needs to be done. There will be lending/borrowing/funds/capital-raising/buying and selling. Finances will be a major preoccupation. You make sustained progress. There will also be travel and a roll in the hay. Nothing serious, says Ganesha, but one never knows with matters of the heart! An innocent dalliance could lead to much more. Expenses soar and there could be medical issues in the family that have to be dealt with. Parents/in-laws/children/partner may cause concern. You may also need to go for a check-up as you are burning the candle at both ends. Take care, says Ganesha. Watch your diet and stress levels.

May 12 - Moon's last quarter in Aquarius

This could be a period of reflection and you could develop a much wider world-view. The sheer immensity of your horizons will be awesome! You will make positive and realistic plans, and will align goals that you can reach. Be prepared to travel as you grow mentally, spiritually and emotionally. There is growth and expansion at all levels. You will concentrate on developing a new, expanded vision of social and personal objectives. You will also be able to share these with like- minded souls. It is the age of ideas and the great fear of the world coming to an end in this present consciousness. You are in tune with the currents. There will be many new ties, bonds, partnerships, collaborations and you grow significantly. You network with one and all as Ganesha continues to bless you. You network with him too!

May 20 - New Moon in Gemini

New ideas continue to pour in. You travel and also make substantial donations to homes for the underprivileged. There will be growth on all fronts as there will be both mental and financial gain. You find yourself much more confident and even charismatic, certainly full of magnetism and drive. Your popularity zooms. More importantly, you will combine and fuse work and play/recreation into a pleasing, pleasant and balanced whole. There is fruition in your affairs and you win applause. Ganesha is happy for you.

May 28 - Moon's first quarter in Virgo

After a long time, you are stable and in one place. You have been moving a lot and this is a good time to get some breathing space. You look at yoga and new mediation techniques. You want to stand still and watch the grass grow. You may even book into a spa or a health resort for rejuvenating massages and therapy. You are also drawn to religion, spirituality, prayer, meditation, rituals, yoga and the esoteric sciences. This is a good move because you are on the verge of a major burn-out. Life has many aspects to it and there is no need to hurry as the road is long. Take it easy, suggests Ganesha. In time, existence will reveal all its plans. We cannot force the pace. It is the law of all life; whatever will be, will be.

June 4 - Full Moon in Sagittarius

You are flying in many directions. You are also swimming with the tide and so making enormous progress too. Your financial affairs are stable and the domestic scene, entertaining and hospitality occupy centre stage. The 4 F's - finance, food, fun and family - are in good order and you are blessed. There is enhanced power and strength, a rise in position and a promotion. The trends are good and Ganesha's blessings are with you. Finances increase but so do expenses and you need to keep a tight lid on spending habits. Watch what you say or you could ruffle feathers! Remember it is not important how much water flows into the bucket. What is important is how much water is used! So plug your leaks. Always save for a rainy day during the good times when the sun is beating down on you.

June 11 - Moon's last quarter in Pisces

The last quarter is in your sign and this could be a very explosive period with emotions and sentiments splayed all over the place like confetti or buntings at a party. Watch your step and your moods. Do not be ego driven and do not retaliate when pushed to a corner. Be calm and the tough patch will pass. You will display the 'slippery' side of your personality. You will swing like a see saw, swimming in opposite directions. There will be periods of introversion and extroversion, of looking both forward and backward. There will be secret meetings, rendezvous, perhaps even a clandestine love affair. You could even manage two homes. One partner is difficult to manage; two can be really tough, more is truly impossible! You withdraw from the hurry of the world and seek a sanctuary as your focus and direction keep shifting. You are not steadfast and are in constant movement. This is a defining period when you have to be careful. Take care, says Ganesha.

June 19 - New Moon in Gemini

In this week, the overall theme of movement is still strong. You will rework many areas of your life --- physical, mental, emotional, even financial. The money scenario will be particularly good. You now have a certain pride in yourself, your assets and your possessions, along with a very strong sense of ownership. You will do very well if you are working with electronics. You are filled with many new and creative ideas. There is solace and joy in times spent with the family. Ganesha blesses you.

June 27 - Moon's first quarter in Libra

This is a beautiful phase of many good tidings, love, warmth and deep, intimate bonding. You are far more committed and determined now. This phase boosts your morale, bolsters your self–belief and confidence and gives you the strength of purpose to overcome your indolent and sometimes careless ways. You really have the magic touch. There will be virtually nothing you can't handle successfully in this spectacular phase. The work arena moves smoothly and you have good interactions with colleagues, peers and bosses. This is a period of power, success, glory and triumph along with lots of energy and enthusiasm. Your outlook on life undergoes a sea change as you bond with near and dear ones deeply. Of course, I must add here that more specific indications depend on your personal horoscope. These are generalizations and I tell every sign that more accuracy will depend on a personal chart. Ganesha wishes you well.

July 3 - Full Moon in Capricorn

As you grow in confidence, you realize that a negative approach or one of withdrawal is not the best solution. You will therefore swing into action in several spheres. There will be deep involvement with finance, assets and liquidity. There is movement and growth. You are eager for change and accept it willingly. There is also likely to be a fair amount of travelling. With more inputs and influences pouring in, there will be a major overhaul in your perspective. You are becoming a new person altogether. There are expenses too and many demands on your time and money. Family has always been a major concern for you. Ganesha's blessings are with you as you go about the long, arduous task of understanding yourself.

July 11 - Moon's first quarter in Aries

You are in the spotlight. You move ahead on all cylinders and are turbo charged. Now that you have decided which way you are headed there will be no stopping you. Also, as a by-product, the image of the company/concern/firm you work for will also improve greatly. The theme of change will now widen to include your social life, relationships and dealings with people. Kudos and plaudits will automatically come your way and you will relish them. The dangers of complacency and over-confidence have to be guarded against. Do not get too brash and cocky. You are a person of many moods and will be very difficult to fathom. But there is no letting up on the work front with many meetings, collaborations and new deals. Go with the flow, says Ganesha. And don't look back. Try to be consistent in all your dealings. You may also be tempted to take an easier route to success. Watch out for the brambly bushes!

July 19 - New Moon in Cancer

The focus is entirely on family affairs. There may be an addition to the family; even adoption is possible. There will be fun times and many moments of celebration. Go for it. The upward trend at work will be maintained. You are also much more involved and committed in your profession and give a good account of yourself. You earn plaudits and rewards for your performance. But the spotlight is on the family. There will be interesting and unusual interactions with parents, in-laws, older relatives. You may also spend time in social work, with the old, sick, infirm and the disabled. Ganesha is happy. Health is stable and it will be wise to keep a tab on it as you are prone to take undue stress and get involved in binges. There could also be tough, emotional moments when you break down.

July 26 - Moon's last quarter in Scorpio

Nothing lasts forever and this phase is very intense with new work, new friends and new romance. Your work will grow in momentum this week. Some truly interesting and promising offers and opportunities will come your way now and you must make the most of all that is thrown on your plate. You will be extremely ambitious, energetic and ebullient. Children will be a source of delight as also the home and family, and you devote a lot of time and attention to them. This is a very successful period. You are shrewd and cunning enough to see through it all and maximize the situation. Believe in Ganesha and go for it!

August 2 - Full Moon in Aquarius

There is a swell in your fortunes. You are certainly laughing all the way to the bank. The feel good factor also reflects positively on your personal life and your marital interactions. This is definitely a happy phase. What makes it even better is that achievement and success will crown almost all your efforts now. Your work will change dramatically and tremendously in nature and scope with many new and exciting turns. Pending assignments will come to a peaceful and successful completion. New projects/ventures/deals will get off to a flying start. You are on a roll but even during such times I suggest you guard against negative and maudlin thoughts which keep troubling you from time to time. Ganesha tells you to clear the cobwebs in your mind.

August 9 - Moon's last quarter in Taurus

The work front is hectic as you make deals, resolve tangled domestic matters, and sort out a variety of problems. Much diplomacy, careful trading and wisdom will be required. Your gentle, softer persona will serve you well now. You will open up the throttles fully where work is concerned. All that kept you busy last month, such as money matters, finances, family affairs will have to be handled imaginatively. You will be like a balm in troubled waters as you express concern and care and soothe hurt feelings. There are stable influences at work but you must also take care not to push too hard and wear yourself out in the bargain. You are much sought after and there are heavy demands on your time and purse. Go slow, suggests Ganesha. This is a particularly good phase for those in the legal profession. You will be in great demand.

August 17 - New Moon in Leo

You enter an expansive phase and many issues will have to be worked out. There is pleasure and progress in both the domestic and work spheres. There will be amusement and entertainment to keep you feeling both fulfilled and happy, and joyous interaction with your children. You will be able to pursue and enjoy new hobbies, leisure-time interests or even take up new fun pursuits. Your sense of adventure will extend to your finances and there will be speculation, spills and thrills! This is a week of both pleasure and excitement. Ganesha is happy for you. Of course, expenses keep mounting, and there could be new romance and bonding too.

August 24 - Moon's first quarter in Sagittarius

You move in many directions. Someone new also enters your life. You will feel and experience true bonding and great love, perhaps more than ever before. There is an intensity and warmth not just in your personal/marital bonds/interactions but in the entire family scene, too. Parents, in-laws, children, all form a fine circle of caring and care. You will truly revel in it. Pisceans are silent, silky romantics and there could be many affairs. This could actually be the theme of your life. Enjoy, says Ganesha, with the necessary precautions. You may even elope or move overseas with someone from another country thanks to a dating site. Once again, it all depends on your personal horoscope!

August 31 - Full Moon in Pisces

The full moon is in your sign and this could be an extremely significant period for you. You feel that you have steadied yourself sufficiently and should now be allowed take some chances. You take risks at work, and also chance your arm and your heart. Dame Fortune smiles on you. There is movement, activity, hustle and bustle in your life. Passion and sex play a very strong part in this configuration. In a paradoxically opposite but more elevated way, equally exciting for you, will be your spiritual pursuits, your interest in meditation and religion. These are genuine and deep. There are also mounting expenses, travel, collaborations and all kinds of communication. At one level, you are at your wit's end. Be calm, says Ganesha, and all will be well.

September 8 - Moon's first quarter in Gemini

There is sustained progress in both the material and non-material spheres of your life. You are on a roll and the luck of the draw favours you without inhibition. Life is good as you combine the best of both worlds easily - of beauty and utility - and enjoy yourself doing it. Money will flow freely, you will enjoy the good things of life, socialise, and fuse work and play with pleasure, fun, joy and closer interactions with people in general and those you love in particular. There is magic in the moment and Ganesha wants you to tug at every heart string and enjoy yourself with passion which you, of course, do without a thought or care in the world.

September 16 - New Moon in Virgo

You steady yourself and worry about the nitty gritty, or the tiny details, at work and at home. You may have to look after the elderly. Children's health may also be a concern. You could get too preoccupied with minor issues and this could lead to unpleasant situations. You could also blow your fuse and create tantrums. A lot depends on your personal horoscope, but it may be a good time to remain calm and balanced. Even in normal times, it is a good idea to keep one's cool. Your attention gets diverted by family, financial matters, work, friendships and other distractions. Keep a steady course through the storm, urges Ganesha. It will pass --- just remember that.

September 22 – Moon's first quarter in Capricorn

This could be a steadying influence. You will however be perturbed by developments at home. There will be many issues with family that need to be sorted out before you embark on other projects. There could be illness and expenses, elderly relatives may have to be hospitalized, and there could be many tense moments. You will have to steer carefully. You may also try to escape from the pressures surmounting you in alcohol, gluttony, mindless shopping or even a relationship. All this will only rebound later and so it may be wise to keep a low profile till the period passes you by as it invariably will. These are testing times but do not worry as Ganesha is with you all the way.

September 30 - Full Moon in Aries

The mood is reasonably belligerent and many things occupy your mind as you realize that a lot needs to be done and you are running out of resources. But the caring, softer side of you will reassert itself. The focus will be on a variety of activities and experiences that conspire to keep you heavily involved. You will be busy with projects, government connections and collaborations, and getting things done through the genuine contacts that you have built up. There is some recreation thrown in too. Social activities, time with children, dependents and pets give both joy and pleasure. There will be happy times with your partner/spouse, friends, companions and loved ones. You are working yourself through uncertain moments but take heart because Ganesha is with you. There is progress in every sphere and some plaudits too.

October 8 - Moon's last quarter in Cancer

There are happy times with the family and genuine fun and enjoyment. There is entertainment, amusement and joy. There will also be journeys, ceremonies, publicity, meetings, interviews and conferences. Romance, and marriage too for the unattached, cannot be ruled out. There are many new associations as you embark on serious planning for the future. The worst seems to be over, at least the cobwebs are being cleared, and the deck is being readied for a brighter tomorrow. Ganesha blesses you.

October 15 - New Moon in Libra

While there are fun and carefree times, spiralling expenses and multifarious activities will make this a busy, demanding, even tiring phase. Take extra care of your health, funds and assets and also of disclosing your plans, projects to all and sundry. Choose your confidants well as even walls have ears and eyes. There could be animosities and rivalries to contend with. Secrecy, surreptitious deals, sly movements, wheels within wheels, subterfuge and strange goings-on are the norm this week, along with 'under-the-table' settlements. There could also be surreptitious emotional entanglements. Here too, there will be a need to keep them under wraps lest they lead to disapproval or social stigma. Of course, I repeat, all this depends on the individual horoscope, and the astrologer is not God or a magician. I am also human and prone to error. But these are indications that should be taken seriously. Every moment in life is fleeting, so do not get bogged down in the unhappy details. Believe that Ganesha will haul you over the coals.

October 22 - Moon's first quarter in Capricorn

Issues build up, gain momentum, and you will be in the throes of a really busy time on the home and property fronts. Having enjoyed your cloak-and-dagger stuff to the hilt, you decide to call it a day; your secret activities will come to an end, too. The trend now remains firmly anchored on the home front. The domestic scene will be given a makeover. There will be refurbishing, renovating, decorating, in short, a complete face-lift to your home. Close relationships will come in for scrutiny and you will seek to improve and enhance them. You will also look to more serious pursuits like your finances, family and parents. There is a new, responsible attitude that will usher many beneficial changes in all spheres of your life. Never take anything for granted, says Ganesha. As we all know, all that glitters is not gold.

October 29 - Full Moon in Taurus

You get steady and make rapid progress. Ties, bonds, partnerships, links and collaborations of all kinds will be strengthened. There could even be a marriage in the family; if you are eligible, it could be yours. There will be all types of romantic/emotional/marital bonds and a grand reaching out to people and places. Travel and journeys will definitely materialize as you zoom around not only for work but also for pleasure. There will be new contacts and tie-ups that will influence and impact you personally as you gain and grow in several ways. You do well and earn applause. You make money too and health is good. What else do you need… asks Ganesha.

November 7 - Last quarter in Leo

As the year ends, your life is again looking up. The trends of the preceding weeks culminate, come to fruition, and reach the best possible conclusion. The themes of work/enjoyment/pleasure will run through this really happy phase and merge into one harmonious and very fulfilling whole. You will try to do full justice to your profession, your talents and potential and your work commitments. There is much to gain on the personal and professional fronts. Pleasure, profit, joy and contentment are yours this week. The new trends at work are beneficial and you manage to make substantial gains. You are also filled with stamina, determination and zest as the temperature mellows and the cold winds blow in. It is winter and there is a spring in your step. Ganesha blesses you.

November 13 - New Moon in Scorpio

A very intense and hectic phase is on the cards. You have restored your faith in yourself, largely by your own efforts. It is a good feeling to know that you have what it takes to get on in this world. You seek new avenues of work but still the focus is mostly on personal matters. There will be great joy from children as you spend your time directing your energy to developing the inputs required for true progress. Ganesha is happy. The home scene is blessed and you are in bliss. If a parent or relative has to undergo surgery, it will come out well.

November 20 - Moon's first quarter in Aquarius

This is a period when the mind and emotions will rule supreme. The higher self is very active in this phase and you will be drawn to religion, spiritualism, prayers, meditation, yoga, healing and the rituals of worship. You truly feel uplifted, consoled and yet, the material world sees you performing wonders. There is no getting away from the fact that you square up more than sincerely to your unusually heavy responsibilities. In doing so, you achieve happiness. You will also deal with occult phenomena even as you face up to your responsibilities and commitments. There are collaborations, companionships and associations. You network furiously and are in touch with people and events on a global scale. You are on a heady run and making rapid headway. Ganesha is with you.

November 28 - Full Moon in Gemini

This is a period of great ideas and you will be at your creative best. You are also full of determination. Finances and funds, joint holdings, realty, stocks, settlements, hypothecation, trusts, loans, even alimony and golden handshakes will make their presence felt in your life. Your mood is upbeat and you give a very good account of yourself in handling work and personal matters. Taking your loved ones/spouse/partner into confidence will help. Ganesha is helping out, moving in mysterious ways to help you. You enthrall audiences with your genius and creativity and get rewards/awards/plaudits/applause. You have money, status and prestige as you zoom ahead vigorously. What a way to begin the end of a year!

December 6 - Moon's last quarter in Virgo

You are greatly loved and appreciated in this lucky phase. You gain much emotional support and happy bonding with your partner or spouse. For the most part, all relationships will be cordial and pleasant. True depth and caring in romance is also foretold and it makes everything that much sweeter. The 5 P's of life – power, pelf, prosperity, progress and position - are also yours for the asking. This is without a doubt going to be a vibrant and busy week in which you zoom ahead with power and purpose. All your earlier initiatives are paying off now. This is a good period for those in industry or electronics or for those working with any type of gadgetry. A good phase, concedes Ganesha.

December 13 - New Moon in Sagittarius

You are in clover as everything is working out in your favour. Hectic times are in store for you. All aspects of your life are energized – home, career, family, entertaining, and money angles will hog your attention. What emerges as the clear winner though will be the angle of finances. You will have to move smartly, indeed, and with savvy, when you are handling money matters. You will handle the entire gamut of financial activities like buying and selling on the bourse, raising capital and even indulging in some speculation. There is a new intensity and a new direction now. You seize the moment with bare hands and make the most of the opportunities thrown your way. Keep at it, says Ganesha.

December 20 - Moon's first quarter in Pisces

Now there will be two prime motivators - work and finance on one hand, and love and romance on the other. These are demanding times and you could be pushed for time. Money and honey will need working on though they are very much on your radar. You could also use some free time for rest, relaxation, health care. Prayers, meditation, solitude and contemplation, tantra and mantra will give you comfort and relief. In the midst of all this will be festivities and even a marriage. A lot is on your cards, agrees Ganesha. This is a fun time and frenetic too.

December 28 - Full Moon in Cancer

This has been an amazing year with many twists and turns. You have worked hard and long, fairly competently and successfully for the most part. You may feel that it is time to give yourself a break. You realize the need to relax, to unwind and to de-stress. Otherwise you could lose out on strength, stamina or just burn out. In the midst of it all, you have fun, host a party, laugh and stay happy. This is certainly not the time for single bliss and solitude. There is fun to be had and a life to be lived. You may travel overseas or on holiday and usher the New Year with loved ones and bubbly. Or you may be working overtime. Which Piscean are you? Ganesha wishes you well either way.

PISCES

KEY DATES

January
2*-3, 6*-8, 11*-13, 16*-18, 21*-22, 25*-26, 29-31.
Ganesha says, you will have the ambition and the luck to carry through any venture you take up. Your creativity will conquer everything.

February
3*-4, 8*-9, 13-14, 17*-18, 21-22, 26*-28
Work is important, and your desire to reach others, as well as to express yourself fully, will be realized. If you are interested in pets, new projects, change of staff/job, this is the right time for it. Health precautions are a must.

March
2*-4 (important), 7-9, 12*-13, 17*-18, 21-22, 25-26, 29*-31.
Both kicks and kisses, partnerships and separations. In short, both the good and the bad have to be dealt with now.

April
1*-5, 8-10, 13*-14, 17-18, 21-22, 26*-28.
April is a collage of loans, funds, romance, joint-finance, journey, children, property. The pace will be hectic. So, safeguard your health.

May
1*-5 (important), 6-7, 10*-11, 14-15, 19*-20, 23*-24, 28-29.
Most important for decisions, a pilgrimage, collaborations, finance and investment, foreign connections. Import-export, tours and trading will come into play.

June
1-3, 7*-8, 11-12, 15-16, 19*-21, 24-26, 29-30.

A turning point, power, fulfillment, gains. Also, disturbances at home, taking care of the health of elders, a time to be brave and forward-looking.

July
1*, 4*-5, 8*-9, 12*-13, 17*-18 (important), 21*-23, 26-28, 31.
You start with a wallop and knock out the opposition. Gains and success are certain for you, says Ganesha!

August
1*, 4*-6, 8*-10, 13*-15 (important), 18-19, 23-24, 27*-29 (important).
A topsy-turvy month. Income, expenses, work, medical care, journeys, buying and selling, are some of the features.

September
1*-2, 5*-6, 9*-11 (important), 14*-16, 19-21, 24*-26, 28-29.
Power gains, promotion, children, hobbies, confidence, victory, says Ganesha.

October
1-3, 7*-8, 11-13, 14-18, 21*-25, (important) 29-31.
New deals, wheeling and dealing, bargain-hunting, furniture, commission, trading, festivals, food, celebrations. After October 14, trips, ties and trading.

November
3*-4, 7-9, 13-14, 18*-19, 22-23, 26-27, 30*.
November is truly action time. Your home, your work and your inner development – all come together. You make personal and spiritual gains.

December
1*, 4*-9 (important), 11, 15-16, 19-20, 23-24, 27*-30.
Home, shop, office (therefore, property, too), immigration, decoration, children, carnival, celebrations, ceremonies, Vaastu, house-warmings are the salient features of *December 2012 to March 2013*.

NASTUR - Bejan's Hanuman

Ganesha says Nastur is the son and also the Hanuman of his father, Bejan. Astrology is all about timing, that is, the right person at the right time and place. No wonder we are now introducing Nastur in the book.

Nastur is a double Scorpio. By Western astrology his sun is in Scorpio, and, by Indian astrology his moon is in Scorpio. Scorpios are intense, magnetic, charming and great at fortune telling. Cheiro, the world's greatest palmist and astrologer was a Scorpio.

We Indians do not say astrology. We say Jyotishi. 'Jyot' means light, 'ish' means God. Therefore Jyotishi is the light of God. Bejan admits that his son Nastur has the greatest possible faith in God. It is this which has made Nastur very solid, steady and sincere. Like his father, he too has mighty powerful intuition. Intuition is the master key to success in predictions. Nastur adds to it numerology and palmistry. Zoroaster, Ganesha, Hanuman, Ambamata are the mighty energies he worships and adores. He also has a great relationship with Sarkar Rooknadin Farokh, Mohammad Chisti, his neighbour. The Chistis of Ahmedabad are the direct descendants of Khwaja Garib Nawaz Chisti of Ajmer. Nastur has great regard for Mohan Patel, President All India Federation of Astrologers, Hemang Pandit of Ganeshaspeaks.com and ace astrologer Vashist Mehta. They teach him astrology and also sponsor him. Bejan says, "I expect good and great things from my son Nastur and his very talented wife Mittu. The future belongs to them. Mittu is perfect in her poojas. That really helps."

MAMATA – Queen of Bengal

Ganesha says Mamata Banerjee has stormed and run over the communists in Bengal. She has mowed them down. May 13, 2011 spelt the end of the rule of 34 years by the CPM. What next?

I predict that she will control her temper, her haste, her rashness and get down to really improve the economy of Bengal, attend to the welfare schemes, build infrastructure, erect a solid edifice for all-round development: In short, she will have a SPECIAL AND COMPLETE PACKAGE FOR BENGAL. Mamata is a solid Capricornian, stubborn and invincible. She has Jupiter in the sympathetic, intuitive, emotional sign Cancer. Her heart is definitely in the right place. Between June 2013 to June 2014, she will change the face of Bengal and Bengal will be beautiful, dynamic, forceful and wonderful. That's the promised and desired CHANGE "PORIBORTON". Yes, she will be the queen of Bengal.

WORLD PREDICTIONS

Ganesha says, this is exactly what my devotee Bejan Daruwalla said on pg 524 of the 2011 Annual book, "Jupiter will be in Aries from **23rd January 2011 to 4th June 2011**. Another, and earlier, lucky period for Obama! Obama will deliver the goods and that is the bottom line!" And I have just heard the news that Obama had sent a search operation to kill Osama Bin Laden and the operation has been successful. **Osama was killed on May 1/2 2011. It falls in the time span 23rd January 2011 to 4th June 2011.**

What has given me enormous satisfaction is that in my 2010 Annual book, I had said on page 9, "Saturn will be in Libra in, by Western astrology, 13th October 2009 to 5th October 2012. We may expect the following happy result for the world. **The poor, the downtrodden, the weak will find prosperity and peace. Justice will be done to them and that, to me, is of vital importance."**

On page 11, under the heading A NEW WORLD ORDER, I had said, **"The main result of this will be the end of tyranny and brute force all over the world."** On 2nd May 2011, as I am dictating these words, we all know the upsurge and rebellion and overthrow of group force in Syria, Libya, Egypt, Yemen and The Middle East. I cried with joy. Sometimes, astrology helps and heals not only the world but the astrologer too. That is the great beauty of predictions. A good and correct prediction for the world is my greatest reward. I thank My Lord and Master Ganesha for it.

Let me go beyond my line of duty, give you glimpses and pictures of world events BEYOND 2012. Saturn, by western astrology, will be in Scorpio from 6th October 2012 to 23rd December 2014. Here are a few pointers about the massive impact of Saturn in Scorpio:

a) Finances, loans, banking as such, jointly held income and all sorts of financial transactions, specially public trust and charities and funds will be hit. I mean 'hit' in the sense of scrutiny, accountability, assessment of debts, assets liabilities and, most certainly, income tax and black money. Black money all over the world will be ferreted and there will be forcible disclosures of it, as well as inducements and attractive opportunities for people to declare their hidden sources of wealth, assets and incomes. It will be unimaginably huge and mind boggling. Even thinking about it makes my head spin!

b) God's blessings, sharp intuition, great skills, solid knowledge, powerful perception, GREAT VISION, and above all, the astrologer's, numerologist's, occultist's or psychic's own destiny, go into predictions. Like the poet, the mystic, the astrologer also leaps from the known to the unknown. I call it THE LEAP OF FAITH AND IMAGES. Saturn in Scorpio will teach the world: 1) Precision and perfection; 2) The best way to get things done; 3) Systematising LIFE itself; 4) Canned, packaged spirituality, salvation; 5) Less is more; 6) Technology, rationality are kings. 7) Health, hygiene, welfare; 8) Managing men and matters; 9) Methodology and perfection. 10) Performance orientation.

c) By fusing Saturn in Scorpio, Jupiter in Gemini and Mars in Virgo, I predict webs of deceit, windows of opportunities and slices of luck, and aggressive, meticulous planning await the world in 2012. Saturn in Scorpio sets the world on fire, as we say. In practical terms, it means spies will be active, terrorists will plan attacks. The State will curtail and limit the freedom of society, the legal system will be strict and phones will most certainly be tapped. Surveillance and control will be the objective of all the states, everywhere. **THIS IS EXACTLY THE FUNCTION AND PURPOSE OF SATURN IN SCORPIO, BY WESTERN ASTROLOGY.**

What does this imply for INDIA?

Our army will specialise in the 4 C's, namely Command, Control, Communication and Computers. I have taken the 4C's from The Sunday Times dated 1st May 2011. Scorpio is an aggressive, war-like, military sign. Saturn gives Scorpio structure, method, management. Therefore, for INDIA, especially Saturn in Scorpio from 6th October 2012 to 23rd December 2014 will give these results.

Lakes, rivers, seas, water as such, AND MOST CERTAINLY CHEMICALS, DNA, DRUGS, MEDICINES, SURGERY, PRIVATE PARTS OF THE BODY, THE BACK, MENTAL ANXIETY AND PHOBIAS, PARANIOD CONDITIONS AND FEAR COMPLEXES, LUNACY, SEXUAL ABERRATIONS AND DEVIATIONS, all sorts of water therapy and mud packs, loss of limbs, anus trouble and surgeries come under Saturn in Scorpio. So does LIFE-DEATH-REGENERATION. That means Karma and Dharma, reincarnation, tantra and mantra come under the influence and impact of Saturn in Scorpio. Longevity may go up to 125 years or so. The mysteries of the sea and the ocean, the fish, the whale and the shark, the submarines will be fathomed, shown and revealed. Why? Scorpio is a powerful water sign. Ganesha has asked me to go a step further and predict that between 27th June 2013 to 16th July 2014, the above predictions will fructify or be realised or come true. It is like a long jumper who springs ahead. I am writing this on 7th May 2011, to the chanting of mantras in the Shiva temple, which is in the same compound as my building. It is a good and lucky omen. It is a sign from God.

It is between 27th June 2013 and 16th July 2014 that results will be obtained, targets achieved, technology will reach out to common humanity. **Why common humanity?** Appliances for homemakers, new and better fuel, oil, gas, gadgets for cookery, laundry, better washing soap, injections, drugs, soft and alcoholic drinks, will be introduced. In other words, household amenities in plenty.

Jupiter in Gemini

Jupiter in Gemini from 12th June 2012 to 27th June 2013 will give a boost, a mighty impetus to technology, especially in America. Throughout the world, the focus will be on communication, coverage, contacts, consciousness, conveyances - that is, all sorts of transport, vehicles and planes, journeys, exploration of space, very particularly, aerodynamics, aviation, kick-starting ventures, plans, and projects.

In addition, Jupiter in Gemini is about Art in every form and shape and context, and most certainly music and dance will have new and innovative significance! Musicians, dancers, sculptors, poets, painters, filmmakers will travel everywhere, including in space, to find the quality, tone, and soul of art, music and dance! **The beauty and the paradox of it all will be that even as we achieve completion and realisation, there will be new discoveries brought about, ignited and inspired by restlessness and the desire to discover.**

I do not believe in needless repetition. The reason is that in my book, "2012, End of The World?" I predicted about India, China, Russia, America and very specially JERUSALEM, which is loved by the Arabs and the Jews, both Semitic races. I admit my heart bleeds with a thousand cuts for JERUSALEM.

For readers who do not know about JERUSALEM, I may say that it is one of the oldest and holiest of cities. It was destroyed twice, attacked 52 times and is only a mere 125.1 sq km of land. There is magic and mystery about JERUSALEM.

THE FINAL TEST

Chanakya says, "As gold is tested in four ways by rubbing, cutting, heating, and beating - so a man should be tested by these four things: his renunciation, his conduct, his qualities and his actions."

ASTRO - ANALYSIS OF SUICIDE BOMBERS

We all know the havoc and panic caused by suicide bombers. It is horrible and nerve wrecking. What gives the suicide bombers the courage and the daring to blow themselves up? Are they not afraid? Do they not value the life of others? Are they so selfish and cruel? The suicide bombers are full of hatred, revenge, and rancor. Rancor means bitterness. This bitterness is caused when others insult you, humiliate you and violate your privacy, your territory, your home and house, your family and friends. Rancor and hatred are exceptionally powerful emotions which motivate the terrorist to kill, go on a rampage, and even destroy himself / herself. The terrorist has been badly hurt, slighted and damaged. He or she seeks revenge. Because the terrorist cannot take revenge openly, he or she does it by stealth, secrecy and cunning. It is his or her way of retaliation.

By astrology Mars, the planet of courage and daring, is linked to violence, killings, explosions and carnage. By killing others, the terrorist gets a perverse feeling of sadism and satisfaction. The terrorist feels that he or she will be recognized by other terrorists. There is also the solace of becoming a martyr. All this comes under the planet Pluto. Pluto means revolution. Pluto is the power house of violence. Pluto means the power of the atom bomb.

But the suicide bomber uses stealth, secrecy and cunning to blow up others and himself / herself. Stealth, secrecy and hidden measures come under the orbit of Neptune. Neptune gives illusions and is also responsible for delusions and hallucinations of grandeur. This gives the martyr complex to the terrorist. The moon shows the subconscious mind; the moon therefore makes it possible for the terrorist to sit in a restaurant, look at the women and children very objectively, and then very coolly and calmly blow up everything.

In other words, the planets which make the mental make-up and actual personality of the terrorist are Mars, Pluto, Neptune and the Moon. The actual making of the bomb will go under technical skills. Technical skills come under the clever and dexterous planet Mercury. By Indian astrology, Rahu also comes into play. Rahu is perverse, sadistic, exceptionally cruel and totally heartless. Rahu is a monster.

Tailpiece:

Ganesha says, "Terrorism will be defeated. The main reason is the Aquarian age means an open mind, tolerating those who are totally different from us in every way, learning to mingle and be friendly and accepting the difference in culture, caste and colour gracefully - yes, that is the message of the New Age. By 2023 latest and 2015-16 earliest, terrorism will trouble us no more. We will be free from it. Terrorism will have no place in our NEW AGE.